EDMU

Conor Cruise O'Brien was born in 1917. A writer and diplomat, he was the United Nations special representative in the Congo in 1961. *To Katanga and Back* (1962), a book drawing on these experiences, is a classic in modern African history. In 1965 O'Brien took a Chair at New York University. He has been pro-Chancellor of the University of Dublin since 1973, and was Editor in Chief of the *Observer* between 1978 and 1981. One of the most outspoken opponents of the IRA, O'Brien has written a number of treatises against the dangers of the myths of Irish republicanism and, in 1996, he was elected to the Northern Ireland negotiating forum as a member of the new UK Unionist Party. Among his many publications are *Parnell and his Party* (1957), *Writers and Politics* (1965), *States of Ireland* (1972), and *The Siege* (1986). He published his autobiography, *Memoir: My Life and Themes*, in 1998.

Conor Cruise O'Brien

EDMUND BURKE

ABRIDGED BY
Jim McCue

VINTAGE

Published by Vintage 2002

2 4 6 8 10 9 7 5 3 1

First published in Great Britain as
The Great Melody: A Thematic Biography of Edmund Burke
in 1992 by Sinclair-Stevenson

This abridged edition first published
in 1997 by Sinclair-Stevenson

Vintage
Random House, 20 Vauxhall Bridge Road,
London SW1V 2SA

Random House Australia (Pty) Limited
20 Alfred Street, Milsons Point, Sydney,
New South Wales 2061, Australia

Random House New Zealand Limited
18 Poland Road, Glenfield, Auckland 10,
New Zealand

Random House (Pty) Limited
Endulini, 5A Jubilee Road, Parktown 2193,
South Africa

The Random House Group Limited Reg. No. 954009
www.randomhouse.co.uk

A CIP catalogue record for this book
is available from the British Library

ISBN 0 09 943344 3

Papers used by Random House are natural, recyclable
products made from wood grown in sustainable forests.
The manufacturing processes conform to the environ-
mental regulations of the country of origin

Printed and bound in Great Britain by
Cox & Wyman Limited, Reading, Berkshire

Contents

v

Contents

Prefatory Note

Conor Cruise O'Brien's preoccupation with Edmund Burke stretches back to the radical years of the late 1960s, when he edited *Reflections on the Revolution in France*. In the 1970s he began and then abandoned an earlier biography. He was not afraid to challenge the accepted account, but neither was he prepared to gloss over questions that troubled him. So when *The Great Melody* was published in 1992, it was the product of prolonged thinking and investigation.

In particular, O'Brien had been vexed by some puzzles about Burke's Irish inheritance and the traps it sprang. It is the solution of these puzzles, beginning on the very first page, that gives the book its structure. No one else is so well placed to understand Burke as O'Brien: their careers have often run in parallel. O'Brien too is the eloquent Irishman active in the fields of politics, literature and journalism; he too left Ireland for a larger stage but found that Ireland never left him; he too understands the pressure that religious bigotry exerts upon politics; he too has been a government minister and yet found much more influence as an adviser to the powerful; he too is wrongly accused of changing sides and reneging on his early liberal commitments; and he too has achieved world renown for his analysis of great matters of state. As O'Brien's own life has been woven with strands of Burke, so his life of Burke is threaded with autobiography.

The Great Melody is a noble and remarkable book, which was published to acclaim and controversy. But it is a book of 750 pages, and even though it has itself engendered new interest, not everyone yet realises how fully Burke repays prolonged study. So the publishers have taken the opportunity of the bicentenary of his death to commission an abridgment, to serve as an introduction to the career and beliefs of one of history's most important political thinkers.

In shortening the text I have made it less personal by omitting the acknowledgements and preface, the introduction, with its survey of historiography, the epilogue, examining Burke's ideas in the light of later events, and the appendix of correspondence between O'Brien and Isaiah Berlin. This means that the background of academic argument against which *The Great Melody* was written – and which required extensive footnotes – has been eliminated: those battles are secondary. The thematic approach of the main chapters has been retained, but the narrative sequence has been made more prominent. A very few episodes (such as Burke's involvement with Maynooth College) have been omitted entirely. Compression has also involved removing recapitulations and a number of avowed speculations, as well as a pruning of some verbal luxuriance.

Spelling has been modernized, because the various sources were not consistent, and punctuation has been regularized where it was difficult or misleading. References to the sources can be found in *The Great Melody*, although unfortunately, with the exception of the complete *Correspondence* under the general editorship of T. W. Copeland (Cambridge and Chicago, 10 vols, 1958–78), there is still no full scholarly edition of Burke's prodigious pronouncements in debate and for publication. Different commentators use different editions, which seem never to match those available in libraries. For the abridgment, a new index and a chronology have been added.

The bicentenary of Burke's death is being commemorated by a reception in the Palace of Westminster hosted by the Speaker of the House of Commons, as well as by events in Dublin, Beaconsfield, the United States and elsewhere. He deserves the official accolades and the scholarly fuss; but more particularly he merits our and our representatives' attention.

Jim McCue
April 1997

Chronology

	Rockingham administration; elected MP for Wendover (December)
1766	Maiden speech (18 January); repeal of the Stamp Act and Declaratory Act passed (March); end of Rockingham adminstration (July);
1767	Townshend Duties imposed
1768	Buys Gregories in Beaconsfield
1769	*Observations on a Late State of the Nation* (February); North administration formed
1770	*Thoughts on the Cause of the Present Discontents* (April); becomes agent to the New York General Assembly
1772	Warren Hastings becomes Governor of Bengal
1773	Boston Tea Party (16 December)
1774	Speech on American Taxation (19 April); Philip Francis arrives in Calcutta (October); elected MP for Bristol (2 November)
1775	Speech on Conciliation with America (22 March); British defeated at Battle of Bunker Hill (17 June); execution of Nuncomar
1776	American Declaration of Independence (4 July)
1777	*Letter to the Sheriffs of Bristol* (April); British surrender at Saratoga (17 October)
1778	France enters American War against Britain (March)
1780	Speech on Economical Reform (11 February); Gordon Riots (June); declines poll at Bristol (September); becomes MP for Malton
1781	Commons Select Committee on Indian Affairs established (January); British surrender at Yorktown; Francis returns from India (October)
1782	Second Rockingham administration formed (March); becomes Paymaster-General; death of Rockingham (July); resigns with Fox from Shelburne administration

1783	Fall of Shelburne (March); Fox–North coalition formed; becomes Paymaster-General again; Fox's East India Bill defeated in Lords and administration dismissed (December)
1784	Pitt the Younger becomes Prime Minister
1785	Speech on the Nabob of Arcot's Debts (28 February)
1787	House of Commons agrees to impeach Warren Hastings (May)
1788	Impeachment begins in Lords (13 February); madness of George III (November–February)
1789	French National Assembly established (June); fall of the Bastille (July); Richard Price extols French Revolution at Revolution Society dinner in London (4 November)
1790	First Commons statement on the French Revolution (9 February); *Reflections on the Revolution in France* (1 November)
1791	*Letter to a Member of the National Assembly* (January); break with Fox (6 May); flight to Varennes (20–21 June); *Appeal from the New to the Old Whigs* (August); *Thoughts on French Affairs*
1792	*Letter to Sir Hercules Langrishe* (February); France declares war on Austria (April), beginning 'universal crusade for liberty'; Louis XVI deposed (August); September massacres in Paris
1793	Execution of Louis XVI (21 January); France declares war on 'the King of England' (1 February); Catholic Relief Act in Ireland (April); *Observations on the Conduct of the Minority* (September); execution of Marie Antoinette (16 October); French Reign of Terror
1794	Portland Whigs break from Fox (January); gives last speech in impeachment of Hastings (May–June); leaves Parliament (20 June); death of brother, Richard (February) and son, Richard (2 August)

I: Ireland 1729–80

FAMILY BACKGROUND

Edmund Burke's biographers all state that he was born in Dublin, and that his father, an attorney, Richard Burke, was a Protestant while his mother, born Mary Nagle, was a Roman Catholic. Edmund's date of birth is now believed to have been New Year's Day 1729. It is not certain, however, that he was born in Dublin; a local tradition has it that he was born in the Blackwater Valley, Co. Cork. And the simple description of his father as a Protestant is misleading if unqualified. At the time, the penal laws against Catholics were in full force, so this was a question not solely of theological or ecclesiastical significance, but of profound importance for Burke's social status, emotional associations and psychology.

Recent converts were in a class by themselves, and neither Protestants nor Catholics thought of them as simply Protestants. As the historian T. P. Power writes: 'Conversions in eighteenth-century Ireland were largely induced by legal requirements and hence were nominal in nature . . . Converts were not fully absorbed into the established order in church and state. Indeed converts came to constitute a hybrid group in Irish society.'

The name 'Richard Burke' appears on the Convert Rolls for 1722, two years before his marriage. In a paper on conversions among the legal profession, Power writes: 'Convert lawyers came to possess a dual capacity: they conformed officially and occasionally outwardly, but on the whole retained their Catholic allegiance and connections.' Power identifies Richard Burke as a member of this class, conforming in March

1722, admitted an attorney in June 1723, and subsequently establishing a respectable legal practice. 'His son, Edmund Burke, following a period of study at Trinity College [Dublin] in the 1740s, entered the Middle Temple.'

Even when he conformed, Richard was not out of the eerie wood of the penal laws. He had moved out of a legally proscribed category, but only into a suspect one. He was still vulnerable, even legally, after he married in 1724, because his wife remained a practising Catholic. Under a law of 1697, a Protestant whose wife remained a Catholic was subject to the same disabilities as if he were a Catholic himself. And in the 1720s and 1730s the Irish Parliament was still trying to make life difficult not only for Papists but for new converts, in the practice of the law.

Richard was vulnerable on another count too: the education of his children. A 1733 Act disqualified any attorney 'educating any of his children or permitting any of his children to be educated in the Papist religion', and Richard's daughter Juliana was certainly brought up as a Catholic. There were rumours that Edmund too had instruction in the Catholic religion as a young child. The legal penalties seem, however, rarely to have been invoked, and were not against Richard. The real penalty was social, in the suspicions entertained towards lawyers who were recent converts.

On 7 March 1727, five years after Richard Burke conformed, Archbishop Hugh Boulter, the Church of Ireland primate, addressed himself to this topic.

> We have had several who were Papists, and on the road from London hither have taken the sacrament and obtained a certificate, and at their arrival here have been admitted to the bar . . . Many of these converts have a Papist wife who has Mass said in the family and the children are brought up as Papists . . . Now this grievance is the greater here because the business of the law from top to bottom is almost in the hands of these converts; when eight or ten Protestants are set aside, the rest of the bar are all converts; much the greatest part of attorneys, solicitors, deputy officers, sub-sheriff's clerks are new converts; and the new Protestants are every day more and more working out the business of the law, which must end in our ruin.

So in Richard Burke's lifetime, the primate of the Church to which he had conformed did not classify him as 'a Protestant', but merely as a most unwelcome and suspect 'convert'.

Edmund and his elder brother, Garrett (*c.* 1725–65) were the first of the family, on either side, to be brought up as members of the Established Church. This made Edmund a lonely and burdened figure. The relation of his whole family to the Ireland of the penal laws was tense, equivocal and secretive. The penal laws and the Protestant domination that they enacted always potentially stood in the family's way. They inhabited a zone of insecurity in which habitual reticence was the norm and dissimulation was an occasional resource.

Reticence in all that concerned his relationship to Catholic Ireland was a marked characteristic of Burke's political career. His occasional appearances in the persona of an English Whig, complete with a gallery of English Whig 'ancestors', may not have been a result of actual dissimulation, but if not they were a flight from distressing and inconvenient reality into a decorous fantasy. He must have realized early on his equivocal relation to the great divide between Catholic and Protestant which governed every aspect of the social, political and juridical life of eighteenth-century Ireland. He was marked for life by the humiliating fact of his father's having conformed, and knew that his own achievements would be based on the consequences of that act of conformity.

The result was a tremendous concentration of mental and spiritual energies in a lifelong struggle not merely against the particular form of oppression that had wounded him in Ireland, but also against abuse of power in America, in India, and above all in France. That struggle was what W. B. Yeats, in his poem 'The Seven Sages', called 'Burke's great melody':

> American colonies, Ireland, France and India
> Harried, and Burke's great melody against it.

Yeats here gives Burke credit for his consistency, which others have unjustly called in question. In all of Burke's great campaigns there was one constant target – Yeats's 'it' – which was the abuse of power, the harrying of peoples. But the forms this took differed from case to case, and his approach to each case differed too.

The Matriculation Register of Trinity College, Dublin, describes Burke as *natus Dublinii* – born in Dublin. A strong tradition in Co. Cork, however, suggests that he was born in the Blackwater Valley, in the townland of Ballywater, Shanballymore, at the house of his uncle, James Nagle. It was customary in certain areas for a married woman who was expecting a child to go to her mother's people for the delivery. (This was almost obligatory for the first child, but it happened also with other children.) As against that, there is the matriculation entry, for which the information must have been supplied by Burke himself. But the record and the tradition may not be irreconcilable. He knew that his background was suspect, and that to give Shanballymore as place of birth would cause eyebrows to be raised. Papist rural Cork was not a place for a proper Protestant to be born. So if he was born there, Burke would probably have preferred to give the place of his father's residence at the time of his birth.

Whether or not Edmund was born in Shanballymore, his parents' connection with the area is firmly attested. The marriage licence bond between Richard Burke and Mary Nagle, dated 21 October 1724, is an Anglican document, from the Church of Ireland diocese of Cloyne. There is no record of a Catholic marriage, but there must have been one. Mary Burke is known to have been a believing Catholic and could not have been content with the Anglican ceremony alone. Catholic marriages and baptisms were illegal under the penal laws, and few records of any such marriages have been found for the early eighteenth century.

Richard Burke is believed to have been descended from a Limerick branch of the Burke family which had settled in Cork, probably in the late seventeenth century. Edmund's great-grandfather settled in the mid Blackwater Valley, the Nagle country, and there was some intermarriage between Burkes and Nagles.

The John Burke who was Mayor of Limerick in 1646 is believed to have been an ancestor of Richard's. Irish Catholics were then divided between those who were prepared on certain conditions to support the royalists, and those who held it sinful to give any allegiance to a heretical prince (Charles I). John Burke belonged in the former category and, as mayor, proposed that Limerick should accept a 'peace' offered by Charles's viceroy, the Earl of Ormonde, under which all Catholics who rallied to the Crown would enjoy equal rights with other subjects. For this proposal John Burke was savagely assaulted by a fanatical mob incited by friars. They cried: 'Kill the rogues and traitors!' A priest cried: 'Kill all and I will absolve you!' Three years later, the moderate Catholics and fanatical Catholics alike went down in common ruin under the sword of Cromwell. The position adopted by the unfortunate mayor is consistent with the position of the mature Edmund Burke in Irish affairs: rejection of all religious and political fanaticism; acceptance of the link between Ireland and the British Crown; determination that all Catholic disabilities should be removed.

Shanballymore is in the heart of what is still known as 'the Nagle country', and Mary's large extended family were the leading Catholics in the area. But the Catholics of Ireland were a defeated people. The Nagles shared in the consequences of that defeat, and coped with it as best they could, with occasional conformity to the Church of Ireland. Mary Burke appears to have conformed shortly after her marriage, but she continued all her life as a practising. Catholic.

Although the eighteenth-century Nagles had come down in the world, and were threatened by the penal laws and their Protestant neighbours, they were far from hopelessly downtrodden. They were part of what the historian Kevin Whelan describes as 'that fusion of long-established rural Catholic families, with close ties to the towns, and links with the Continent and the new world'. This was to be the backbone of Irish Catholicism in the late eighteenth century.

One of the most marked features of Burke's mind, as it developed, was a sense of the contrast between social realities and the abstract systems that claim to govern them. His Ireland must have been, in that respect, a good school. At the age of six, he was sent by his parents to live with his maternal uncle, Patrick Nagle, in Ballyduff, at the foot of the Nagle Mountains, in Co. Cork. It is said that he was sent there as a sickly child, for the sake of his health, since the city of Dublin was then an unhealthy place. But there was probably also another reason, no less important. As a devout Catholic, Mary Burke must have wanted her son to get the basics of a Catholic education, in spite of the ostensible and constrained conformity of the Burke family.

For this purpose, the move to Ballyduff was highly advantageous. Dublin, in those days, was the capital of an Ireland that was officially entirely Protestant, since the law presumed no such person as an Irish

Roman Catholic to exist, except for the purpose of punishment. The law was very strong in Dublin, much less strong in rural Co. Cork. Throughout Ireland, in theory, the penal code still prohibited and penalized Catholic education, the presence of Catholic priests and attendance at Mass. But in practice the authorities had not seriously attempted to enforce the provisions of the religious side of the anti-Catholic laws since Cromwellian times. The provisions that were rigorously applied from 1691 onwards were those pertaining to wealth and power: those that made it advantageous for a Catholic landowner, or relative of a Catholic landowner, to become a Protestant; those that denied Catholics access to the franchise, Parliament, the military profession and – somewhat less rigorously – the legal profession.

In the 1730s, places such as Ballyduff were openly Catholic as far as the profession and practice of religion were concerned. Protestant neighbours were vigilant and repressive about what they perceived as subversion – social, agrarian or political – but they did not attempt what would have been the daunting and dangerous task of interfering, or asking the government to interfere, with the religious life of their far more numerous Catholic neighbours. So there was never any danger that a party of redcoats would be sent down to Ballyduff to stop little Edmund from attending Mass with his uncle.

Richard Burke must have had no great objection to Edmund's being brought up by Catholics, or he would not have allowed him to be sent to Ballyduff for five years. Whilst there, Edmund attended a 'hedge school' conducted by a teacher named O'Halloran, under the walls of the ruined castle of Monanimy, formerly a Nagle stronghold. The Blackwater Valley is one of the most beautiful regions in Ireland; it was the home of Edmund Spenser and became the landscape of *The Faerie Queene*. Monanimy Castle is on an escarpment, rising above the north bank of the Blackwater, about a hundred yards from the river. Looking south-east across the river from the grounds of his school, the young Burke would have seen, less than a mile away across the river, the forfeited demesne lands and woods of his Jacobite kinsman, Sir Richard Nagle of Carrigacunna, James II's Attorney-General. Behind those lost Nagle lands he could see the range of hills still known as the Nagle Mountains.

Hedge schools were Catholic institutions in their general ethos, and the only places Catholics could get an education. They were illegal, and were conducted in the open air, originally so that master and pupil could disperse more promptly if the law was enforced, as sometimes it had been in the very early years of the penal code – and might still be to vent some personal spite. At the hedge school, Burke's education was probably from an itinerant friar, who was most likely a Dominican or Franciscan. It is very unlikely that he was taught by Jesuits, as later hostile rumours had it.

The mid Blackwater Valley, where Burke was brought up from his sixth to his eleventh year, was in the early eighteenth century different from the anglicized East Coast, not only in religion, but in language. The vernacular of the Nagle country was Gaelic. Edmund's Nagle relatives spoke Gaelic, although they also spoke English, and probably some French as well. In the hedge school, which prepared children for the real world, English would have been the medium of instruction, but at times of recreation the language would have been Gaelic. During this period, the young Burke was living in a culture quite distinct from that of the English Pale in Ireland, the area where the English writ had traditionally run, in which his parents lived and where all his later schooling took place. It was quite different, too, from southern England, where he spent his maturity.

Such an experience, in early boyhood, could not fail to leave an abiding mark on his personality. In later life, when his deep early involvement with Catholic Ireland would have been considered compromising, Burke did not refer in any utterances that have been preserved to these childhood experiences, mentioning only the later, safely Protestant, phases of his education.

To be brought up in Ballyduff and to love his Nagle relatives was to share in a considerable part of the experience of the Gaelic-speaking Catholic Irish, and to be at least somewhat affected by Irish Catholic aspirations and interpretations of history. Among the Nagles, this meant an acceptance of the Revolution of 1688 and the Protestant Succession as *faits accomplis*, but also a bitter resentment of the broken Treaty of Limerick, the penal laws and Protestant domination. The Nagles hoped for the rehabilitation of the Catholic Irish within a revised 'revolution settlement'. These views were suspect in the world in which the young Burke had to make his way as a young man, both in Ireland and England, but they were generally those avowed by the mature and successful statesman.

Linguistically and culturally, where concealment was less imperative than in religious matters, the continuity is clear. All his life Burke retained an interest in the Irish language and its literature. He played an important part in the preservation of its monuments and in rendering them accessible to scholars. In 1765 at Beechwood, Hertfordshire, he discovered in the library of his friend Sir John Sebright some important early manuscripts in Irish. Realizing their value, he borrowed them and sent them for evaluation to the librarian of Trinity College, Dublin. Sebright later presented them to the college library, where they are now recognized as being among the foundations of the Irish manuscript collection. So it was through Burke that an important part of the source material for the great scholarly advances of the nineteenth century in this field was made available.

LATER SCHOOLING

At the age of twelve, in 1741, Burke was moved out of the Catholic environment to a boarding school kept by a Quaker, Abraham Shackleton, at Ballitore, Co. Kildare. This was much nearer Dublin and in more 'settled' country. Presumably his father thought it was time for him to be preparing for a career, as a Protestant. The school was well chosen. At Ballitore, Burke received a good classical preparation for Trinity College, Dublin. The atmosphere was Protestant but not strictly so, since the Shackletons were dissenters, and Abraham Shackleton, a pacifist, was as remote as possible from any tendency to polemical theology.

The contrast between Ballyduff and Ballitore was not a collision; many people of various denominations and of considerable note sent their children to Ballitore (Paul Cullen, later Roman Catholic Archbishop of Dublin, and Cardinal, was a pupil there in 1812). It is clear that Abraham Shackleton was a man of independence and integrity, and that the school was run on his principles rather than on conventions dominant in the society from which he drew his pupils. In a published advertisement for the school he stated that from conscientious motives he declined 'to teach that part of the academic course which he conceives to be injurious to morals and subversive of sound principles, particularly those authors who recommend in seducing language the illusions of love and the abominable trade of war'.

In April 1744, Burke sat successfully for entrance to Trinity College,

8

Dublin. The earliest letter that survives from his pen – to his friend at school and university, Richard Shackleton, Abraham's son – tells of his examination, in Horace, Virgil and Homer, by an 'exceeding good humoured cleanly civil fellow – N.B. I judge by outward appearances.' It also tells of the cleanly fellow's comments: 'He was pleased to say (what I would not say after him unless to a particular friend) that I was a good scholar, understood the authors very well and seemed to take pleasure in them (yet by the by I don't know how he could tell that) and that I was more fit for the college than three parts of my class.'

Most of what we know of Burke's life as an undergraduate at Trinity, and all we know of the early working of his mind, comes from a series of sixty letters to Richard Shackleton, written between April 1744 and January 1748/9. Thomas Copeland, the editor of Burke's *Correspondence*, says that Shackleton 'was an unusually intelligent and serious boy, steadier and more settled than Burke was ever to become'. On Burke's letters to Shackleton, Copeland justly remarks that they are disappointing to those hoping for precocious revelations of genius.

Critics [he writes] often speak of their eagerness to witness the trial flights of genius. Burke's sixty undergraduate letters, thirty-five of them written before his seventeenth birthday, are the rare case of the critics being given their hearts' desire. Alas for romantic hopes! The undergraduate letters are an entirely creditable series, but they are not much more vivid or interesting than other people's undergraduate letters. They do not record much of their writer's experience, perhaps because he had had very little. They do not give proof of a precocious sensitivity to language, being in fact rather carelessly written. What is most remarkable in them, a ranging energy of mind that was always a characteristic of Burke, is not in its adolescent phase an unusually winning virtue.

Yet though Burke's genius by no means shines out, it is quite clear from these adolescent letters that certain lifelong habits of mind and certain attitudes or prejudices were already formed. There is already the Burkean emphasis on *circumstances*, the awareness that the nature of things is a sturdy adversary: 'How little avails this freedom [of man's will] if the objects he is to act upon be not as much disposed to obey as he to command, what well-laid and better executed scheme of his is there but what a small change of nature is sufficient to defeat and entirely abolish.' He is aware already of the necessity of considering the substance of things rather than an abstraction:

> Your office of a schoolmaster throws you amongst the ancient authors who are generally reputed the best. But as they are commonly read and taught, the only use that seems to be made of 'em is barely to learn the language they are written in, a very strange inversion of the use of that kind of learning: to read of things to understand words, instead of learning words that we may be the better enabled to profit by the excellent things which are wrapt up in 'em!

He is already distrustful of human nature, and of those who are confident in their own virtue; he expresses himself about the 'inner light' in terms which must have been somewhat wounding to his Quaker friend: 'I don't like that part of your letter wherein you say you had the testimonies of well-doing in your breast, whenever such motions rise again, endeavour to suppress 'em. It is one of the subtlest stratagems that the Enemy of Mankind uses to delude us, that by lulling us into a false peace his conquest may be the easier.' There are clear traces here of a deposit of Catholic instruction from his Ballyduff years.

Copeland writes of the tentativeness and uncertainty that characterize many of these letters, in which the adolescent Burke tries on various styles and manners, devotional, facetious, oriental, romantic, and so on. Most of these exercises are unremarkable. What is striking, however, is that the few passages expressing attitudes and convictions that were to be lasting are marked by a greater maturity, vigour and determination, even testiness, than the surrounding matter.

Burke probably did not express himself with the same freedom to anyone other than Richard Shackleton. For a very young man, he already knew only too well the need to be on guard. In one of the letters he writes: 'We live in a world where everyone is on the catch, and the only way to be safe is to be silent – silent in any affair of consequence; and I think it would not be a bad rule for every man to keep within what he thinks of others, of himself, and of his own affairs.' Adherence to this rule may well account for the large gaps in our knowledge of Burke's early career. It is clear that although he was two years younger than Richard, Edmund considered himself to have more experience of the need for distrust, and that this opinion was well-founded. The passage advising silence was written during the Forty-Five Jacobite rebellion, but Burke did not refer explicitly to that event until his next letter to Richard, dated 26 April 1746, ten days after Culloden:

> This Pretender who gave us so much disturbance for some time past is at length with his adherents entirely defeated and himself, as some say, taken prisoner. This is the most material or rather the only news here. 'Tis strange to see how the minds of people are in a few days changed, the very men who but a while ago, while they were alarmed by his progress, so heartily cursed and hated those unfortunate creatures are now all pity and wish it could be terminated without bloodshed. I am sure I share in the general compassion; 'tis indeed melancholy to consider the state of those unhappy gentlemen who engaged in this affair (as for the rest they lose but their lives) who have thrown away their lives and fortunes and destroyed their families for ever in what I believe they thought a just cause.

Although loyalty to the Stuart cause was much less strong in Ireland than in Scotland, where loyalty was sustained by national sentiments, all Catholics had strong reasons for wishing for a restoration of the Catholic dynasty. Deep down, Burke may well have shared that wish, but he knew that it was worse than useless to indulge such an unrealistic hope.

TRINITY COLLEGE, DUBLIN

Burke's university career was distinguished. He became a Scholar of the House in his senior freshman year, in June 1746. Between then and taking his degree in January 1748, and for a short time after that, he busied himself to some purpose with the debating club which he founded and with a miscellany paper, *The Reformer*, which he also founded and largely wrote. Both were moralistic, preoccupied with improvement in taste and knowledge, rather earnest, determined, talented, a bit priggish, with the air of a rising middle class about them. Both were exercises and preparations for success in the world. Both carry the imprint of Burke's will and purpose, yet the specific imprint of his quality of mind is generally not much more discernible in them than in the 'exercise' portions of his letters to Shackleton.

The club, founded on 21 April 1747, was a small one: the seven members included William Dennis and Andrew Buck, who both became Church of Ireland clergymen. The others were Burke's old friend Richard Shackleton, Matthew Mohun, Joseph Hamilton and Abraham Ardesoif. If it was not a group entirely of intimates, or even altogether like minds, it was at least an exclusive club of mutually acceptable acquaintances, significantly different from a modern college debating society such as the Trinity College Historical Society, which claims descent from it and has preserved its records. The preamble to its laws begins: 'The improvement of the mind being the proper employment of a reasonable creature . . .' and makes it clear that the members were conscious of the club as a training ground for life, so that 'when years draw us further into the cares and business of life, we would be thereby enabled to go with more ease through the duties of it; and more largely to contribute to the good of the public and to the increase of our private interest'. The club's business included the reading of prepared papers, reading aloud of suitable poetry (with a preference for speeches from *Paradise Lost*) and debating on set themes.

Little more than a week after its foundation, the club experienced a conflict between the freedom of debate and training for success in life. It was the third meeting, with Burke acting as secretary. In the course of a debate on 'whether the woollen or linen manufacture be best for Ireland', it happened that 'some expression' was 'dropped with some warmth concerning the conduct of the English in denying us a free commerce'. Andrew Buck then argued that no subjects should be set 'which in the discussion of the question will make us show any dislike to His Majesty or his ministry' and that 'questions related to the government of our country are ticklish points and not fit to be handled'. Burke argued against this, holding that 'to restrain us in considering what would be more useful to our country would take away a most considerable part of our improvement and that there is no danger of our showing any disloyalty to His Majesty'. A long debate followed. Further consideration of the question was adjourned to the next committee meeting. When it came up again, at a meeting on 8 May, Buck, who received 'thanks for his diligence in promoting the good of the society', proposed a new club law: 'No questions relating to the government of our country which may possibly affect our loyalty to be handled in this assembly.' Burke's minutes record simply that the new law 'was carried'; we do not know whether a debate occurred or what the voting was.

The minutes do record a debate, however, on another proposal by Buck, 'to restrain us from throwing any personal reflection on each other'. Burke opposed this, saying that

> we act here not in our real but certain personated characters, and that any reflection on Mr Buck of this society does not hurt him as Mr Buck of the [incomplete], that confining us will destroy our oratory and consequently the society, as it only flourished in great states, which he confirmed by examples. This law were it to pass would take away our spirit by reducing our speeches to dry logical reasoning, as otherwise it is almost impossible to condemn bad actions without also condemning him from whom they proceed.

Buck and Hamilton were for the motion, Burke and Mohan against. It was defeated by the casting vote of the chairman, William Dennis.

The incident is interesting both for the pressure brought to bear on Burke and for his response. Buck's introduction of a loyalty test on subjects for debate – a sanction from the world outside the club – must have been disconcerting, unwelcome, even a little frightening. Someone with Burke's background was not in a good position to argue about loyalty, as conceived by the Protestant Ireland of his day. In the first phase of the argument he had had to accept defeat: the constitution of the club is modified in an important way, against his will. But he shifts his ground and wins on the question of personalities. And in the course of this debate he re-established what Buck had shaken, the fictitious nature of the proceedings of the club: 'We act here not in our real but certain personated characters.' If there was felt to be something doubtful or dangerous about his contribution to the previous debate, or to any debate, the 'personated character' would cover it. At no time in his life was Burke a stranger to what he was to describe in his *Reflections on the Revolution in France* as the 'politic well-wrought veil'. Yet through the veil, at this moment of difficulty, we have a rare early glimpse of the enduring Burke, in his rejection of anything that would have the effect of 'reducing our speeches to dry logical reasoning', and his assertion that 'it is almost impossible to condemn bad actions without also condemning him from whom they proceed'.

As a preparation for 'the cares and business of life', these early proceedings of the club were relevant enough. Perhaps they were felt to be all too relevant. It may be significant that the most ticklish debates all occurred in the first month of the club's life. Later, the discussions took a more academic turn, and where politics were touched on, it was in a harmless fashion, as for instance in a panegyric Burke gave on Chesterfield's lord lieutenancy.

In Burke's next enterprise, early the following year, he avoided the kinds of point that had proved ticklish in the club. The miscellany called *The Reformer* did not concern itself with specific political reforms. The penal laws which Burke passionately resented, as he was to show later, were not touched on – no doubt wisely, for Burke was not yet strong enough to attack them effectively, and had he attacked them prematurely he might never have become strong enough. Rather, *The Reformer* set out to improve taste, arguing that the reform of taste was the first and surest method of reforming morals. As yet the case was not very clearly made, but it was to be a consistent conviction, and during the French Revolution he was to write that taste and elegance were 'among the smaller and secondary morals'.

Inevitably *The Reformer* imitated Addison, and it was done skilfully enough. Its tone was middle-class, but unlike the club, and unlike everything in Burke's subsequent career, it was also provincial, making use of the typical argument that the citizens of the province enjoy exceptional virtue and good sense, which are menaced with corruption by the ephemeral and immoral productions of London. The journal's thirteen numbers (28 January to 21 April 1748) were exercises again – but even the exploration of a blind alley can be an exercise. Burke was, however, consistent with himself in seeing morality as dependent on religion, and both as menaced by the two great enemies, 'infidelity and blind zeal'. As he wrote, 'the first gives rise to the free-thinkers, the latter to the sectarians'. These were the apparently opposing forces which, towards the end of his life, he was to see joined in an unholy alliance in the English response to the French Revolution. The explosion of *Reflections* had an exceptionally long fuse.

It was Richard Burke's intention that his son should follow in his footsteps into the law. At eighteen, Edmund was accordingly enrolled as a student of the Middle Temple. He left Dublin at twenty-one to begin his studies; his bond in the Middle Temple is dated May 1750. Not long after his enrolment, he had written to Shackleton, apparently about their friend William Dennis: 'Don't you think, had he money to bear his charges, [that] 'twere his best course to go to London? I am told that a man who writes can't miss there getting some bread, and possibly good. I heard the other day of a gentleman who maintained himself in the study of the law by writing pamphlets in favour of the ministry.' He may have seen the school of 'personated' characters as fitting its graduates for such employment. At any rate it is clear that he saw not only law but writing and politics, or a combination of the two, as outlets for talent, and London, not Dublin, as the place of greatest scope.

THE MISSING YEARS

Hardly anything significant is known about Burke's life for nine years after his graduation. As Copeland writes in his introduction to the *Correspondence*,

> the well-recorded period of Burke's youth ends when he takes his B.A. at Trinity in January 1748. There is a single short letter written in the following month, and after that Burke's whole surviving correspondence for the two last years he remained in Ireland consists of two sentences and part of a third which biographers have quoted from letters now lost . . . We have six letters – two of them highly uninformative poetic epistles – to tell us of his activities in his first two-and-a-half years in England. Then between the autumn of 1752 and the summer of 1757 comes the darkest period of all. To illuminate those five years there remains a single letter, which happens to be torn and incomplete.

With so little to go on for this period, a piece of gossip may be worth recording. Sir Richard Musgrave, in his *Memoirs*, wrote that a year after Burke had gone to the Temple, an apprentice of Richard Burke noted that Edmund 'seemed much agitated in his mind and that when they were alone, he frequently introduced religion as a topic of conversation'. The apprentice believed Burke 'was become a convert to P[opery]'. Burke's father was 'much concerned' at this report, and had his brother-in-law, Mr Bowen, make 'strict enquiry about the conversion of his son'. Bowen reported that Edmund had indeed converted. 'Mr Burke became furious, lamenting that the rising hope of his family was blasted, and that the

expense he had been at in his education was now thrown away.'
Musgrave continues that it was

> possible that Mr Burke, in the spring of life . . . might have conformed to the
> exterior ceremonies of Popery to obtain Miss Nugent, of whom he was very
> much enamoured; but it is not to be supposed that a person of so vigorous
> and highly cultivated an understanding would have continued under the
> shackles of that absurd superstition.

Because of Musgrave's obsession with Catholicism, he is often treated as
an unreliable witness. Yet Richard Burke's reported reaction to his son's
reported conversion (or regression) to Catholicism has a ring of truth.
And destruction of relevant correspondence by Burke himself might
perhaps account for some of what is missing in these missing years.

Certainly, in the spring of 1757, Edmund Burke married Jane Nugent,
the daughter of a well-known Irish Catholic physician, Christopher
Nugent, who was a friend both of Burke and Samuel Johnson. Characteristically, Musgrave describes Nugent as 'a most bigoted Romanist bred at
Douay in Flanders'. Jane Nugent appears to have conformed at one time to
the Established Church, but like Burke's mother, she practised the Catholic
religion throughout her married life. No record of the marriage has been
found. If it were a Catholic marriage, as Jane would have insisted, it could
not have been legally solemnized in England or Ireland. It may have been a
Catholic marriage in France. In any case, the marriage of Edmund Burke
and Jane Nugent, over its forty years, was to be an extremely happy one.
Two sons, Richard and Christopher, were born in 1758, but only Richard
survived infancy.

In his late twenties, Burke published two books, which were well
received: *A Vindication of Natural Society* (1756), a satirical anticipation
of the great melody of his life's works, and *A Philosophical Enquiry into
the origin of our Ideas of the Sublime and Beautiful* (1757). *The Sublime and
Beautiful* has been described by Jerry C. Beasley as 'a brilliant study of
the emotional responses called forth by a variety of images and effects'.
It is also an implicit rejection of the limitations of Burke's Quaker
education. Abraham Shackleton had refused to teach 'those authors who
recommend in seducing language the illusions of love and the
abominable trade of war'. Burke, however, found the origin of 'the
beautiful' in love, and the origin of 'the sublime' in war.

By the early 1760s, Burke was laying the foundations of his political career in London. In 1759, he became an assistant to a well-known parliamentarian and almost exact contemporary, William Gerard Hamilton (1729–96). In April 1761, Hamilton became Chief Secretary for Ireland under the Lord Lieutenant, the Earl of Halifax, and asked Burke to accompany him as his private secretary. Burke accepted. As private secretary to the Chief Secretary, he had a minor role in the government of Ireland until 1764, when Hamilton was dismissed, and was in Dublin for sessions of the Irish Parliament in the winters of 1761 and 1762.

To the extent that he could influence policy, his principal objective was to improve the condition of the Catholics. In the autumn of 1761, he is said to have been already at work on a *Tract Relative to the Laws against Popery* in Ireland. This was not completed, nor was any part of it published during his lifetime, but the known fragments of it occupy some seventy pages. In the main, the *Tract* is a synopsis and an indictment of the penal code as it existed in the 1760s. The code then stood in full rigour on the statute book, though it was not enforced with the severity seen earlier in the century. Burke had studied it closely, and was to write about it during the American Revolution, during the French Revolution and during the incubation of the Irish Rebellion of 1798. So his *Tract* is important as a first investigation of the penal code. Burke's formal position – unlike that he adopts in all his later comments – is that some measures of exclusion of Catholics are just and necessary. Exclusion 'from all offices in church and state', he writes, is 'a just and necessary provision'. But when it comes to their exclusion from the army and the law 'in all its branches', he offers some extreme examples of 'scrupulous severity' – which, by implication, were neither just nor necessary.

It is hard to believe that Burke ever really thought that the exclusion of Catholics from all state offices was 'just and necessary', and his later writings on the penal code are incompatible with such a belief. We may infer from this that the *Tract* was prepared to be shown to someone, probably Hamilton, who did believe in such exclusion. Presumably Burke hoped that his concession would make Hamilton more willing to listen to the rest of his argument. For while Burke generally argued from deep and strong conviction, he was not above the occasional tactical adjustment if it might serve to carry the rest of his argument. (He himself was later to acknowledge publicly that 'an economy of truth' was permissible in certain circumstances.) The rest of the *Tract* is then made up of powerful arguments against various aspects of the penal code. It stresses that its victims are the majority of the people of Ireland:

> The happiness or misery of multitudes can never be a thing indifferent. A law against the majority of the people is in substance a law against the people itself; its extent determines its invalidity; it even changes its character as it enlarges its operation: it is not particular injustice but general oppression, and can no longer be considered as a private hardship which might be borne, but spreads and grows up into the unfortunate importance of a national calamity. Now as a law directed against the mass of the nation has not the nature of a reasonable institution, so neither has it the authority: for in all forms of government the people is the true legislator; and whether the immediate and instrumental cause of the law be a single person or many, the remote and efficient cause is the consent of the people, either actual or implied; and such consent is absolutely essential to its validity.

Burke points out that those in Ireland who most fiercely condemned the bigotry of the French monarchy in matters of religion were the first inclined to practise it themselves.

> For my part, there is no circumstance, in all the contradictions of our most mysterious nature, that appears to be more humiliating than the use we are disposed to make of those sad examples which seem purposely marked for our correction and improvement. Every instance of fury and bigotry in other men, one should think, would naturally fill us with an horror of that disposition: the effect, however, is directly contrary. We are inspired, it is true, with a very sufficient hatred for the party, but with no detestation at all of the proceeding. Nay, we are apt to urge our dislike of such measures as a reason for imitating them and, by an almost incredible absurdity, because some powers have destroyed their country by their persecuting spirit, to argue, that we ought to retaliate on them by destroying our own.

Having shown the code to be ineffective in its declared objective of penalizing Papists into becoming Protestants, he finds the lapidary phrase: 'Ireland, after almost a century of persecution, is at this time full of penalties and full of Papists.' He then takes on the Protestant argument that any suffering that the Catholics endure is their own fault, because they are free to escape all penalties simply by becoming Protestants:

> Now as to the other point, that the objects of these laws suffer voluntarily, this seems to me to be an insult rather than an argument. For besides that it totally annihilates every characteristic, and therefore every faulty idea of persecution, just as the former does; it supposes, what is false in fact, that it is in a man's moral power to change his religion whenever his convenience requires it. If he be beforehand satisfied that your opinion is better than his, he will voluntarily come over to you, and without compulsion; and then your law would be unnecessary; but if he is not so convinced, he must know that it is his duty in this point to sacrifice his interest here to his opinion of his eternal happiness, else he could have in reality no religion at all. In the former case, therefore, as your law would be unnecessary; in the latter, it would be persecuting; that is, it would put your penalty and his ideas of duty in the opposite scales; which is, or I know not what is, the precise idea of persecution.

From the son of Richard Burke, a convert to the Established Church, this passage has a poignant ring. It seems that Richard had failed, in Edmund's view, in his 'duty ... to sacrifice his interest here to his opinion of his eternal happiness'. And Edmund's political career, then just beginning, was open to him only by virtue of that failure in his father. Here he is writing in the persona of a strong but fair-minded Protestant, the better to expose the absurdity and injustice of the anti-Catholic code: 'We found the people heretics and idolaters; we have, by way of improving their condition, rendered them slaves and beggars: they remain in all the misfortune of their old errors, and all the superadded misery of their recent punishment.'

A passage about some of the Irish Protestants' habitual arguments in defence of the penal laws may also have an autobiographical resonance:

> The great prop of this whole system is not pretended to be its justice or its utility, but the supposed danger to the state which gave rise to it originally, and which they apprehend would return if this system were overturned. Whilst, say they, the Papists of this kingdom were possessed of landed property, and of the influence consequent to such property, their allegiance to

the Crown of Great Britain was ever insecure, the public peace was ever liable to be broken, and Protestants never could be a moment secure either of their properties or of their lives. Indulgence only made them arrogant, and power daring; confidence only excited and enabled them to exert their inherent treachery; and the times, which they generally selected for their most wicked and desperate rebellions, were those in which they enjoyed the greatest ease and the most perfect tranquillity.

Such are the arguments that are used, both publicly and privately, in every discussion upon this point. They are generally full of passion and of error, and built upon facts which in themselves are most false.

How often, and with what a sinking heart, Burke must have listened to people talking in that vein, full of passion and error. But he was constrained to reply to them on the basis of assumptions common to Protestants in general – and not of the Catholic assumptions which were so much nearer his heart. In his predicament, straddling the great divide between Protestant and Catholic, and listening to a Protestant bigot's views about Papists, the most insistent and painful question must always have been, did the bigot know of Burke's close Catholic connections? If he didn't, the situation was relatively harmless; but if he did, then Burke was listening to a personal enemy obliquely taunting him, menacing him with a hint of exposure. His position was comparable to that of a person of Jewish origin brought up as a Christian in a country with a legal system saturated with anti-Semitism and having to listen to fellow Christians holding forth about 'the Jews' in hostile and contemptuous terms. In the light of that predicament, he was courageous in taking up the cudgels against the powerful enemies of his people (or, at the very least, of his mother's people). Political courage is an expensive commodity, and he was to pay a heavy price for it in parliamentary terms nearly twenty years later.

The tenor of the 1761–62 administration of Halifax and Hamilton in Ireland was exceptionally mild and enlightened. Some of the credit for that should go to the private secretary to the Chief Secretary, Edmund Burke. The main problem they faced was the Catholic 'Whiteboy' disturbances in Munster in the early 1760s. The Irish Protestant landlords and oligarchs insisted that these disturbances were seditious, and of Jacobite and French inspiration – a heavy imputation at a time when

Britain and Ireland were at war with France. The Jacobite-French interpretation of Whiteboyism had, and was meant to have, a tendency to raise suspicions that the Irish Catholic gentry – the natural leaders of their people in political matters – bore some responsibility for the disturbances. But the administration resisted the pressure from the Protestant oligarchy, and treated the disturbances instead as essentially agrarian in character (correctly, in the view of most historians). This tended to exonerate the Catholic gentry, most of whose economic interests were opposed to those of the impoverished Whiteboys. As Burke's biographer Carl B. Cone writes, the Whiteboy outrages

> marked the beginnings of the agrarian disturbances that remained a baneful feature of Irish life for another century and a half. Against the protests of angry Protestants and frightened Francophobes, Lord Halifax steadfastly refused to consider the disorders of the early 1760s as either sectarian or political in nature. So did Sir Richard Aston, Chief Justice of the Common Pleas in Ireland. After making a judicial circuit of the embroiled counties, Aston wrote to Hamilton that the disturbances in which 'Papist and Protestant were promiscuously concerned' were not caused by 'disaffection to his Majesty, his government, or the laws in general', but arose mainly from bad economic conditions.

Burke probably contributed a good deal to the thinking of the Halifax–Hamilton administration about the Whiteboys, despite his lowly position. It is a mistake to equate his political importance with the importance of the offices he held, which was never great. His contemporaries were well aware of his gifts, even though they sometimes disparaged his use of them. Burke was the only man of whom Samuel Johnson stood in awe. 'That fellow calls forth all my powers,' he said on a day when he was ill. 'Were I to see Burke now, it would kill me.' Lesser mortals were less inclined to stand in awe, and the lesser they were, the less in awe they stood; but William Hamilton was intelligent enough to understand Burke's unique combination of gifts. It was as an adviser, not an amanuensis, that Hamilton employed him. So it is probably no coincidence that this major policy of the administration in which Hamilton was Chief Secretary followed the advice that we know Burke would have given.

It is possible, however, that Hamilton came to resent the intellectual superiority of his adviser, and to chafe under his advice. In any case, the two men quarrelled irrevocably in April or May of 1765. The rift appears to have originated, at least in part, in a feeling on Burke's side that Hamilton had let him down on a matter of concern to Irish Catholics.

INTO PARLIAMENT

Burke soon acquired a more lasting patron. On 11 July 1765, he became private secretary to Charles Watson-Wentworth, 2nd Marquess of Rockingham (1730–82), who was just then forming a government, which was to last for a year. He was leader of that section of the Whigs which Burke regarded as the most principled element in Parliament. To the end of Rockingham's life, Burke remained a loyal Rockingham Whig, and the party's chief policymaker and publicist. But the relationship came near to foundering within its first week, because of his Irish connections, as interpreted by his enemies. On 16 July, he quotes *Macbeth* to his actor friend David Garrick: 'So far at least, I thank God, the designs of my enemies, who not long since made a desperate stroke at my fortune, my liberty, and my reputation (All! Hell-kite! All at a swoop), have failed of their effect, and their implacable and unprovoked malice has been disappointed.'

According to the *Memoirs* of the Earl of Charlemont, who may have heard the story from Burke himself, the Duke of Newcastle warned Rockingham that Burke was a dangerous person to associate with. He was an Irish Papist, said to have been educated by the Jesuits at St Omer and sent to England as a spy. Burke was able to satisfy Rockingham that the allegations were unfounded, Rockingham refused his offer of resignation, and the episode was closed. We don't know what exactly Burke said in his explanation to Rockingham. He probably practised 'an economy of truth'. Yet he had an acute sense of personal honour, and he was being questioned about a matter of intimate concern to him, over which he observed habitual reticence. Fortunately, Newcastle's specific 'Jesuit' charges were unfounded. He had never been near St Omer, so he could deny that flatly, which presumably placated Rockingham. But Rockingham might not have been so satisfied if he had understood the extent of Burke's connections with Catholic Ireland. Throughout his career, cartoonists would continue to portray Burke in the garb of a Jesuit, and the whiskey bottle and the potato joined the Jesuit cassock as identifying props.

Burke was elected to Parliament for the Borough of Wendover in December 1765, and attracted public attention with the brilliance of his first Commons speech in January 1766. The first Rockingham administration fell in July 1766, and shortly afterwards Burke went to Ireland for three months.

The Rockingham Whigs were to remain in opposition for sixteen years. Political parties were not at the time as formal as they were to become, and some former Rockinghams took office in other administrations during this period. Overtures were made to Burke, and his political career could have been much more superficially brilliant than it proved if he had chosen to abandon Rockingham in or after 1766. That is the course he would have followed had he been the venal opportunist that some historians suggest. Instead he remained loyal to Rockingham, whose principles he admired.

In 1767, Lord Townshend became Lord Lieutenant of Ireland, ruling much more directly than any of his predecessors. Unlike them, he resided in Ireland and set himself, successfully, to curb the autonomy of the Protestant governing caste – which hated him accordingly. Burke and his Nagle relatives must have been hugely relieved by Townshend's advent, and yet he had reason to be careful even into the 1770s. In April 1770, on the floor of the House, a country gentleman, Sir William Bagot, asked of some debating point of Burke's: 'Such an idea, such a picture, where could it be formed? I should only think it came from one bred at St Omer's.' Lord John Cavendish, on behalf of the Rockinghams, rebuked Bagot, who then apologized. This did not save him from a stinging retort from Burke, who avoided calling his antagonist a liar, but only by the nicest of margins: 'He thought gentlemen above the invention of a lie would scorn to adopt the dirty falsehood that a newspaper was probably paid for propagating.'

Just over a week after that scene in the Commons, the *London Evening Post* published an article based on particulars innocently supplied four years earlier by Burke's old schoolfriend Richard Shackleton, who had still not learnt the discretion Burke had urged upon him at university. Of Burke's mother, Shackleton had written: 'She was of a Popish family; I cannot say whether she legally conformed to the Church of England, but she practised the duties of the Romish religion with a decent privacy.' He described Burke's wife Jane as 'a genteel, well-bred woman, of the Roman faith, whom he married neither for her religion, nor her money, but from the natural impulse of youthful affection'.

Shackleton had supplied the information in May 1766 in response to a letter from a Quaker correspondent in Dublin, at the request of 'a particular friend' of a 'kinsman' of the correspondent. The 'particular friend' asked to be advised of 'the family connections, religion (if any) and general character' of 'Edwd Bourk, Secretary to the Marqu of Rockinham', adding, 'this enquiry is not made with any design to prejudice E. Bourk but, as he apprehends, quite the contrary; therefore I request thou will give me such an answer as thou thinks proper and post per return.' The unworldly Shackleton duly supplied the information requested in this peculiar letter. Thomas Copeland writes: 'Having no suspicion whatever that the facts he had to relate might be used maliciously, Shackleton wrote a most complimentary short sketch of his friend.'

Later in 1766, Burke had got word of the enquiry, and was sufficiently concerned to ask Shackleton about it: 'I am given to understand that you have received at some time a letter from England, some way relating to me. Have you ever received such a letter?' No reply to this enquiry appears to have been preserved, and there seem to have been no immediate repercussions. But in 1770, when it all came out in public, Burke was furious. The episode temporarily strained the friendship, and it revealed Burke's extreme sensitivity to public discussion of his Catholic family connections. Replying to a letter from Shackleton, he wrote:

I confess a little weakness to you. I feel somewhat mortified at a paper written by you which some officious person has thought proper to insert in the *London Evening Post* of last night. I am used to the most gross and virulent abuse daily repeated in the papers – I ought indeed rather have said, twice a day. But this abuse is loose and general invective. It affects very little either my own feelings, or the opinions of others, because it is thrown out by those that are known to be hired to the office of my enemies. But this appears in the garb of professed apology and panegyric. It is evidently written by an intimate friend. It is full of anecdotes and particulars of my life. It therefore cuts deep. I am sure I have nothing in my family, my circumstances, or my conduct that an honest man ought to be ashamed of. But the more circumstances of all these which are brought out, the more materials are furnished for malice to work upon: and I assure you that it will manufacture them to the utmost. Hitherto, much as I have been abused, my table and my bed were left sacred, but since it has so unfortunately happened, that my wife, a quiet woman, confined to her family cares and affections, has been dragged into a newspaper, I own I feel a little hurt. A rough public man may be proof against all sorts of buffets, and he has no business to be a public man if he be not so. But there is as natural and proper a delicacy in the other sex which will not make it very pleasant to my wife to be the daily subject of Grub Street, and newspaper invectives; and at present, in truth, her health is little able to endure it.

In his reply, the mortified Shackleton attains an eloquence which his Quaker principles would have suppressed under ordinary circumstances. The letter also gives a vivid impression of how Edmund Burke, in an angry mood, appeared to a quiet friend. Shackleton wrote:

My dear Friend, if I may take the liberty still to call thee so, I have received thy letter written in the vexation of thy spirit, cutting and wounding in the tenderest parts, and ripping open a sore which I thought was long ago healed. I know nothing in the world about the publication of that unfortunate paper, but what thou tells me; nor who could be the publisher of it. I have used thee and thy family grossly ill. I acknowledged it as fully as I could. I am covered with grief, shame, and confusion for it. It was done in the simplicity of my heart: I mean the writing of it. The giving a copy of it I will not call indiscretion, but madness and folly. With the same simplicity I before let thee know how I came to write it, and why I gave a copy of it. When I had given it to my friend, and he had given a copy to his friend, it very probably circulated out of the power of either of us to recall. It passed like money through the hands of people, good and bad, friends and enemies, and because the matter was gold, though bunglingly coined, and possibly still more defaced in the circulation, it was too precious to be lost. I am sure I had no more thoughts of its spreading as it has done, nor of its ever being published, than I have of the publication of this letter. If what has been published varies at all from the copy which I sent thee, or if I can do anything by way of atonement or amendment, grant me this last favour of putting it in my power to do it . . . I said thy letter cut and wounded me: it did indeed effectually. It was dictated by a perturbed mind: it was calculated to punish and fret me, and it has obtained its end. Thy family, thy circumstances, thy conduct, thy bed, thy board: I am indirectly or directly charged with defaming and vilifying them all; not indeed as a false friend, but as a very foolish one. I could bear even all this, whether deserved or not, from thee. Thou art so used to lay about thee, and give and take no quarter with thy enemies, that it is unsafe for thy friends to be near thee. If there be any of the language of friendship in thy letter, it is only like oil, to make the edge more keen; if the voice be anywhere like Jacob's, the hands are Esau's. Thou art grown a rough public man, sure enough – I say I could bear even this from thee (for I know both my own heart and thine), and if the affair lay only between ourselves, there might some time be an end of it. But thy mention of my interfering in thy domestic connections and dragging the partner of thy bed and the softener of thy busy scenes of life into a newspaper is wounding to the last degree. Whatever thou art pleased to think of me, I have, perhaps, and (for aught I know) ever had as great delicacy in these matters as any man. Look into that ill-advised, impertinent paper which I stupidly wrote, and see is there anything that offends against the nicest delicacy?

Burke's reply of 6 May 1770 is worthy of himself and of Shackleton. It also gives some idea of the stress Burke was under:

My dear Friend, I am now in the place from whence I was weak and blameable enough to write you a very angry, a very cruel, and in all respects a very improper letter. I will not be more dilatory in making all the amends in my power for the offence than I was in offending. So I write immediately on the receipt of your letter. But let my apology be, if it be one, that a spirit not naturally over-patient had about that time ten thousand things to mortify it, and this coming on the back of them did for a while put me beside myself. I assure you I am so concerned for what you have felt that I could not bear to read through your description of it. A little trifling mere imprudence, at worst, did by no means deserve anything like a reproof, much less so harsh an one. As to my wife, you needed to make no apology at all to her. She felt nothing but good wishes and friendship to you, and is by no means liable to those spurts of passion to which I am unfortunately but too subject.

Burke, though reconciled and magnamimous, is also characteristically wary, for he adds:

> burn the letter I wrote, which deserves no better fate; and may I beg – since it is one of the drawbacks on those who get a little consideration in the world that every little matter relative to them, how unfit soever for the public eye, is dragged before it by one means or other – that you would commit to the same flames any other letters or papers of mine which you may find and which you think liable through some accident to be so abused. It is hardly credible how many people live by such publications and how hard it is altogether to escape their interested diligence.

Apart from the exchange in the House with Sir William Bagot, Burke came well out of what had been a stormy parliamentary session for him personally. He wrote to Charles O'Hara on 21 May 1770:

> After saying so much of the general state of things, you will expect I should say a word of myself. I must say, that the session ended well for me, I thank God. I have no doubt that a plan had been formed, by general calumny of every kind, as well as by personal attacks in Parliament, to reduce my little consideration to none at all. So it has happened that (notwithstanding I find everything which goes through the Irish Channel is very unfavourably reported for me) the malice of my enemies has not overpowered me; on the contrary it has been of service to me.

Burke was still deeply interested in Ireland, and in particular in the disabilities of the Irish Catholics, but in the early 1770s he needed to keep his distance. Detachment and even dissimulation were desirable, both in the interests of his personal career and in order to help Ireland, and specifically the Catholics, as he signally did later, in the persona of a disinterested and liberal observer of the Irish scene.

In 1773, a tax on absentee Irish landlords was mooted in Parliament. Nominally, Burke was the owner of a small estate in Ireland at Clogher, Co. Cork. More significantly, Rockingham owned large estates in Ireland, and stood to lose heavily by the passage of the Bill. It may therefore look as though their opposition to the Bill was dictated by material interests. However, opposition to the tax was entirely compatible with the principles on which Burke acted in matters concerning the relationship between Britain and Ireland (and indeed Britain's relations with America and with India). His guiding principle was the exact reverse of that of the father of Irish republicanism, Theobald Wolfe Tone (1763–98). Tone wanted 'to break the connection with England, the never failing source of all our political evils'. Burke wanted to strengthen that connection by making it more equitable, both in general by abolishing restraints on trade between the two countries, and specifically, in relation to the majority of the Irish people, by dismantling the penal code. He thought that objective much more likely to be achieved through the British Parliament than through an Irish Parliament of Protestant resident landlords. He thought that what Ireland needed was the removal of existing restraints and penalties, rather than the introduction of new ones, and the strengthening, not the weakening, of relations between the two countries. He did not want Members of Parliament to be forced to choose between one country and the other as their place of residence.

His writings on the absentee tax have the ring of conviction, and are animated by the same spirit as the rest of his writing about Ireland. To Rockingham, he wrote on 29 September 1773:

> I never can forget that I am an Irishman. I flatter myself perhaps, but I think I would shed my blood rather than see the limb I belong to oppressed and defrauded of its due nourishment. But this measure tends to put us out of our place and not to improve us in our natural situation. It is the mere effect of narrowness and passion, and if it should take effect would bring on the natural consequence of these causes ... There is a superficial appearance of equity in this tax, which cannot fail to captivate almost all those who are not led by some immediate interest to an attentive examination of its intrinsic merits.

Characteristically, Burke does not deny the existence of an 'interest', but finds it conducive to the kind of 'attentive examination' that exposes the weaknesses of the proposed tax.

Responding both to the force of the examination and to the weight of the interest behind it, the government – after the measure had been defeated in the Committee of Ways and Means of the Irish House of Commons in November 1773 – dropped the proposal, and Burke did not have to return to the matter.

In 1774, Burke was elected Member for Bristol. This was a great step forward in his career, and a great enhancement of his parliamentary status. Hitherto, he had been member for the insignificant pocket borough of Wendover. Now he was the representative of a thriving port, the second city in Great Britain. If he had been the opportunist some historians depict, or just an ordinary politician, he would have nursed this new and prestigious constituency with the utmost care, avoiding advocacy of anything that might run counter to the perceived interests of his constituents or offend their prejudices. But Burke failed to follow this prudent course. In April 1778, in relation to Irish commerce, he put free-trade principles ahead of the perceived interests of his most powerful constituents. And the following month he went on to offend their prejudices by helping to bring about the first legislative measure to relax the penal code against Catholics.

At the beginning of that April, British reverses in America and France's entry into the war led to the suggestion of various parliamentary measures. One set of proposals provided for direct importation of Irish goods, except woollens, into the colonies, and of colonial products, except tobacco and indigo, into Ireland; for the exportation of Irish glass, and for abolition of duties on cotton yarn, sailcloth and cordage imported into Britain from Ireland. Burke supported them, and they were approved in committee. Realizing that this would not go down well in Bristol, where the traders wished to maintain a protected trade, Burke wrote to one of his most prominent constituents and supporters, Samuel Span, of the Society of Merchant Adventurers:

> It is found absolutely necessary to improve the portion of this empire which is left, so as to enable every part to contribute in some degree to the strength and welfare of the whole. Our late misfortunes [in America] have taught us the danger and mischief of a restrictive coercive and partial policy. The trade in some degree opened by the resolutions is necessary, not so much for any benefit thereby derived to Ireland as to satisfy and unite the minds of men at this juncture by the sense of a common interest in the common defence. If nothing of this kind should be done, I apprehend very serious consequences. Ireland may probably in some future time come to participate of the benefits which we derive from the West India trade. But Ireland being a country of

the same nature with this can never be beneficial to this kingdom but by pursuing several, if not all, of the objects of commerce and manufacture which are cultivated here. The world, I apprehend, is large enough for all, and we are not to conclude that what is gained to one part of it is lost of course to the other. The prosperity arising from an enlarged and liberal system improves all its objects, and the participation of a trade with flourishing countries is much better than the monopoly of want and penury. These opinions I am satisfied will be relished by the clear understanding of the merchants of Bristol, who will discern that a great empire cannot at this time be supported upon a narrow and restrictive scheme either of commerce or government.

Constituents don't generally care to be addressed in such a way by their parliamentary representative, and it seems that Span was no exception. His reply of 13 April strikes an ominous note with respect to Burke's prospects in the next election:

Mr Burke's letter of the 9th Instant, transmitting copy of the Resolutions of the Committee of the House of Commons on the Trade of Ireland, was this day read at a general meeting of this society. The city are greatly alarmed at the measure, and intend to oppose it all in their power, and we are sorry that we are likely to be deprived of so able an advocate as Mr Burke. Ireland has many local advantages over us, and their duties are not in some instances (particularly sugar) above one fourth of ours, the difference between English and Irish money considered. The revenue in England will likewise be greatly diminished, and then additional taxes will be laid on. It strikes us at present that it would be much better for this kingdom that an union should take place rather than this very prejudicial measure, and then we should be on a more equal footing. The interest of your constituents and of the English manufactures call for your strenuous opposition to this plan.

Burke replied to Span on 23 April 1778, in a long, earnest and impressive letter. He took up Span's point about a union between Britain and Ireland:

You tell me, sir, that you prefer an union with Ireland to the little regulations which are proposed in Parliament. This union is a great question of state, to which, when it comes properly before me in my parliamentary capacity, I shall give an honest and unprejudiced consideration. However, it is a settled rule with me to make the most of my *actual situation*, and not to refuse to do a proper thing because there is something else more proper, which I am not able to do. This union is a business of difficulty, and, on the principles of your letter, a business impracticable. Until it can be matured into a feasible and desirable scheme, I wish to have as close an union of interest and affection with Ireland as I can have; and that, I am sure, is a far better thing than any nominal union of government.

He tries to get Span to see that Bristol, as well as Ireland, can benefit from increased Anglo-Irish trade:

If I thought you inclined to take up this matter on local considerations, I should state to you, that I do not know any part of the kingdom so well situated for an advantageous commerce with Ireland as Bristol; and that none would be so likely to profit of its prosperity as our city. But your profit and theirs must concur. Beggary and bankruptcy are not the circumstances which invite to an intercourse with that or with any country, and I believe it will be found invariably true, that the superfluities of a rich nation furnish a better object of trade than the necessities of a poor one. It is the interest of the commercial world that wealth should be found everywhere.

He ends with a notable declaration of the duty of a public representative:

I have written this long letter in order to give all possible satisfaction to my constituents with regard to the part I have taken in this affair. It gave me inexpressible concern to find that my conduct had been a cause of uneasiness to any of them. Next to my honour and conscience, I have nothing so near and dear to me as their approbation. However, I had much rather run the risk of displeasing than of injuring them, if I am driven to make such an option. You obligingly lament that you are not to have me for your advocate, but if I had been capable of acting as an advocate in opposition to a plan so perfectly consonant to my known principles, and to the opinions I had publicly declared on a hundred occasions, I should only disgrace myself, without supporting, with the smallest degree of credit or effect, the cause you wished me to undertake. I should have lost the only thing which can make such abilities as mine of any use to the world now or hereafter, I mean that authority which is derived from an opinion that a Member speaks the language of truth and sincerity, and that he is not ready to take up or lay down a great political system for the convenience of the hour; that he is in Parliament to support his opinion of the public good, and does not form his opinion in order to get into Parliament or to continue in it. It is in a great measure for your sake that I wish to preserve this character. Without it, I am sure, I should be ill able to discharge, by any service, the smallest part of that debt of gratitude and affection which I owe you for the great and honourable trust you have reposed in me.

Statements should always be read in context, and in this case the context proves the sincerity of the principle asserted. Any politician can utter noble principles that cost him nothing. But Burke, under pressure, is holding firm to a principle that brings him no material or career advantage, and which he knows may be about to cost him the greatest prize of his political career to date, his seat as Member of Parliament for Bristol. The principles he maintains, under Span's pressure, are those which he had declared on his election for Bristol in 1774:

Certainly, gentlemen, it ought to be the happiness and glory of a representative to live in the strictest union, the closest correspondence, and the most unreserved communication with his constituents. Their wishes ought to have great weight with him, their opinions high respect, their business unremitted attention. It is his duty to sacrifice his repose, his pleasure, his satisfactions, to theirs – and above all, ever and in all cases to prefer their interest to his own.

But his unbiased opinion, his mature judgement, his enlightened conscience, he ought not to sacrifice to you, to any man, or to any set of men living. These he does not derive from your pleasure – no, nor from the law and the constitution. They are a trust from providence, for the abuse of which he is deeply answerable. Your representative owes you not his industry only, but his judgment; and he betrays, instead of serving you, if he sacrifices it to your opinion.

Burke was distressed but not daunted by Span's threat. To a more friendly correspondent, John Noble, he wrote on the very next day:

You are so good as to say that you wish to see me Member for Bristol at the next general election. I most sincerely thank you, and beg leave to add this friendly wish to the innumerable obligations which I have to you already. To represent Bristol is a capital object of my pride at present. Indeed I have nothing external on which I can value myself but that honourable situation. If I should live to the next general election, and if being a Member of Parliament at that time should be desirable to me, I intend to offer myself again to your approbation. But far from wishing to throw the memory of the present business into the shade, I propose to put it forward to you and to plead my conduct on this occasion as a matter of merit on which to ground my pretentions to your future favour. I do not wish to represent Bristol, or to represent any place, but upon terms that shall be honourable to the chosen and to the choosers.

Not only will Burke not compromise or gloss over any differences, but he wishes to persuade his constituents, and insists on being judged on the very issue where he has offended.

In the summer of 1778, the first reform of the penal code passed through the British Parliament. Burke drafted the Bill, but it was introduced by Sir George Savile, a shrewd and influential Yorkshire gentleman and a close friend of Rockingham. The essence of what became the Catholic Relief Act was the relaxation of the restrictions upon the ownership of property by Catholics, and the abolition of the threat of forfeiture to Protestant relatives and informers. It repealed one of the earliest and most effective of the penal laws. At the time it passed, Burke wrote a letter explaining the strategy:

Some people who heartily agreed with us in the principle of our proceedings were of opinion that in an affair like this, involved in a multitude of penal regulations and disabilities, we ought not to have satisfied ourselves with the repeal of a single Act of Parliament, whilst we suffered grievances to continue under other unrepealed Acts, which were of as harsh an nature as those to which we had given a remedy. I admit this larger plan would have been theoretically preferable, and was most suitable to the firm and systematic mind of the Attorney-General who recommended it. But it was too large for the time and it would inevitably have entangled us in the speculations of every rash and busy mind. In a popular assembly we should never have found an end to a work of this kind. It was necessary to come with simplicity and directness to the point, and to repeal that Act which, with

33

the least apparent cruelty, had the most certain operation; leaving those laws which from their very savageness and ferocity were more noisy than effective to wait for a time of greater leisure. Neither was the choice of this method wholly blind and without a principle, for it affirmed that *property* was to be encouraged in the acquisition, and quieted in the holding, whatever might become of religious toleration . . .

The Attorney-General referred to in this letter was almost certainly Edward Thurlow, who left a striking record of what it felt like to be lobbied by Burke over the penal laws. To Burke himself, Thurlow wrote, after talking with him: 'I am ashamed to confess how much emotion your display of the Popery laws in Ireland raised and how much it unfitted me to form any *judgment* upon them. If one so . . . phlegmatic as myself feels in that, is it impossible that all your knowledge may not find a formidable adversary in your feeling?'

Burke's management of the first repeal of a penal law was conducted mainly behind the scenes, but it attracted the favourable attention of the Irish Catholic Committee, which voted at its November meeting in Dublin to present him with 500 guineas. He civilly declined the offer (he was acting, after all, according to his conviction, not at the behest of 'any set of men living'), and urged the committee to use the money 'to give some aid to places of education for your own youth at home, which is indeed much wanted'.

His activities attracted less favourable attention from other quarters. Although Burke's role in the passing of the Catholic Relief Act had been discreet, he soon marked himself out by presenting to the Commons the petition of the Scottish Catholics in March 1779. Inevitably, the passage of the Relief Act had aroused great resentment among fervent Protestants, who wanted to reimpose the Catholic disabilities. In the first week of June 1780, Lord George Gordon, accompanied by a riotous crowd of some 60,000, brought to the House of Commons the petition of the Protestant Association for the repeal of the Relief Act. Lord George addressed supporters outside the House at intervals as the petition was debated within. Burke's responsibility for the relief measure was known to the petitioners, many of whom took part in the riots. Lord Frederick Cavendish noted Lord George's 'inflammatory speeches' to his supporters, 'particularly against Burke'. Burke's life was threatened on several occasions during the riots, and witnesses attested his courageous conduct.

He was not injured physically, but he was injured politically. Most Englishmen condemned the rioters, but some also blamed those whose imprudent sponsorship of the measure had provoked the riots. And some of the people who were thinking along these lines lived in Bristol, where Burke was to face an election in the autumn.

Between the riots of June and the elections in September, we find Burke writing to a Bristol hosier, Job Watts:

> You tell me besides that religious prejudices have set me ill in the minds of some people. I do not know how this could possibly happen, as I do not know that I have ever offered either in a public or private capacity, an hardship or even an affront to the religious prejudices of any person whatsoever. I have been a steady friend, since I came to the use of reason to the cause of religious toleration, not only as a Christian and a Protestant, but as one concerned for the civil welfare of the country in which I live, and in which I have for some time discharged a public trust. I never thought it wise, my dear Mr Watts, to force men into enmity to the state by ill-treatment, upon any pretence, either of civil or religious party; and if I never thought it wise in any circumstances, still less do I think it wise when we have lost one half of our empire [America] by one idle quarrel, to distract, and perhaps to lose too, the other half by another quarrel, not less injudicious and absurd. No people ought to be permitted to live in a country who are not permitted to have an interest in its welfare by quiet in their goods, their freedom, and their conscience.

Next day, 11 August, writing again to Noble, Burke refers sardonically to 'the rout made about my conduct relative to the late *Acts of scanty and imperfect toleration*', and asks, if the Act 'was of a nature so distasteful to any of my constituents why did none of them express their dislike of it until two years after it was passed?' The answer is of course that the Gordon Riots of June 1780 had given a new and lurid salience to Burke as an agent for the promotion of Catholic interests. And this view of Burke mingled, in a manner most awkward for him, with the perhaps more deep-seated resentment of his promotion of Irish trade.

We can never be certain that the Irish issue was the principal cause of the loss of support in Bristol that led Burke to withdraw from the contest in September. However, the leading Victorian authority on Burke, John Morley, thought that they were. 'He had lost his seat in Bristol in consequence of his courageous advocacy of a measure of toleration for Catholics and his even more courageous exposure of the enormities of the commercial policy of England towards Ireland.' Burke himself in his Speech at Bristol, in the Guildhall previous to the Election, discusses 'matters which have been at various times objected to me in this city': 'These charges, I think, are four in number: my neglect of a due attention to my constituents, the not paying more frequent visits here; my conduct on the affairs of the first Irish trade Acts; my opinion and mode of proceeding on Lord Beauchamp's Debtors' Bill; and my votes on the late affairs of the Roman Catholics.'

Of the fifty-six pages of this Bristol speech, forty-three are devoted to replying to the two Irish charges: six pages on Irish trade and thirty-seven on 'the late affairs of the Roman Catholics'. It is clear that Burke attached by far the most importance to the charge concerning the Catholics. Accurately, but disingenuously, he denied having proposed or seconded the Catholic Relief Bill of 1778:

> I will now tell you by whom the Bill of Repeal was brought into Parliament. I find it has been industriously given out in this city (from kindness to me, unquestionably) that I was the mover or the seconder. The fact is, I did not once open my lips on the subject during the whole progress of the Bill. I do not say this as disclaiming my share in that measure. Very far from it. I inform you of this fact lest I should seem to arrogate to myself the merits which belong to others.

Burke had indeed neither proposed nor seconded the Bill, nor had he spoken in favour of it. All the same, he had shaped it and organized its passage: Lord George Gordon's Protestant Association suspected as much, and that was what had raised Edmund Burke to what he called 'a degree of evil eminence' which some of his constituents did not care for.

Crude anti-Catholicism was no longer fashionable. People of substance, such as those who came to the Guildhall to listen to Edmund Burke, did not want to be associated with such riff-raff as the supporters of Lord George Gordon. Yet some of these respectable citizens of Bristol were disposed to blame Burke for having provoked the Gordon Riots by an untimely and unnecessary zeal for removal of Catholic disabilities. They may not have realized the extent of his responsibility for the passage of the Bill, but his support for it was avowed and defended by him. And that, for some of his constituents, appears to have been enough. In retrospect, from the autumn of 1780, to have voted for the Catholic Relief Bill of 1778 was to have a share in the responsibility for the Gordon Riots of June 1780. A Bristol merchant, thinking of himself as a moderate and deprecating the extremism of Lord George Gordon, might well bracket the Member for Bristol with that half-crazy incendiarist.

This must have been high among the factors that convinced Burke that he could not win and so induced him to withdraw from the election in Bristol. Even on the day of his withdrawal, he still had some warm friends there. One of these, Richard Champion, described the proceedings for Rockingham:

> I never was present at a more moving scene. There were, my lord, very few dry eyes in court. When he finished, it was not so much a plaudit as a burst of affectionate regard. A general silence succeeded, and we all returned with him to the Town House, with the same degree of solemnity as if the people had lost their best friend and were following him to the grave. The streets were crowded with people, who though of different parties and of different descriptions, universally joined in the solemn and silent tribute of affectionate regard.

Burke had made a sacrifice, as he was to do again and again. But he had done more than simply stand up for a just principle, as another MP might have done. In justifying his support for repeal, Burke gave his constituents an extensive review of the character and history of the Irish penal laws. The culmination of this review came in a semi-autobiographical paragraph about their impact:

> In this situation, men not only shrink from the frowns of a stern magistrate, but they are obliged to fly from their very species. The seeds of destruction are sown in civil intercourse, in social habitude. The blood of wholesome kindred is infected. Their tables and beds are surrounded with snares. All the means given by providence to make life safe and comfortable are perverted into instruments of terror and torment. This species of universal subserviency, that makes the very servant who waits behind your chair the arbiter of your life and fortune, has such a tendency to degrade and abase mankind, and to deprive them of that assured and liberal state of mind which alone can

make us what we ought to be, that I vow to God I would sooner bring myself to put a man to immediate death for opinions at once than to fret him with a feverish being, tainted with the jail-distemper of a contagious servitude, to keep him above ground an animated mass of putrefaction, corrupted himself, and corrupting all about him.

In this extraordinary, Swiftian passage, Burke is not simply inveighing against bad laws. He is talking about something that has touched him personally and caused him deep anguish. The emphasis on contamination – 'corruption', 'infection', 'contagious' – is significant, for the bulk of Roman Catholics, those who openly adhered to their religion and neither conformed nor pretended to conform to Anglicanism, could not reasonably be described as 'corrupted' or 'infected'. They were straightforwardly oppressed. The people whom the penal laws had a clear tendency to corrupt and infect were those who either conformed or pretended to conform to the Established Church, for reasons of worldly ambition, social acceptability or fear. The corrosive effects of these measures had been felt most by people such as Burke's father. Edmund himself had benefited from his father's act of conformity, and his own consequent Anglican baptism. Without that, he could not have become a Member of Parliament, for Bristol or anywhere else. And Burke's beloved wife also belonged to the category of those who had once pretended to conform, in her case presumably for the sake of her husband's career. It is reasonable to assume that her husband asked her to do so. So when Burke spoke of 'infection' and 'corruption' in this context, he had his own family uncomfortably in mind. He loathed the penal laws not merely for being unjust, but because of the false position in which they had placed the Burkes.

In such circumstances, a lesser man would have turned his back on Ireland, and this would have been wholly to the advantage of his political career in Britain. It would have freed him from the 'Jesuit' albatross which he carried round his neck throughout his career. It would almost certainly have saved his seat at Bristol. Above all, by never saying or doing anything that could remind people of his Irishness, Burke would have become less suspect in the eyes of his English contemporaries, and therefore eligible for the high office to which his talents entitled him. Edmund Burke chose otherwise. He often spoke in the persona of an Englishman, but he never dropped Ireland altogether. Specifically, he failed to drop the cause of the Irish Catholics, the most compromising and disabling of his Irish associations.

So why did he cling to an Ireland which inspired in him such lively sentiments of shame and horror? My guess is that he needed to cling to Ireland to exorcize the shame for the sake of his kinsfolk, of himself, and especially of his beloved son Richard, by leading the repeal of the penal laws. There was also, probably, a more intimate motivation: that Burke, who often used spectral metaphors, was haunted by the conversion – or apostasy – of his father. He did not refer to that transaction in particular, but he did refer to this category of transactions years later in the course of a private letter to his son – and in a tone very similar to that of this passage about contamination in his Guildhall speech.

The letter to his son was written early in 1793. Burke was writing about Protestant domination in Ireland, and specifically about the Oath of Conformity:

> Let three millions of people but abandon all that they and their ancestors have been taught to be sacred, and to forswear it publicly in terms the most degrading, scurrilous, and indecent for men of integrity and virtue, and to abuse the whole of their former lives, and to slander the education they have received, and nothing more is required of them.

The Oath of Conformity, 1704, was brought in under Queen Anne by 'An Act to prevent the further growth of Popery'. It runs:

> I [Richard Burke] do solemnly and sincerely, in the presence of God, testify and declare that I do believe that in the sacrament of the Lord's Supper there is not any transubstantiation of the elements of bread and wine into the body and blood of Christ, at or after the consecration thereof by any person whatsoever, and that the adoration or invocation of the Virgin Mary, or any other saint, and the sacrifice of the Mass, as they are now used in the Church of Rome, are superstitious and idolatrous.

In taking that oath, in Burke's opinion, his father had forsworn all that his Burke and Nagle ancestors had been taught to hold sacred. The Oath of Conformity was essentially a required act of submission and a ritual humiliation, designed to deter conversions rather than bring them about. The conforming party, in the words of Francis Finegan, 'made his appearance at a public service in a place of Protestant worship and before the assembled congregation read his renunciation'.

The penal laws had obliged his father to insult his mother's faith in order to make possible his own and his son's career. To avenge this, Edmund was in honour bound to subordinate that career, to a significant and costly degree, to the service of his mother's people. Finally, there was the question of his own son, Richard, who was the apple of his eye. The penal code had, in different ways, 'ensnared the soul and body' of Burke's mother, his father and of Burke himself. To save his son from that snare, he had to weaken, and if possible destroy, the penal code.

Edmund Burke was a proud man, with a strong sense of family honour, and we may infer that he felt his father's conformity as a stain on the family escutcheon which had to be erased. The idea of chivalry was important to him. Contemporaries sometimes saw him as Don Quixote, and within limits the comparison is apt. The difference is that the foes Burke had to fight were real, not imaginary. He seems to have seen himself as a man with a dragon to slay, and he dealt it some swingeing blows, notably in the Catholic Relief Act of 1778 and in the removal of most of the remaining Catholic disabilities in 1793.

Thus, at some cost to his own political career, Burke rendered considerable services to the Irish Catholic people, services which most of that people have now entirely forgotten. But the services inspired by his experiences of Ireland were to extend to the world.

II: America

PARLIAMENTARY DEBUT

On 23 December 1765, Burke was elected MP for Wendover, a pocket borough belonging to Lord Verney, a patron friendly to Rockingham. The next day he wrote to the Irish MP Charles O'Hara: 'This is only to tell you in a few words that yesterday I was elected for Wendover, got very drunk, and this day have a heavy cold.'

His election coincided with the start of the American crisis that was to lead to war and end with American independence from Britain. A new MP would usually take a lead from his party, especially if, like Burke, he was private secretary to the party leader, so it might be expected that at least his early speeches on America would be dominated by party considerations. But Burke made up his mind on the main issue of the day before his party did, and with one exception, in 1770, his American speeches were all delivered from conviction.

In American affairs, Burke began as the leading exponent of conciliation. He wanted to see the British Empire run for the benefit of its inhabitants generally, and not just for the benefit of those represented in the Parliament of Great Britain (or the Parliament of Ireland). He was interested not only in the tranquillity and prosperity of the empire, but also in its freedom, by which he meant that the full benefits of the British constitution should be extended to all subjects of the Crown. Conciliation was a means not merely of preserving the empire, but of extending its freedom. And when, with the outbreak of the revolutionary war, it came to a stark choice between preservation of the empire and the freedom of the Americans, he and his friends openly chose the freedom of the

Americans. They did so at the cost of isolating themselves from the rest of Parliament and from the great majority of the English people for the duration of the war.

As Burke took his seat, Parliament's immediate contention with America focused on the Stamp Act, a measure adopted in 1765 on the recommendation of the administration of George Grenville, who was shortly afterwards replaced by Rockingham. The object had been to raise revenue in the colonies and to relieve the burden on British taxpayers. The Act extended to the colonies the system of stamp duties on legal and other documents that was already in force in Britain. Parliament saw this at the time as a simple matter of ensuring that the colonists bore their share of the expenses of the empire. But having paid what they considered to be enough during the Seven Years War of 1756–63, which ended French power in North America, the colonists were in no mood to accept fiscal burdens about which they had not been consulted. No longer under threat from the French, the Americans no longer felt a need for British government, and the Stamp Act had shifted them from passivity to resistance.

The Americans had raised the cry of 'No taxation without representation' and mobs had gathered to destroy the stamps and to menace and sometimes molest would-be collectors of the duty. The resistance was effective. Collecting the duty became impossible. Equally effective was a boycott of British goods, to last until the repeal of the Stamp Act. Trade between America and the western ports of Great Britain was at a standstill. So when Burke took his seat for the opening of the new session on 14 January 1766, Parliament was meeting at a time of crisis. This was the earliest prelude to the American Revolution.

The issue of the hour was whether to repeal the Stamp Act. Before his election to Parliament, Burke had already questioned its wisdom. 'This sullenness in the colonies should alone, one would imagine, have prevented the laying of any additional burden on them.' He was already ahead of Rockingham opinion. Writing to Charles O'Hara eight days after his election and before the Rockinghams had decided what to do about the Act, Burke notes the overwhelming importance of the American issue, and states his intention of voting in accordance with his own opinion, irrespective of what his party may think:

There are wonderful materials of combustion at hand; and surely, since this monarchy, more material point never came under the consideration of Parliament. I mean the conduct which is to be held with regard to America. And there are difficulties in plenty interior and exterior. Administration has not yet conclusively (I imagine) fixed upon their plan in this respect, as every day's information from abroad may necessitate some alteration. In the meantime the Grenvillians rejoice and triumph as if they had gained some capital advantage by the confusions into which they have thrown everything. With regard to myself and my private opinion, my resolution is taken, and if the point is put in any way in which the affirmative or negative become the test of my vote I shall certainly vote according to them, though some of my very best friends should determine to the contrary.

Doubtless Burke meant what he said, and was prepared to vote according to conscience and in defiance of party, as he did a quarter of a century later over the French Revolution. Fortunately, he was spared any need to defy his party at the outset of his career, because the Rockinghams soon decided to repeal the Act, in conformity with his views. The Rockingham administration's Bill for the repeal of the Act received its first reading in February.

The debate on Burke's first day in the Commons was one of the most dramatic of the century. Formally, it concerned the King's Speech, which, since the Rockingham administration had not yet decided what to do about the Stamp Act, was non-committal. William Pitt the Elder (1708–78) had come to demand repeal of the Act. His presence was an event in itself, for he had been absent because of illness all the previous year: the year in which the Act was passed. Pitt was the hero of the nation, having led it to victory in the Seven Years War. He was also the greatest parliamentary speaker of his time. George Grenville, the author of the Stamp Act and a tenacious and formidable politician, was in Parliament to defend himself and his Act against Pitt, and to attack Rockingham's government for its weakness in failing to impose the stamp duty on the refractory colonists. A striking feature of this debate was the agreement by the different sides that the issue at stake was enormously important and that revolution in America was a serious possibility if Parliament took the wrong decision. They were divided only over what the right decision was. Pitt thought it right to repeal the Stamp Act. Grenville thought it right to impose it by military force.

Pitt said he rejoiced that the colonists were forcibly resisting taxation by a Parliament in which they were not represented, and compared the resisting colonists to those who had carried out England's own Glorious Revolution. He called the American resistance to the Stamp Act 'a subject of greater importance than ever engaged the attention of this House, that subject only excepted, when near a century ago it was the question whether you yourselves were to be bound or free!'

Grenville neatly took up an understatement by the Rockingham administration. The King's Speech had referred to what was happening in America as 'disturbances'. Grenville said: 'the "disturbances" began in July and now we are in the middle of January; lately they were only "occurrences", they are now grown to "disturbances", to "tumults and riots". I doubt [suspect] they border on open rebellion; and if the doctrine I have heard this day [in Pitt's speech] be confirmed, I fear they will lose that name to take that of revolution. The government over them being dissolved, a revolution will take place in America.' Less than a year before, Parliament had passed the Stamp Act without a division and almost without a debate. Yet now the Act was the central issue of British politics.

On 18 January, three days after the opening of the Stamp Act debate, Burke made his maiden speech. No published record exists, and there is no draft since he was speaking impromptu. Our only information about that speech – or rather speeches, for he spoke more than once that day – is in a letter written next day to Charles O'Hara:

That day I took my first trial. Sir William Meredith [a senior Rockingham Whig] desired me to present the Manchester petition [of merchants against the Stamp Act]: I know not what struck me, but I took a sudden resolution to say something about it, though I had got it but that moment and had scarcely time to read it, short as it was; I did say something – what it was, I know not upon my honour; I felt like a man drunk. Lord Frederick Campbell made me some answer to which I replied; ill enough too; but I was by this time pretty well on my legs. Mr Grenville answered, and I was now heated, and could have been much better, but Sir G[eorge] Savile [another Rockingham Whig] caught the Speaker's eyes before me and it was then thought better not to proceed further, as it would keep off the business of the day. However I had now grown a little stouter, though still giddy, and affected with a swimming in my head, so that I ventured up again on the motion, and spoke some minutes, poorly but not quite so ill as before. All I hoped was to plunge in, and get off the first horrors; I had no hopes of making a figure. I find my voice not strong enough to fill the House; but I shall endeavour to raise it as high as it will bear.

It is a measure of Burke's performance that Grenville answered him. We would not expect the head of a former administration to reply to the argument of a maiden speaker. Clearly something that Burke said struck home to the author of the Stamp Act. Burke was, from the beginning, an unusually aggressive debater, and he treated Grenville's arguments with casual contempt.

This debut surpassed the high expectations of such friends as David Garrick and Samuel Johnson. Burke won the praise of Pitt, and even Horace Walpole, the cynical son of Britain's first Prime Minister, could scarce forbear to cheer. And yet Burke was speaking for a party that had yet to make up its mind about its American policy. Soon, however, the Rockinghams decided on a policy in conformity with his views. They would repeal the Stamp Act, but first they would pass a Declaratory Act affirming Parliament's legislative supremacy over the colonies. They believed that repeal of the Act could not be carried through Parliament unless accompanied by a solemn expression of British superiority over the colonies. Otherwise the party might have been split.

In March, Burke wrote happily to O'Hara, telling him of his work on the revision of the commercial laws: 'This you see will find me at least as much business as the evidence on the Stamp Act; but it is a business I like, and the spirit of those I act with is just what I could wish it, in things of this kind.'

So could Burke, having entered Parliament a bare two months earlier, have influenced his party's policy over the Stamp Act? Most twentieth-century British historians have thought not. Burke, they say, was too low in the political and social hierarchy to have much influence over party policy on a major issue. Lucy Sutherland writes of him at this stage that he was of 'far too slight consequence to be a deciding factor in the policy of the party', yet goes on to say that 'By the end of the ministry, in spite of his occasional rashness, he had become, together with Dowdeswell, the Chancellor of the Exchequer, the most noted man of his group. It was indeed said in the last months of the ministry that Burke, "not . . . Lord Rockingham's right hand, but . . . both his hands", was a metaphysical visionary.' But if Burke was merely an industrious and inconsequential drudge, how was it that when the Rockingham administration ended, only four months later, he could be compared to the Chancellor of the Exchequer? If a contemporary could see Burke as 'not ... Lord Rockingham's right-hand but ... both his hands', why should we, many generations later, assume that Burke had little influence over Rockingham?

On the contrary, when Parliament was in session, and urgent political choices had to be made, the Rockinghams met regularly. They talked. Such influence as any one of them exerted over the others, other than the influence conferred by higher social standing, had to be exerted in conversation. And we know, on high authority, that Burke's conversational powers were extraordinary. Dr Johnson stood in awe of him, which suggests that Burke would have been heard with close attention by his political associates, even this early in his political career. Furthermore, his first speeches in the Commons were met with rapture, almost astonishment, by men such as Pitt and Garrick. Years later, at a time when his own judgment was diverging momentously from Burke's – over the French Revolution – Charles James Fox paid tribute to Burke's influence over him. He said that 'if he were to put all the political information which he had learnt from books, all which he had gained from science, and all which any knowledge of the world and its affairs had taught him, into one scale, and the improvement which he had derived from his right hon. friend's instruction and conversation were placed in the other, he should be at a loss to decide to which to give the preference.' These witnesses, who were among the leading spirits of the age, are telling us about a man they knew well. Their impressions of Burke and the force of his character are likely to be reliable, especially when they are unanimous.

Burke's formidable persuasive powers were backed by a wealth of information, acquired as a result of his enormous capacity for hard work. Nobody in his party could match that combination. Rockingham needed him for information. Rockingham was a high-minded nobleman, but intellectually indolent, so he needed help in finding what to be high-minded about. Shortly after Burke became his secretary, Charles O'Hara, who then knew Rockingham better than Burke did, offered some advice, which Burke clearly took to heart: 'You have pride to deal with, but much softened by manner and exceeding good sense, but you must feed it, for it can't feed itself.'

Once the decision to repeal the Stamp Act had been taken, Burke told O'Hara that 'the spirit of those I act with is just what I would wish it', and this remained so (with one brief and partial exception in 1770) for sixteen years, through the incubation of the American Revolution, and the whole of the Revolutionary War. From the moment of the decision on the Stamp Act, in February 1766, to the end of 1782, the Rockinghams, at every critical juncture, favoured conciliation as against coercion. As the American historian Ross Hoffman says, Burke's 'American politics remained unchanged from the time he argued for the repeal of the Stamp Act until he opposed the ministerial and parliamentary measures of 1774–5 that plunged the empire into a civil war'. They also remained consistent throughout that war, until 1782, when George III accepted defeat by calling on Rockingham to form an administration.

At the beginning of the crisis, however, Burke must have been ambivalent about the English and the Americans. He admired America's energy, audacity, ingenuity and hardihood, and he celebrated these qualities in major speeches. He warned the English that if they used force against the Americans, they might be taking on adversaries who would eventually prove too much for them. During the early phases of the pre-revolutionary process, he tried to persuade the English not to provoke the Americans into rebellion; later he tried to dissuade them from using force against the Americans; and during the war itself he tried, with little hope up to 1778, and no success up to 1782, to persuade them to concede independence to America. At no stage of this prolonged effort would it have been helpful or relevant for him to give expression to negative feelings about America. Yet he did have such feelings, especially in relation to the southern colonies and New England.

Burke hated slavery, and he argued against having representative Americans in the British Parliament, on the ground that this would mean having slave-owners as MPs. In 1765, the seating of Americans in Parliament had been offered as a possible response to the cry of 'No taxation without representation'. In the *Annual Register*, which Burke edited and largely wrote for many years, he argued against this expedient: 'Common sense, nay self-preservation, seem to forbid that those who allow themselves an unlimited right over the liberties and lives of others should have any share in making laws for those who have long renounced such injust and cruel distinctions.' Hoffman aptly comments that 'Burke's feelings towards American slave-owners thus were not unlike his feelings towards the "bashaws" who as a master class ruled the people of his native Ireland.'

Feeling as he did about American slavery, Burke must have been uncomfortable with the copious American revolutionary rhetoric about freedom – especially when it came from the slave-owners, as did the momentous 'Virginia resolves' of 29 May 1765, which began America's campaign of defiance against the Stamp Act. Burke favoured repealing the Act on rational grounds, but he is unlikely to have been impressed by an assertion of the importance of 'American freedom' coming from Virginia's House of Burgesses. Burke's friend Samuel Johnson – who disagreed with him on the American question – was sarcastic on the subject of the freedom-loving slave-owners. Burke did not join in the sarcasm, which was a weapon in the armoury of those who wished to repress the free Americans, but he must have felt the force of Johnson's point.

As well as slavery, Burke's feelings about America before the outbreak of the war must have been tempered by its anti-Catholicism. In general, America in this period was more anti-Catholic than Britain, and the revolutionaries exploited and fanned anti-Catholicism, especially in the pulpits of New England, for their own political purposes. Burke appears only once to have referred directly – and then not publicly – to the religious intolerance prevalent in America. Anglicanism was seen by American Congregationalists and Presbyterians as a creeping form of Popery, and in 1772 militant American dissenters denounced an alleged plot to introduce Anglican bishops into the American colonies. Burke wrote privately to John Cruger, the Speaker of the New York Assembly, for which he was acting as a British agent, about the defeat in the Lords of a measure for the relief of dissenters. This gave him an opportunity, and a practical reason, to refer to American intolerance. He explained to Cruger how a display of intolerance by American dissenters had given members of the Lords a pretext for exercising their own, retaliatory intolerance: 'I have no doubt that in time [the relief measure] will be carried, and that this spirit of intolerance will vanish away by degrees both on our side of the water and on yours.'

Later, in 1774–75, on the eve of war, the American leaders were seeking to legitimize their own recent revolutionary loyalties, bringing them in line with England's Glorious Revolution of 1688. They cast

George III in the role of James II, the last Roman Catholic King of Great Britain. It was hard to pretend that the strongly anti-Catholic George was really a Catholic, but the emerging revolutionaries found a plausible argument in the Quebec Act of 1774, which recognized and tolerated Catholicism as the religion of Canada. Most Americans resented this Act, and accepted the revolutionary argument that it was part of a great British and Catholic conspiracy against the freedoms and religion of American Protestants. In that way, revolution became a religious duty as well as a political cause.

On 21 October 1774, the Continental Congress issued an Address to the People of Great Britain, condemning Parliament for establishing in Canada a religion which had deluged England with blood and 'disbursed impiety, bigotry, persecution, murder and rebellion through every part of the world'. Burke must have read that address with disgust. This was the language of the enemies of his people. The American revolutionaries apparently wanted the Catholics of Canada to be submitted to the same treatment as was endured by the Catholics of Ireland.

Burke's party, the Rockingham Whigs, had opposed the Quebec Bill in Parliament, not of course on pro-Catholic grounds, but mainly because it enlarged the powers of the Crown (which were a central preoccupation of the party at the time). In Parliament, Burke had said:

> Give them English liberty, give them an English constitution – and then, whether they speak French or English, whether they go to Mass or attend our own communion, you will render them valuable and useful subjects of Great Britain. If you refuse to do this, the consequence will be most injurious: Canada will become a dangerous instrument in the hands of those who wish to destroy English liberty in every part of our possessions.

Yet although he had opposed the Quebec Act personally, Burke reported its passage to the New York Assembly in a manner intended to reconcile his American audience to the measure. Hoffman writes: 'The whole tone of his letter breathed a hope that New York might find cause for satisfaction rather than for grievance in the Quebec Act. On the subject of the French Catholic establishment – politically the most inflammatory feature of the law – he said not a word.' That pregnant silence was Burke's only comment on the anti-Catholic agitation that swept America on the eve of the revolution. And this is characteristic.

While he showed high courage in his personal efforts to remove the disabilities of Catholics in Ireland and England, he had to be very guarded about his personal connections with Catholicism. Unless there was some practical purpose to be served, he avoided any utterance that might suggest, or betray, a Catholic or pro-Catholic attitude.

Though it has generally been forgotten, the anti-Catholic paroxysm of 1774–75 was an important phase of the American Revolution. Once the serious fighting began, however, George Washington sternly discouraged any manifestation of anti-Popery in the army. He wanted recruits, whatever their religion, and he wanted allies, whatever their religion.

Awareness of religious intolerance on both sides of the Atlantic may account for the consistently cool and cerebral tone of Burke's speeches and writings on America before the penal Acts of 1774–75 and the outbreak of war. His emotions were not so much detached from the contest as almost evenly distributed between the parties. Passionate outbursts such as occur in his speeches and writings on France, India and (more rarely) Ireland are absent from those on America, until the war. In the pre-war period, as Hoffman says, 'his indignation at ministerial mismanagement of the colonies had always been a great deal warmer than his sympathy for their grievances'. Yet Burke's correspondence shows that once the fighting broke out his feelings were strongly aroused. He shed his reservations and became fully committed – to the American side. When the Americans resisted British aggression, he could forget his fears about their attitudes towards Papists and slaves. From then on, his statements on America are fully in harmony with the other parts of the great melody. He knew which side he was on.

CIRCUMSTANCES NOT RIGHTS

Some historians say that while the repeal of the Stamp Act had a soothing effect in the short run, the accompanying Declaratory Act was productive of great evils in the longer term. What was certainly productive of great evils was the domineering attitude towards the colonists of George III, of most Members of both Houses of Parliament, and probably of the people of England. That attitude predated the Declaratory Act and would have prevailed even if it had never been passed. Even with the addition of the Declaratory Act, repeal of the Stamp Act would probably not have carried had it not been for the crisis in British commerce caused by the American boycott. The Rockinghams did more than any other group to force that crisis on the attention of Parliament, and Burke was the link between Rockingham and the merchants, indefatigable in the preparation and presentation of merchant petitions. Both by his activities behind the scenes and in Parliament itself, he deserves much of the credit for the only successful measure of conciliation passed by Parliament after the dispute with America began. That the success did not prove lasting was not his fault or that of his friends.

Burke spoke in Parliament on the Declaratory Resolution on 3 February. As his friends had by then made up their minds, and to his satisfaction, he was able to speak in terms of the general principles that should govern Parliament's approach to the colonies. He made a strong impression. That speech and others shortly afterwards established him as a leading parliamentarian. His central theme was that Parliament should content itself with affirming the principle of legislative supremacy, and refrain from any further practical exercise of it.

However, Rockingham's administration fell in July 1766, and its successors tried to govern the colonies according to completely different principles. The Rockinghams did not return to office again until 1782, after Yorktown, when the bankruptcy of American policies pursued for sixteen years by their successors had been conclusively demonstrated, at a heavy cost in life and treasure.

Part of the surviving draft of Burke's speech on the Declaratory Resolution reads:

This speculative idea of a right deduced from the unlimited nature of the supreme legislative authority, very clear and very undeniable, but when explained proved and admitted little to the purpose.

The practical, executive, exertion of this right may be impracticable, may be inequitable and may be contrary to the genius and spirit even of the constitution which gives this right, at least contrary to the principles of liberty.

This practical idea of the constitution of the British Empire to be deduced from the general and relative situation of its parts. The purposes for which they were formed. The law of England and examples of other countries not applicable here. It must be governed upon principles of freedom. There is not a more difficult subject for the understanding of men than to govern a large empire upon a plan of liberty...

Besides the abstract point of right there is in every country a difference between the ideal and the practical constitution – they will be confounded by pedants, they will be distinguished by men of sense; they may not follow from the rules of metaphysical reasoning but they must be rules of government. The practical exertion of many clear rights may by change of times and circumstances become impossible, may be inequitable; may clash with the genius of the very constitution that gives them, or at least may clash entirely with liberty; and those who are not for governing with an attention to the circumstances of times, opinions, situations and manners, they will not govern wisely, they cannot govern long...

Neither, I apprehend, will it be sufficient to resort for rules of the present practical constitution of the British Empire to our old laws and law books; to resort to contracted ideas, operating in dark times on a limited object; not in the broad daylight of science, for governing a tract of the world that our ancestors so far from knowing how to govern did not know it existed in the Universe.

'Govern America as you govern an English corporation which happens not to be represented in Parliament.' Are gentlemen really serious when they propose this? Is there a single trait of resemblance between those few towns disseminated through a represented county, and a great, a growing people spread over a vast quarter of the globe, almost from the Polar Circle to the Equator, separated from us by a mighty ocean, neither actually or by a possibility a part in our government. The rule of their constitution must be taken from their circumstances: not by oppressing them by the weight [of a] gross dead body, but by applying as far as the rules of subordination will permit the principles of the British constitution. The eternal barriers of nature forbid that the colonies should be blended or coalesce into the mass of the particular constitution of this kingdom. We have nothing therefore for it, but to let them carry across the ocean into the woods and deserts of America the images of the British constitution; the penates of an Englishman, to be his comfort in his exile, and to be the pledges of his fidelity and to give him an interest in his dependency on this country.

This and Burke's other pronouncements on America, right up to the end of the war, are all strongly and consistently anti-authoritarian. He found all authoritarianism abhorrent, morally, politically, philosophically and temperamentally. The 'it' in Yeats's line 'And Burke's great melody against it' is authoritarianism. Burke hated it in the Irish Protestant Ascendancy; in Warren Hastings; in the Jacobins; and in the attitude towards America of Grenville, North and George III. If Parliament had followed Burke's advice, as given here and elsewhere, there would have been no American Revolution.

He spoke again four days later, opposing Grenville's demand for enforcement of the Stamp Act forthwith. This was an effort to pre-empt repeal, and it was a dangerous one, because of the mood of exasperation in the House at the colonists' insubordination. The motion was a tactical one, and Burke's speech in reply was also tactical: not an oration but a debating speech. Burke desperately needed to influence votes, and for this purpose the most effective part of the speech was probably the conclusion, which drew attention to the plight of English merchants rather than the misbehaviour of the American colonists: 'Before we do determine, we must have our preparatory grounds before us. Our merchants object to it as having brought them to the brink of ruin. Let us hear them. Let us consider the subject in its full extent before a single resolution if possible should reach America.' Burke's tactics worked. Grenville's motion was rejected. Some of the colonists' grievances could now be met. The Declaratory Bill and the Bill repealing the Stamp Act received the royal assent on 18 March 1766. The work of the first Rockingham administration in relation to America was substantially complete.

The session came to an end on 6 June. There was much opposition bitterness, especially against Burke. Grenville was more bitter than anyone, and raked up Burke's Irish past and that of his kinsman Will Burke. Grenville sarcastically questioned the sanity of the Rockingham leadership in designating 'for their men of business and of confidence in the two great offices of the Treasury and the Secretary of State, the two Mr Burkes, whose Whig pedigree, history and qualifications for this unlimited trust may be learnt from those who have been lately in Ireland'. Will Burke (1728–98) was a distant relation with whom Edmund long worked closely. Grenville referred to him as well as Burke's Catholic connections because Will represented another chink in Burke's armour. His financial reputation was dubious and his finances were entangled with Edmund's in ways that sometimes brought Burke to the brink of disaster. The sneer at the Whig pedigree is a reference to Burke's Jacobite connections, through the Nagles.

After the end of the session, the King dismissed Rockingham and called on Lord Chatham to form a new administration. What George III liked about Chatham was that he, like George, was opposed to 'connection'. 'Connection' meant acting like a political party. When a connection formed an administration, it meant that its members acted in concert, in a manner approaching what would later be known as 'Cabinet responsibility'. The Rockinghams formed a connection on principle, and the King felt that this interfered with the exercise of his own proper authority. Chatham believed in 'measures not men' – a piece of cant, in Burke's view – and drew his ministers from every faction represented in Parliament. The King believed that an administration so composed would leave more scope for the exercise of his personal authority than had existed under the Rockinghams. He was right about that, but the consequences of his enlarged power were to prove unfortunate for his realm.

A few days after the Rockingham administration was dismissed, Burke published *A Short Account of a Short Late Administration*, celebrating its achievements. This pamphlet includes the sentence: 'The passions and animosities of the colonies, by judicious and lenient measures, were allayed and composed, and the foundation laid for a lasting agreement amongst them.' The foundation was strong, but sadly his wording would soon sound too optimistic. News of the repeal of the Stamp Act was greeted with rejoicing in America, while the Declaratory Act was ignored. Burke's name was among those toasted both then and on anniversaries up to 1770. The disturbances in America came to an end for the time being, and commerce was restored between Britain and the colonies.

But disputes continued in the years that followed. One arose in New York, where the Assembly had refused to make appropriations for barrack supplies, so defying the 1765 Mutiny Act, which required colonial legislatures to provide facilities for imperial troops at their own expense. Charles Townshend, the new Chancellor of the Exchequer, was determined to quell insubordination in the colonies and to raise revenue there. He decided to make an example of New York, introduced resolutions condemning the Assembly and approved a Bill to suspend it. On 13 May 1767, Burke spoke against the proposal to suspend the New York Assembly. It was a forceful, unequivocal attack:

> It is with unaffected sorrow of heart I see the business of America come again before the House. Because every such event affords a new, a convincing, and surely a most humiliating proof of the utter insufficiency of public debate to discuss, and of parliamentary regulation to settle anything upon a subject of so very intricate and so very delicate a policy.
>
> The proposition which is made to you is liable to every objection which can be brought against an executive plan as violent, unjust, and ineffective . . . After you have made this law to enforce your last, you must make another to enforce that – and so on in the endless rotation of vain and impotent efforts. Every great Act you make must be attended with a little Act, like a squire to carry his armour. And the power and wisdom of Parliament will wander about, the ridicule of the world . . . By suspending their legislature – observe that during this suspense of their authority, you suspend your own.

Townshend's proposal for suspension was, nonetheless, easily carried. As it happened, it did no harm, because the New York Assembly, before word of the proposal reached them, had decided to comply with the Mutiny Act after all. On 15 May, however, Townshend introduced new revenue duties, which were to renew the revolutionary process in America that had been halted by the Rockinghams' repeal of the Stamp Act. Naturally, Burke expressed his vexation:

> I confess I feel myself not a little affected to find again before [us] an American tax upon a principle of supply – as tending in my opinion further to unsettle America, and to weaken the opinion they ought and I hope will have of the constancy, equity and wisdom of Parliament . . .
>
> You [repealed the Stamp Act] solely from an opinion that a general tax upon the colonies was not suitable to their circumstances at that time and not consistent with the principles of commercial policy on which they were founded.
>
> You examined merchants from every part of your extended dominions, you examined tradesmen in every part of your extensive manufactures. The

examination was long and in detail . . . What facts are now before you from whence you can infer a difference in their circumstances or a change in your own policy? – None!

The Rockinghams did not divide the House over the Townshend duties. Probably they were themselves divided about them and reluctant to advertise a division in their ranks. In any case, there was now no chance of defeating the duties, which were extremely popular in Parliament. The country gentlemen looked to the new revenue from America to relieve their tax burden; the placemen – Members holding lucrative posts, usually sinecures, at the pleasure of the monarch – saw the prospect of jobs for their relatives. Most parliamentarians were probably thinking about their own affairs, and how America might be used to their advantage, rather than about American affairs in themselves.

Burke's speech against the passing of the Townshend duties lacks the cutting edge of his replies to Grenville over the Stamp Act. One reason for this is personalities, which mattered a lot to Burke. He did not like George Grenville, but he did like Townshend, whose secretary he had almost become in 1765. He was not so constituted as to be able to deploy against Townshend the cold and cutting condescension that had enraged George Grenville.

But there was another personality checking him too. This was William Dowdeswell, whom Burke respected and worked with closely; their partnership was at the heart of the Rockingham opposition in the Commons. On the question of the duties, Dowdeswell agreed with Townshend, not Burke. For Burke to oppose them at all must have strained the relation with Dowdeswell; to be scathing about them might have strained that relationship to breaking point, which would have been a disaster for the Rockinghams.

A third factor was also making for moderation. Burke knew that the duties would carry, and that they would probably be resisted in America. But he also knew that if he specifically predicted resistance, he would later be accused of having stimulated what he had predicted. Grenville had made precisely that charge against the Rockinghams over the Stamp Act. So when Burke delivered his warning against the duties, he did so quietly.

On 8 November 1768, Burke delivered a powerful speech analysing the disastrous effects of the Townshend duties. He reminded the House that in the previous year he had 'expressed the little opinion I had', and went on: 'I shall prove a true prophet, that you will never see a single shilling from America.'

He made his case again the following February in his pamphlet *Observations on a Late State of the Nation*:

> North America was once indeed a great strength to this nation, in opportunity of ports, in ships, in provisions, in men. We found her a sound, an active, a vigorous member of the empire. I hope by wise management she will again become so. But one of our capital present misfortunes is her discontent and disobedience. [To what] this discontent is owing, we all know but too sufficiently. It would be a dismal event if this foundation of ... all of our public strength should, in reality, become our weakness ...
>
> Without ever doubting the extent of its lawful power, Parliament always doubted the propriety of such impositions. And the Americans on their part never thought of contesting a right by which they were so little affected. Their assemblies in the main answered all the purposes necessary to the internal economy of a free people, and provided for all the exigencies of government which arose amongst themselves. In the midst of that happy enjoyment, they never thought of critically settling the exact limits of a power which was necessary to their union, their safety, their equality, and even their liberty. Thus the two very difficult points, superiority in the presiding state, and freedom in the subordinate, were on the whole sufficiently, that is, practically, reconciled, without agitating those vexatious questions which in truth rather belong to metaphysics than politics, and which can never be moved without shaking the foundations of the best governments that have ever been constituted by human wisdom. By this measure was let loose that dangerous spirit of disquisition, not in the coolness of philosophical enquiry, but enflamed with all the passions of an haughty resentful people who thought themselves deeply injured, and that they were contending for everything that was valuable in the world.

In this pamphlet, which was widely acclaimed, Burke may have been trying to fend off an emerging parliamentary commitment that cannot have been to his liking. This was the drift towards an alliance between the Rockinghams and Grenvilles. In terms of America, such an alliance was monstrous: an alliance between the author of the Stamp Act and the authors of its repeal. Grenville still maintained the wisdom of the Stamp Act, while the Rockinghams maintained the wisdom of its repeal. But in terms simply of domestic politics, such an alliance made some sense. The Grenvilles and the Rockinghams were in *de facto* alliance against the refusal of the government to allow the elected Member for Middlesex, John Wilkes, to take his seat in Parliament, on the grounds that he was disreputable and had insulted the King. Unlike opposition on the American issue, opposition on the Wilkes issue attracted significant support outside Parliament, so it is not altogether surprising that the Rockinghams, who were isolated and unpopular, were tempted to fudge the American issue in order to coalesce with the Grenvilles.

This cannot have been congenial to Burke, either politically or personally. Apart from the American issue, he must have remembered Grenville's sneer in the House in June 1766 at his Irishness and his Catholic connections. In his correspondence one can sense something of his concern about rapprochement with Grenville. In May 1769 he writes to Charles O'Hara: 'You probably hear that there is a perfect coalition between us and Grenville; but there is nothing more than good humour towards one another, and a determination to act with joint forces against this new, usurped, and most dangerous power of the House of Commons, in electing their own Members.' Burke here is clearly trying to limit the alliance to an *ad hoc* one over Wilkes. However, he did not succeed with Rockingham, and the united front came into being early in 1770. For the brief time that it lasted, Burke was no longer free to speak his mind or to take initiatives over America.

Meanwhile, in the previous autumn Lord North (1732–92) had become head of the administration, and he now decided to try to restore calm in the colonies by removing most of the Townshend duties. On 5 March 1770, he moved the repeal of them all, except the one on tea. In the Commons, three speakers urged the repeal of the tea duty as well. Everything they said conformed to the principles Burke had laid down in his speech on the Declaratory Act and had often reaffirmed since. But in that debate, he was silent.

George Grenville, however, did speak, and what he said may have been the reason why Burke was silent. Having reproached the administration with inconsistencies, Grenville added: 'I cannot on the one hand suppose that a partial repeal of the present tax will reduce the colonies to temper [i.e. calm], nor on the other by forcing government into a total repeal, can I suppose we have sufficiently provided for the dignity of the nation.' Less than two years before, Burke had savagely attacked the cant of those who argued that it was necessary to collect the taxes in the colonies in order to preserve the dignity of the nation: when peace had been achieved by repealing the Stamp Act, he had said, 'they began to pine, and whine for their dignity, for some little thing that would give them back their dignity'. Now, however, in 1770, he was obliged to give a respectful hearing to just this sort of thing when it fell from the lips of a temporary ally. Grenville's words meant that the Rockinghams could not call for a repeal of the tea duty as long as they wanted their parliamentary alliance to hold. Yet it was the attempt to collect the tea duty that was to keep the colonies in turmoil for the next five years, until turmoil grew into revolution. On the principles laid down by Burke from 1766 on, repeal of the tea duty was as clear a necessity in 1770 as the repeal of the Stamp Act had been in 1766. But Burke was silenced on the topic.

Rockingham and Grenville reached agreement, probably in April 1770, on a set of opposition resolutions on America to be introduced in Parliament. In them they accused the administration of giving 'ill-judged and inconsistent instructions ... to the governors of some of the provinces in North America'. But their own agreement too was inconsistent. Basically, all the Rockinghams and the Grenvilles could agree upon in relation to America was that they should charge the administration with being inconsistent and following toughness with leniency. But Grenville was in favour of the toughness, Rockingham of the leniency. So the two leaders were themselves inconsistent.

Two of the resolutions, which proclaimed Parliament's freedom to tax the colonies, were incompatible with everything that Burke had been saying for four years, and yet it was Burke who was assigned the task of introducing them. Having accepted out of loyalty to Rockingham, he did so on 9 May 1770. His speech was a polished professional performance and won applause at the time. Horace Walpole, who disliked him, called it 'a fine speech', and it was certainly adroit, as shown in his assessment of the repeal of the Stamp Act, where Burke had to allow for two contradictory points of view: 'The consequences of this Act appeared in two views, one immediate, the other remote. It brought present peace. It might encourage to future disturbance. The first was certain, the latter was contingent and problematical.'

In his survey of past events, Burke then passed on to the Townshend duties, which had undone the good of the Stamp Act repeal.

In the next session, it was not thought right to leave this matter to its natural operation; we began to tire of the tranquillity which we enjoyed. It was said we purchased peace by dignity, and now we must purchase dignity at the hazard of peace. At all hazards, America must be taxed again, and reasons [were] given for it which . . . were calculated to irritate them much more than the taxation. Thus after we had been in harbour we had got to sea again on this new traffic for dignity. We were on a rotten bottom. The winds began to blow.

The trouble with this was that it made no mention of the only one of the Townshend duties still in force: the tea duty which was now the centre of controversy. Burke could not allude to it, for Grenville wanted to keep it, precisely for reasons of dignity. The very evil Burke was denouncing existed within the alliance on whose behalf he was speaking.

Perhaps the strongest passage in the speech makes a point that is coercive, as Grenville wished, rather than concessive, as Burke wished: that the administration ought not to have introduced duties without providing means for their enforcement.

If ever there was in all the proceedings of government a rule that is fundamental, universal, invariable, it is this, that you ought never to attempt a measure of authority you are not morally sure you can go through with. For by doing otherwise you risk the whole stock and fund of government at a single cast of chance. Its providence you forfeit in not foreseeing the difficulties it was to engage in, its wisdom in not providing against them, its powers in not overcoming them. All is lost, all the machines of government shown to be without force . . .

In this speech of 9 May 1770, Burke descends from his habitual intellectual and moral level. On this single occasion during the sixteen years of his American involvement, he appears as a party spokesman, dressing up in fine language policies laid down for him by others. Ross

Hoffman comments: 'No doubt Burke wished to maintain the empire – which certainly was not yet collapsing – but his immediate aim was to use America as a stick to beat the ministers, for his speech was a mixture of the fundamentally unfusable opinions of the Grenvilles and Rockinghams on America.' This is quite true, and it was most unlike Burke.

Usually, Burke influenced Rockingham more than Rockingham influenced him. But Rockingham under the potent influence of Grenville was a different man. Burke was now feeling, through Rockingham, the pressure of an imperious, alien will, and of a system of ideas inimical to his own. I suspect that he could not have submitted to that pressure for long. As it was, he didn't have to. On 13 November 1770, George Grenville died, and the alliance died with him. The repealer of the Stamp Act was no longer the prisoner of the author of the Stamp Act.

Remarkably, American affairs were not raised in Parliament for nearly four years, from May 1770 to March 1774. The administration had no occasion to bring them forward, and the opposition knew that if it did so it would receive a drubbing in terms of parliamentary votes without impressing public opinion. Throughout this period, the public was profoundly indifferent to American affairs. As Burke wrote to Rockingham on 2 February 1774: 'Your lordship remarks very rightly on the supineness of the public. Any Remarkable Highway Robbery at Hounslow Heath would make more conversation than all the disturbances of America.' Burke, however, did not cease to think about America. Indeed, as London agent for the New York Assembly, he was paid to think about it.

New York was one of the more moderate of the colonies, and so appreciated his efforts, as over the repeal of the Stamp Act, to avert the threat of revolution. But he is frank in 1772, in a letter to John Cruger of the New York Assembly, about the inability of himself and his friends to do much for America under present conditions:

The strength of opposition remains nearly the same as ever – unexerted indeed, but unimpaired. You know that everything in political conduct depends upon occasions and opportunities. In the present state of things it has been thought advisable to be less active than formerly. Since it has appeared upon a multitude of trials and upon a great variety of matters that there is a determined, systematical, and considerable majority in both Houses in favour of the court scheme [to coerce America], an unremitted fight would only

serve to exhibit a longer series of defeats. It was therefore thought advisable
to attend to circumstances and to pitch only upon those where the advantage
of situation might supply the want of numbers, or where, though without
hope of victory, you could not decline the combat without disgrace. This
was, during the last session, the measure of our conduct.

Then, on 16 December 1773, an event occurred which was to bring
the parliamentary calm to an end. The Boston Tea Party, when tea from
three ships was thrown into Boston harbour, was a conspicuous act of
defiance, to which North's administration decided to respond by a series
of coercive measures. This created a situation in which, in Burke's
opinion, 'you could not decline the combat without disgrace'.

As it happened, the Boston Tea Party linked the American crisis with
the next of Burke's great global preoccupations, for the tea was the
property of the East India Company. On this imperial conjunction, one
of Warren Hastings' biographers, Sir Alfred Lyall, wrote with insight:

It is useful to recollect that the tea thrown into Boston harbour in December
1773 belonged to the East India Company, and had been allowed free export
by way of helping them commercially; for the incident fixes important dates,
and marks a curious point of connection between eastern and western
complications. And while it is remarkable that a petty concession to the
Indian trading company should have been the signal for rebellion in the
American colonies, such an electric reverberation across the horizon
illustrates the tempestuous condition of the whole political atmosphere.

ZEALOUS ADVOCATE FOR LIBERTY

The first of the North administration's coercive measures after the Tea
Party was the Boston Port Bill, which proclaimed the closure of the port
until Bostonians accepted the tea duties and paid compensation for the
Tea Party. When this Bill was introduced in the Commons in March
1774, Burke spoke in opposition to it. He conceded that the perpetrators
of the Tea Party might properly be punished, but he argued strongly
against the collective punishment of an entire city:

You can't pursue this example, if other towns should do the like. Have you
considered what to do if this example should not operate as you wish?

Would you put a total proscription to the whole trade of America. Virginia does not mean to pay our taxes, as it's asserted. If we stop the trade there, we lose £300,000 per annum revenue, as well as a great loss by many other means. I do not say punishment ought not to be inflicted on America, and I think it might, and on the offenders too. If punishment is not just but rigorous it's a double cause of complaint ... Every punishment is unjust that is inflicted on a party unheard. The distance of the party is no argument for not hearing. It's a devilish doctrine that every person is punishable where a riot is committed, even though it should be out of his power to prevent it. We punish the governed for the faults of the governors.

Or, as Burke puts it elsewhere: 'We whip the child until it cries, and then we whip it for crying.'

The Rockinghams did not divide the House on the Bill, and Burke explained in a letter to the committee of the New York Assembly that 'Those who spoke in opposition did it more for the acquittal of their own honour and discharge of their own consciences, by delivering their free sentiments on so critical an occasion, than from any sort of hope they entertained of bringing any considerable number to their opinion.'

However, with Grenville gone, Burke was again influencing Rockingham, who was also temperamentally disinclined to support coercive measures. Active opposition on American issues was now resumed, even though the Whigs knew it was even more hopeless than it had been in 1770. The Rockinghams took the decision from which they had flinched in 1770 and decided to call for the repeal of the duty on tea. This decision set Burke free once more to speak on America with the full force of his mind – as he had done in 1766 over the Declaratory Resolution, but had been unable to do in 1770 when introducing the hotch-potch of Rockingham–Grenville resolutions. A sense of release may partly account for the splendour of Burke's eloquence in the two famous speeches On American Taxation (1774) and On Conciliation with America (1775).

On American Taxation was delivered on 19 April, in support of a motion for the repeal of the tea duty. It was part of Burke's strategy, in all his American pronouncements after his maiden speech, to review the history of the question, showing that non-taxation of the colonists, exemplified by the repeal of the Stamp Act, had been a wise policy, and that taxation, as exemplified by the Townshend duties, had been proved unwise. Immediately before he rose, Charles Cornwall, a member of North's administration, had tried to pre-empt such an argument by affirming that it was the present, not the past, that should be of concern to the House. Burke's reply, which must have been impromptu, is remarkable both for its concentrated and polished argument and for the sudden stinging epigram of its conclusion:

> He asserts that retrospect is not wise, and the proper, the only proper subject of enquiry is 'not how we got into this difficulty, but how we are to get out of it'. In other words, we are, according to him, to consult our invention, and to reject our experience. The mode of deliberation he recommends is diametrically opposite to every rule of reason, and every principle of good sense established amongst mankind. For that sense and that reason I have always understood absolutely to prescribe, whenever we are involved in difficulties from the measures we have pursued, that we should take a strict review of those measures, in order to correct our errors if they should be corrigible; or at least to avoid a dull uniformity in mischief, and the unpitied calamity of being repeatedly caught in the same snare.

Burke is debating, not just delivering what Horace Walpole called a 'fine harangue'. And perhaps the most remarkable feature of this speech is the way impromptu debating points are made to fit into and embellish a pattern of which the general lines were clearly thought out in advance. The phrase 'a dull uniformity in mischief' is both an effective reply to Cornwall's particular objection and a devastating characterization of the policies towards America pursued by every administration since 1766. To be able to respond to an objection on the floor of the House so that the reply blends indistinguishably into the texture and pattern of a prepared speech is a sure mark of personal conviction.

Over and over, Burke recommends friendship and co-operation rather than strife, pride and the kind of theoretical divisions which he knew would divide peoples too:

> Revert to your old principles – seek peace and ensue it – leave America, if she has taxable matter in her, to tax herself. I am not here going into the distinctions of rights, nor attempting to mark their boundaries. I do not enter

into these metaphysical distinctions; I hate the very sound of them. Leave the Americans as they anciently stood, and these distinctions, born of our unhappy contest, will die along with it. They and we, and their and our ancestors, have been happy under that system. Let the memories of all actions in contradiction to that good old mode, on both sides, be extinguished for ever. Be content to bind America by laws of trade; you have always done it. Let this be your reason for binding their trade. Do not burthen them by taxes; you were not used to do so from the beginning. Let this be your reason for not taxing. These are the arguments of states and kingdoms. Leave the rest to the schools [of metaphysics]; for there only they may be discussed with safety. But if, intemperately, unwisely, fatally, you sophisticate and poison the very source of government by urging subtle deductions and consequences odious to those you govern, from the unlimited and illimitable nature of supreme sovereignty, you will teach them by these means to call that sovereignty itself in question.

The motion for repeal of the tea duty was defeated by 182 to 49. As Paul Langford observes: 'Considering that Rockingham had taken particular pains to rally the forces of his party for that day, this represented a crushing defeat for the opposition.' There must have been some among the Rockinghams who felt that the margin of defeat vindicated the previous practice of keeping quiet about America.

Burke, however, persevered. In April he spoke against the Massachusetts Bay Regulation Bill, the second and toughest of North's coercive measures. This Bill removed the appointment of the Massachusetts Council from popular to royal control, and dealt similarly with juries. Burke rose late at night, at 11.45, and spoke for an hour and a quarter. He had a rough ride. One report shows him feeling the pressure:

I do feel myself, what with the weight upon me and the temper of the House, under a difficulty to go on. I shall endeavour to contract as narrowly as I can to comply with the temper of the House and with my own weakness; to comply with the temper of the House [a great noise] my respect to the House absolutely makes me silent: my respect to my duty absolutely pushes me on. First the magnitude of the subject, my mind saturated with it I scarce know where to begin or where to end. I will jump into the middle of it.

Another report has him defiant: 'The House being noisy, several

Members going out, soon after which he got up and said: I find, sir, I have got my voice and I shall beat down the noise of the House.' The Massachusetts Bay Regulation Bill was overwhelmingly carried, by 239 votes to 64, and the other excise Acts were carried by similar margins.

'Within doors', opposition on American issues was futile and unpleasant. But outside Parliament there were, for the first time since 1766, signs that some people were attending favourably to what Burke was saying. At the end of June 1774 he received an enquiry from Dr Thomas Wilson, Rector of St Margaret's, Westminster, as to whether he would stand as candidate for Bristol if his friends there were strong enough to nominate him. The main reason, though not the only one, why Burke had attracted support in Bristol was that he was known there as 'an able opponent of many odious measures – especially those injurious to American trade'. Bristol was the principal port trading with America, and although its merchants seem on the whole to have shared in the general merchant acquiescence in the Townshend duties, some were apparently alarmed by North's coercive measures. Burke replied cautiously, expressing willingness to stand, but not eagerness. This correspondence was to lead, after a number of vicissitudes, to his winning Bristol in the general election of November 1774.

That new position, as Member for the second greatest commercial city of Great Britain, greatly enhanced Burke's prestige and influence in Parliament, and his authority in the councils of the Rockinghams. Yet he had not at first entertained much hope of winning Bristol, though he needed to find a seat, because his patron, Lord Verney, was in financial difficulties and was compelled to sell Wendover to someone else. In September, Burke wrote a long and unusually personal letter to Rockingham. He wrote in a despondent vein, which is also unusual, about America, about British politics, and about his own situation. In America, he correctly foresaw a long-drawn-out struggle. But Britain, he wrote, remained blind to the strength of feeling in America:

> But in the present temper of the nation, and with the character of the present administration, the disorder and discontent of all America, and the more remote future mischiefs which may arise from those causes, operate as little as the division of Poland. The insensibility of the merchants of London is of a degree and kind scarcely to be conceived. Even those most likely to be overwhelmed by any real American confusion are amongst the most supine.

As regards his personal situation, Burke mentioned his troubles at Wendover (but not the Bristol possibility):

> Sometimes when I am alone, in spite of all my efforts I fall into a melancholy which is inexpressible; and to which if I gave way, I should not continue long under it, but must totally sink. Yet I do assure you, that partly and indeed principally by the force of natural good spirits, and partly by a strong sense of what I ought to do, I bear up so well that no one who did not know them could easily discover the state of my mind or my circumstances. I have those that are dear to me, for whom I must live as long as God pleases; and in what way he pleases. Whether I ought not totally to abandon this public station for which I am so unfit, and have, of course, been so unfortunate, I know not. It is certainly not so easy to arrange me in it, as it has been hitherto. Most assuredly I never would put my feet within the doors of St Stephen's Chapel without being as much my own master as hitherto I have been, and at liberty to pursue the same course.

Burke could hardly have used the expression 'my own master' in a letter to his party leader if they did not know one another very well indeed and trust one another completely.

Early in October, Burke was formally nominated for Bristol. He expected this so little that before the news arrived he had set out for Malton, a borough offered to him by Rockingham. On learning of the nomination, Burke chose to fight for Bristol. It was a hard campaign, and inevitably his opponents attacked him for his Irish Catholic connections. Ironically, one of the things that had initially commended him to his Bristol supporters was the anti-Papist zeal they attributed to him. Dr Wilson, in making the original tentative offer, had said that 'the Quebec Affair' had aroused the Bristol Quakers and Dissenters, 'making the time especially favourable for such an intervention as he proposed'. Almost all the commotion in America and Britain against the Quebec Act of 1774 had been anti-Papist in character. Since Burke had voted against the Quebec Bill, these Quakers and Dissenters of Bristol made the simplistic assumption that he was a sound anti-Papist. But he had made it clear in his speech of 10 June that his opposition to the Bill was not on anti-Catholic grounds. Probably no one in Bristol had read that speech, so in July, from a distance, Burke looked like a good Protestant. By October, and in the throes of a contested election, his opponents were busy trying to clear up that misconception.

Burke's younger brother Richard (1733–94), who acted as his election agent, was so worried about the 'Saint Omer & Popery' stories that he sought the help of Burke's Quaker schoolfriend Richard Shackleton. The faithful Shackleton promptly came to the rescue with the following, addressed to William Fry, a prominent Quaker preacher in Bristol:

> I this day (and not before) was informed that Edmund Burke had offered himself a candidate to represent your city in Parliament ... Having had a particular intimacy with Edmund Burke from our early youth ... I think then thou mayst with great truth assure our friends there, and anyone else in thy freedom, that Edmund Burke is a man of the strictest honour and integrity; *a firm and staunch Protestant*; a zealous advocate (not an enthusiastic brawler) for that which rightly deserves the name of liberty.

The words 'a firm and staunch Protestant' and the emphasis given to them were probably suggested by Richard Burke. Shackleton would not have meant those words to imply that Burke was a bigoted anti-Papist. He knew that Burke was no such thing, and would not have lied, even to protect his friend. All the same, that was what the words meant in the context of the Bristol election, and they must have helped Burke's chances with the Quakers of Bristol. Not for the first time, Ballitore and its Quaker school were being used to filter out from Burke's past his unacceptable associations with Catholic Ballyduff and the hedge school under the ruins of Monanimy Castle.

Despite the rumours, Burke was elected for Bristol on 2 November. Presumably his American services outweighed his Irish associations. But some of the Quakers and Dissenters who voted for him must have regretted their decision four years later, when their 'firm and staunch Protestant' discreetly piloted the first Catholic Relief Act through the British Parliament. Their revenge came at the general election of 1780. At the end of 1774, however, Burke was at the height of his political career. His victory at Bristol, and the fatal illness of the Rockinghams' long-time leader in the Commons, William Dowdeswell, made him effectively their new leader in the House. Fortified by his success – and by the support it demonstrated for his position on America – he could once more turn his attention to American affairs.

Burke now tried to induce the Rockinghams to be more active over America. He failed, because the aristocratic leaders were not capable of organizing themselves to pursue a political campaign. However, they were at least now consistently taking a policy lead from him on American affairs, in the Commons. On 22 March 1775 he introduced a series of resolutions on America in the speech later published as On Conciliation with America. Unlike the 1770 Grenville–Rockingham resolutions, which were the product of an inter-party pact, these resolutions were clearly Burke's work, at least in the main. They are comprehensive and far-reaching. If passed, they would have repealed the tea duty and all the recent penal Acts, known in America as 'the Intolerable Acts'. The resolutions would also have acknowledged the claim of Americans to tax themselves, and not to be taxed by the Parliament of Great Britain. The resolutions were a serious effort to get to the root of the matter and to avert an impending war. Four weeks after they were rejected, war broke out at Concord, Massachusetts.

On Conciliation with America is more of a set speech than On American Taxation, because of the parliamentary context. In On American Taxation, in 1774, Burke had been intervening in the debate on the unsuccessful motion to repeal the tea duty, answering previous speeches and thinking on his feet. But in the Speech on Conciliation he was moving a set of resolutions. On American Taxation is all in Burke's own voice, but in moving the resolutions On Conciliation he was speaking partly in the persona of the Rockinghams collectively. In the following passage he is speaking not out of his own personality and actual ancestry, but in the person of a proper English Whig:

> In forming a plan for this purpose, I endeavoured to put myself in that frame of mind which was the most natural and most reasonable, and which was certainly the most probable means of securing me from all error. I set out with a perfect distrust of my own abilities, a total renunciation of every speculation of my own, and with a profound reverence for the wisdom of our ancestors, who have left us the inheritance of so happy a constitution and so flourishing an empire, and, what is a thousand times more valuable, the treasury of the maxims and principles which formed the one and obtained the other.

When On Conciliation was published in the summer of 1775, some copies must have found their way into Nagle country in the Blackwater Valley of Co. Cork. Did anyone smile, I wonder, at the phrase 'the wisdom of our ancestors'? Such Whiggish ancestors as Richard Nagle of Carrigacunna, James II's Attorney-General? So thoroughly does Burke renounce 'every speculation of my own' and enter into the frame of mind of an English Whig, in this section of his speech, that he even offers us an idyllic view of Ireland as it might appear to a Whig constitutional lawyer who had never visited the place and who accepted the penal laws as perfectly in order:

It was not English arms but the English constitution that conquered Ireland. From that time, Ireland has ever had a general Parliament, as she had before a partial Parliament. You changed the people, you altered the religion, but you never touched the form or the vital substance of free government in that kingdom. You deposed the kings; you restored them; you altered the succession to theirs, as well as to your own Crown; but you never altered their constitution, the principle of which was respected by usurpation, restored with the restoration of monarchy, and established, I trust, forever by the Glorious Revolution. This has made Ireland the great and flourishing kingdom that it is, and, from a disgrace and burden intolerable to this nation, has rendered her a principal part of our strength and ornament.

Burke here temporarily talks himself out of existence. Yet he struck precisely the right note as far as the Rockinghams were concerned, as a letter from the Duke of Richmond shows:

Since I saw you I have read your last speech and cannot too strongly express my admiration of it. It is so calm, so quiet, so reasonable, so just, so proper, that one cannot refuse conviction to every part. At other times, wit, or strong pictures, or violent declamations may be proper. There may be a season for poetry, but in the present awful moment, the grave sober language of truth and cool reason is much better timed. And you appear in this speech not that lively astonishing orator that some of your works show you to be, but the most wise, dispassionate, and calm statesman.

If On Conciliation with America is less thoroughly Burkean than On American Taxation, it is the finest example of one of Burke's manners:

that of polished gravitas. It contains, for example, some of the best specimens of the Burkean aphorism:

> If you do not succeed, you are without resource: for, conciliation failing, force remains; but, force failing, no further hope of reconciliation is left. Power and authority are sometimes bought by kindness; but they can never be begged as alms by an impoverished and defeated violence.

> I do not know the method of drawing up an indictment against an whole people.

> Man acts from adequate motives relative to his interest and not on metaphysical speculations.

> Magnanimity in politics is not seldom the truest wisdom; and a great empire and little minds go ill together.

On Conciliation also contains one of the finest examples of the Burkean oratorical set-piece, expressing his admiration for the American spirit:

> Pass by the other parts, and look at the manner in which the people of New England have of late carried on the whale-fishery. Whilst we follow them among the tumbling mountains of ice, and behold them penetrating into the deepest frozen recesses of Hudson's Bay and Davis's Straits, whilst we are looking for them beneath the Arctic Circle, we hear that they have pierced into the opposite region of polar cold, that they are at the Antipodes, and engaged under the frozen serpent of the South. Falkland Island, which seemed too remote and romantic an object for the grasp of national ambition, is but a stage and resting place in the progress of their victorious industry. Nor is the equinoctial heat more discouraging to them than the accumulated winter of both the poles. We know that whilst some of them draw the line and strike the harpoon on the coast of Africa, others run the longitude, and pursue their gigantic game along the coast of Brazil. No sea but what is vexed by their fisheries. No climate that is not witness to their toils. Neither the perseverance of Holland, nor the activity of France, nor the dexterous and firm sagacity of English enterprise, ever carried this most perilous mode of hard industry to the extent to which it has been pushed by this recent people – a people who are still, as it were, but in the gristle, and not yet hardened into the bone of manhood.

The core of Burke's case is contained in this passage, near the conclusion:

> My hold of the colonies is in the close affection which grows from common names, from kindred blood, from similar privileges, and equal protection. These are ties which, though light as air, are as strong as links of iron. Let the colonies always keep the idea of their civil rights associated with your government, they will cling and grapple to you, and no force under heaven will be of power to tear them from their allegiance. But let it be once understood that your government may be one thing and their privileges another, that these two things may exist without any mutual relation – the cement is gone, the cohesion is loosened, and everything hastens to decay and dissolution.

The resolutions were negatived without debate, by 270 votes to 78. Burke had expected no other result: 'I have this comfort, that in every stage of the American affairs, I have steadily opposed the measures that have produced the confusion, and may bring on the destruction, of this empire. I now go so far so to risk a proposal of my own. If I cannot give peace to my country, I give it to my conscience.'

Richard Burke, writing to Richard Shackleton on the day the speech was delivered, gives an impression of its impact, which was quite distinct from its capacity to influence the vote: 'He began at half past three, and was on his legs, until six o'clock. From a torrent of Members rushing from the House when he sat down, I could hear the loudest, the most unanimous, and the highest strains of applause. That such a performance even from him was never before heard in that House.' Richard goes on to make a comment which shows that the family had been worried by the way American affairs had been preying on Burke's mind since the drift to war had begun with the passage of the penal Acts at the end of 1774:

> In short, by what I can learn, he has done himself infinite credit – I know that he has discharged his conscience of a load that was on it. I do not use the word conscience other than in its ordinary acceptation; believe me America was not on his mind only as a politician, it hung on his conscience as being accountable for his actions and his conduct. That is now satisfied – may he be satisfied – it will be highly necessary that he should, to his health and to his peace.

In May, the second Continental Congress met in Philadelphia, set up a Continental Army, and appointed George Washington Commander-in-Chief. The battle of Bunker Hill followed on 17 June, with heavy British casualties. George III declared the colonies to be 'in open rebellion'. In July, before the news of Bunker Hill had reached London, Burke wrote to Richard Champion in Bristol:

> Things are come to a crisis in America. I confess to you that I cannot avoid a very great degree of uneasiness in this most anxious interval. An engagement must instantly follow this proclamation of [General] Gage's. If he should succeed, and beat the raw American troops, which from his superiority in discipline and authority as well as his present considerable numbers I think he probably will, then we shall be so elevated as to throw all moderation behind us and plunge ourselves into a war which cannot be ended by many such battles, though they should terminate in so many victories. If we are beat, America is gone irrecoverably.

Whether the war was to be short or long, it could not end well for Britain. By August, Burke is sure of an eventual American victory: 'The spirit of America is incredible,' he writes to Rockingham. 'God knows they are very inferior in all human resources. But a remote and difficult country and such a spirit as now animates them may do strange things. Our victories can only complete our ruin.' He is deeply distressed by the almost universal acquiescence in Britain in the prosecution of the war against the colonies. He sees it as acquiescence rather than support, but the political effect is the same: 'No man commends the measures which have been pursued, or expects any good from those which are in preparation; but it is a cold, languid opinion, like what men discover in affairs that do not concern them. It excites to no passion; it prompts to no action.' He saw no allies in Britain for his own policy. The allies of the days of the Stamp Act repeal – the merchants – were no longer sympathetic. Out of his Bristol experience, he warned:

> We look to the merchants in vain. They are gone from us, and from themselves. They consider America as lost, and they look to administration for indemnity. Hopes are accordingly held out to them that some equivalent for their debts will be provided. In the meantime the leading men among them are kept full fed with contracts, remittances and jobs of all

descriptions . . . They all, or the greater number of them, begin to snuff the cadaverous *haut goût* of a lucrative war. War indeed is become a sort of substitute for commerce.

Burke's admonitions take on an almost frantic tone:

I shall therefore make no apology for urging again and again how necessary it is for your lordship and your great friends most seriously to take under immediate deliberation what you are to do in this crisis. Nothing like it has happened in your political life. I protest to God I think that your reputation, your duty, and the duty and honour of all who profess your sentiments, from the highest to the lowest of us, demand at this time one honest, hearty effort in order to avert the heavy calamities that are impending, to keep our hands from blood, and if possible to keep the poor, giddy, thoughtless people of our country from plunging headlong into this impious war.

Rockingham's long reply shows him anxious to live up to Burke's expectations of him, but incapable of doing so. He writes about presenting some kind of memorial or address, but goes on: 'I have no conception that we can do anything by a constant attendance on Parliament . . . at any rate, I think we should show fully our adherence to our opinions of the impending ruin of this country if the violent measures are continued towards America, and after we have done so . . . I think we should abstain from going to either House of Parliament when the American affairs are the subject of debate.' Burke seems to have hoped for more. He had indeed advocated secession from Parliament, but he wanted this to be accompanied by an extra-parliamentary effort to gain support: 'All opposition is absolutely crippled if it can obtain no kind of support without doors.'

Having failed to galvanize Rockingham, Burke did his best with the next most important member of the party, the Duke of Richmond, to whom he wrote near the end of September:

I am perfectly sensible of the greatness of the difficulties and the weakness and fewness of the helps in every public affair which you can undertake. I am sensible too of the shocking indifference and neutrality of a great part of the nation. But a speculative despair is unpardonable where it is our duty to act. I cannot think the people at large wholly to blame; or if they were, it is to no purpose to blame them. For God's sake, my dear lord, endeavour to mend them. I must beg leave to put you in mind ... that no regular or sustained endeavours of any kind have been used to dispose the people to a better sense of their condition. Any election must be lost, any family interest in a country would melt away, if greater pains – infinitely greater – were not employed to support them than had ever been employed in this end and object of all elections, and in this most important interest of the nation and of every individual in it. The people are not answerable for their present supine acquiescence. Indeed they are not. God and nature never made them to think or to act without guidance and direction. They have obeyed the only impulse they have received. When they resist such endeavours as ought to be used by those who, by their rank and fortune in the country, by the goodness of their characters and their experience in their affairs, are their natural leaders, then it will be time enough to despair and to let their blood lie upon their own heads.

Richmond's influence with the Irish Parliament was considerable, and Burke wanted him to use it to get that body to come out against the war:

Ireland is always a part of some importance in the general system; but Ireland never was in the situation of real honour and real consequence in which she now stands. She has the balance of the empire, and perhaps its fate for ever, in her hands. If the Parliament which is shortly to meet there should interpose a friendly mediation, should send a pathetic address to the King, and a letter to both Houses of Parliament here, it is impossible that they should not succeed. If they should only add to this a suspension of extraordinary grants and supplies for troops employed out of the kingdom, in effect employed against their own rights and privileges, they would preserve the whole empire from a ruinous war, and with a saving rather than expense prevent this infatuated country from establishing a plan which tends to its own ruin by enslaving all its dependencies. Ministry would not like to have a contest with the whole empire upon their hands at once.

Nothing came of this idea. Irish, American and British politics did not begin to interact profoundly until 1778, after Burgoyne's defeat at Saratoga.

By now Burke was perhaps clutching at straws so as to prevent himself falling into 'a speculative despair'. Frustrated in his efforts to galvanize his party leaders, he fell back on a parliamentary initiative of his own. Foredoomed though this was, in terms of votes, he could still hope that it might make some impression in the country, as On American Taxation had, at least in Bristol. He introduced his 'Bill for Composing the Present Troubles in America' on 16 November. It contained substantially the same set of measures as his March resolutions, but embodied them in somewhat more explicit form. The speech introducing his Bill was in a low key, analytical and businesslike. The most remarkable part of it was a prediction that was to be fulfilled three years later. The 'predatory war' waged by the government, he said, 'did not lead to a speedy decision. The longer our distractions continued, the greater chance there was for the interference of the Bourbon powers, which in a long protracted war may be considered not only as probable but in a manner certain.' He was sure the country was 'utterly incapable of carrying on a war' with America, France and Spain acting together.

Exposing the danger of the ministerial policy of forcing the Americans to consent to terms, he argued that

> if the ministers treated for a revenue, or for any other purpose, they had but two securities for the performance of the terms: either the same force which compelled these terms, or the honour, sincerity, and good inclination of the people. If they could trust the people to keep the terms without force, they might trust them to make them without force. If nothing but force could hold them, and they meant nothing but independency, as the Speech from the Throne asserted, then the House was to consider how a standing army of 26,000 men, and 70 ships of war, could be constantly kept up in America. A people meaning independency will not mean it the less because they have, to avoid a present inconvenience, submitted to treaty. That after all our struggles, our hold in America is, and must be, her good inclination. If this fails, all fails . . .

Cogent reasoning, which fell on deaf ears. In the debate that followed, the first ministerial speaker, one of the King's friends, Welbore Ellis, gave the standard ministerial answer to the case for conciliation. He urged that 'the greater disposition Great Britain showed towards conciliation, the more obstinate, rebellious, and insolent America would become'. Burke's Bill was rejected by 210 votes to 105. The defeat was immediately followed by Lord North's American Prohibiting Bill, forbidding 'all traffic and intercourse with the American colonies'. On that disheartening note, the session of 1775 ended, so far as American business was concerned.

PROGRESS OF THE AMERICAN WAR 1776–78

The first months of 1776 went badly for the British in America. General Sir William Howe, who had been sent to punish Boston, was cooped up there, surrounded by the bitterly hostile population of Massachusetts and besieged by Washington's forces. In mid March, he withdrew to Halifax in Nova Scotia. For several months, all thirteen colonies were 'clear of redcoats'.

In the meantime, the Rockingham Whigs had a new and brilliant convert, largely thanks to Burke. Charles James Fox (1749–1806) had been so impressed by Burke's 1774 speech On American Taxation, that he became Burke's political pupil. From now on, in relation to much American business, and in the Commons, Burke was to play second fiddle to a first violin he himself had trained. The relationship was exceptional – if not unique – in political history. It was Fox who now applied the Burkean principles to each new situation, while Burke backed him up with the necessary historical facts and figures. On 20 February 1776, Fox proposed a 'motion for an enquiry into the causes of the ill success of British arms in North America'. He spoke eloquently, and was followed by Burke, who, according to the *Parliamentary History*, 'showed from the records of Parliament and from history, that nothing was more frequent than enquiries of the kind now proposed; and observed, at no time within the course of his reading, did he ever recollect a period at which such a proceeding was more absolutely necessary than the present'.

Fox would not have taken the lead without the approval of his friend and guide, and it was probably Burke's idea that he should do so. The policies Burke believed in would carry more weight with Parliament and the public when advocated by a well-connected Englishman than by an Irish adventurer. Fox was the only contemporary in Burke's class as an orator, and that Burke did not mind taking second place to him is a measure of his commitment to his beliefs. Policies consistently came ahead of considerations of personal advantage or advancement.

Throughout the spring and summer of 1776, forces were being

mobilized for the American War. Burke was distressed for both sides, but his emotions were definitely engaged on the side of the Americans. 'The worst about Canada is certainly true,' he wrote to Rockingham in June. 'And much more of the same bad kind, not very improbable.' The 'worst' had been a British victory and the retreat of the American forces from Canada. The next month he wrote: 'I received your letter before I was up this morning, and not having passed a good night, I tried to sleep after it, but the hurry and bustle of the march of the first division and second division of Pennsylvania troops, of the fortification of Boston, and all the din of war, disturbed me in such a manner that I courted sleep in vain.' That letter was written on the day of the Declaration of Independence, 4 July 1776.

The war was temporarily going against the Americans. Having landed his forces on Staten Island, General Howe defeated Washington in the Battle of Long Island, and Washington retreated into Pennsylvania. In Britain, supporters of the war were triumphant. Parliament resumed late in October. Ministerial speakers urged that since the Americans had declared independence, there could be no negotiating with them. Burke held that Britain's delay in starting serious negotiations had been at the root of all the trouble:

> By this delay you drove them into the declaration of independency ... and now they have declared it, you bring it as an argument to prove, that there can be no other reasoning used with them but the sword ... In order to bring things to this unhappy situation, did not you pave the way, by a succession of acts of tyranny; for this, you shut up their ports, cut off their fishery, annihilated their charters, and governed them by an army. Sir, the recollection of these things being the evident causes of what we have seen is more than what ought to be endured. This it is that has burned the noble city of New York, that has planted the bayonet in the bosoms of my principals, in the bosom of the city where alone your wretched government once boasted the only friends she could number in America.

Clearly in a towering passion, Burke then fell into one of the extravagances that occasionally embarrassed his friends. The King had ordered church services and a public fast in support of the war. Burke commented: 'Till our churches are purified from this abominable service, I shall consider them not as the temples of the Almighty but the synagogues of Satan.' This was extravagant, no doubt, but it was an extravagance that revealed a furious commitment, such as no man can simulate.

The opening weeks of 1777 were the nadir for British friends of America. On 15 January, Sir George Savile reported to Rockingham: 'We are not only patriots *out of place*, but patriots out *of the opinion of the public*. The repeated successes [of British arms], *hollow* as I think them and the more *ruinous* if they *are real*, have fixed or converted ninety-nine in one hundred.' A few days earlier, Burke had written to Rockingham:

> The affairs of America seem to be drawing towards a crisis. The Howes are by this time in possession of, or able to awe, the whole middle coast of America, from Delaware to the western boundary of Massachusetts Bay; the naval barrier on the side of Canada is broken; a great tract of country is open to the supply of the troops; the River Hudson opens away into the hearts of the provinces; and nothing, in all probability, can prevent an early offensive campaign. What the Americans have done is, in their circumstances, truly astonishing. It is indeed infinitely more than I expected from them. But having done so much, for some short time I entertained an opinion that they might do more. But it is now evident that they cannot look [British] standing armies in the face.

That last opinion was based on the information available in Britain at the time. In America, it had already been disproved. Crossing the Delaware on Christmas Day, Washington had captured Trenton from the regulars who had occupied it, and he had then won another victory at Princeton on 2 January.

In his letter, Burke went on to discuss Benjamin Franklin's recently begun mission to Paris, and mentioned an idea of his own about possible mediation:

> If the Congress could be brought to declare in favour of [the Rockinghams'] terms for which 108 Members of the House of Commons voted last year, with some civility to the party which held out those terms, it would undoubtedly have an effect to revive the cause of our liberties in England, and to give the colonies some sort of mooring and anchorage in this country. It seemed to me that Franklin might be made to feel the propriety of such a step; and as I have an acquaintance with him, I had for a moment a strong

desire of taking a turn to Paris. Everything else failing, one might obtain a better knowledge of the general aspect of things abroad than I believe any of us possess at the present. The Duke of Portland approved the idea. But when I had conversed with the very few of your lordship's friends who were in town and considered a little more maturely the constant temper and standing maxims of the party, I laid aside the design, not being desirous of risking the displeasure of those for whose sake alone I wished to take that fatiguing journey at this severe season of the year.

It is tempting to see Burke here as deferring excessively to the Rockingham aristocrats. But this putative mission would have been of interest to Franklin only if Burke could speak for the most significant section of the British opposition. In any case, Burke would not have proposed such a mediation if he had known about the American successes at Trenton and Princeton. Still, we may feel a sense of loss: Edmund Burke and Benjamin Franklin in diplomatic negotiations in Paris in the winter of 1776–77 would have been a dramatic set-piece. Their reports to London and to Philadelphia would have made marvellously instructive and entertaining reading. But it was not to be.

At this time, the Rockinghams were staying away from Parliament, finding opposition hopeless as long as the British appeared to be winning in America. But if inactive in the Commons, Burke continued to exert himself outside by writing (as he was to do again during a period of parliamentary silence after the French Revolution). In April, he published *A Letter to the Sheriffs of Bristol*. This tract was partly to justify to his constituents the policy of parliamentary abstention, though that policy ended shortly afterwards, when the news of the American victories at Trenton and Princeton arrived, shaking the government and heartening the opposition. But it is for Burke's thinking at a time when the American cause seemed at its lowest ebb that this pamphlet is important. With the speeches on the Declaratory Act (1766), On American Taxation (1774), and most of On Conciliation with America (1775), *A Letter to the Sheriffs of Bristol* completes the quartet of his major pronouncements on America. Taken together, they make up the burden of the American part of his great melody, though there were also a great number of occasional speeches and devastating debating replies.

To the Sheriffs of Bristol differs from the other three major pronouncements in that it was written, not spoken. The difference is not so great, since most of Burke's fully recorded speeches are highly structured, as if on parade, with each subordinate clause firmly in line. Still, there is a difference of texture. The *Letter to the Sheriffs of Bristol* is even more tightly argued than his other statements. In all the parts directly addressed to America, it is in Burke's essential style: grave, sober, aphoristic, energetic. The stately, courtly manner, prominent in On Conciliation, appears only in a complimentary flourish about the Rockinghams. There are no jokes. Burke's anger, though lowering as often on the horizon, is under control; there are no 'synagogues of Satan' here. The tract – which was sent to the sheriffs with copies of the penal Acts against America – begins:

> It affords no matter for very pleasing reflection to observe that our subjects diminish as our laws increase . . .
>
> I think I know America – if I do not, my ignorance is uncurable, for I have spared no pains to understand it – and I do most solemnly assure those of my constituents who put any sort of confidence in my industry and integrity that everything that has been done there has arisen from a total misconception of the object: that our means of originally holding America, that our means of reconciling with it after quarrel, of recovering it after separation, of keeping it after victory, did depend, and must depend, in their several stages and periods, upon a total renunciation of that unconditional submission which has taken such possession of the minds of violent men.

There is a wealth of painful experience behind Burke's arguments:

> When any community is subordinately connected with another, the great danger of the connection is the extreme pride and self-complacency of the superior, which in all matters of controversy will probably decide in its own favour . . .
>
> They have been told that their dissent from violent measures is an encouragement to rebellion. Men of great presumption will hold a language which is contradicted by a whole course of history. *General* rebellions and revolts of an whole people were never *encouraged*, now or at any time. They are always *provoked*.

Burke harks back to the repeal of the Stamp Act in 1766, and cites a relevant declaration of Congress, which has been ignored by the many historians who depreciate the importance of that measure:

> The Congress has used an expression with regard to this pacification which appears to me truly significant. After the repeal of the Stamp Act, 'the colonies fell', says the Assembly, 'into their ancient state of *unsuspecting confidence in the mother country.*' This unsuspecting confidence is the true centre of gravity amongst mankind, about which all the parts are at rest. It is this *unsuspecting confidence* that removes all difficulties and reconciles all the contradictions which occur in the complexity of all ancient puzzled political establishments. Happy are the rulers which have the secret of preserving it.

He goes on, with reference to the Declaratory Act which accompanied the repeal:

> If this undefined power has become odious since that time, and full of horror to the colonies, it is because the *unsuspicious confidence* is lost, and the parental affection, in the bosom of whose boundless authority they reposed their privileges, is become strange and hostile.

Burke refutes the claim that there is a contradiction between his support for the Declaratory Bill in 1766 and his advocacy of the denial of Parliament's power to tax the colonists in 1775:

> It will be asked, if such was then my opinion of the mode of pacification, how I came to be the very person who moved not only for a repeal of all the late coercive statues but for mutilating, by positive law, the entireness of the legislative power of Parliament, and the cutting off from it the whole right of taxation. I answer, Because a different state of things requires a different conduct. When the dispute had gone to these last extremities (which no man laboured more to prevent than I did), the concessions which had satisfied in the beginning could satisfy no longer, because the violation of tacit faith required explicit security. The same cause which has introduced all formal compacts and covenants among men made it necessary: I mean habits of soreness, jealousy, and distrust. I parted with it as with a limb, but as a limb to save the body; and I would have parted with more, if more had been necessary: anything rather than a fruitless, hopeless, unnatural civil war. This mode of yielding would, it is said, give way to independency without a war. I

am persuaded, from the nature of things, and from every information, that it would have had a directly contrary effect. But if it had this effect, I confess, that I should prefer independency without war to independency with it; and I have so much trust in the inclinations and prejudices of mankind, and so little in anything else, that I should expect ten times more benefit to this kingdom from the affection of America, though under a separate establishment, than from her perfect submission to the Crown and Parliament accompanied with her terror, disgust, and abhorrence. Bodies tied together by so unnatural a bond of union as mutual hatred are only connected to their ruin.

By using the term 'civil war', he emphasizes that the mother country could never profit from its military campaigns, even if could win them. The war was inevitably destructive to both sides, just as the bonds of trade and affection had been of mutual benefit.

By the summer of 1777, after the news of Trenton and Princeton, the opposition was back in business. There were no more parliamentary set-pieces from Burke that year: he knew better than to attempt a repeat of On Conciliation. Rather, he followed up the thesis of that speech – which he left Fox to reassert – by crushing interventions in debate. Thus, in a debate on the Budget in May, Charles Jenkinson, the King's closest political confidant and a *bête noire* of Burke's, had argued that 'if America was to remain a part of the British Empire, she ought most certainly to bear a proportionate share of the expense of general protection'. Burke retorted that 'it would be extremely difficult for him to show that the surest steps towards conquering America or inducing the colonies to come to terms of accommodation would be to apprise them that, conquer or submit, they must pay the expense of conquest . . .'

That summer, Burke was preoccupied with America to the exclusion of almost everything else, and conscious of the forces impelling France towards intervention in America. To Philip Francis in India, with whom he was later to collaborate closely, he wrote:

The affairs of America, which are as important [as Indian affairs] and more distracted, have almost entirely engrossed the attention which I am able to give to anything. I wished and laboured to keep war at a distance; never having been able to discover any advantage which could be derived from the greatest success; I never approved of our engaging in it, and I am sure it might have been avoided. The ministers this year hold out to us the strongest hopes of what they call a victorious campaign. I am, indeed, ready enough to believe that we shall obtain those delusive advantages which will encourage us to proceed but will not bring matters nearer to an happy termination. France gives all the assistance to the colonies which is consistent with the appearance of neutrality. Time is to show whether she will proceed further, or whether America can maintain herself in the present struggle without a more open declaration and more decided effort from that power. At present, the ministers seem confident that France is resolved to be quiet. If the Court of Versailles be so pacific, I assure you it is in defiance of the wishes and opinions of that whole nation.

The 'delusive advantages' duly materialized, shortly before disaster struck. In July, Burgoyne captured Ticonderoga on his southward march from Canada towards, as he believed, a junction with Howe, the isolation of New England, and comprehensive victory. In September, Howe, who was not giving much thought to a junction with Burgoyne, won the battle of Brandywine and entered Philadelphia. Burke wrote to Richard Champion: 'The worst of the matter is this: that let Howe's success be what or where it may, it will be sufficient to keep up the delusion here, and to draw in Parliament deeper and deeper into this system of endless hopes and disappointments.'

In November, shortly before news of Brandywine reached Britain, Burke appealed to Parliament to take advantage of her position of relative strength to attempt to achieve a compromise. This was clearly a powerful speech, but the *Parliamentary History* gives only part of it:

If it were possible, we would give a detail of a speech which in the course of almost two hours commanded the attention, excited the laughter, and sometimes drew tears from the sympathizing few ... but we must ... touch only on that pathetic supplication which he made to the House to seize the present happy moment to attempt an accommodation, when, neither elated with insolent victory nor debased with abject defeat, we could without dishonour to ourselves make such proposals to our colonists as they could without dishonour accept ... Shall we give them no alternative but unconditional submission? A three years' war has not terrified them, distressed as they are, from their great purpose. Let us try the power of lenity over those generous bosoms.

The chance, which would not have been taken, was already lost. Burgoyne's army had surrendered at Saratoga on 17 October, though the news did not reach England until 2 December, the day before the Commons convened. On 3 December, Lord George Germain, the disastrous Secretary of State for the Colonies, had 'a piece of very unhappy intelligence to report'. The ensuing angry and excited debate brought Burke into personal danger. He had attacked North's Solicitor-General, Alexander Wedderburn, calling him 'counsel' to the despised Germain. During Wedderburn's reply, Burke laughed loudly. Wedderburn exclaimed that 'if the gentleman did not know manners, *he as an individual* would teach them to him.' Burke made a sign to Wedderburn to follow him out of the House, and a duel was averted only by the intervention of Fox and other friends. On learning that it had been averted, Rockingham wrote: 'My dear Burke, My heart is at ease. Ever yours, most affectionately, Rockingham.'

The entry of France into the war, which had long been foreseen by Burke, was now inevitable. In the Commons on 10 December, he spoke of 'our natural and avowed enemy the French, negotiating the treaty – perhaps not negotiating but even perfecting a treaty by which America will be irrevocably lost to this country'.

On 6 February 1778, he proposed in the Commons a 'motion relative to the military employment of Indians in the civil war with America'. This was no side-issue; it referred to the principal cause of the Battle of Saratoga. Burgoyne's proclamation explicitly threatening the use of his Indian (or Native American) allies against the settlers, many of whom hitherto had been neutral, caused the settlers to embody as militia and to rally to the aid of the revolutionary army in overwhelming the British forces. The unctuous ferocity of that proclamation chills the blood. Burgoyne threatened to use the Indians not just against the rebels, but against any settler families who should fail to assist his army. It was that threat which doomed his army. As reported in the *Parliamentary History*, Burke said: 'The fault of employing [Indians] did not consist in their being of one colour or another, but in their way of making war, which was so horrible that it not only shocked the manners of all civilized nations, but far exceeded the ferocity of any other barbarians that have been recorded either by ancient or modern history.' He attributed the fatal catastrophe at Saratoga 'to the cruelties exercised by these barbarians, which obliged all mankind, without regard to party or to political principle, and in despite of military indisposition, to become soldiers, and to unite as one man in the common defence'.

Horace Walpole, in his *Last Journals*, provided a vivid impression of this speech and its impact:

> The 6th was memorable for the *chef d'oeuvre* of Burke's orations. He called Burgoyne's talk with the Indians the 'sublimity of bombast absurdity' in which [Burgoyne] demanded the assistance of seventeen Indian nations, by considerations of *our holy religion*, by regard for our constitution; and though he enjoined them not to scalp men, women, or children alive, he promised to pay them for any scalps of the dead, and required them to repair to the King's standard ... Seventeen interpreters from the several nations, said he, could not have given them any idea of his reasons – but, added Burke, the invitation was just as if, at a riot on Tower Hill, the keeper of the wild beasts had turned them loose, but adding, 'My gentle lions, my sentimental wolves, my tender-hearted hyenas, go forth, but take care not to hurt men, women, or children.' He then grew serious; and as the former part had excited the warmest and most continued bursts of laughter even from Lord North ... and the ministers themselves, so he drew such a pathetic picture of the cruelties of the King's army – particularly in the alleged case of a young woman on whose ransom, not beauty, they quarrelled and murdered her – that he *drew iron tears* down Barr's cheek ... Governor Johnston said he was now glad that strangers were excluded, as, if they had been admitted, Burke's speech would have excited them to tear the ministers to pieces as they went out of the House.

On 17 February, the Commons debated Lord North's Conciliatory Propositions to the Americans. Ironically, the propositions were in substance identical, as Fox pointed out in the debate, to those put forward by Burke in 1775: repeal of the tea duty and the penal Acts – abandonment of the right to tax. Offered in 1775, these concessions would probably have led to peace; offered in 1778, after Saratoga, they were hopeless. There is a description in the *Annual Register*, probably by Burke himself, of the scene in Parliament when North had finished his appeal: 'A dull melancholy for some time followed this speech. It had been heard with profound attention, left without a single mark of approbation to any part from any description of men, or any particular man in the House. Astonishment, dejection and fear overwhelmed the whole assembly.' The fear was due to the general belief that North would never have made such an offer, reversing his (or rather George III's) entire policy of the past three years, unless he had had word that a treaty between the Americans and the French was well on the way to conclusion, meaning that war with France would follow.

On 16 March, seconding a 'motion for all communications touching a treaty between France and America', Burke demanded 'a discovery of the councils, and of the persons who gave them, by which [Britain] had been reduced from the pinnacle of honour and power to the lowest ebb of wretchedness and disgrace'. The next day, George III publicly acknowledged that he had been informed of the conclusion of 'a treaty of amity and commerce between the Court of France and certain persons employed by His Majesty's revolted subjects in America'. The British ambassador was withdrawn from Paris. Great Britain and France were in a state of war. The British Isles were under threat of invasion.

The government had now to give some urgent attention to the affairs of that island where a French invasion would be likely to find a welcome. Burke would in future be simultaneously involved in the political affairs of America and of his native Ireland.

III: America, Ireland

From the very beginning of Burke's parliamentary career, Ireland and America were connected in his mind. On 31 December 1765, shortly after his election for Wendover, he wrote to Charles O'Hara: 'One thing however is fortunate to you, though without any merits of your own, that the liberties (or what shadows of liberty there are) of Ireland have been saved in America.' He presumably meant that America's resistance to the Stamp Act had averted a possible decision by the British Parliament to tax Ireland. What exactly he may have meant by the liberties of Ireland, '(or what shadows of liberty there are)', is puzzling – and seems to have puzzled Burke himself.

On 4 March 1766 we find him writing to O'Hara: 'Could not Ireland be somehow *hooked* into this system?' By 'this system', he appears to be referring to a revision of the commercial laws affecting North America and the West Indies which the first Rockingham administration was then working on. (He later dropped the idea of including Ireland in the commercial revision.) But he refers, virtually in the same breath, to his exertions over the repeal of the Stamp Act. Clearly what is attracting him, in this exhilarating dawn of his parliamentary career, is the idea of stimulating some kind of benign and free interaction between the affairs of his native Ireland and those of the rest of the British Empire, and especially of America.

In 1775 Burke again had such an interaction in mind when he tried, in vain, to get the Irish Parliament to declare itself opposed to the American War by a 'pathetic address' to the King and by a 'suspension of extraordinary grants' for troops employed overseas. This bid failed; the Irish Parliament probably assumed at this time, as did most people in Britain, that the American rebellion would be speedily snuffed out.

An interaction between America and Ireland did begin with the outbreak of the American War, but it was limited and of limited interest to Burke. Only one set of people in Ireland was passionately concerned about the outcome of the American War, and Burke did not have emotional ties with them: the Dissenters, most of them in Eastern Ulster (now Northern Ireland). Many of their kinsmen, along with many from Scotland, had emigrated to America, mostly to Pennsylvania, where they became known as the Scotch–Irish and formed an important part of Washington's armies. Accordingly, most of their people back in Ireland made the American cause their own.

So support in Ireland for the American cause was mainly Protestant. Taking note of that, Catholic leaders, especially among the gentry, sought to take advantage through declarations of loyalty to the Crown and contributions to the war effort. The implicit message was that the people whom Britain had treated as disloyal were really the loyal ones, while those who had been regarded as loyal were now shown to be disloyal – so the disabilities imposed on the Catholics for supposed disloyalty should be removed.

Burke understood these tactics well; years afterwards, during the French Revolution, he was to use similar arguments himself, to the advantage of the Catholics. In general, however, the disposition of the different groups among the Irish over the American War was uncomfortable for him. The people whose interests he had most at heart, the Catholics, supported the British forces in a war he opposed – or at least those who claimed to speak for them did, without reported contradiction. And the people who were most opposed to George III's war were anti-Catholic.

Such were the Irish responses to the American War between its beginning in 1775 and Burgoyne's surrender at Saratoga in 1777. During this period, British politicians from George III down noted with moderate gratification the assurances of Catholic loyalty. They were not unduly alarmed by support for the Americans among Dissenters, who were a minority and unlikely to stage an insurrection on their own. The insurrection most to be feared was one by the great majority of the population, the Catholics. Since the British Parliament was not preoccupied with Irish affairs, Burke was under no obligation to take up positions about them, and probably felt no great inclination to do so, given the uncongenial alignment of forces in Ireland. However, after the news of Saratoga had reached Britain in 1777, Ireland became overnight a matter of acute concern to the people and Parliament of Great Britain. The interaction of Ireland and America had begun in earnest, and it proved more disconcerting than Burke had once hoped.

The Franco-American Treaty, the principal consequence of Saratoga, was concluded in March 1778. Britain and France were now at war, and the British Isles were exposed to an imminent threat of invasion. The army and navy were heavily committed in America. The Treasury was depleted. England was in danger, and every soldier and ship had to be committed to its defence. The Royal Navy would try to repel a French landing in any port, but if the French succeeded in landing in force in Ireland, the government had little means to resist them. Irishmen themselves would have to do the resisting.

This was the emergency that led to the creation of the armed force that became known in 1779 as the Irish Volunteers. The Volunteers were to dominate Irish politics for the duration of the war with France. They were also to have a powerful effect on British politics, and to bring about two important pieces of legislation, of great concern to Burke.

With the lucidity of fascinated malice, Horace Walpole put his finger on the nub of the matter. In October 1779, when the Volunteer movement was at its height, Walpole wrote: 'The Irish have 28,000 men in arms ... I dare to say that Mr Edmund Burke does not approve of these proceedings, for the 28,000 are all Protestants.' Burke must indeed have watched the emergence of the Volunteers with foreboding. The situation bore an ominous resemblance to the Whiteboy disturbances in 1766, the year of persecution, when some of his Nagle relations had come close to the gallows. Now, as before, a French invasion of Ireland was expected, this time with much greater reason. As in 1766, it was expected that if the French did land in force, there would be an Irish Catholic rising in support of them. And as in 1766, Protestant vigilantes were on the look out for 'Papist Whiteboys' who might be in league with the French.

That vigilante movement was the origin of the Irish Volunteers. And the Volunteers themselves, at their inception, were not just incidentally Protestant: they were militantly and triumphantly so. The Volunteers were accordingly strongly opposed to an occupation of Ireland by France, for although in reality the France of the late 1770s was only nominally Catholic, anti-Catholics still thought of it as Papist. The Protestants possessed almost everything that was worth possessing in Ireland, and stood to lose it if the French landed in force and were supported by large numbers of Irish Catholics. So the determination of the Protestant Volunteers to resist a French landing was sincere. With respect to resistance to the French, George III had no more loyal subjects than the Irish Protestants in 1778–80.

The red-letter days of the Protestant Volunteers, on which they held their great winter and summer parades, were 4 November (the birthday of William III) and 12 July (the anniversay of the Battle of the Boyne). These were the days – as the latter still is in Northern Ireland – on which Protestant Ireland annually celebrated its decisive victories over its Irish Papist enemies and their French allies (1689–91). And the Volunteers of 1778 were clearly looking forward to yet another victory over the same combination of enemies.

Protestant vigilantism might have turned into a witch-hunt against the Irish Catholic gentry, as had happened in 1766. In the event, however, persecution was avoided. Partly at least, this was because the Catholic leadership chose to support the Volunteers, for tactical reasons. Catholic declarations of loyalty and offers of assistance to the Volunteers – and, in a very few cases, actual enlistment – were motivated by calculation rather than by a true common cause. After all, if what the Protestants feared were to come to pass, Catholics would be the gainers. The Catholic gentry seem to have judged it prudent to assume either that the French would not land at all, or that they would not land in sufficient strength to overthrow the existing system. On either assumption, the safest course for the subject people was to demonstrate their solidarity with their Protestant neighbours against the threatened French invasion.

The Catholics' real attitude can be judged from the response of Maurice O'Connell to the invitation of a Protestant neighbour to help to establish a corps of Volunteers in the borough of Iveragh. His reply is masterly in its use of the style and vocabulary of absolute loyalty and submission to constituted authority to convey a refusal of any practical support:

I am fully convinced that the Roman Catholic gentlemen of Iveragh would readily unite with their Protestant neighbours . . . to form a corps did they think such a measure would meet the approbation of the legislature. They would, in common with every Catholic of standing in Ireland, be exceedingly happy by every means in their power to give additional weight and strength and security to the kingdom; but what can they do while the laws of their country forbid them the use of arms? Under such circumstances, I look upon it to be their duty to confine themselves to that line of conduct marked out for them by the legislature, and with humility and resignation wait for a further relaxation of the laws, which a more enlightened and liberal way of thinking, added to a clearer and more deliberate attention to the real interests and prosperity of the country will, I hope, soon bring about.

The leaders of the Irish Volunteers understood the feelings of their Catholic countrymen well enough to have little belief in their professions of loyalty to the Crown, and at first local Volunteer commanders rebuffed Catholic overtures. After a while, however, Catholic support for the Volunteers became officially welcome. With that, the possibility of a 1766-style witch-hunt against Catholics receded.

Yet the danger to the established order in Ireland was far greater in 1778, with its real threat of invasion, than it had been in 1766, with its fantasy threat. Three years after the triumphant conclusion of the Seven Years War, with the conquest of Canada and India, England's power, and its authority over Ireland, looked invulnerable. In 1778, after Burgoyne's defeat by the unaided Americans at Saratoga, England looked vulnerable indeed. To a conquered people such as the Irish Catholics, the news that their conquerors had undergone a defeat at the hands of some of their former subjects must have been exciting. After Saratoga, and especially after France's entry into the war, Irish Catholics naturally took a keen interest in the course of events. Most probably hoped for a French victory.

From England, however, the politics of Ireland in 1778 presented, on the surface, a spectacle of unprecedented harmony. Protestants were arming for the defence of their country, and Catholics were supporting their Protestant defenders. The political conjuncture in Britain was more favourable than ever before to the two Irish causes closest to Burke's heart: free trade and Catholic emancipation. Frightened by possible disaffection in Ireland in the context of the threatened invasion, the North administration decided on a limited relaxation of the restrictions on Irish trade. It also decided on a limited measure of Catholic relief, which went through in 1778. Burke spoke in the Commons in April and May in support of the Irish Trade Bills, explicitly linking them to events in America: 'Ireland was now the chief dependency of the British Crown, and it particularly behoved this country to admit the Irish nation to the privileges of British citizens.' Burke's point here is that America is as good as lost, and all because Parliament failed to conciliate the colonists. Now, with Ireland taking the place of America as the chief dependency, Parliament must learn from its mistake and conciliate the Irish.

But the Irish Trade Bills were unpopular in Britain, and a reaction set in. Burke writes: 'A strong opposition was forming against the Irish Bills ... A general alarm was spread, through most of the trading and manufacturing parts of the kingdom ... It ran like an infection every-where and took such absolute possession of the mind, that the recent, and immediately sore-felt example of America, with respect to any general application of cause to effects, was totally forgotten.' The 'infection' had spread to Burke's own constituency of Bristol. He acknowledged in the Commons that his support for the Irish Trade Bills might result in his being 'deprived of his seat ... his conduct being disapproved by many of his chief friends and supporters, as well as by all who had opposed him at his election'. Burke added that

> He should not blame [his constituents] if they did reject him: the event would afford a very useful example, on the one hand, of a senator inflexibly adhering to his opinion against interest and against popularity; and, on the other, of constituents exercising their undoubted right of rejection; not on corrupt [grounds], but from their persuasion that he whom they had chosen had acted against the judgment and interest of those he represented.

More frightened, now, by the general alarm in Britain than by any danger in Ireland, North's administration decided in effect to drop the Trade Bills, by voiding them of all substance. It was a decision the government was to regret, and to rescind, in the following year.

Burke first publicly adverted to the existence of the Volunteers when speaking on 12 March 1779 in the Commons on a motion 'respecting the state of Ireland':

> Were there not at this very time 11,000 land-forces actually under arms in

Ireland without any kind of subordination to the government or any part thereof? . . . Not that he blamed those soldiers. Both the officers and the men, he was sure, deserved every compliment that could be paid them. But was it possible for that House to sit down tamely under such a fact? For his part, he was determined not to sit down before he had sifted the matter to the bottom. With respect to the influence of the noble lord [North], if it produced anything at all, it was one eternal scene of anarchy and confusion. But what alas! was that compared with the anarchy that the noble lord had raised through the whole continent of America?

In expressing alarm about the anarchic potential of the Irish Volunteers, Burke seems to have been alone at this date. Most people in authority in Britain and Ireland seem to have found them reassuring. But Burke had reasons of his own, which he was not about to acknowledge explicitly, for being anything but reassured by the thought of large bodies of armed Irish Protestants patrolling the countryside, for whatever declared purpose.

A great expansion of the Volunteers now began. From 11,000 in March, they grew to 18,000 in July, and at least 25,000 by October. As they expanded, the Volunteers added to their original role of defenders of Ireland against French invaders a new, political role, that of armed reformers, whose immediate aim was free trade: principally, the removal of the burdensome restrictions on Irish exports to Britain. In Dublin, the Lord Lieutenant, the Earl of Buckinghamshire, who had been hearing that the Volunteers had begun to 'moulder away', became alarmed when he found, late in May, that 'on the contrary, within these days, intelligence has reached me, that additional companies are forming; and it has been asserted, that this arises from the insinuations which are daily circulated in the public prints, that the idea of their numbers may conduce to the attainment of political advantages to their country.' The Lord Lieutenant was now dependent for the defence of that part of the King's realms on a force not under his control and with a political programme of its own.

The Volunteers' importance to the defence of Ireland became even more acute when Spain entered the war as France's ally. In early June 1779, the French fleet, with twenty-four ships of the line, left Brest to rendezvous with the Spanish fleet. The combined fleet outnumbered British ships in home waters. The British Isles were now in greater danger of invasion than at any time since 1588. It was thought that the enemy might be bound for Ireland, in which case the fate of the empire would be in the hands of the Irish Volunteers. In late July, Burke thought that the fleet – 'the greatest force ever got together' – was bound either for Ireland or the West Indies. The French had indeed made contingency plans for a landing in Ireland, but the Spaniards ruled that out because it would mean a long war, for which Spain was not prepared. The objective of the combined fleet was the occupation of a port in southern England, followed by a dictated peace.

In August, the fleet lay off Plymouth. London was believed to be in imminent danger; we find Burke thanking his friends the Champions for offering his wife Jane 'asylum' in Bristol. About a week later, the danger was over, at least for that year. The great fleet returned to Brest and never put to sea again. There had been no naval engagement. The enterprise had been defeated by disease.

With the invasion threat out of the way, for 1779 at least, the Volunteers were free to concentrate their abundant energies on political agitation in the last months of the year. For Burke this was a most uncomfortable period. He had expressed some reservations about the Volunteers in March, but his political friends had difficulty understanding him. From the viewpoint of a typical English Whig, the Irish Volunteers were a thoroughly admirable body. That the Volunteers were themselves Whigs was attested by their pious observation of the Whig festivals of 12 July and 4 November. Their patriotism was demonstrated by their voluntary enlistment to resist the French. They were a standing demonstration that Whigs could be pro-American and anti-French at the same time. And the Volunteers' political objective, free trade, was a Whig objective too: its most eloquent advocate in the British Parliament was Burke. The Irish Volunteers seemed to be acting in the best Whig tradition, and Charles James Fox accordingly became an enthusiast. 'The Irish associations [i.e. Volunteers] had been called illegal,' he declared; 'legal or illegal, he entirely approved of them.'

Burke anxiously tried to restrain similar tendencies in Rockingham, and to keep Whig support in Parliament for free trade altogether separate from the Volunteers' agitation in Ireland. It was to the British Parliament, and specifically to the English Whigs, that he looked for the emancipation of the Irish Catholics. The first measure towards that end had just come from the British Parliament, in 1778, and the Irish Parliament had only reluctantly and partially followed suit. If the power of the Irish Volunteers – the armed power of an exclusive, dominant caste – were to be substituted for the ultimate authority of Britain, the Irish Catholics would be trapped, at the mercy of the caste whose interest it was to keep them permanently disfranchised. So for Burke it was of the utmost importance that the British Parliament should not be seen to yield to the Volunteers.

To Burke, the Volunteers represented a specific system of injustice, weighing on the Catholic majority in Ireland. But in 1778–82, while his colleagues engaged in animated discussion of matters about which they knew little, Burke knew far more than he could tell. With Rockingham in particular, communications broke down. As an Irish landlord, Rockingham supported the Irish Volunteers, without thinking very deeply about them, both as defenders of Ireland against French invasion and as Whigs protesting against unjust laws. He armed and equipped his tenants at Shillelagh, Co. Wicklow, as a Volunteer corps, and the idea that the Volunteers might pose a threat to the Catholics probably never occurred to him. When Burke urged the need for a 'light and delicate' touch in handling them, Rockingham couldn't see what he was talking about. Although Burke's influence over Rockingham remained great, even decisive, it was frustratingly limited over Whig policy towards Ireland. He became a tongue-tied and irritable passenger in a vehicle he felt was travelling in the wrong direction.

On William III's birthday in 1779, the Volunteer campaign reached a climax with a great parade through Dublin. The historian R. B. McDowell writes:

On 4 November the Dublin Volunteers corps (one of them commanded by the Duke of Leinster) paraded in College Green before an immense crowd of spectators. The pedestal of King William's statue was decorated 'with labels in large capital letters', one of which read 'A short money bill' and another 'A free trade or else'. There were 900 men on parade and the precision of their firing, it was said, was not surpassed by any army in Europe. Ten days later there was a cruder display of public feeling when some thousands of artisans, assembled it was rumoured by printed handbills, beset the Parliament House demanding a free trade, and a party of rioters, trying to find the attorney-general, stormed his house in Harcourt Street and swept through the Four Courts.

The Irish agitation was now led by Henry Grattan (1746–1820), a young Member of the Irish Parliament, who worked in concert with the commander of the Volunteers, the Earl of Charlemont. Grattan was one of the most admired orators of the day. His best-known speeches resemble the more ornate of Burke's, though he lacked Burke's range and variety, as well as his intellect. In this quasi-revolutionary phase of his career especially, he was a skilful and audacious politician. By the end of 1779, the Volunteers were said to number 50,000 men. The British government had no force in Ireland to match them, and no force elsewhere available for Ireland. Grattan and the Volunteers were therefore masters of the Irish scene. He could dictate to the Irish Parliament, and he laid down the law in terms which, drawing on Rousseau, prefigure the imperious and absolute language of the French Revolution ten years later. An MP, according to Grattan, was 'the servant of his constituents, whose commands he was bound to obey, as the servants of the Crown were the royal authority. If a member deviate[d] from the intentions of his constituents, they were authorized to associate against him to reprobate his proceedings – and never trust him with their rights again.'

This was the doctrine that Burke had resonantly rejected in his famous speech to the electors of Bristol in 1774. So although on the face of it Burke and Grattan were agreed over the question of the hour, free trade for Ireland, they were deeply at odds over principles. In any case, Grattan was using the term 'constituents' in a somewhat specialized sense. When he spoke of 'constituents . . . authorized to associate against' a 'deviating' Member 'to reprobate his proceedings', he was, given the brute realities of the time, threatening to unleash the violence of the largely Protestant Dublin mob, backed by the Irish Volunteers, against any parliamentarian who dared to vote against free trade. The Irish Parliament understood and capitulated. An amendment to the address demanding free trade was carried unanimously on 12 October 1779. As the Irish Parliament was usually subservient to the British administration of the day, this was symptomatic of a near-revolutionary situation in Ireland.

The centre of this political storm then shifted to the British Parliament, which met on 25 November. Burke spoke on the question of free trade, linking Ireland to America.

> However the noble lord [North] . . . might pretend to disunite the American War from the present affairs of Ireland and the temper and disposition of the people there, his lordship would find the mad, cruel and accursed American War written in the most legible characters in every single cause, circumstance and step which had contributed to call further the spirit, the resentment and resolution of the Irish nation, whether already in actual existence or in embryo, ready to burst forth in tenfold mischief, or in a storm strike the nation and shake it to its very foundations.

The phrase about 'the spirit, the resentment and resolution of the Irish nation' is immediately qualified by the words 'whether already in actual existence or in embryo' which must have puzzled Burke's audience. This was because Burke could not accept the Protestants' idea of themselves as the Irish nation. But with the Catholics fully behind the Volunteers' demand for free trade, he grasps at this as the 'embryo' of something yet to be born: the real Irish nation, made up of both Catholics and Protestants. He cherished a hope that such a nation might come into being in his time. As he wrote to Edmund Sexton Pery, Speaker of the Irish House of Commons, in August 1778, congratulating him on the progress of the Catholic Relief Bill in the Irish Parliament: 'You are now beginning to have a country and I trust you will complete the design.' This was the new nation in embryo.

Burke continued to point out to the Commons the lessons that could be learnt from the American experience and applied to Ireland.

> The people of Ireland have reasoned fairly and justly: the colonies, they know have been offered the most that their own most sanguine expectations could aspire to, a free trade with all the world. America, for her revolt, has had a choice of favours. This reward of rebellion . . . Though an Irishman by birth, he was urged, he said, from real sentiment, to express his warmest gratitude to this country, which had raised him from a humble situation, from obscurity to a seat in the national great council: and declared that he must be the most ungrateful and worthless man existing if he ever forgot the

profusion of favours she had heaped upon him; he would not say totally unmerited, but infinitely beyond anything his most sanguine expectations ever held out to him ... He was induced, from every consideration which struck him, to believe, that what ever measure would serve Ireland essentially would and must in the end serve England ...

Passages such as this, in which Burke emphasizes his loyalty to England and the British Parliament, have often been found insincere and been interpreted to his disadvantage. He has been seen as turning his back on his native country to fawn on its oppressors. But this is a misreading. The Ireland on which Burke here turns his back is not his native country, but the Ireland of its oppressors: the exclusively Protestant nation, armed and embodied in the Irish Volunteers. The England whose interests he prefers is the enlightened England, whose best representatives were the Rockingham Whigs. The British Parliament had given Catholics a significant measure of emancipation in the previous year, and Burke looked to it to complete that work, overruling expected opposition from the forces represented by the Volunteers. There are false and inconsistent passages in this difficult and troubled speech, but this passage is not among them, even if some of its expressions are strained.

Continuing his address, Burke went on to say that 'if ever any concessions on the part of his native country should be insisted upon, derogatory to the interest and prosperity of this country, he would be one of the first men in this House, in the character of a British senator, to rise and oppose in the most peremptory and decisive manner, any proposition tending directly or indirectly to any such point.' This was a warning. Burke correctly foresaw that the next demand from the Irish Volunteers would be for independence for Ireland – meaning Protestant Ireland – and he here served notice that he would oppose any such demand. Explicitly, he opposed the idea on purely British grounds – 'concessions ... derogatory to the interest and prosperity' of England – and he did indeed believe that independence for Ireland, like independence for America, would diminish Britain. Yet he had still stronger grounds for opposition. A fully independent Parliament in Ireland would have been a Protestant Parliament, incompatible with Catholic enfranchisement. Burke's hopes for his people would be extinguished, at least for his lifetime. Thus he is nowhere more profoundly Irish than in this extravagantly pro-British passage. As he clutches round him his toga as 'a British senator', he is articulating the hopes and fears of the Nagle country in the Blackwater Valley.

On 15 December, North's administration caved in before the Volunteers' demand for free trade. In Ireland, the news was greeted with general enthusiasm. Yet Burke was silent. His difficulty was how to reconcile his satisfaction at the attainment of free trade with his repugnance and foreboding at this revelation of the apparently irresistible power of the Volunteers. Having studied reports about the Volunteers, George III concluded that 'there is an end of all government in that country', and for once Burke agreed with him.

IRELAND 1780–81

On 19 April 1780 Henry Grattan formally launched the struggle for legislative independence in Ireland. He introduced the resolution 'that His most excellent Majesty by and with the consent of the Lords and Commons of Ireland [is] the only power competent to enact laws to bind Ireland'. This was what Burke had been dreading. But the threat did not immediately become pressing. The resolution of 19 April was defeated in the Irish Commons, through a negative amendment, by 136 votes to 97, so the question of Irish independence did not come immediately before the British Parliament. Nevertheless, an astute move on the part of Grattan's patriot party brought the issue to Westminster.

Ever since the Glorious Revolution of 1688 there had been annual Mutiny Bills in the British Parliament, designed to ensure the continuity of parliamentary control over the armed forces. It had long been assumed that the British Parliament's Mutiny Act covered all the Crown forces, in whatever parts of His Majesty's dominions these might be stationed. In 1780, however, the opposition in the Irish Parliament successfully challenged that assumption by passing the first Irish Mutiny Bill. The idea of such a Bill – 'a political stroke of almost Machiavellian cleverness', Maurice O'Connell calls it – was probably prompted by the course of the debate in the Irish Parliament in April on Grattan's resolution for legislative independence. All those who spoke in that debate, even those who voted against Grattan, denied the right of the

British Parliament to legislate for Ireland; that was a normal part of Irish parliamentary rhetoric. But if the British Parliament had no right to legislate for Ireland, the Irish opposition argued, then the Mutiny Act did not apply to the British forces in Ireland, and these therefore escaped all legal control. The Irish Mutiny Bill was accordingly passed in Dublin on 2 June and transmitted to London for approval on 3 July. Frightened by the thought of a lawless soldiery, the British Parliament decided to be on the safe side and pass an Irish Mutiny Act.

Grattan and his friends had failed to carry a resolution explicitly challenging the right of the British Parliament to legislate for Ireland, but they had now succeeded in bringing about the passage of an Act of the Irish Parliament which implicitly challenged that right. In the Commons on 20 February 1781, Burke pounced on the implications of this partial abdication of British power. America, he argued, was already lost through the follies of government, and now Ireland was being lost too. He spoke in elegiac vein:

> Mr Burke said so many and such great revolutions had happened of late, that he was not much surprised to hear the right hon. gentlemen treat the loss of the supremacy of this country over Ireland as a matter of very little consequence. Thus one star, and that the brightest ornament of our orrery [America], having been suffered to be lost, those who were accustomed to inspect and watch our political heavens ought not to wonder that it should be followed by the loss of another:

> > So star would follow star, and light light,
> > Till all was darkness and eternal night.

Charles James Fox, who was clearly disturbed by the implications of what Burke was saying, intervened to say that 'it was not his purpose to attack the claim which [the Irish] had set up to legislative independency.' Having followed Burke in supporting liberty for the Americans, Fox now supposed that he was supporting liberty in Ireland too. He did not understand that independence for Ireland meant for the majority not freedom but repression. His intervention only made matters worse. It provoked Burke to change from a relatively harmless elegiac speech to an expression of determination to oppose legislative independence for

Ireland: 'It became him to be firm and to look on the preservation of what yet remained as their first duty.'

Burke was now committed to supporting American independence while opposing the independence of his own country, Ireland. This bewildered contemporaries, including some of his friends, and it is among the puzzles that some twentieth-century historians have 'solved' by assuming his motives to be purely opportunistic and venal. However, his position on the two kinds of independence was perfectly consistent in principle. He supported independence for America because he saw it as a genuine case of a people demanding its freedom. But Grattan's demand for independence for his version of the Irish nation was bogus: it meant only exacerbated oppression of the Catholic majority in Ireland.

The distinction is absolute, yet Burke's position remained a puzzle to his contemporaries because he never explicitly articulated the distinction in a parliamentary debate – and knew that he could not without compromising himself. His position was most peculiar, and in the debate on the omission of the word 'Ireland' from the Mutiny Bill, he tied himself in a rhetorical knot; if we are to believe the record of the *Parliamentary History*, he said that 'He thought himself called upon not to decline giving his opinion on a subject in which local attachments might be supposed to interfere with his duty.' Now if 'local attachments' were likely to interfere with his duty, he might have felt obliged to decline giving an opinion; but instead he feels obliged 'not to decline' to give it. That double negative is indicative of a disingenuous position: he was not supporting the moves towards Irish independence, as the Commons expected an Irishman to do; nor was his principal consideration the maintenance of British power, as he pretended. The persona of an impartial imperial legislator in the Roman style, deaf to all local considerations and bound by no ties of personal affection, is a disguise. Burke's 'local attachments' did not, as he implies, join him to those in Ireland who were demanding legislative independence, but to the unwilling subjects of those who were making that demand.

A truthful man in other respects, Burke was in this regard living a lie. The artificiality of his public position must have been a torment to him. But a new Irish crisis was in the making, and would break once the news reached the British Isles, at the end of the year, of Cornwallis's surrender to Washington, on 17 October.

Between Saratoga and the yielding of the King to the inevitable through his acceptance of the second Rockingham administration, the parliamentary struggle over America consisted essentially of a battle of wills between George III and Edmund Burke. At first sight Burke and the King may appear quite incommensurate, as indeed they were in some important respects. George was the star around which the whole system revolved, and Burke was no more than an occasionally visible moon, revolving around a minor planet, Rockingham, at a great distance from the star. But there is another way of looking at things. In terms of intellect and imagination, Burke was the star and George, at best, a moon. There are, however, politically relevant ways in which they were commensurate and alike. They were alike in will-power and continuity of purpose. They were deeply committed, on opposing sides, on the great questions of the day. They both rightly identified the two crucial political issues and the relationship between them. The issues were the American War and what would now be called Cabinet responsibility.

Burke and his friends were determined to bring the American War to an end at the first opportunity. George was determined to bring it to a victorious conclusion, despite every setback. Burke's view of the constitution was what later became the accepted one: that the monarch must do as advised by his ministers, collectively responsible to Parliament. George's view was that ministers could advise the monarch, but that once the monarch had made up his mind, even if against that advice, ministers must comply with his decisions. And the test case, for the constitutional question, was the American War. George saw that if the Rockingham party were ever to form an administration he would be under pressure to end the American War, unless Rockingham could be persuaded to drop his opposition over America. The attempt was tried, but it failed completely. Rockingham not only refused to give the necessary assurances but demanded that the King drop his attempt to assert a royal veto on American independence. It is of course to Rockingham, not to Burke, that George refers in his correspondence when complaining about factious opposition to the royal will. But Rockingham was so strongly under Burke's influence as to be virtually controlled by him.

Up to Saratoga Burke had hoped that America might be kept within the British Empire through the concessions he had unsuccessfully proposed before the Declaration of Independence in 1776: essentially, the end of all attempts to tax Americans, and repeal of all penal Acts against them. In 1775 these concessions had a good chance of being accepted by the Americans but were withheld. After Saratoga, North's administration offered the Americans these concessions, only to have them contemptuously rejected. By then nothing less than independence would do. After that rejection, Burke concluded that recognition of American independence had become unavoidable. Speaking in December 1778, he told the Commons how reluctantly he had reached that view:

> With regard to acknowledging the independency of America, gentlemen looked at the position in a wrong point of view, and talked of it merely as a matter of choice, when, in fact, it was now become a matter of necessity . . . It was incumbent on Great Britain to acknowledge it directly. On the day that he first heard of the American states having claimed independency, it made him sick at heart; it struck him to the soul, because he saw it was a claim essentially injurious to this country, and a claim which Great Britain could never get rid of: never! never! never! It was not, therefore to be thought that he voted for the independency of America. Far from it. He felt it as a circumstance exceedingly detrimental to the fame – and exceedingly detrimental to the interest, of this country. But when, by a wrong management of the cards, the gamester had lost much, it was right for him to make the most of the game as it then stood, and to take care that he did not lose more.

Burke also challenged George directly, in the Commons, when he led the drive for 'economical reform' which was directed against the King's influence over Parliament through holders of sinecures. And that struggle was linked in Burke's mind to the American War. The intention was to bring down North's administration and to force George to accept one led by Rockingham, and to recognize American independence.

As long as the crisis remained confined to matters of taxation – roughly, up to 1774 – the Americans themselves directed their protests against Parliament, not against George. They even, on occasion, appealed to the King over the heads of his Parliament. As the crisis developed, however, George came increasingly to feel that his personal dignity was at stake as a result of the defiance of his subjects. He strongly supported (and probably prompted) the penal Acts: the passage of the Boston Port Act gave him 'infinite satisfaction'. Before that, an unfinished memorandum, perhaps of 1773, shows the depth of his resentment against the party of Rockingham and Burke for its encouragement of the Americans:

> Perhaps no one period in our history can produce so strange a circumstance, as the gentlemen who pretend to be patriots, instead of acting agreeable to such sentiments, avowing the unnatural doctrine of encouraging the American colonies in their disputes with their mother country; this so plainly shows that men not measures decide their opinions, that it is not necessary to deduce the total want of principle which this motley tribe by their conduct ... [unfinished].

The actual coming of the war, and the Rockingham Whigs' continued support for the Americans, inevitably aggravated this resentment. The King was determined that the only tolerable end to the conflict would be unconditional surrender by the colonists. And after Saratoga his will was the main force that sustained the war, which was by this time no longer popular, though opposition to it was not popular either. The effort to tax the Americans, which had been the source of the popularity of the American measures, had clearly failed, and was explicitly abandoned by North after Saratoga. The war itself, especially after the entry of the French, then of the Spaniards, then the Dutch, was costing far more than could conceivably have been raised by taxing the Americans.

After Saratoga it would have made sense for Britain to cut her losses in America and concentrate on fighting her other enemies at sea. But the King was bent on beating the Americans. North's heart was not in the struggle; he begged repeatedly to be allowed to resign, but the King would not let him. During 1777 North had been confident that the Americans would be looking for peace terms 'before winter', and he was correspondingly unnerved by Saratoga, 'this most fatal event'. But George was not unnerved. Writing to North on 11 June 1779, he expressed his determination to resist independence, not least because of the precedent: 'step by step the demands of America have risen – independence is their object ... that [this] country can never submit to; should America succeed in that, the West Indies must follow them; Ireland would soon follow the plan and be a separate state ... then this island would be reduced to itself, and soon would be a poor island indeed.'

Writing to North again, the King lays down his conditions for admission to his administration: 'before I will ever hear of any man's readiness to come into office, I will expect to see it signed under his hand that he is resolved to keep the empire entire and that no troops shall be consequently withdrawn from thence nor independence ever allowed.' The person George had in mind was Rockingham, the leader both of parliamentary opposition in general and specifically of opposition to the war in America. Before allowing Rockingham into power, the King insists that he undertake never to grant independence to America. But Rockingham, guided by Burke, counter-insisted that the King drop his veto over American independence. Rockingham had been regarded as a rather vacillating politician, but there was nothing vacillating about him when fully under the influence of Burke over the American War.

For a while after Saratoga, the war appeared to go well for the British. British troops overran large parts of Georgia and South Carolina. This phase culminated in Britain's greatest victory, the capture of Charleston, with 3,000 American prisoners, in June 1780. It would therefore have been unprofitable, at this time, to concentrate opposition activity on America. In late 1779, an opportunity arose to challenge and perhaps reduce the King's influence without raising the unpopular American issue. Burke now prepared his plan for 'economical reform', a huge and complex task, and led the parliamentary struggle for it. He introduced his 'Plan for the Better Security of the Independence of Parliament and the Economical Reformation of the Civil and other Establishments' in the Commons on 11 February 1780.

Burke's speech occupies seventy-two columns in the *Parliamentary History*, and made a great impression on the minds of the Members, though not quite so great an impression on their votes. Sir Nathaniel Wraxall records the occasion:

Whatever opinion might be entertained respecting the necessity or the eligibility of those proposed regulations in the royal household, only one sentiment pervaded the House and the nation on the unexampled combinations of eloquence, labour, and perseverance which had been displayed by their enlightened author. They covered with astonishment and admiration even those who from principle or from party appeared most strenuous in opposing the progress of the Bill itself through every stage.

In his speech, Burke avoided direct references to America, and even his indirect references to the war are extremely cautious; he was after all looking for votes for reform even from habitual supporters of the war. The only substantial direct link he made between his proposals and America was the proposal to abolish the post of Secretary of State for the Colonies, then held by the extremely unpopular Lord George Germain, on the grounds that the American colonies were already lost. Yet even though he played it down in the speech, America was central to his strategic objective: a Rockingham administration and peace with America, through an attack on the corrupting influence of the Crown. If his proposals had carried, George III would have lost about sixty placemen. That would have rendered Lord North's administration far more vulnerable, and the monarch's will much less formidable.

In this parliamentary engagement Burke was defeated, but narrowly. North, who was a master of parliamentary tactics, attacked the plan piecemeal, removing most of its sections in a series of divisions. Yet the defeat of the plan rebounded into a defeat for the King. On 6 April 1780, Dunning's resolution 'that the influence of the Crown has increased, is increasing and ought to be diminished', was carried by 233 votes to 215. John Dunning was a follower of the minority Whig leader Shelburne, but an admirer of Burke. In introducing his resolution, he explicitly linked it to Burke's plan and paid tribute to Burke. Probably Dunning had discussed the wording of his motion with Burke, and the wording may actually be Burke's in whole or in part.

North reported the passage of Dunning's resolutions to the King in a letter dated

April 7; 2 o'clock a.m.: Sir – It has happened as I expected, and the House of Commons have come to three resolutions on the motion of Mr Dunning by a considerable majority. Ayes 233. Noes 215. If I had not for four years past apprised your Majesty that this event would happen and if I had not made it my constant prayer that I might be allowed to quit your Majesty's service, I should feel very unhappy now at what has happened and may further be expected. I humbly submit once more to your Majesty that it is absolutely necessary that I should be permitted to retire at the end of the session, and some other arrangement take place.

There was still some chivalry among ministers. However, the King, as usual, refused North permission to resign.

Then in June 1780 came news of the greatest British victory of the war, the defeat of Charleston. The administration, naturally, used the news to proclaim that a victorious end to the war was in sight. Yet the King and Lord North were less confident than they appeared. North had been deeply shaken by the effectiveness of the opposition in the spring. To avert the resumption of such attacks, he now, with the King's approval, tried to bring Rockingham and others, including Burke, into his administration. The attempt failed – as a result of the intransigence of both Rockingham and George – but it sheds light on the real positions of both parties. Rockingham stipulated

> that peace was in every respect most desirable – that a fundamental obstacle to peace must exist if His Majesty had, or continued to have, a decisive objection against acknowledging the independency of America at any rate or risk: I therefore desired to premise that if any new administration were to be formed, that it should be known, whether His Majesty would put a *veto* on the acknowledgement of the independency of Am: and *on the other hand* I stated that what seemed requisite was, that it should be understood both by H.M. and his ministers that the *ultimatum* upon that business must, and was, to depend on the circumstances of, and at, the time.

The wording sounds like the result of careful rehearsal with Burke.

In conveying Rockingham's reply to the King, Lord North seems to have drastically toned down Rockingham's message about America, since the King describes this as 'evasive', which it certainly was not. North had reasons for modulating the message, for he desperately wanted the negotiations to succeed and knew they could not if the King received Rockingham's message *en clair*. So he garbled it.

Even garbled, it would not do for George. He commented on 3 July 1780 that 'the dependency of America need not also be mentioned as it could not at the present hour be necessary to be taken into consideration' (meaning that the British seemed to be winning). He added: 'it is absolutely necessary, if any coalition is to be attained, that those who come into office must give assurance that they do not mean to be hampered by the tenets they have held during their opposition. I fear I am not wrong in suspecting that those gentlemen wish to bring at least part of their tenets with them.' The assurances sought by Rockingham from the King, and by the King from Rockingham, were almost grotesquely incompatible, and both were unobtainable, so the coalition idea died.

In George's letter there is one sentence of high significance for Burke's career. Discussing who might be admitted to the coalition, the King notes: 'Mess Townshend and Burke would be real acquisitions.' This is remarkable, since George regarded Burke's Economical Reform Bill as having been levelled against himself personally. Clearly he was more impressed by the desirability of acquiring Burke's talents – minus his 'tenets' – than he was deterred by personal rancour. That sentence, in George's own handwriting, puts paid to the theory that Burke's political activities were motivated merely by personal ambition. He didn't need to thrash around for sixteen years in opposition in order to force himself into office: he could have had office for the asking. George appreciated, needed and would have been happy to use Burke's parliamentary skills, and would have rewarded him richly. All Burke had to do was to convey to North that he was prepared to drop his principles and adopt the King's.

Having failed to widen the basis of his administration by bringing in the Rockinghams, North now decided on a parliamentary dissolution, in the hope that the ensuing elections, influenced by the favourable war news, would bring him additional parliamentary support. In the event, the parliamentary balance was unchanged but Burke lost his seat at Bristol.

The election also saw the first sign of a rift between Burke and Fox (who was re-elected for Westminster). In his electoral campaign, Fox made a bid for what might be called 'the Gordon vote'. He publicly declared: 'I never have supported nor ever will support any measure prejudicial to the Protestant religion, or tending to establish Popery in this kingdom.' Once he was safely re-elected, however, his conscience smote him. It is revealing of the relationship then existing between the two men that, in this distress of conscience, Fox asks Burke to be his judge: 'If anyone were to think that I had given up in the smallest degree the great cause of toleration for the sake of a point of my own I should be the most miserable man in the world ... Pray judge me severely and say whether I have done wrong.' No reply by Burke has been preserved. It would have been in character for Burke to have reassured a friend, in conversation, over a lapse which troubled him. It would be in character also for him to forgive the lapse, but not forget it. He may have remembered this occasion ten years later, when Fox first gave public expression to his enthusiasm for the French Revolution, the anti-Catholic character of which was linked in Burke's mind to the Gordon Riots.

On 23 January 1781 Burke was returned to the new Parliament as Member for Rockingham's borough of Malton. He at once resumed his attack on the King's influence by preparing a Bill for the Regulation of the Civil List Establishments. He introduced it on 15 February, almost exactly a year after introducing his Plan for Economical Reform, and he emphasized the identity of purpose of the two measures. 'It remained', he said, 'for the present Parliament to accomplish and fulfil what the others had but begun, that the resolutions ... might not stand upon the journals, public monuments to their disgrace.' Having set out the financial savings that would result from the Bill, he added: 'What he valued more than all this saving was the destruction of an undue influence over the minds of sixty Members of Parliament in both Houses.' But the new measure, not being supported by a great flow of petitions as the old one had been, was easily defeated. Fox commented: 'The design was very wise and proper, but, like every other design of that description it had failed by means of that very influence which it was calculated to prevent.'

In May, a motion to restore peace with America was defeated by 72 to 106, which shows that it was supported only by the Rockinghams. In June, Burke introduced a petition on behalf of American prisoners of war: 'Mr Burke ascribed the ill usage of those poor men to the rancour that had pervaded our whole system of politics with regard to America, and contended that it would be as pernicious to our cause as it was inhuman in its nature.' The motion was lost. Burke was right about the 'rancour', and its prime source was the King's determination that his rebellious subjects should be made to suffer to the greatest possible extent.

For the King, 1781 was a good year, almost to its close, even though he had doubts about whether 'the nation is equally determined with myself' to pursue the American War. But in the last week of November, a few days before Parliament resumed after the summer recess, news reached London of the surrender of Cornwallis and his army to Washington at Yorktown.

AFTER YORKTOWN

Summary accounts of the American Revolution generally end with Cornwallis's defeat at Yorktown, as if British recognition of American independence followed automatically. This was not so. On 25 November, two days after the news arrived, the King opened Parliament. In his speech he treated the event as simply a setback to British arms: 'The events of war have been very unfortunate to my army in Virginia, having ended in the loss of my forces in that province.' He added, 'I retain a perfect conviction of the justice of my cause.' Burke rightly interpreted the speech as conveying a determination to continue the war. 'Victories gave us hopes, defeats made us desperate, and both instigated us to go on,' he said.

The obstinacy of trying to persist with the war after Yorktown inspired an Aesopian fable from Burke:

Oh, says a silly one, full of his prerogative of dominion over a few beasts of the field, there is excellent wool on the back of a wolf, and therefore he must be sheared. What! Shear a wolf? Yes. But will he comply? Have you considered the trouble? How will you get this wool? Oh, I have considered nothing, but my right: a wolf is an animal that has wool; all animals that have wool are to be shorn, and therefore I will shear the wolf.

The Commons address, drafted by ministers, left open the question of future American policy, but George decided to treat the carrying of the address, by 218 votes to 129, as a mandate to continue the war. On 12 December, a motion for ending the war, on which Burke spoke, was defeated by 220 votes to 179. The increased opposition vote showed that the country gentlemen were beginning to desert the administration.

When Parliament resumed after the Christmas recess, which had given Members an opportunity to hear the views of their constituents and neighbours, the pressure on the administration drastically increased. On 27 February 1782, the House debated a resolution moved by General Henry Conway 'against the further prosecution of offensive war with

America', and this was carried without a division. Seeing a vote of no confidence looming, North reported the news to the King 'with the utmost concern'. The House then submitted to the King an address reflecting its resolution, to which he replied on 4 March:

> You may be assured that, in pursuance of your advice, I shall take such measures as shall appear to me to be most conducive to the restoration of harmony between Great Britain and the revolted colonies – and that my efforts shall be directed against our European enemies, until such a peace can be obtained as shall consist with the interest and permanent welfare of my kingdom.

Observing that the King's reply 'was not quite so explicit as he could have wished', Conway moved a second resolution, 'declaring the advisers of the further prosecution of offensive war in America to be enemies to the King and country'. Because of the memorable wording, the passage of this resolution is sometimes seen as the breaking point in the parliamentary struggle over whether to persist with the fight. But again this was not so. Nobody now really favoured 'the prosecution of offensive war in America'. Even the King wanted only a war of containment, and the Conway resolutions would not prevent him from continuing this. Conway had explained the object of his first resolution as being to make the administration 'renounce the war on the continent of America for the impracticable object of reducing the colonies by force'. That formula was not incompatible with the King's position.

What finally rendered North's position untenable in his own mind was a motion that was actually not carried. This was proposed by Lord John Cavendish on 8 March, and declared 'that the calamities and expense of the times have proceeded from want of foresight in the ministers'. This was a motion of no confidence. Cavendish was a leading Foxite and a nominal leader of the Rockingham party in the Commons. By proposing this motion, the Rockinghams were clearly establishing their claim to the succession. The wording too bolstered that claim. The accusation of 'lack of foresight' carried weight because the foresight of Burke and his friends, in their unheeded warnings about American policy, was only too well known to the House.

The motion was worded so as to attract as many votes as possible, since it recorded an opinion almost universally held. It did not refer directly, as previous motions had done, to the corrupting influence of the Crown, but Burke was on hand to make that point in a speech, in a context in which it would go home. It was his practice, in critical debates, to mark a particular speaker on the other side, and rise to speak after him. In this case, the speaker was Charles Jenkinson, who moved an administration amendment – 'that the other orders of the day be now read' – designed to defeat the Cavendish motion. As the King's confidential agent in the Commons, Jenkinson was a principal part of the system that Burke aimed to destroy. Answering him now, Burke said: 'There was no man in that House, unless he had a place, a contract, or some such motive to speak, that attempted to defend [North's administration].' Jenkinson's amendment carried, but by a perilously narrow margin of ten votes. North wrote to George: 'After such division Lord North is obliged to repeat his opinion that it is totally impossible for the present ministry to conduct His Majesty's business any longer.'

The King asked for time, and sent the Lord Chancellor, Edward Thurlow, to sound out Rockingham about 'forming an administration, upon a broad bottom and public views'. Thurlow reported to George III Rockingham's conditions for entering an administration. The report began 'On Thursday, March 14, the Marquess came to the Lord Chancellor and said: "The King must not give a veto to the independence of America".' The style is Burke's. Rockingham, left to himself, would either have set no precondition at all or would have wrapped it up in such courtly phraseology that the King would be able to wriggle out of it. But this formula makes its meaning utterly plain, and in terms of the conventions of the time, pushes discourtesy to the verge of treason. George may well never before have read or heard a sentence beginning with the words 'The King must not'. The substance of that curt message must have been as startlingly obnoxious as the style. Parliament was still not calling for the independence of America; the topic had not been mentioned in any of the resolutions carried or even proposed; it had not even been a theme of debate. Nor was the King at all prepared for any such demand. For although Rockingham had tried to lay down this precondition before, in the abortive negotiations of 1780, North had apparently compromised the message so much that George thought Rockingham 'evasive' about America. But the message received through Thurlow is so far from being evasive that it is designed to preclude evasion on the part of the King.

George did his best to resist. He wrote to Thurlow: 'The King feels the indignity offered to his person by such propositions and cannot direct any further conversation to be held with the Marquess ... H.M. cannot offer up his principles, his honour and the interests of his good subjects to the disposal of any set of men.' On the same day, however, North warned the King, in language of unprecedented firmness and gravity, that as a constitutional monarch he had no choice: 'Your Majesty is well apprised that, in this country, the prince on the throne cannot, with prudence, oppose the deliberate resolution of the House of Commons ... There are no persons capable or willing to form a new administration except Lord Rockingham and Lord Shelburne with their parties.'

The King's mind, as he later avowed to North, was 'truly tore to pieces'. Rather than send for Rockingham, he even drafted an instrument of abdication, which was found among his papers after his death. On consideration, however, he swallowed his pride, accepted North's advice, and called on Rockingham and Shelburne.

Shelburne was a consolation, from the King's point of view. He had been opposed to American independence, and was still not committed to it, and he habitually addressed the King in the soothing language of a courtier. But it was Rockingham, as the leader of far the largest section of the opposition, who had to be First Lord of the Treasury and chief minister. And before accepting office, Rockingham again spelt out his conditions, in a letter to Shelburne which was sent on to the King:

> Lord Rockingham ... desires to explain clearly to his lordship his opinion that such a Cabinet should be formed as is suitable to the execution of the very important measures which Lord Rockingham had the honour of submitting to His Majesty, through the Lord Chancellor.
>
> Upon Lord R——m's being assured that His Majesty consented to these measures, and that he shall have this consent confirmed to him by His Majesty himself, Lord R——m is willing to state to Lord Shelburne his ideas of a Cabinet likely to concur in the principles of those measures, and therefore fit for the execution of them.

This sounds less like the spontaneous letter of a marquess to an earl than a document drafted by the man of business of a marquess – Edmund Burke – making absolutely sure that his principal does not get cheated. Burke's radical distrust of Shelburne shows in the almost insulting provision 'that he shall have this consent confirmed to him by His Majesty himself', which was vitally necessary because the King had been trying to deal with Rockingham exclusively through Shelburne.

George finally accepted Rockingham on Rockingham's terms, though he still hoped to get round them. On 27 March 1782, North's administration resigned and the second Rockingham administration was sworn in, with Rockingham as First Lord of the Treasury and Shelburne and Fox as Secretaries of State. Burke became Paymaster-General. It was a minor post, but probably the one he wanted. It was lucrative and he needed the money. What mattered more to him was his securing of a minor Treasury post for his beloved son, Richard. Burke never seems to have craved major office. He didn't need to. As long as Rockingham was First Lord of the Treasury, his policies were shaped by his confidential adviser. This should have meant that once Rockingham took office Burke was the effective head, but in practice this was not the case, for Rockingham himself was not fully in control of the administration. The time when Rockingham, guided by Burke, had really wielded power, and to tremendous effect, was during the four days before the formation of the administration. In office, Rockingham could proceed with the policy already laid down in his preconditions, but that was all. Having been forced to comply with Rockingham's demands, the King wanted no further advice from him, and denied him access. George communicated with the Rockingham administration, not through its head, but through a Secretary of State, Shelburne. It was Shelburne, therefore, who controlled its patronage.

From its beginning, the second Rockingham administration was poisoned for Burke by Shelburne's presence. Burke deeply distrusted Shelburne, and with reason. On the eve of the formation of the administration, Shelburne was signalling to George his intention of siding with him against Rockingham. A letter from Shelburne beginning 'I was with Lord Rockingham till very late last night' ends by expressing the hope 'that I shall have been able to keep things within the bounds prescribed by Your Majesty'. Shelburne was widely distrusted, and was more disliked than any other contemporary politician, partly because of his oily manners. His biographer and kinsman, Lord Edmund Fitzmaurice, lists among Shelburne's 'liabilities' an 'overstrained affectation of extreme courtesy and a habit of issuing unnecessary compliments in conversation': clearly a man one would go round corners to avoid.

Burke's loathing of him, however, verged on the obsessive. And as always when Burke's feelings are stronger than one might expect and there is a hint of obsession in the air, there is an Irish aspect. Both men were Irish.

Common Irishness is always a bond of some kind, but not always one of affection. Both men were jeered at by some of the English for their Irishness, and the same stereotype was applied to both: Shelburne was labelled 'the Jesuit of Berkeley Square'. Yet the 'Jesuit' taunt, which came near the bone for Burke, was wide of the mark for Shelburne. William Petty (1612–87), the founder of the Shelburne family fortunes, had acquired his enormous wealth and vast estates in Co. Kerry through services to Oliver Cromwell. In his *Memoirs*, Shelburne refers to the 'good breeding' of his own family as the only acceptable feature of Ireland. As for the rest, he saw only 'those uncultivated, undisciplined manners which make all Irish society so justly odious all over England'. This attitude was, of course, anathema to Burke. The Irish Catholic gentry were intensely proud of their Norman blood – both Burke and Nagle are Hiberno-Norman names – and regarded the great Cromwellian landlords as upstarts who had usurped the lands of their betters.

But there was more than atavistic resentment in Burke's loathing. Burke also knew that Shelburne, far from being a Jesuit, was an anti-Papist. Shelburne wore his anti-Popery discreetly, as 'good breeding' required in the late eighteenth century, but both Papists and anti-Papists were aware of his feelings.

The danger Shelburne posed as Rockingham's Secretary of State was that he would throw away the constitutional gains made by Rockingham's preconditions. If the royal influence, which Burke had done so much to curtail, was about to be restored, Shelburne was its willing agent. Just as he concealed religious bigotry behind a façade of enlightenment, so he concealed Tory sensibility behind a façade of Whig principles. With a small and shaky majority, the administration needed the ten votes that Shelburne commanded, and as a politician Burke could understand that; but spiritually, the thought of being in partnership with Shelburne was a contamination he could scarcely bear.

In the months after the formation of the second Rockingham administration, the King honoured the condition that had brought him to the verge of abdication, and ceased to impose a barrier on the conclusion of a peace with America on the only terms available: recognition of the independence of the United States of America. But even now he tried for a while, through Shelburne, to avoid concluding a peace. Shortly after his acceptance of Rockingham's precondition, the fortunes of war changed in Britain's favour. On 12 April 1782, at the Battle of the Saints in the West Indies, Rodney defeated and captured the French admiral, the Comte de Grasse. By altering the balance of forces at sea, this favoured the kind of war that George wanted to continue, and he duly tried to use the victory to retract recognition of America's right to independence. He wrote to Shelburne: 'He must see that the great success of Lord Rodney's engagement has again so far roused the nation, that the peace which would have been acquiesced in three months ago would now be matter of complaint.' Shelburne, not surprisingly, concurred. A courtier to his fingertips, he did his best to comply with his royal master's wish.

Reflecting the division at the heart of the Rockingham–Shelburne administration, the British peace negotiations with the Americans in Paris were in two parts, led by the two Secretaries of State: Fox, whose agent was Thomas Grenville, and Shelburne, whose agent was Richard Oswald. On 23 May 1782, the Cabinet decided to offer unconditional independence to the Americans. Fox instructed Grenville to inform the Americans of this Cabinet decision, but Shelburne did not inform Oswald, who thus could not confirm Grenville's account. The Americans knew that Oswald's silence might be more significant than Grenville's words, since Oswald's master was close to George, while Grenville's master was anathema to him. The negotiations stalled, and the state of war continued. This was a prime example of Shelburne's intolerable subservience to the King and untrustworthiness as a member of the administration.

Shortly afterwards, at the beginning of July, Rockingham unexpectedly died. Burke had lost a friend and leader, whom he still loved and respected, although he had become somewhat disenchanted with him in the last months. But he had also lost the medium through which he had exercised his influence. Rockingham had been the Archimedean lever with which Burke had moved the King and broken his will to pursue the American War. Burke still had a very strong influence over Charles James Fox, who was to become the leader of the Whigs in the Commons in succession to Rockingham, but it was not the same as the continuous, closely controlling influence that he had attained over Rockingham in the last seven years of the marquess's life. Burke's party-political career had now passed its peak. He soon began to move into the role of political prophet – over India, France and Ireland – which he occupied for most of his latter years.

Soon, but not immediately: in the eighteen months immediately after Rockingham's death, Burke was extremely busy politically in a brisk and brilliantly conducted feud with Shelburne, whom the King now made head of the administration. Burke saw that it was imperative to remove Shelburne before he conceded back to the King powers over Parliament which Burke considered unconstitutional. So Burke resigned immediately, on 4 July, as did Fox. This entailed a heavy financial sacrifice for Burke, and to his distress it also nipped Richard Burke's political career in the bud. Flames of rage against Shelburne leap out in Burke's resignation speech of 9 July 1782:

> On the late change of ministry, the people, he said, looked up to the Marquess of Rockingham as the only person who must be at the head of affairs, as the clearness of his head, and the purity of his heart, made him universally beloved ... But as fate had so ordained it as to take that great and virtuous statesman from us, the first step His Majesty's ministers should have done was to seek out some person like him in sentiment and integrity; but unfortunately for the country it had turned out just the reverse; they had pitched on a man, of all others the most unlike to him ... He was a man that he could by no means confide in, and he called heaven and earth to witness, so help him God, that he verily believed the present ministry would be fifty times worse than that of the noble lord, who lately had been reprobated and removed [Lord North]. He would ask the gentleman [Conway] whether if he had lived in the time of the immortal Cicero, he would have taken Cataline upon trust for his colleague in the consulship, after he had heard his guilt so clearly demonstrated by that great orator? Would he be co-partner with Borgia in his schemes after he had read of his accursed principles? If Lord Shelburne was not a Cataline or a Borgia in morals, it must not be ascribed to anything but his understanding.

Shelburne, in other words, was too stupid to be a first-class villain. This Cataline and Borgia passage may sound excessive to us, but it may not have done so to many of Burke's auditors. The whiff of brimstone that Burke detected as emanating from Shelburne's person was perceptible to other contemporary nostrils. Horace Walpole too compared Shelburne to both Cataline and Borgia.

The resignation of Fox and Burke was followed by the defection of most of the parliamentary support on which the administration had been based. This left Shelburne in an exceedingly weak parliamentary position, but paradoxically that meant he was in a much stronger position *vis-à-vis* the King. George needed Shelburne because he was desperately afraid that the Rockinghams, headed by the odious Fox, might come back. Shelburne, hoping to strengthen his parliamentary position, was able, without loss of favour, to persuade the King to accept the independence of America, and the Provisional Articles of Peace were signed. On 5 December 1782, the King signified his capitulation in his address to Parliament: 'Finding it indispensable to an entire and cordial reconciliation with the colonies, I did not hesitate,' he said, not quite accurately, 'to go the full length of the powers vested in me, and offered to declare them free and independent states.' At every stage in George's long rearguard action after Yorktown, it had been pressure from the Rockinghams that had induced him to concede, and in 1783 it was dread of a Rockingham comeback – under Fox – that brought his capitulation.

Burke and Fox, now on the opposition benches, were in partnership, bent on the destruction of their detested former colleague, Shelburne. Their opportunity came in March 1783, when they joined with Lord North to drive him from office, and soon afterwards from political life altogether. A letter from Burke to his old friend Richard Shackleton reflects his sombre satisfaction:

> We have demolished the Earl of Shelburne, but in his fall he has pulled down a large piece of the building. He had indeed undermined it before. This wicked man, and no less weak and stupid, than false and hypocritical, had contrived to break to pieces the body of men, whose integrity, wisdom, and union, were alone capable of giving consistency to public measures, and recovering this kingdom from the miserable state into which it is fallen. To destroy him was a necessary preliminary to everything that could be devised beneficial for the public.

The administration that took over now was nominally headed by the Duke of Portland, but is known as the Fox–North coalition. Burke served in it, again as Paymaster: the Fox–North coalition had three heads; not just two. The King drew up another putative abdication on learning of the coalition, so implicitly ratifying its continuity with Rockingham's administration of 1782.

Contemporaries were shocked, or affected to be shocked, by the sudden reconciliation of Burke and Fox with their old adversary Lord North, who had so long followed the King's policy of war with America. But in 1783 the vehicle of the corrupting royal influence was no longer North but Shelburne, who by grace and favour of the King had usurped and corrupted the Rockingham administration. What was important now was to drive Shelburne from office. If North was prepared to assist in that, so much the better. The memory of battles fought and won should not be allowed to distract from the task of winning the battle that needed to be won now.

The continuity of principle in Burke's opposition to Shelburne is quite genuine, though his hostility to Shelburne does not derive solely from it. There is a continuity of feeling, as well as of principle. Burke had long hated Shelburne, not least when they were colleagues under Rockingham. But he had never hated North; even in the years of strong political opposition, the two were personally on friendly terms, and sometimes terms of banter. Burke regarded North as a good but weak man, under the domination of a more powerful mind and will than his own – the King's.

In the political termination of the American War, the crucial moment had been Rockingham's laying down of terms for acceptance of office, in March 1782, and this moment was of lasting constitutional importance, as Burke clearly saw. North had advised the King, in effect, that he could not reject Rockingham without a constitutional crisis. After toying with abdication, George flinched and accepted Rockingham's terms. The battle of wills between the monarch and the Commons was more important even than securing an early end to the American War. The nature of royal authority was at stake. By accepting the conditions, George was accepting the view of his legitimate authority which Burke had laid down on the Rockinghams' behalf twelve years before. The King was beginning to assume the character of a constitutional monarch as the Rockinghams, and not George himself, understood the constitution. And that was the sense in which later generations were to understand it too. The King's acceptance of Rockingham's conditions is a milestone in British constitutional history. It took a first-class political mind to identify the ground on which the royal authority could be successfully challenged and the moment to do it. There was only one such mind in the Rockingham party, and it was not Lord Rockingham's.

As for George, the loser in that long battle of wills, he remained bitter for many months over the loss of so substantial a part of the vast dominions he had inherited at his coronation in 1760, but eventually consoled himself with the following reflection:

> I cannot conclude without mentioning how sensibly I feel the dismemberment of America from this empire, and that I should be miserable indeed if I did not feel that no blame on that account can be laid at my door, and did I not know that knavery seems to be so much the striking feature of its inhabitants that it may not in the end be an evil that they become aliens to this kingdom.

The Fox–North coalition fell in its turn in December 1783. The successor, William Pitt, was truly the head of his own administration, not under the control of the King. Rockingham had prepared the way for the role of Prime Minister in the modern sense, though the term was not yet in use. Shelburne had become head of the administration by compliance as a court favourite. But William Pitt the Younger (1759–1806) was the first Prime Minister as we know the position today. He owed more to Rockingham and Burke for the King's acceptance of this than he probably realized, for they had forced George III to become (more or less) a constitutional monarch. The King grew a bit frisky again under Shelburne's permissive handling, but was again reduced to submission – after a second threat of abdication – by the Fox–North coalition. In terms of Burke's vision, the termination of Shelburne's political career and the forced submission of George III were the two great and principled achievements of the coalition with North, and fully justified an alliance that some had seen as opportunist.

IRELAND 1782–83

The agitation of the Irish Volunteers for legislative independence acquired a new momentum in early 1782 as a result of Cornwallis's surrender at Yorktown. A Catholic Relief Bill – modelled on the 1778 British Catholic Relief Act that Burke had guided through Parliament –

was then going through the Irish Parliament. Resolutions welcoming this development were drawn up by Henry Grattan, and carried at a great convention of Volunteers at Dungannon in February. The resolutions read:

> Resolved, that we hold the right of private judgement in matters of religion to be equally sacred in others as in ourselves.
>
> Resolved, therefore, that as men and as Irishmen, as Christians and as Protestants, we rejoice in the relaxation of the penal laws against our Roman Catholic fellow-subjects, and that we conceive the measure to be fraught with the happiest consequences to the union and prosperity of the inhabitants of Ireland.

The pseudo-liberalism of the Dungannon resolutions was not of a nature to win Burke over to the Volunteer movement. It probably reminded him of Shelburne's liberalism. The very wording of the second resolution is a reminder of the direction of a Volunteer movement which was aiming at independence for an exclusively Protestant Parliament. Burke's tongue-tied incapacity to communicate his reservations about the Volunteers and their objective had permitted Rockingham and Fox to commit themselves to the cause of legislative independence for Ireland. It was the second Rockingham administration that carried legislative independence through the British Parliament in an address declaring 'no body of men competent to bind this nation [Ireland] except the King, Lords and Commons of Ireland'. Thus the British Parliament at length ratified the proposition which Grattan had put to the Irish Parliament on 19 April 1780.

Grattan genuinely thought of himself as struggling for 'the liberties of his country', which he was brought up to think of as Protestant, so he could not understand Burke's resistance to liberties which did not include liberty for Catholics. The address, recognizing the legislative independence of Ireland, was moved by Fox, who declared that 'he would rather see Ireland totally separated from England, than kept in obedience only by force'. Burke spoke in this debate, but without reference to the specific content of the address. His language is unusually vague, diffuse and emollient:

> Mr Burke said that it was not on such a day as that, when there was not a

difference of opinion, that he would rise to fight the battle of Ireland; her cause was nearest his heart; and nothing gave him so much satisfaction, when he was first honoured with a seat in that House, so that it might be in his power, some way or other, to be of service to the country that gave him birth . . . He was a friend to his country, but gentlemen need not be jealous of that, for in being the friend of Ireland, he deemed himself of course the friend of England; their interests were inseparable. He spoke also of his friendship to the natives of India, whom he did not know, and who could never know him, and by proving himself their friend, he was convinced that he must prove himself also the friend of England.

Burke's acquiescence in the passage of a measure to which he had been so vehemently opposed at its original introduction may appear tame. But what had alarmed him about Grattan's proposal in 1780 was its tendency to break the connection with Britain by granting real independence for the Irish Protestants. What was passing through the British Parliament in 1782 was very much less than that. 'Legislative independence of Ireland', if it went no further, was largely a sham. The British Parliament could at any time withdraw the independence it was granting, and did so eighteen years later. In the meantime, the British government maintained its control over the Irish executive and so exercised a very powerful influence over the legislative process.

So Burke could accept 'legislative independence', though without enthusiasm. There was no need for him to be dismayed by Grattan's glittering language, based on the Rockingham administration's concessions to Ireland. As a working parliamentarian, Burke understood the dependent relationship which that rhetoric concealed. He was determined, however, that his friends should make no further concessions to the Irish Protestant version of the Irish nation. Even before legislative independence was conceded, his influence over future Rockingham policy is discernible in a letter written by Fox, as Secretary of State, to Richard Fitzpatrick, the new Chief Secretary in Dublin: 'My opinion is clear for giving them all they ask, but for giving it them so as to secure us from further demands, and at the same time to have some clear understanding with respect to what we are to expect from Ireland in return for the protection and assistance which she receives from those fleets which cost us such enormous sums, and her nothing.' Fox's enthusiasm for 'Irish independence' had been brought under control, and his aim, tactics and language are here similar to Burke's with respect to America. The intention is the eminently Burkean one of maintaining friendly and mutually beneficial ties by granting freedoms.

In Ireland, Henry Flood – Grattan's great rival – disparaged the concessions won by Grattan and demanded that the British Parliament 'renounce for ever any right to legislate for Ireland'. With this demand, Flood gained in popularity over Grattan in the second half of 1782. From Burke's point of view Flood was now the dangerous man and Grattan the safe one. The concession demanded by Flood would be a long step from the sham independence of 'Grattan's Parliament' in the direction of real independence. Burke therefore did his best to help Grattan, against Flood, by maximizing the importance of the concessions already granted, in order to stave off more demands. In a Commons debate in December 1782, Burke

> spoke of the repeal of the Dependency of Ireland Act of 1719, on which the Declaratory Act of 1766, on America, was modelled, and declared that however mistaken motives to the contrary have been since excited and fomented in Ireland [by Flood], the repeal of that Act was meant by those who proposed it, to be considered as a total dereliction on the part of this country of all claim to the right of legislative, or judicial power over Ireland, in every case whatsoever.

When Burke was back in office, in the Fox–North coalition, he advised the new Chief Secretary that the success of the new Lord Lieutenant of Ireland, Lord Northington, would depend 'not only on Grattan's formal assistance but upon his cordial and earnest support'. The 'madman' of 1780 had become a prop and stay by 1783.

In that year, however, a new tendency appeared among the Irish Volunteers, which outdid Flood in extremism, just as Flood had outdone Grattan. The new tendency was to put pressure on Grattan's Parliament to widen the franchise to include the middle classes. To give this demand more credibility, and widen the basis for its support, spokesmen for the tendency, led by the brilliant eccentric Frederick Augustus Hervey, Earl of Bristol and Bishop of Derry, asked that the franchise reform include Catholics, provided they possessed adequate property qualifications. But Hervey's concessions were not as radical as they may sound. It has been reckoned that if Grattan's Parliament had been reformed in the way

Hervey intended, only some 300 to 500 Catholics would have been enfranchised. On that basis, the Irish Parliament might have remained exclusively Protestant, and would certainly have remained overwhelmingly so. The people the proposals really aimed to emancipate were middle-class Protestants. These were generally more enthusiastic for the Protestant nation than the landlords were, and their representation in the Irish Parliament would have increased the pressure for real independence for that nation. Burke's reservations about franchise reform were by no means modified by the emergence of the Hervey tendency. Quite the contrary. The Fox–North administration, in office through most of 1783, strongly opposed this radical tendency in the Irish Volunteers.

A great national convention of the Irish Volunteers was announced, to open in Dublin on 10 November. The 1779 national convention had demanded free trade, and won it with little delay. The 1780 convention had demanded legislative independence, and that too had been conceded, at least in form, in 1782. The radicals now hoped that the 1783 convention would demand parliamentary reform, giving the vote to the Protestant middle class, plus a few Catholics. If the convention approved that demand, it was expected that the Irish Parliament would concede this too. Real independence for Protestant Ireland would be likely to follow.

The Fox–North administration was alarmed by these developments. Fox wrote two letters on the eve of the convention, one to General Burgoyne, of Saratoga fame, who was now commanding the British forces in Ireland, and one to Lord Northington, the Lord Lieutenant. To Burgoyne he wrote:

If either the parliamentary reform in any shape, however modified, or any other point claimed by the Bishop of Derry and his Volunteers be conceded, Ireland is irrevocably lost for ever, and this would be my opinion if I were as fond of the measures themselves as their most enthusiastic admirers. The question is not whether this or that measure shall take place, but whether the constitution of Ireland, which Irish patriots are so proud of having established, shall exist or whether the government shall be purely military, as ever it was under the Praetorian bands.

To Northington he wrote that unless the Volunteers were to

dissolve in a reasonable time, government, and even the name of it, must be at an end ... If they are treated as they ought to be – if you show firmness, and that firmness is seconded by the aristocracy and Parliament – I look to their dissolution as a certain and not very distant event; if otherwise, I reckon [the Volunteers'] government, or rather anarchy, as firmly established as such a thing is capable of being ... Volunteers, and soon, possibly, Volunteers without property, will be the only government in Ireland, unless they are faced this year in a manful manner ... All other points appear to me to be trifling in comparison of this great one of the Volunteers.

Coming from Fox, these robustly anti-Volunteer sentiments are remarkable. In 1779 he had made Burke uneasy by his enthusiasm for the Volunteers, and from 1780 to 1782 he had strongly supported the demand for legislative independence. From then on, however, he adopted Burke's line of no further concessions, and by 1783 he was urging the dissolution of the Volunteers. It looks as if Burke had been working on him and had finally brought him round. However that may be, he must have consulted Burke, the acknowledged expert on Irish affairs, about despatches to Ireland with such major implications as these had for the policy of the Fox–North coalition.

Burke and Fox need not have been so worried. The national convention was a fiasco. Unlike 'free trade' and 'legislative independence', parliamentary reform including a Catholic franchise was deeply divisive. Apart from the Bishop of Derry, none of the Irish leaders favoured it. Grattan, who theoretically favoured Catholic enfranchisement, was in practice opposed, at this time, to any further parliamentary reform. Flood and the nominal commander of the Volunteers, Lord Charlemont, were in favour of reform but opposed to any franchise for Catholics. And that also seems to have been the position of most of the delegates.

The convention heard conflicting reports about what the Catholics wanted – there were of course no Catholic delegates present – and afterwards did not vote on a franchise for Catholics, but simply sent to the Irish Parliament 'resolutions ... which proposed the grant of votes to Protestant freeholders and leaseholders exclusively'. As the convention had shown the Volunteers to be deeply divided over this, the Irish Parliament felt it could safely defy its resolutions, which were defeated by 158 votes to 49.

On the failure of the 1783 Volunteers' convention, their last, Wolfe Tone wrote:

> The government seeing the convention by their own act separate themselves from the great mass of the people who could alone give them effective force, held them at defiance; and that formidable assembly, which, under better principles, might have held the fate of Ireland in their hands, was broken up with disgrace and ignominy, a memorable warning that those who know not to render their just rights to others, will be found incapable of firmly adhering to their own.

It is worth noting that Tone does not blame Dublin Castle or the British government. It was 'by their own act' that the Volunteer delegates separated themselves from 'the great mass of the people'.

In the retrospect of Irish nationalism, Burke's hostility to the Volunteers has been portrayed as treacherous: an Irishman siding with England. But Burke, who had to deal with contemporary realities, did not see it that way. He and Tone, who deeply disagreed about so much, had one basic objective in common. Both wished, and strove hard in their different ways, to bring about the end of the penal laws. Tone tried to achieve this by agitation in Ireland and later by revolutionary action breaking the connection with England. Burke, by contrast, and with some success, tried to utilize the connection with England for the benefit of all the Irish, Catholic and Protestant, as well as England. His approach to the Irish and American questions was the same. From 1765 to 1775 he tried to stay the movement towards American independence through timely concessions and the renunciation of imprudent British pretensions. Only in 1778, when all that had failed, did he reluctantly decide that American independence would have to be recognized. And in 1782 he and Rockingham succeeded in imposing the acceptance of that conviction on George III. So with Ireland. In 1778, at the cost to himself of his seat at Bristol, he had achieved the Catholic Relief Act. But though his approach to the two questions was identical, he saw the circumstances – always a key idea with him – as vastly different. With the awkward exception of slaves and slave-owners, the Americans were a people, fighting for their freedom. The Irish Volunteers were merely a caste, which denied to a majority of the Irish people the freedom it demanded for itself.

Rather than recognize the kind of independence that seemed to be emerging in 1783, the Fox–North coalition, advised by Burke, would have been prepared to use force. And in 1783, with the American War over, the use of force by Britain was a practical option, as it had not been in 1779; General Burgoyne could have had a victory at last. As it was, the Volunteers dissolved themselves. The movement had begun spontaneously to defend Ireland against the French and to put down potential rebels, the Whiteboys. The war with France was over and these original purposes had disappeared, and meanwhile the political purposes on which the Volunteers had been able to agree – free trade, which was real, and a version of 'legislative independence' which was largely spurious – had been secured.

So the Irish Volunteers disappear from history in 1783. A residue, however, remained, consisting of those – mainly Dissenters – who had hoped to enlist Catholic support for a radical programme. This was the seed-bed of the Irish Jacobins, with whom Burke would have to contend in the following decade.

IV: India 1767–90

THE LONGEST CAMPAIGN

Burke's active concern with Indian affairs lasted even longer than his concern with America. It was first recorded in 1767, the year he entered Parliament, and it lasted almost until his death, thirty years later. But the record of his concern with India differs greatly from that of his concern with America. Over America Burke is consistent from 1766 to 1782, but with regard to India there is no such overall consistency. There is some consistency in Burke's statements from 1767 to 1773, and there is complete consistency from 1781 to 1795. Between these two periods, however, there is no consistency, but rather a great contradiction. Up to 1773, we find Burke again and again defending the East India Company against ministerial attempts to control it. From 1782 on, we find him insisting that the Company be brought under parliamentary control, and then that its most powerful figure – 'servant', in theory – the Governor-General of Bengal, Warren Hastings, should be impeached.

Both in Burke's time and since, hostile writers have tried to account for this inconsistency as they do for each of the perceived anomalies in Burke's career: by arguing that venality and personal ambition were Burke's main motives throughout his political life. As there are many such anomalies in his career, a writer who never considers any other possible explanation for any of them can build up what may look like an impressive pattern, discreditable to Burke. But when one takes account, in each case, of other possible explanations, which in turn interrelate, a much more complex and subtle pattern appears.

The basic difference between Burke on America and Burke on India is that Burke found his way – his own personal way – very quickly over America but only very slowly over India. As Lucy Sutherland, the editor of volume II of Burke's *Correspondence*, wrote when commenting on a letter of November 1772:

> This and the rest of Burke's correspondence on East India affairs at this time make it clear that the attitude adopted by the Rockingham group was not the result of reliance on his knowledge of and opinion on these matters, and that he himself began with no clearly defined views on the right line to adopt, nor any particular inside knowledge of the Company's concerns. Nor is there any suggestion that Burke felt that he had personal issues at stake.

So why was Burke so quick to find his way over America and slow over India? The reason may lie partly in the unparalleled urgency of American affairs at the very beginning of Burke's career in 1766, and partly in the existence of a collective Rockingham orthodoxy over India which it did not have on America. When Burke took his seat in the Commons, the Rockinghams did not have an American policy. Their customary touchstone – resisting the influence of the Court – was hardly relevant to America in 1766, though it later became so. But Burke had already made up his mind against the Stamp Act, and was present at the formation of his party's policy. Towards India, however, there was a definite Rockingham policy already, laid down without Burke's participation, and accepted by him for six years. The essentials of this were that ministerial efforts to regulate the East India Company were to be regarded with intense suspicion. The motive behind any such proposals was deemed to be a desire, on the part not merely of ministers but of persons connected with the Court, to get their hands on the vast patronage and loot of India. If they got hold of that, and of the power that went with it, England would be on its way back to absolute monarchy. So maintaining the independence of the East India Company was the Rockingham policy, never entirely disavowed during Rockingham's lifetime, though it ceased to be followed in practice after the Madras crisis of 1776.

The Rockingham line over India in the 1760s and 1770s was not senseless, as has sometimes been suggested, but it did lack balance, for it tended to magnify a threat to India from ministers and the Court, while minimizing abuses already luxuriantly established in India by the

Company's 'servants'. After Burke made a study of the Company, in 1781, he emerged as the most determined, passionate and eloquent enemy of that oppressive system, but the system was at least as oppressive in the 1760s and 1770s, when Burke was defending it. So some difficult questions arise. In the years 1767–73, can Burke's acute, attentive mind really have failed to see that very serious abuses were going on in India under the Company's rule? If so, why did he fail? Or if he saw the abuses, how could he fail to speak out against them if he really felt the horror that he later proclaimed?

BURKE UNDER RESTRAINT, 1767–73

Burke's first recorded speech on Indian affairs was made in 1767, although it appears that he had already spoken several times in Parliament in a similar vein. On 25 November 1766, for example, he opposed a motion that there be a committee of enquiry into the Company's affairs. On 16 May 1767 he opposed the East India Dividend Bill, which levied an annual sum of £400,000 on the Company and restricted the Company's right to declare a dividend. Burke at once takes high Rockingham ground:

> You are going to restrict by a positive arbitrary regulation the enjoyment of the profits which should be made in commerce. I suppose there is nothing like this to be found in the code of laws in any civilized country upon earth – you are going to cancel the great line which distinguishes free government.

He is not known to have spoken on Indian affairs again until nearly two years later, when the arrangement of 1767 expired and the government presented a new 'East India Settlement' similar to the earlier one. Burke adheres to his line, but awkwardly, and without his previous confident resonance. Lord Clive had spoken before him, and Burke was clearly taken aback by part of what he had to say. Clive had begun by speaking in glowing terms of the potential of Britain's Indian Empire – of which he himself was the founder – but he went on to demand 'sweeping reforms of the Company, with rigorous central control of the officials both in London and in India'.

This was precisely the policy which Burke and his friends were to follow energetically when in office fourteen years later. But in 1769, what

Clive demanded ran clean contrary to Rockingham policy. And Clive's authority, in an Indian debate, at that time, overshadowed that of anyone else. In this distressing situation for a debater, even Burke is driven to dither. He opens by asserting that 'the committee are bound by the noble lord's arguments', and goes on to resist the noble lord's recommendations. He eulogizes Clive, and then tries to dissent from the views of the man eulogized. This is a difficult rhetorical feat to bring off, and Burke duly fails. The following passage from this speech, evading a commitment for or against Clive's proposed statute making the Company's Court of Directors responsible to Parliament, rather than to the stockholders, is perhaps the weakest in the entire canon of Burke's oratory:

> This Company is grown under such directors; it is become a great, a glorious Company. Men continually watched by their constituents, it works them into vigour. The body has not been so fluctuating, some have been changed. They may be formed into a body against their country. They are apt to form themselves into cabals. I do not say this in opposition to the noble lord. But I hope whenever the committee sit upon that, they will not be too quick in adopting that idea.

The uncharacteristic irresolution of these remarks shows that Burke was shaken by Clive's ideas and beginning to doubt the Rockingham line.

He did not return to Indian affairs for more than three years, until he spoke on the East India Select Committee on 13 April 1772. This was a polished performance. There are elements in it of both the old Rockingham line and the Clive doctrine. It is not easy to reconcile these, but Burke at least manages to combine them effectively in a smooth piece of advocacy. By now, there was considerable public concern at the maladministration and corruption disfiguring the Company's rule in India. The matter immediately under discussion was a private Member's motion calling for an enquiry into the Company's affairs. As the motion was supported by Lord North's administration, Rockingham principles dictated opposition to it, and Burke supplies this in a confident, scornful, debating style:

> He liked to see his way before him, and would never plunge himself into any business without knowing how he was to get through it. He would not beat

the cover merely to see what game might start out; neither would he consent to go barking and questing about the East India Company, or any other corporations, in order to drive them into the toils of administration.

The principles on which Burke now defends the Company are different from those on which he had defended it in 1766, and half-defended it in 1769. He now embraces, in principle, the Clive doctrine he had half-opposed in 1769. He blames North's administration for not having taken that advice, and then he uses the culpability he imputes to the administration to exonerate the Company and its servants for any irregularities they may have committed, in an inherently irregular situation:

When discretionary power (said he) is lodged in the hands of any man, or class of men, experience proves, that it will always be abused. This was the case with the East India Company. That charter, which was well enough calculated for the purposes of a factory, becomes totally insufficient upon the acquisition of extensive territories. Hence unlimited authority fell necessarily into the hands of their governors. The directors, attentive to the extension of their trade, had not time, nor perhaps capacity, to make general regulations sufficient for the good government of so great an empire: and, had they been possessed of both these requisites, yet they wanted the power to exert them. Else why have they now applied for a new charter? The thing speaks for itself. They could only act within their charter, and send to their governors directions, and directions that were not binding in law, no competent authority having been delegated to them by the legislature. Does it not follow from this that they were obliged to leave their governors a discretionary power? But how was the governor to keep in awe the Company's servants, who knew that he did not derive his authority from law, and that they could not be punished for disobedience beyond the ditch of Calcutta? In order to preserve some kind of subordination, he was forced occasionally to act the despot, and to terrify the refractory by the arm of power or violence. This, I believe, you will find to be the genuine source of that arbitrary conduct charged upon the late governors in Bengal. Where no laws exist, men must be arbitrary; and very necessary acts of government will often be, in such case, represented by the interested and malevolent as instances of wanton oppression. Suppose some examples of real tyranny to have occurred, does it thence follow that the governors were culpable? Is it not possible that they were misinformed? In such a multiplicity of affairs, and in a government without laws, some enormities must have been committed. But who are the blameable persons? Not the Company, nor the Company's servants, who have not done what experience tells us is above the reach of humanity, and what they had not legal right to do; but those who did not, upon the acquisition of such vast territories, compose for their use a comprehensive and well-digested code of laws for the rule of every man's conduct. Had the ministry, upon a former occasion, adopted this plan, as they were advised, we should not now be debating this point, nor should we have heard that the neat revenues of Bengal are sunk to less than two hundred thousand pounds. In fact, administration is, in this case, the only culprit. The East India Company is not punishable for not performing what no body of men in their circumstances ever did or will perform. It is the men who are at the helm of affairs, and who neglected, or wanted capacity and inclination to make the proper arrangements that ought to be the objects of public and parliamentary vengeance.

Warren Hastings could have used that line of argument, to great effect, in his defence in the following decade when he was being impeached by Burke. But then Hastings might never have been impeached if Burke had been heeded, for towards the end of this speech Burke argues for 'a general amnesty or act of oblivion' for the Company's servants in India.

A few months later, in August, Burke received an offer from the East India Company. Laurence Sulivan, its powerful Deputy Chairman – and chief protector of Warren Hastings – urged Burke to accept the appointment of head of a commission of three supervisors to be sent out to investigate and correct abuses in their Indian presidencies. It is interesting, and altogether characteristic of the Company, that a person who had recently argued for an amnesty for the Company's servants should have been asked to lead a commission 'to investigate and correct abuses'. Quite clearly, what was intended was a whitewash. This offer came with an enormous financial incentive. If Burke had accepted the invitation, and done what the Company expected of him, he could have returned from India a wealthy man. But he turned it down.

The series of Burke's early Indian speeches was now drawing to a close. Several broke no new ground and simply continued to blame North's administration: 'They pretended reformation and they meant nothing but plunder.' His next major speech came on 5 April 1773. It contains one highly significant passage, revealing the real state of his feelings about the Company he had been defending. The speech was clearly impassioned. A newspaper account of it begins: 'Mr Edmund Burke next arose, and with a vehemence uncommon amongst our modern orators, he arraigned, as usual, the conduct of administration.' The report refers to Burke as speaking 'with the *verbum ardens*, or glowing expression of the ancients'. For most of the speech the *verbum ardens* is indeed directed against the government, but then it suddenly takes a different and startling turn, with a warning that

> the East India Company tied about their necks, would, like a millstone, drag them down into an unfathomable abyss; that it was well if it dragged not this nation along with them . . . that for his part, he always had had his fears, and would now venture to prophesy his apprehensions, that this cursed Company would at last, viper, be the destruction of the country which fostered it in her bosom.

If the Company was a viper, it was one that Burke had been fostering in his own bosom. That is the nature of the horror he is experiencing, as he 'prophesies his apprehensions'. The peroration of this strange speech may be seen as an attempt to bring together Burke's warnings about the administration with his newly acknowledged loathing for the Company:

> . . . as to the East India Company, he foresaw it would be the *destruction of this country*, but that for his part he would sooner have the Company itself totally overthrown; he would sooner see it fall to ruin about his ears, than have *the base of the English constitution undermined, or a single pillar which contributed to the support of so excellent a structure receive the slightest fracture, or defaced in the minutest part*.

To that he added, according to another report, 'I have eased my conscience.' No doubt he had. Burke did not again, in this period, attack the East India Company. That 'viper' passage remains isolated: a lonely harbinger of the tremendous barrage he was to unleash against the Company ten years later.

On 10 June 1773 he found himself again defending what he had called 'this cursed Company'. The circumstances of this speech, on the East India Regulating Bill, were rather special. It was Lord North's major

Indian measure of the 1770s, and was peculiarly obnoxious in terms of what was still the general Rockingham doctrine of non-intervention in Company affairs, for many believed that the government was attempting to take unwarranted control of the Company.

Burke spoke late in the debate. 'Mr E. Burke got up next, and made an apology to the House for his having been silent hitherto concerning this momentous and important business.' This is an unusual parliamentary opening, and implies an unusual parliamentary context. Under normal conditions, an MP who apologized for 'having been silent hitherto' would be laughed at for his self-importance. Burke's opening implies that his silence had been the subject of comment, and had worried his friends. There was nothing unusual in his speaking late – that was his habitual procedure. But on this occasion he seems to have hung back so long as to excite speculation that he might not speak at all. Such speculation would have been unlikely unless Members on both sides were aware that he was having difficulty with the Rockingham line. He was being watched, by both friends and foes; he often was. He may well have hoped to avoid speaking at all. The prospect of fostering that viper once more must have been exceedingly distasteful. Yet he held his nose, did his duty by his party, and defended the Company. He referred to 'the affairs of the India Company, which he in his opinion deemed not improperly managed; nor that the abuses complained of either at home or abroad were existing in the manner represented'. Later, as if feeling that that formula might sound a bit grudging, he adds that 'if the House, would but allow a short time, these disorders, few as they are, would be able to correct themselves; that the Company surely had done great things, and would still do greater, if they were suffered to go on.' It was hardly an inspiring case.

Fortunately for Burke, he never again felt obliged to defend the Company or to minimize the abuses committed in India. For nearly four years he had nothing to say in public about India, as he became more and more committed to American affairs. He probably welcomed the change of theme from an uncongenial subject to one on which he could speak with an unconstrained mind and heart. When he returned to the subject of India, in May 1777, it was in a changed context. The dramatic arrest and deposition of Lord Pigot, the newly appointed Governor of Madras, by his colleagues in the Madras Council, had ended the Rockinghams' enthusiasm for the independence of the Company. Burke was now free to chastise its masterful 'servants' and expose abuses. And this was the role he was to sustain for the rest of his career, even against the growing reluctance of his party.

Until 1773 he had been defending the Company's independence in most of his speeches; and even in the one speech, in 1772, where he temporarily abandoned that line, he opposed any enquiry into abuses in India, and even called for a general amnesty. But when he breaks his silence in 1777, it is to demand enquiry into the abuses and punishment of the offenders. The four years' silence is a chasm separating two incompatible policies.

In retrospect, Burke must have experienced shame and guilt whenever he came to think of the things he had said about India earlier. He can hardly have avoided some remembrance of these in 1781, when he settled down to a serious study of how India was being governed. Many of the outrages he then identified, and subsequently exposed, were being perpetrated while he was still defending the Company's independence, opposing enquiry, proposing amnesties for offenders and even protesting against the 'blackening' of Warren Hastings. Burke would have tried to suppress such memories – he was never one to acknowledge past errors – but they probably go a long way towards accounting for the elemental fury of his Indian speeches of the 1780s, and above all for the compulsion of his attack on Warren Hastings.

Hastings had committed terrible crimes in India, as the Burke of the 1780s passionately argued. But in the 1770s Burke had been a partner in that guilt, for he had condoned the crimes, and sought to conceal them and to protect the perpetrators. In punishing Hastings, Burke was also punishing himself. His party, too, was punished, for having made him adopt its line up to 1773. Contemporaries noted, in 1783, his driving rage in pursuing his Indian concern, with reckless disregard for the risks to his party and the government of which he was part. As a result, that government was overthrown, and in the subsequent general election Burke's party and its allies lost eighty-nine seats and were consigned to opposition for the rest of Burke's life. Far from being dismayed by these drastic political consequences, Burke immediately reasserted the primacy of his Indian concern in the new Parliament, and managed to induce the remnants of his party to join him in pressing for Hastings's impeachment. He may have had to toe the party line in the early 1770s, but from 1784 to 1795 he made the party toe his line over India.

His passion over India in the 1780s was fuelled by a need to atone for a personal dereliction in the previous decade. But it was also fuelled by forces deeper in his psyche. His concern for the suffering people of India also had to do with his concern for his own suffering people, the Catholics of Ireland. Partly, this was a matter of being able to empathize with another cowed people from experience of an oppressive system. But the forces at work were more complex and more dynamic. It was not just a question of championing an oppressed people or sympathizing with them, but of defecting from and so betraying them.

Burke came from an oppressed people, but as a privileged Protestant he colluded with the oppressive system, to the extent of his personal exemption from the penal laws. He responded by a long, heroic, skilful and largely successful effort to demolish those laws, and by engaging his energies against other oppressive systems. At the outset of his career, however, he found himself precluded by Rockingham policy from any intervention in defence of the Indians. I believe that as he looked back on that period, he came to feel that he had betrayed the oppressed of India just as his father had betrayed the oppressed of Ireland. By betraying the Indians, he had re-enacted the apostasy of his father. And I believe that it was this thought, and a compulsion to atone for it, that drove him on in his Indian crusade from 1781 to 1795. In the person of Warren Hastings, Burke was punishing not only himself, but also his father – and was vindicating the people wronged by him and his father, as well as the people wronged by Hastings. All this may seem somewhat feverish, and indeed there is something feverish about it. But the fever is in Burke himself.

AN INDIAN AGON, 1750-80

Warren Hastings (1732–1818) had first gone to India at the age of eighteen as a 'writer', the lowest rank in the East India Company's service. It was then a straightforward commercial company, selling British goods to the Indians and buying the products of India with the money. The Nabob of Bengal was then in reality an independent prince, owing nominal fealty to the Moghul Emperor. But in 1757, following Clive's decisive victory over the last fully independent Nabob of Bengal, at the Battle of Plassey, the Company became, in effect, the sovereign power in Bengal. As its objectives remained purely commercial, it used this power to maximize its profits. The 'investment', as the moneys sent home to England were paradoxically known, was based on the land revenues of Bengal. The Company, collectively, had the incentive to squeeze the Bengalis as hard as possible. Individually, its servants each had an incentive to squeeze the natives still further, in order to accumulate the personal fortunes which each had come to India to seek. In short, the Company's government of Bengal, under the Nabob's nominal authority, had become a gigantic extortion racket at the expense of the Indians.

Clive had detected the abilities of Hastings, and in 1758 appointed him to the key post within the system of the Company's Resident at the Court of the Nabob. The then Nabob, Mir Jafar, had been appointed by Clive, and accepted a subservient role. But from 1760 on, a new Nabob, Mir Qasim, while accepting the Company's collective hegemony, sought to curb the individual depredations of the Company's servants. Henry Vansittart, Clive's successor as Governor, backed Mir Qasim in this, and was supported by Hastings, now a member of the Company's council. But Hastings and Vansittart were in a minority. The majority on the council – who were doing very well out of the system – demanded that all the Company's servants and agents be entirely exempt from control by the Nabob's government. Hastings vigorously opposed this demand, using language that would have earned Burke's warm approbation:

It is now proposed absolving every person in our service from the jurisdiction of the government. This it is true will prevent their suffering any oppression; but it gives them a full licence of oppressing others, since, whatever crimes they may commit, the magistrate must patiently look on, nor dare even to defend the lives and properties of the subjects committed to his care, without a violation of our rights and privileges. Such a system of government cannot fail to create in the minds of the wretched inhabitants an abhorrence of the English name and authority, and how would it be possible for the Nabob, whilst he hears the cries of his people which he cannot redress, not to wish to free himself from an alliance which subjects him to such indignities?

Hastings' support for Mir Qasim made him very unpopular with his colleagues, and this unpopularity was heightened when Mir Qasim, reacting to provocation by some of the Company's servants, massacred

200 Europeans at Patna. The Company's forces defeated Mir Qasim at Buxar in October 1764. He was deposed, and his predecessor, the pliant Mir Jafar, was reinstated. The Company's system was now restored in Bengal in its full rigour, and with full licence for its servants to rob the natives to their hearts' desire.

Hastings' position had become untenable. In December 1764, after Buxar, he and Vansittart resigned and returned to England. Hastings was to spend the next four years in England, where he made valuable contacts among the Company's Court of Directors, and renewed his acquaintance with Clive. He seems to have convinced Clive that if he were allowed to return to India, he would follow the line Clive had advised for him in 1758, which he had ignored. The line was one of severity towards the natives: 'These people will do nothing through inclination,' Clive advised. 'Ten sepoys now and then will greatly expedite payment.' He added that nothing but fear would make the Muslims 'do justice to the Company's claims'. Before returning to Bengal as Governor in 1772, Hastings wrote to Clive: 'I cannot wish to profit by a surer guide than your counsel and your example.'

So the Warren Hastings who returned to India in 1772 as Governor – and who was elevated to Governor-General the next year – was a very different person from the reform-minded man who had stood out against the majority on Vansittart's council. He would never again challenge powerful Company servants who were using their positions to accumulate fabulous personal fortunes. He did not take many bribes himself: his personal fortune when he left India was modest by their standards. He was more interested in power than in money. But because he was interested in power, he sought allies among those who had power-bases in India: men like Richard Barwell at Calcutta, and Paul Benfield at Madras. And these were the people who were most successful in enriching themselves at the expense of the natives. Ambition and avarice go well together, as Burke was later to observe. Once the Barwells and the Benfields realized that the new Governor represented no threat to their interests, they rallied to his support. So did the rest of the Company's servants, who hoped, in the course of time, to become Barwells and Benfields themselves. Hastings had been a pariah in British India at the end of his first term, but he became its hero in his second.

He was an excellent servant of the East India Company, in that he was more interested in raising revenue for the Company than for himself, and was good at it. His operations now ranged far beyond Bengal, westward up the Ganges valley, through Oudh and Rohilkhand and out to Benares. As Governor-General of Bengal, he was responsible, at least ostensibly, to the Company's Court of Directors in Leadenhall Street. But in dealing with the territories he informally acquired, he was responsible to no one. In these territories he exercised arbitrary power through his absolute control of a nominally sovereign prince, the Nabob of Oudh. He used this power to extort as much money as possible from the Nabob's subjects. Then he leased the Company's troops to the Nabob, at a stiff price, to annex Rohilkhand to the Nabob's territories – that is, to his own. These new domains were then devastated, as well as being systematically looted.

Hastings practised collective extortion from the natives of India on behalf of the Company, and extended the area of its operation. He also connived at individual extortion, for private enrichment, by the Company's servants. He thus presided over a system of double extortion from the natives. And this system of extortion sometimes involved torture. Mostly this arose spontaneously. Hastings did not have to instruct his agents to use torture if it seemed the only way to extract money, though in at least one case he seems to have been personally implicated.

Hastings' personal inclinations towards Indians were surprisingly benevolent. He had a deep respect for Indian culture, Hindu and Muslim. He was a pioneering patron of oriental scholarship, and in general an enlightened and cultivated person. Yet he was part of a system which was inimical to the interests of the Indians, as he well recognized. In a letter to Alex Elliot, he wrote in February 1777: 'In my government I face an endless and a painful choice of evils. The primary exigencies of the Company conflict with the interests of the Indian peoples who are subject to its authority.' That last sentence sums up what Company rule in India represented.

As a civilized human being, Warren Hastings might – and occasionally did – spare a sigh for the sufferings of the peoples of India. But as Governor-General he was required to satisfy 'the primary exigencies of the Company', by increasing and extending the sufferings of the peoples of India. Hastings had not invented the East India Company's system of extortion, and he had made some efforts to reform it during the first of his two terms in India. But after the failure of those efforts had brought his first term to a disastrous close, he returned to India as the practitioner-in-chief of the system. This was the Warren Hastings whom Burke, in the 1780s, was to see as the personification of the evil system. In denouncing and later impeaching Hastings, Burke used some exaggerated language and was mistaken over particular incidents; but he was basically right in his analysis of the system over which Hastings presided.

The legislation that elevated Warren Hastings to Governor-General of Bengal also hemmed him in. Lord North's East India Regulating Act of 1773 – which Burke opposed, lamely and reluctantly – foisted upon Hastings a council of four members (in addition to himself) and stipulated that decisions should be taken by a majority in council. One of the councillors, Richard Barwell, was in Hastings' pocket. The three other councillors named in the Act were not. They were General Sir John Clavering and Colonel George Monson – who have been aptly described as 'third-rate politicians of considerable parliamentary influence' – and Philip Francis.

Francis (1740–1818) was a man of remarkable ability and soon took the lead in the new council. As he had the support of Clavering and Monson, he had the legal authority to overrule Hastings. Burke was impressed by Francis's position at this time. He wrote to Rockingham on 20 October 1773: 'Francis will be here, by appointment, today ... I find that this Mr Francis is entirely [in the] interests of Lord Clive. Everything contributes to the greatness of this man, who whether government or the Company prevails will go near to govern India.' 'Go near' turned out to be right.

The new councillors arrived in Calcutta on 19 October 1774. Francis described their reception as 'mean and dishonourable'. Why was there no guard of honour? And why was there a salute of only seventeen guns, instead of twenty-one? This wasn't just a matter of hurt vanity, though that came into it. The niggardly reception was a signal from Hastings to all Calcutta, as well as to the councillors themselves, that the council was of much less consequence than the Governor-General.

The councillors had a mandate to enquire into past abuses. Hastings obstructed them, and the struggle between Francis and Hastings began. It was to last twenty-one years.

Superficially, the two men appear ridiculously mismatched. Warren Hastings was the absolute ruler of vast territories. Philip Francis, for all of Burke's tribute to his 'greatness', had at that time done nothing more than serve in minor government posts. However, his pseudonymous writings, the *Letters of Junius*, were the talk of the British political world. The letters, a brilliant series of political polemics with a whiff of blackmail, appeared in the *Public Advertiser* between 21 January 1769 and 21 January 1772. They were directed mainly against the Duke of Grafton's administration from the point of view of a supporter of George Grenville, and the political argument is on a high intellectual level. But Junius's readers were less interested in political argument than in the damaging personal allegations, couched in a tone of silky menace, which intersperse the argument. Politicians read Junius with bated breath, in fear of what might be coming next, and wondered and worried about who was penning them.

The letters are superbly written, and some of the finest writers of the time, including Burke, were among those credited with the authorship. But the identity of the author remained in dispute until 1962, when Alvar Ellegard, on the basis of statistical linguistic tests, established conclusively that Junius was Francis.

Philip Francis gave up his relatively lowly War Office job in 1772, and in the following year he accepted the offer of the lucrative and honourable post of a member of the new Council for Bengal, created by North's Regulating Act. This was a political plum, hardly to be expected by a minor official. So it seems probably that while two of the fellow councillors who set out with him were being rewarded for political services, Francis was being rewarded for political disservices and for agreeing to curtail them. His blackmail was being rewarded. The Philip Francis who landed at Calcutta in October 1774 was a dangerous and unscrupulous man. But he was to find a man awaiting him there who was even more unscrupulous.

TRIAL OF NUNCOMAR

When the new councillors arrived in India, they had a mandate to enquire into past abuses, and Francis and his colleagues, Clavering and Monson, let it be known that their doors were open to people with charges to make against Hastings. By February 1775, Hastings knew that his enemies on the council were in close touch with an Indian whom he had been making use of in the murky politics of Oudh: 'the principal theatre of his iniquities', as Francis called it later. Hastings wrote: 'Nuncomar, whom I have this long protected and supported, whom against my nature I have cherished like a serpent, is now in close connection with my adversaries.' Maharaja Nandakumar, known to Burke, Hastings and other contemporaries as Nuncomar, was an astute Brahmin of business, whom Hastings at one time opposed, and later used. Now he was turning against Hastings, intending to explain how they had conspired in extortion.

At a meeting of the council, Francis produced a letter from Nuncomar containing charges of bribery against Hastings. Nuncomar asked permission to appear before the council to produce his evidence. Francis and his associates demanded that Nuncomar be heard. The Governor-General, naturally, declined to submit to this procedure, which would have meant acquiescence in his own trial in a council dominated by his enemies. He asked the council, 'Shall I sit at this board to be arraigned in the presence of a wretch whom you all know to be one of the basest of mankind? I will not.' The Governor-General and his supporter, Barwell, left the council board, while Francis and his colleagues listened to Nuncomar.

For more than two centuries Hastings' biographers and admirers have echoed his indignation at the willingness of Francis and his allies to listen to such a notorious scoundrel as Nuncomar. Unfortunately for the admirers, this argument has a pronounced tendency to rebound against their hero. If Nuncomar was such a scoundrel, why had Warren Hastings 'long protected and supported him', cherishing him 'like a serpent'?

Hastings had made use of Nuncomar for several purposes, all with extortion as their aim. His principal use was for the purpose of conducting, in 1772, what Hastings called 'an enquiry' into the affairs of Mohammad Reza Khan, formerly chief minister of the Nabob of Oudh. Hastings accused this man of embezzlement, and ordered him to be imprisoned. He also ordered an enquiry into Reza Khan's affairs, and put Nuncomar, 'the basest of mankind', in charge of it. He left a candid statement of his reasons for doing so. 'It would be superfluous to add other arguments to show the necessity of pressing the enquiry by breaking Reza Khan's influence, removing his dependants, and putting the direction of all the affairs which had been committed to his care into the hands of the most powerful and active of his enemies.' He added: 'You will be pleased to recollect that the charge was general, without any specificates of time, places or persons. I had neither witnesses nor vouchers, nor materials of any sort to begin with. For these I relied chiefly on the abilities, observation, and active malignity of Mahraja Nuncomar.' In other words, Reza Khan was a political prisoner, and Nuncomar was Hastings' agent of terror.

Reza Khan was imprisoned for two years while the enquiry proceeded. Hastings then declared Reza Khan 'acquitted', for lack of evidence. It may seem odd that an enquiry entrusted by Hastings to Reza Khan's enemy precisely because he was his enemy, should fail to come up with evidence that would satisfy Hastings of Reza Khan's guilt. Nuncomar himself, however, had the explanation. The charges were dropped, Nuncomar told Francis and his allies in the council, because Hastings had taken a bribe to drop the charges. This was the most plausible of Nuncomar's allegations, and indeed hardly anything else could account for the phenomenon of such an 'enquiry' followed by such an 'acquittal'.

Hastings had put the frighteners on Reza Khan by setting Nuncomar on him, and it worked. Francis, in setting Nuncomar on Hastings, in 1775, was acting in very much the same way. If the word 'scoundrel' is to be used, it should not be confined, as it generally is, to the Indian partner in these transactions. But just as Nuncomar had apparently been let down by Hastings over Reza Khan, he was now to be let down by Francis, and with lethal effect. Six weeks after Nuncomar had formulated his charges, he himself was arrested by Hastings' men. The unfortunate Nuncomar was being crushed by Hastings as a deterrent to others: notably to Francis and his allies.

The East India Company Act, which had created the new council, also created a new Bengal Supreme Court, before which Nuncomar was brought for trial. The Chief Justice was Sir Elijah Impey, a friend of Warren Hastings since their schooldays at Westminster. The first critical decision was taken by Impey before the trial properly began, when he decided that the jury would consist not of Nuncomar's Indian peers, but of Englishmen. He then decided, dubiously, that English law applied in Calcutta, and so that forgery, being then a capital offence in England, was a capital offence in Calcutta too.

Now Nuncomar knew that he was doomed unless the majority in the council, who had enticed him to his ruin, came to his aid. So he sent a petition to the councillors, and a pathetic personal appeal to Francis. Nuncomar's letter, dated 31 July 1775, begins: 'Most Worshipful Sir, – In the perilous and unhappy circumstances I am now reduced to at present ... I am now thinking I have but a short time to live.' It ends: 'As I entirely rely on your worship's endeavour to do me all the good you can, I shall not, according to the opinion of the Hindus, accuse you in the Day of Judgment of neglecting to assist me in the extremity I am now in.'

We know that Francis opened the private letter, for it is preserved in his letter-book. But he did not open the petition. Instead, he sent it to be burned by the common hangman, and allowed it to be known that he had treated it in this way. So Nuncomar himself was, as Hastings commented, 'in a fair way to be hanged'.

It may well be that Francis and his colleagues were afraid for their own lives, as they had cause to be. Any intervention in the Nuncomar case – even an attempt at a stay of execution – would be likely to be construed by Impey as contempt of court and interference with due process. A jail sentence would follow, and a term in a Calcutta jail, guarded by the agents of Warren Hastings, was not an attractive prospect for Philip Francis. Francis was indeed in deadly danger. In the following year Lord Pigot, who was a threat to the interests of Paul Benfield in the Carnatic as Francis was to Hastings in Bengal, was to be thrown into jail in Madras, where he shortly died. Francis, facing the combination of Hastings and Impey, knew that his only hope was to send out, to all of British India, an unmistakable signal that he had abandoned Nuncomar to his fate, and was no longer a threat to the power of Warren Hastings. Francis sent this signal by letting it be known that he had handed over Nuncomar's petition to the common hangman.

Nuncomar was duly found guilty by the British jury and sentenced to death by Sir Elijah Impey. The sentence was carried out immediately. For good measure, and in case anyone should miss the point, the defence witnesses, who were Indians, were all prosecuted for perjury. No one else in India was now likely to come forward to the council with allegations against Hastings.

Burke described the execution of Nuncomar and its repressive effects to the House of Commons in his great speech on Fox's East India Bill:

Hanged in the face of all his nation, by the judges you sent to protect that people; hanged for a pretended crime, upon an *ex post facto* British Act of Parliament, in the midst of his evidence against Mr Hastings. The accuser they saw hanged. The culprit, without acquittal or enquiry, triumphs on the ground of that murder: a murder not of Nuncomar only, but of all living testimony, and even of evidence yet unborn. From that time not a complaint has been heard from the natives against their governors. All the grievances of India have found a complete remedy.

Men will not look to Acts of Parliament, to regulations, to declarations, to votes, and resolutions. No, they are not such fools. They will ask, what conduct ends in neglect, disgrace, poverty, exile, prison, and gibbet? These will teach them the course which they are to follow. It is your distribution of these that will give the character and tone to your government. All the rest is miserable grimace.

In their private communications, Hastings' familiars made no secret of the connection between Nuncomar's death and the stopping of the mouths of Hastings' accusers. As an enthusiastic supporter of Hastings wrote, 'With the life of [Nuncomar] has ended the prevalent spirit of informants and the litigants: the blacks know not which way to look; everyone cautious and reserved. The change which the execution has worked is easily perceived and felt [by] the different ranks of the inhabitants in this settlement – and I hope they may continue in their timid disposition.' Or, as Burke put it years afterwards: 'Mr Hastings observes, that no man in India complains of him. It is generally true. The voice of India is stopped. All complaint was strangled with the same cord that strangled Nuncomar.'

Burke and his friends, in 1787, tried to persuade the Commons to impeach Impey, but the attempt failed. Even more than the case against Hastings – which succeeded in the Commons – the case against Impey depended on legal interpretation. The lawyers in the House were naturally inclined to exonerate Impey, who had presided over the trial with a satisfactory appearance of decorum. Burke was censured by the Commons, years after the acquittal, for having said that Warren Hastings had 'murdered' Nuncomar 'by the hands of Sir Elijah Impey'. But the censure of the Commons has worn less well than Burke's terse summary of Nuncomar's end.

A Duel

Once Nuncomar had been made an example to those inclined to oppose or accuse Hastings, a less determined character than Philip Francis would have swiftly left India. But Francis stayed on for a further six years, even though he soon lost his only institutional asset, the majority on the council. The death of Colonel Monson in September 1775 meant that the division in the council was now 2–2, issues then being resolved by Hastings' casting vote. Opposition to Hastings was now quite hopeless, so Francis offered a show of co-operation. Hastings accepted this for some years, though of course he didn't trust Francis: 'Even the apparent levity of [Francis's] ordinary behaviour is but a cloak to deception.'

Yet if Francis was willing to stay, Hastings had good reason for wanting him to. Hastings' enemies were in the ascendant in North's administration, and if Francis were to return to England bearing a credible account of recent transactions, he might well precipitate Hastings' own recall. So Francis stayed on, compiling a dossier against Hastings, as the Governor-General probably knew. (Presumably he thought that the longer Francis remained in India, the longer it would be before the dossier could be used against him.) But after five years of this, and some symptoms of renewed intrigue by Francis, Hastings decided to provoke a duel, kill Francis if he could, and if not, frighten him into going home. The occasion was an adverse vote by Francis in the council, when, thanks to the temporary absence of Hastings' man Barwell, Francis momentarily had a majority.

Hastings believed that Francis's vote violated an agreement entered into between the two men in the previous year. The sequel is well told by Sir Alfred Lyall, who clearly had access to the recollections of eye-witnesses:

Hastings unquestionably believed that he had been tricked, and took his measures characteristically. He conveyed his wife to Chinsurah, at a short distance from Calcutta, and returning alone sent to the Council a minute redolent with the bitterness and resentment distilled out of their long personal altercations. 'But in truth', he said, 'I do not trust to [Francis's] promise of candour; convinced that he is incapable of it, and that his sole purpose and wish are to embarrass and defeat every measure which I may undertake, or which may tend even to promote the public interests, if my credit is connected with them. Such has been the tendency and such the manifest spirit of all his actions from the beginning; almost every measure proposed by me has for that reason had his opposition to it. When carried against his opposition, and too far engaged to be withdrawn, yet even then and in every stage of it his labours to overcome it have been unremitted; every disappointment and misfortune have been aggravated by him, and every fabricated tale of armies devoted to famine and to massacre have found their first and most ready way to his office, where it is known they would meet with most welcome reception . . .'

· Then came the homicidal provocation: 'I judge of his public conduct by my experience of his private, which I have found void of truth and honour. This is a severe charge, but temperately and deliberately made.'

These words produced the effect intended; for after the meeting of council at which the minute was read, Francis drew Hastings aside and read him a written challenge, which was accepted. On the second day following they met at a spot still well remembered in Calcutta tradition, taking ground at a distance of fourteen paces, measured out by Colonel Watson, one of the seconds, who said that Charles Fox and Adams had fought at that distance; although Hastings observed that it was a great distance for pistols. The seconds had baked the powder for their respective friends; nevertheless Francis's pistol missed fire. Hastings waited until he had primed again and had missed, when he returned the shot so effectively that Francis was carried home with a ball in his right side. The remarkable coolness of Hastings was noticed; he objected to the spot first proposed as being overshadowed by trees; and probably those were right who inferred from his behaviour that he intended to hit his man. That the single English newspaper then published in Calcutta should have made no mention of so sensational an incident as the Governor-General's duel, is good evidence of the kind of censorship then maintained over the Bengal press. But the editor had recently been in jail for a smart lampoon upon Hastings and Impey, a formidable pair of magnates to cut scandalous jokes upon in those days . . .

The duel served Hastings well, since it removed the last and strongest of the three adversaries against whom he had been contending in council since 1774. Such a mode of dealing with political opponents may be thought questionable, but governors and high officials of that period had to be as ready with the pistol as with the pen, for a challenge was often the resource not only of irritated rivals but of disappointed subordinates. Fox had met Adams, and Lord Shelburne, Colonel Fullerton; Lord Macartney was called out by General Stuart to account at twelve paces for some censure which he had passed on the General during his Madras governorship; and Sir John Macpherson, who held the Governor-Generalship for a time after Hastings, met an offended Major Brown in Hyde Park. Hastings sent Francis a friendly message, offering to visit him; but Francis declined any private intercourse with his adversary, and some months later he returned to England, where he prosecuted his feud against Hastings with pertinacious and inveterate malignity.

Although Hastings knew that Francis was going home 'to prosecute his feud', he was by now hardly troubled. He probably thought his political position in London at this time too strong to be shaken by the likes of Philip Francis, and in 1780 this was a reasonable assumption. Hastings' position had been alarmingly shaky in the mid 1770s when the North administration had sent out three hostile councillors to check him. But his political fortunes recovered dramatically in London from 1778 onwards. This was because of the dramatic weakening in Britain's world position after Burgoyne's defeat at Saratoga, followed by the French alliance with America. As Hastings' Victorian biographer G. R. Gleig put it: 'The minister who had lost America did not care to risk the loss of India likewise, and therefore sought to represent matters as great and prosperous there by way of a counterpoise to the evils which had overtaken the nation elsewhere.'

Yet there was more involved than Lord North's public relations. From 1779 on, the loss of India was a real possibility, together with the loss of America. The French hoped that through a confederation of Indian military princes against the British, they themselves might recover the position they had lost in India more than twenty years before. The government was in no position to send help to India. British shores were threatened with a French invasion and Britain had almost lost control of Ireland. Hastings was on his own. Whether Britain was to retain its hegemony in India or not depended on him.

As Francis had found, Hastings was at his ruthless best in a tight corner. He responded to the crisis created by the degenerating American War by going on the offensive in India, against the major remaining native Indian military force, the Mahratta confederacy, with its centre at Poona, in the west. He chose his military commanders well, and instructed them as to their objectives with a lucidity not often found in relations between political leaders and military executants. In their terseness and clarity, his military despatches recall the style of Julius Caesar. Like Caesar, he was also lucky. All his operations were successful and, by the time he had done, there was no longer any military opposition to British power in India.

One important ingredient in these formidable military successes was Hastings' experience and skill as an extortionist. That is how he raised the money to win the wars; no money was forthcoming, or to be expected, from home; the traffic was always the other way. And those military successes constitute the best case for Hastings' reputation. He may have had to resort to extortion, but he saved India for Britain.

So in 1781, with Philip Francis sailing home from Calcutta, Hastings thought himself safe. He had done the state some service, and he thought they knew it. He had held out in the Old World, while the New World was being lost. At the nadir of England's imperial fortunes, he alone could show a record of victory. He had a right to look forward with confidence to a peerage, which had been Clive's reward, and then to a position, such as Clive's had been, of uncontested authority in England over Indian affairs. That Francis could instead have him put on trial would have been inconceivable to him. He believed he had taken the measure of Francis when Nuncomar's petition was handed over to the common hangman. But Hastings had yet to take the measure of the ally Francis was about to enlist.

BURKE AND FRANCIS, 1781–85

Burke and Junius were not made to be soulmates. Burke was eleven years older than Francis, but the gap between the two was much wider in terms of outlook. Burke had grown up in the first half of the century, when Montesquieu and Locke were in the ascendant, and enlightenment was felt to be fully compatible with tolerant forms of Christianity. Burke's Christian faith was of profound importance to him, underlying his thoughts about India. Francis, by contrast, had matured in the second half of a century of momentous ideological change. He belonged to the militant Voltairean phase of the Enlightenment, and was contemptuous of Christianity – so contemptuous that he called it 'priestianity'. The religious difference between the two men did not prevent a close and long working alliance over India, but together with moral and political differences, it prevented the alliance from developing into a genuine friendship, despite efforts on both sides to make it so.

The moral gap was related to the religious one. Francis was what his French contemporaries called a *libertin*: a person so enlightened as to regard himself superior to moral considerations. Junius certainly behaved as if he thought of himself in this way. Politically too, their differences were important. Junius had opposed the repeal of the Stamp Act, and therefore the whole Rockingham policy towards America, a matter of the greatest consequence to Burke. Even worse, Junius was of the school of Shelburne: so much so that C. W. Everett, who edited the *Letters of Junius* in 1927, believed that Shelburne actually was Junius. And Shelburne, for Burke, was an embodiment of evil, on a par with Warren Hastings himself. (Appropriately, Shelburne ordered a bust of Hastings, with an inscription commemorative of the ingratitude of his countrymen, to be set up in Lansdowne House.)

Despite these weighty differences, a powerful and complex emotional bond, less than friendship, but also more, developed between Burke and Francis in the matter of punishing Hastings. Contemporaries didn't think so. They thought that Francis was coldly manipulating, for his own ends, Burke's genuine indignation in regard to the oppression of Indians. This suspicion crystallized in two Commons decisions, when the managers of the impeachment of Warren Hastings were being chosen in 1787. When Burke was proposed as chief manager, the House did not divide; the choice was unanimous. But when Burke nominated Francis as a member of his team, his name was rejected by a large majority, much to Burke's dismay and Francis's mortification.

In reality, their motives were more similar than contemporaries supposed. The Francis who had returned from India was no longer altogether the cool and calculating Junius; he was now a tormented, driven man – a man with a mission. Contemporaries might see him as bent on revenge for personal injuries, but that is not how he saw himself. How he saw himself appears in an extraordinary passage in a letter, written about a month after his return from India, to his friend Sir John Day: 'Nuncomar is returned and, like Caesar's ghost with Ate by his side, is now raging for revenge.' This suggests a soul in pain. He had brought back to England Nuncomar's letter to him with its desperate appeal for the council's intervention and the implicit contingent curse in its last sentence. If we can imagine the real Nuncomar returning, it is certainly on Francis, not Hastings, that he would wish to be revenged. Nuncomar had attacked Hastings, and could hardly blame him for striking back. But Francis had incited Nuncomar to take the bold step that was to lead to his destruction. Then, when Nuncomar called on Francis for help, Francis had not merely declined to help, but spurned his appeal in the most spectacular fashion.

Francis's conduct had been so outrageous as to arouse feelings of guilt even in the bosom of Junius. His imagination coped with the guilt by turning himself into the man he had incited and betrayed, and then seeking revenge on Hastings. So the common factor between Burke and Francis was a genuine indignation, partly fuelled by a sense of personal guilt. While in India, Francis had not shown any concern over the oppression of Indians, but once back in England, and clothed in the imagined robes of Nuncomar, he is in the grip of a genuine indignation, which feeds Burke's as well.

On India, the two men were in total sympathy. In the pursuit of Warren Hastings, they worked in unbroken harmony for nine years, until the French Revolution disrupted their personal relationship. Even after that, they continued to collaborate on the impeachment. But the relationship was always somewhat strained when anything other than India was in question. There is something in Burke's surviving letters to Francis that sets the teeth on edge. The tone is different from anything else in Burke's correspondence. There is a touch of effusiveness, an affected jocularity – even, in one or two letters, an affectation of rakishness – most uncharacteristic of him, and unbecoming. It is as if he is trying to take his tone from Francis, and not managing to bring it off. Probably the explanation is that he was distastefully aware that Francis was Junius but tried to suppress the thought for the sake of the invaluable partnership over India. Burke sensed that he was yoked, for a particular purpose, with an alien spirit. Significantly, the first explicit sign that he knew that Francis was Junius comes only in the letter that breaks off their friendship, or attempted friendship, in 1790.

Even the partnership over India had something disturbing about it. There is a hint of *folie à deux* in the shared guilt, and the compulsion to project all of it onto the person of Warren Hastings. Yet it is no more than a hint. Curiosity about motivations should not obscure the fact that the system of extortion against which Burke and Francis campaigned so indefatigably really did exist in India, and that it was Hastings who presided over it, ably and ruthlessly. Burke, aided by Francis, did far more than anybody else to bring that system to an end; and also to establish the accountability of the rulers of India, and the principle that the welfare of its natives was a criterion of government. These were great public services and it took an extraordinary expenditure of energy to bring them about. It may be that so much energy could not have been generated without the driving force of guilt.

When Burke turned his attention to Indian affairs once more in 1777, it was in a new situation. In 1775, the East India Company, in one of its fitful attempts to restrain the excesses of its servants, sent Lord Pigot out to be Governor of Madras, with instructions of a reformist tendency. Pigot was instructed to restore the Rajah of Tanjore to his territories, which had been annexed in 1773 in the name of the Nabob of the Carnatic (also known as the Nabob of Arcot).

The restoration of the Rajah of Tanjore was a perilous undertaking, comparable to setting Nuncomar on Warren Hastings. The Company's system worked in essentially the same way in the Carnatic, the region around Madras, as in Bengal. The Nabob of the Carnatic was as powerless as the Nabob of Oudh. In the Carnatic, as in Oudh, real power was in the hands of Europeans, who used it for extortion, and extended the supposed domains of the Nabob so as to widen their own scope. In the Carnatic, the practitioners and beneficiaries of this system had a majority on Lord Pigot's council, a group of speculators led by the notorious Paul Benfield (c.1740–1810), who amassed one of the largest fortunes ever brought home from India.

Benfield and his friends saw Pigot's instructions over Tanjore as a threat to their interests. So on 24 August 1776, they had Pigot seized by Company troops and thrown into jail in Madras, where he died in May 1777. In Madras, as in Bengal, the Company's servants in India wielded more power than their putative masters, the Court of Directors, in Leadenhall Street, London.

When news of Pigot's incarceration reached Britain, the Rockinghams began to organize a campaign for the release and rehabilitation of one who, along with his brother Admiral Hugh Pigot, had been a political supporter of theirs. Burke eagerly joined in this campaign. Yet, although the Rockinghams had changed course, they did not wish to acknowledge that they had done so. In his Speech on Restoring Lord Pigot, Burke still paid lip-service to the old policy: 'Far from meaning to take away I mean to strengthen the authority of the Company – to preserve respect to its orders, obedience to its governors, honesty in its councils, and discipline in its armies, not to subject her to ministerial jobs, but to take her out of the bondage of court cabals.' However, while putting on record the formal continuity of policy, Burke was discreetly logging the actual change of course: 'I wished to see the Company free from court influence that it might always be under public control.'

The key words here are 'public control'. Favoured by the new situation, Burke has revived the policy he had adopted – following Clive – five years before, but had abandoned, presumably under party pressure. There was one aspect that remained continuous, however: the emphasis on breaking the influence of 'court cabals'. The personal influence of George III, exercised mainly through his confidential agents Charles Jenkinson and John Robinson, was a potent force in the affairs of the Company, as well as in Parliament itself. Burke and his friends would feel the full weight of that influence, to their discomfiture, years later, in 1783–84.

The situation was now complicated by the appearance on the Indian scene of Burke's kinsman and close friend, Will Burke. Will was a goose whom Edmund took for a swan. He was not without abilities, and he seems to have been good company and beloved by all the Burkes, but he was forever thinking up schemes and speculations that ended in disaster. Edmund so doted on him that he backed him up in all his undertakings, to the misfortune of them both.

Now Will determined to go to India to repair his shattered fortunes. He went out as the bearer of a message from Admiral Pigot to his imprisoned brother – hardly the most promising introduction, for the purposes of making money in a Carnatic dominated by Lord Pigot's jailers. By the time Will Burke reached Madras, Lord Pigot was already dead, but Will did manage to see the Rajah of Tanjore, and was appointed his agent in London. (Presumably he got some money for this, but it cannot have been much. The Rajah, like Will himself, was a loser.) As Warren Hastings backed 'the Nabob of the Carnatic' – which is to say, Paul Benfield – against the Rajah of Tanjore, it has inevitably been suggested that Burke's hostility to Hastings was a result of the financial interests of his kinsman. That idea is now generally dismissed, but in the late 1770s, before Burke had identified Warren Hastings as his quarry, he was certainly affected by concern for Will's interests. He collaborated with him in preparing a curious and rather regrettable pamphlet, *The Policy of making Conquests for the Mahometans*. There was no such policy; as Burke was soon to realize, the conquests in question were all planned by Britons for their own benefit.

Poor Will seems to have realized, to some extent, that he was getting in Edmund's way. In a letter to Edmund's son Richard he expressed dismay at the rumours that Edmund's Indian exertions were motivated by concern for Will's interests. 'Oh my God,' he wrote, 'there is something sad and at the same time ridiculous, that the foreign papers ... should consider me as the spur and motive of your father's Eastern exertions, when in fact, his alarms for me are the only stay or reserve that hangs on his mind, in that noble walk of his.'

By early 1781, well before Philip Francis's return, Burke was beginning to grasp the nature of the system of extortion in India. The focus of his attention was still Madras, and not yet Bengal, but the system in both places was essentially the same. In October 1780, Burke had acquired a £1,000 holding of East Indian Company stock, the minimum required for a vote in the Court of Proprietors, the supreme body in the affairs of the Company (since it could overrule the Court of Directors, the executive body). He acquired this so as to have a say in the deliberations of the Court of Proprietors in the matter of Paul Benfield.

Benfield had been recalled as a result of the scandal over Pigot's death, and was seeking reinstatement. When the Court of Proprietors met to consider the case, on 17 January 1781, Burke presented seventeen 'Heads of Objection' to Benfield. The first three charges read:

That a dealing by the Company's servants in money transactions with the country powers in India hath been prohibited by strict and repeated orders from the Court of Directors and hath been productive of mischievous consequences to the revenues of the Company, to those of the country powers in alliance with the Company, to the trade, prosperity, population and safety of the countries on the coast of Coromandel.

2nd. That Paul Benfield Esquire appears to have been a dealer in money transactions, to an enormous extent, with one of the country powers in India, contrary to the letter and spirit of the Company's orders.

3rd. That the immense magnitude of the sums alleged by him to be due as aforesaid in the year 1775 to the said Paul Benfield, furnishes a just cause to doubt whether the money (if really advanced as pretended) could be acquired by lawful means, considering Mr Benfield's rank in the service, the nature of his trade, and the time of his residence in India.

Burke tried to have witnesses examined in support of the charges, but the Court of Proprietors decided, by 109 votes to 90, not to hear witnesses. Burke protested against 'sending Mr Benfield again to India with such charges upon him, and refusing so much as to hear the grounds of those charges that had a tendency to drive thirty or forty millions of distressed people into absolute despair'. The court decided to put the question of Benfield's reinstatement to a ballot of the shareholders. With Lord North's government urging its supporters to vote for him, Benfield won his reinstatement by 368 votes to 302.

Defeated at Company level, Burke now threw himself into parliamentary investigation of India. On 15 January 1781, North set up a Select Committee of the House to consider a number of petitions from Bengal. Government supporters were not interested in unprofitable things like petitions from Bengal, and the Select Committee consisted mostly of opposition Members. Burke joined it immediately, and soon came to dominate its proceedings. Three of the committee's reports are believed to have been written by him, including the Ninth Report on the economic exploitation of India and the Eleventh Report (November 1783), which is an indictment of Warren Hastings for accepting bribes. On 23 March 1781, Burke wrote to Sir Thomas Rumbold, Lord Pigot's successor as Governor of Madras:

I feel, as a member of this community, and as a member of the community of mankind at large, your merit in discountenancing, as I understand you have done, the present ruinous Mahratta War; and I shall ever acknowledge it as a public service. In condemning the perverse policy which led to that war, and which had before given rise to the still less justifiable war against the Rohillas, I do not speak from the smallest degree of prejudice or personal animosity against the respectable person (for such in many particulars he undoubtedly is) who was so unhappy as to be the author of both these measures [Warren Hastings]. I rather gave him my little voice as long as I thought it justifiable to afford him the smallest degree of support. I was always an admirer of his talents, and the farthest in the world from being engaged in a faction against him.

Most Englishmen would see the Mahratta War as a glorious episode in Hastings' career: through his victory, he had ended serious native resistance to British rule in India, and so denied any possible foothold to the hostile French. Hastings had, quite simply, 'saved India'. But for Burke, 'saving India' meant something quite different, having to do with the welfare of the Indian people.

Already there is a sign that at a deep level in Burke's psyche, his horror at the oppression of the Indians was merging with his horror at oppression of the Irish Catholics. The sign is a compulsive resort in Indian speeches to imagery of physical corruption – the imagery that had dominated his Bristol Guildhall speech of 1780 on the Irish penal laws. In a speech on the establishment of a secret committee on Indian affairs, Burke attacks the idea of secrecy:

> Secrets of inefficacy, of treachery, or of corruption, were the bane of governments. He never knew of a state that had been ruined by the openness of its system; by its readiness to search into its distempers, and to lay bare its wounds; but he had heard and read of many that had been ruined by the timorous secrecy of their proceedings, by the concealments which they observed in their inferior branches and dependencies; by which corruption and disease were suffered to gather head, until, when they burst into eruptions, they were too formidable for remedy, and withstood all the powers of physic.

And again, later in the speech:

> These are the mere pustules, the eruptions on the skin, and while you are intent on the examination of these, you neglect the real seat of the disease, which is in the blood, from the corruption of which these appearances have their rise.

From now on, Burke will allow nothing to deflect him from his pursuit of the oppressors of India. And it is in this same speech that he gives the first hint that he is about to attack Hastings: 'Let us enter on this enquiry with a determined spirit to screen no delinquent from punishment, however high.'

In June and July 1781, he was able to carry through Parliament a major piece of Indian legislation, the Bengal Judicature Bill, designed to restrict the use of English law in Bengal. The occasion for it had been the extension – by Elijah Impey, in collusion with Hastings – of English law over the natives of Bengal. This was greatly resented, and gave rise to the petitions which had led to the creation of the Select Committee. The committee had reported adversely on 8 May on the consequences of this extension of English law. Burke, speaking on the Bill in Parliament on 27 June 1781, said:

> The House had, in the report of the committee, an account of the proceedings of those judges. They were arbitrary in the extreme. The encroachments which they made on the most sacred privileges of the people, the violation of their dearest rights, particularly in forcing the ladies before their courts; the contempt that was shown for their religious ceremonies and mysteries; and the cruel punishments inflicted upon them in case of their disobedience; new, strange, and obnoxious to them; all these things contributed in fact, to compel the British legislature to restore peace, order, and unanimity to the extensive territories of India, by giving them the laws which they approved.

Burke went on to identify a common principle, applicable to the governance of countries as different from one another as the American colonies and India: 'We had suffered enough in attempting to enervate the system of a country, and we must now be guided as we ought to have been with respect to America, by studying the genius, the temper, and the manners of the people, and adapting to them the laws that we establish.'

It is remarkable that Burke, as a private Member, and in opposition, should have been able to carry such an important measure through Parliament. Partly this was thanks to having acquired, through the Select Committee, considerable influence over the Commons. Almost all the committee's members had become converts to Burke's views, and they spread the word, principally among the Rockinghams, of whom Burke became the *de facto* leader on Indian affairs in the summer of 1781. On the other side around this time, North was trying to conciliate Burke and his friends in the hope of enlisting their support for his administration. He probably didn't greatly care whether English law was extended to the natives of India or not. Finally, Burke had concluded a tactical working alliance with Henry Dundas, North's specialist on India, who for reasons

IV: India 1767–90

of his own was anxious to change the system of governing India. The Bengal Judicature Act of 1781, Burke's achievement, was the first parliamentary blow to the Hastings–Impey system in Bengal.

On Francis's return from India in October, he became the Select Committee's principal witness. His collaboration with Burke was, however, shortly disrupted by the news from America. The news of Yorktown, arriving at the end of November 1781, changed the face of British politics. For the next six months Burke was principally preoccupied, first with achieving peace with America and then with the affairs of the shortlived second Rockingham administration of March to July 1782. Yet even at this period he was working hard on Indian affairs. On 15 January 1782, Jane Burke describes him as having been 'full as busy since we came into the country as he was in town; he is trying whether he shall have more success in saving the East than he had in his endeavours for the West; he has been drawing Acts of Parliament and Bills, and reports ever since we have been here.' He was probably working on the First Report of the Select Committee, which was published on 5 February. This was a strong indictment of the corrupt bargain between Hastings and Impey, giving Impey jurisdiction over the native courts but making him removable (in that capacity) at Hastings' discretion. As P. J. Marshall points out, this arrangement was 'open to criticism; a royal judge intended to be an independent check on the Company was accepting a salaried post from it to preside over one of its own courts'. Resolutions highly critical of Impey were passed in April by the Commons.

The Rockinghams were now in power, and Burke was directing Indian policy. In May, the House voted for the recall of both Hastings and Impey. The Court of Directors was prepared to comply with the Commons demand, but the Court of Proprietors overruled it on 19 June. The proprietors took the audacious constitutional line that the Company was not bound by decisions of the Commons alone, only by decisions of both Houses of Parliament.

It is not likely that it would have taken such a dangerous line without indications of support from the House of Lords and the King, so we may suspect that Charles Jenkinson, the liaison between George III and the Company, had been at work. George bitterly resented what Rockingham had forced upon him over America, and a wish to frustrate Rockingham's designs concerning the Indian part of his domains would have been instinctive with him. In the Lords, George's influence was even stronger than in the Commons. The position adopted by the Court of Proprietors was the first warning sign of an impending confrontation between the two Houses, with the King making use of the Lords against the Commons. That confrontation took dramatic shape, at the end of 1783, with disastrous political results for Burke and his friends.

The momentum of the drive towards Indian reform was sweeping Burke into dangerous constitutional waters, as he surely knew from the Company's unprecedented defiance of a Commons decision. But neither that nor any other consideration could deflect him. By the end of 1782, with American affairs no longer an issue in British politics, India became his constant concern until the French Revolution in 1789. On 29 December 1782 he wrote to Francis: 'I have undertaken a vast task, but with your assistance I may get through it.' And the same month, in the House, he defined that vast task by insisting not merely on Hastings' recall 'but on his trial and punishment'. In 1783, Burke also moved to bring the Company system under 'public control'. In March he was back in office again, as part of the Fox–North coalition, which lasted until December. He made sure that Indian legislation was the centrepiece of the legislative programme. By August he had convinced Fox of the need for the measure, and in the same month he began drafting it, at Fox's house. This was the measure known to history as Fox's East India Bill, providing for the punishment of abuses, the observance of Indian rights and customs, and much stricter control from London.

The East India Company detested all this, of course, and it had powerful friends. The Court of Proprietors' defiance of the Commons in June was a strong signal of danger ahead. Several of Burke's colleagues advised caution, and by mid November, three weeks before the Bill was due to be introduced, Fox was beginning to be worried. Charles Jenkinson had attacked the plan of the Bill as 'injurious to the interests of the Crown'. Jenkinson was officially a supporter of Lord North – and consequently of the coalition – but he was also George III's chief confidential political agent, and he was signalling the King's opposition. It was now clear that the East India Bill, even if it passed the Commons, would run into trouble in the Lords. Some members of the coalition, probably with the support of Fox, now made overtures to Hastings' friends to see if there was any way of buying them off.

On 18 November, however, any hope of conciliation was shattered.

As P. J. Marshall puts it: 'On the day the [East India] Bills were presented, the Select Committee produced a report with the sole purpose of proving Hastings' personal corruption. The Eleventh Report was quickly put on sale to the public in an edition produced by Debrett and copies of it were later distributed "under blank covers to several (if not all) Members of the Upper House of Parliament".' The Select Committee was dominated by Burke; the Eleventh Report is known to be his work: the timing of its publication and the publicity ensured for it also bear Burke's mark. The report is a political landmine, detonated by Burke on the day of the publication of the East India Bill in order to destroy the effort to do a deal with Hastings.

This drastic and successful intervention is a measure of Burke's political autonomy in Indian affairs by late 1783. He, not Fox or North, had laid down the coalition's Indian policy, and by his coup with the report he made sure that there would be no deviation from it. This was a bold stroke, because the negotiations attempted with Hastings had, at the least, the blessing of the party leader, Fox. But where Indian affairs were concerned, Burke, with his power-base in the Select Committee, dominated Fox and, through him, the coalition. Fox was never Burke's leader except in name (and in the Commons). He stood in awe of Burke, morally and intellectually, and Burke was well aware of this. He could call Fox to order – as he implicitly did with the Eleventh Report – but Fox never successfully called him to order, though he was to try in 1791, over France.

Burke's colleagues had every reason to be worried about the dangerous course he had charted for them. Before the end of the year, his Bill would bring down the coalition, and many of his colleagues and allies would lose their seats in the subsequent general elections. Burke could see the danger as well as anyone else, or better; of all men, he best understood the ominous implications of Charles Jenkinson's phrase 'injurious to the interests of the Crown'. Yet he drove his colleagues on remorselessly.

Fox introduced his East India Bill on 18 November with a fine Burkean speech. Burke spoke only briefly in the debate on the second reading. When the two men were in agreement – that is to say, when Fox agreed with Burke – Burke had always been happy to leave the speaking honours to Fox, even in the days when Fox had been only an ally of the Rockingham party and not, as now, its leader in the

Commons. The Bill substituted a commission appointed by Parliament, and responsible to Parliament, for the Company's Court of Directors, which was responsible only to the Company's Court of Proprietors. That is to say, the Bill sought to end the Company's autonomy.

Few who opposed the East India Bill tried to defend the Company: it was unpopular and its abuses were by now notorious. The strongest argument of the Bill's opponents was that a legislative encroachment on the Company's charter implicitly undermined all charters, and so all the rights guaranteed by these. Burke came powerfully to grips with this argument on 1 December 1783, when for the first time his mature understanding of Indian affairs was unleashed on the Commons, in his great Speech on Fox's East India Bill.

As to the first of these objections; I must observe that the phrase of 'the chartered rights *of men*', is full of affectation; and very unusual in the discussion of privileges conferred by charters of the present description. But it is not difficult to discover what end that ambiguous mode of expression, so often reiterated, is meant to answer.

The rights of *men*, that is to say, the natural rights of mankind, are indeed sacred things; and if any public measure is proved mischievously to affect them, the objection ought to be fatal to that measure, even if no charter at all could be set up against it. If these natural rights are further affirmed and declared by express covenants, if they are clearly defined and secured against chicane, against power, and authority, by written instruments and positive engagements, they are in a still better condition: they partake not only of the sanctity of the object so secured, but of that solemn public faith itself, which secures an object of such importance. Indeed this formal recognition, by the sovereign power, of an original right in the subject, can never be subverted, but by rooting up the holding radical principles of government, and even of society itself. The charters which we call by distinction *great* are public instruments of this nature; I mean the charters of King John and King Henry the Third. The things secured by these instruments may, without any deceitful ambiguity, be very fitly called the *chartered rights of men*.

These charters have made the very name of a charter dear to the heart of every Englishman – But, sir, there may be, and there are charters, not only different in nature, but formed on principles the *very reverse* of those of the great charter. Of this kind is the charter of the East India Company. *Magna Charta* is a charter to restrain power, and to destroy monopoly. The East

India charter is a charter to establish monopoly, and to create power. Political power and commercial monopoly are *not* the rights of men; and the rights to them derived from charters, it is fallacious and sophistical to call 'the chartered rights of men'. These chartered rights (to speak of such charters and of their effects in terms of the greatest possible moderation) do at least suspend the natural rights of mankind at large; and in their very frame and constitution are liable to fall into a direct violation of them.

Burke then refers to the extensive powers to be retained by the Company once the Bill becomes law.

But granting all this, they must grant to me in my turn, that all political power which is set over men, and that all privilege claimed or exercised in exclusion of them, being wholly artificial, and for so much, a derogation from the natural equality of mankind at large, ought to be some way or other exercised ultimately for their benefit.

If this is true with regard to every species of political dominion, and every description of commercial privilege, none of which can be original self-derived rights, or grants for the mere private benefit of the holders, then such rights, or privileges, or whatever else you choose to call them, are all in the strictest sense a *trust*; and it is of the very essence of every trust to be rendered *accountable*, and even totally to *cease*, when it substantially varies from the purposes for which alone it could have a lawful existence.

This I conceived, sir, to be true of trusts of power vested in the highest hands, and of such as seem to hold of no human creature. But about the application of this principle to subordinate *derivative* trusts, I do not see how a controversy can be maintained. To whom then would I make the East India Company accountable? Why, to Parliament to be sure; to Parliament, from whom their trust was derived; to Parliament, which alone is capable of comprehending the magnitude of its object, and its abuse; and alone capable of an effectual legislative remedy. The very charter which is held out to exclude Parliament from correcting malversation with regard to the high trust vested in the Company is the very thing which at once gives a title and imposes a duty on us to interfere with effect, wherever power and authority originating from ourselves are perverted from their purposes, and become instruments of wrong and violence.

Having systematically demolished the strongest argument of his opponents, Burke appears to pause for a moment in his act. He refers to the reluctance he had felt about interfering with the Company's rights:

> The strong admission I have made of the Company's rights (I am conscious of it) binds me to do a great deal. I do not presume to condemn those who argue *a priori* against the propriety of leaving such extensive political powers in the hands of a company of merchants. I know much is, and much more may be said against such a system. But with my particular ideas and sentiments, I cannot go that way to work. I feel an insuperable reluctance in giving my hand to destroy any established institution of government, upon a theory, however plausible it may be.

In that last sentence, Burke states the principle on which, seven years later, he will denounce the destructive theorists of the French National Assembly.

In this part of the speech, where he is referring to the reluctance with which he approached the problem, Burke adopts a calm detached tone, resembling that of a neutral. He even defends the Company, at one point, against the aristocratic criticism that merchants are not fit persons to exercise political power. 'I have known merchants with the sentiments and the abilities of great statesmen; and I have seen persons in the rank of statesmen, with the conceptions and character of pedlars' (a hit at Shelburne). But Burke's explanation of his reluctance to interfere with the Company is a prelude to a recital of the enormities which alone could have overcome the depth of his reluctance:

> To justify us in taking the administration of their affairs out of the hands of the East India Company, on my principles, I must see several conditions. First, the object affected by the abuse should be great and important. Second, the abuse affecting this great object ought to be a great abuse. Third, it ought to be habitual, and not accidental. Fourth, it ought to be utterly incurable in the body as it now stands constituted. All this ought to be made as visible to me as the light of the sun, before I should strike off an atom of their charter.

Burke then establishes his four conditions. For his first condition he describes the extent of the Company's dominions:

> With very few, and those inconsiderable intervals, the British dominion,

either in the Company's name, or in the names of princes absolutely dependent upon the Company, extends from the mountains that separate India from Tartary, to Cape Comorin, that is, one-and-twenty degrees of latitude!

In the northern parts it is a solid mass of land, about eight hundred miles in length, and four or five hundred broad. As you go southward, it becomes narrower for a space. It afterwards dilates; but narrower or broader, you possess the whole eastern and north-eastern coast of that vast country, quite from the borders of Pegu – Bengal, Bahar, and Orissa, with Benares (now unfortunately in our immediate possession) measure 161,978 square English miles; a territory considerably larger than the whole kingdom of France. Oude, with its dependent provinces, is 53,286 square miles, not a great deal less than England. The Carnatic, with Tanjore and the Circars, is 65,948 square miles, very considerably larger than England; and the whole of the Company's dominion comprehending Bombay and Salsette, amounts to 281,412 square miles; which forms a territory larger than any European dominion, Russia and Turkey excepted. Through all that vast extent of country there is not a man who eats a mouthful of rice but by permission of the East India Company.

Having estimated the population of British India in 1783 at around thirty millions, he continues:

My next enquiry to that of the number, is the quality and description of the inhabitants. This multitude of men does not consist of an abject and barbarous populace; much less of gangs of savages, like the Guaranies and Chiquitos, who wander on the waste borders of the river of Amazons, or the Plate; but a people for ages civilized and cultivated; cultivated by all the arts of polished life, whilst we were yet in the woods. There, have been (and still the skeletons remain) princes once of great dignity, authority, and opulence. There, are to be found the chiefs of tribes and nations. There is to be found an ancient and venerable priesthood, the depository of their laws, learning, and history, the guides of the people whilst living, and their consolation in death; a nobility of great antiquity and renown; a multitude of cities, not exceeded in population and trade by those of the first class in Europe; merchants and bankers, individual houses of whom have once vied in capital with the Bank of England; whose credit had often supported a tottering state and preserved their governments in the midst of war and desolation; millions of ingenious manufacturers and mechanics; millions of the most diligent, and not the least intelligent, tillers of the earth.

Burke clearly senses some resistance from his parliamentary audience to this phase of his argument, for he adds that he has been trying 'to awaken something of sympathy for the unfortunate natives, of which I am afraid we are not perfectly susceptible, whilst we look at this very remote object through a false and cloudy medium'. There follows the recital of abuses by the Company, which makes up the bulk of the speech. There is a magnificent passage, contrasting the effects of Company rule with those of previous Asian rulers of India:

The several irruptions of Arabs, Tartars, and Persians, into India were, for the greater part, ferocious, bloody, and wasteful in the extreme: our entrance into the dominion of that country was, as generally, with small comparative effusion of blood; being introduced by various frauds and delusions, and by taking advantage of the incurable, blind, and senseless animosity, which the several country powers bear towards each other, rather than by open force. But the difference in favour of the first conquerors is this; the Asiatic conquerors very soon abated of their ferocity, because they made the conquered country their own. They rose or fell with the rise or fall of the territory they lived in. Fathers there deposited the hopes of their posterity, and children there beheld the monuments of their fathers. Here their lot was finally cast, and it is the natural wish of all that their lot should not be cast in a bad land. Poverty, sterility, and desolation are not a recreating prospect to the eye of man, and there are very few who can bear to grow old among the curses of a whole people. If their passion or their avarice drove the Tartar lords to acts of rapacity or tyranny, there was time enough, even in the short life of man, to bring round the ill effects of an abuse of power upon the power itself. If hoards were made by violence and tyranny, they were still domestic hoards; and domestic profusion, or the rapine of a more powerful and prodigal hand, restored them to the people. With many disorders, and with few political checks upon power, Nature had still fair play; the sources of acquisition were not dried up; and therefore the trade, the manufactures, and the commerce of the country flourished. Even avarice and usury itself operated both for the preservation and the employment of national wealth. The husbandman and manufacturer paid heavy interest, but then they augmented the fund from whence they were again to borrow. Their resources were dearly bought, but they were sure, and the general stock of the community grew by the general effort.

But under the English government all this order is reversed. The Tartar invasion was mischievous; but it is our protection that destroys India. It was their enmity, but it is our friendship. Our conquest there, after twenty years, is as crude as it was the first day. The natives scarcely know what it is to see the grey head of an Englishman. Young men (boys almost) govern there, without society, and without sympathy with the natives. They have no more social habits with the people, than if they still resided in England, nor indeed any species of intercourse but that which is necessary to making a sudden fortune, with a view to a remote settlement. Animated with all the avarice of age, and all the impetuosity of youth, they roll in one after another; wave after wave; and there is nothing before the eyes of the natives but an endless, hopeless prospect of new flights of birds of prey and passage, with appetites continually renewing for a food that is continually wasting. Every rupee of profit made by an Englishman is lost for ever to India. With us are no retributory superstitions, by which a foundation of charity compensates, through ages, to the poor, for the rapine and injustice of a day. With us no pride erects stately monuments which repair the mischiefs which pride had produced, and which adorn a country, out of its own spoils. England has erected no churches, no hospitals, no palaces, no schools; England has built no bridges, made no high roads, cut no navigations, dug out no reservoirs. Every other conqueror of every other description has left some monument, either of state or beneficence, behind him. Were we to be driven out of India this day, nothing would remain to tell that it had been possessed, during the inglorious period of our dominion, by anything better than the orang-outang or the tiger.

There is nothing in the boys we send to India worse than the boys whom we are whipping at school, or that we see trailing a pike, or bending over a desk at home. But as English youth in India drink the intoxicating draught of authority and dominion before their heads are able to bear it, and as they are full grown in fortune long before they are ripe in principle, neither nature nor reason have any opportunity to exert themselves for remedy of the excesses of their premature power. The consequences of their conduct, which in good minds (and many of theirs are probably such) might produce penitence or amendment, are unable to pursue the rapidity of their flight. Their prey is lodged in England; and the cries of India are given to seas and winds, to be blown about, in every breaking up of the monsoon, over a remote and unhearing ocean.

Entering into particular abuses, Burke comes to the case of the Begums of Oudh, and therefore to Hastings. He does not denounce him directly, but he quotes from him, copiously and effectively, and details a number of his extortions. The following is a lucid summary of the Company's system under Warren Hastings:

> The invariable course of the Company's policy is this: either they set up some prince too odious to maintain himself without the necessity of their assistance, or they soon render him odious by making him the instrument of their government. In that case troops are bountifully sent to him to maintain his authority. That he should have no want of assistance, a civil gentleman, called a Resident, is kept at his court, who, under pretence of providing duly for the pay of these troops, gets assignments on the revenue into his hands. Under his provident management, debts soon accumulate; new assignments are made for these debts; until, step by step, the whole revenue, and with it the whole power of the country, is delivered into his hands. The military do not behold without a virtuous emulation the moderate gains of the civil department. They feel that, in a country driven to habitual rebellion by the civil government, the military is necessary; and they will not permit their services to go unrewarded. Tracts of country are delivered over to their discretion. Then it is found proper to convert their commanding officers into farmers of revenue. Thus, between the well paid civil and well rewarded military establishment, the situation of the natives may be easily conjectured. The authority of the regular and lawful government is everywhere and in every point extinguished. Disorders and violences arise; they are repressed by other disorders and other violences. Wherever the collectors of the revenue and the farming colonels and majors move, ruin is about them, rebellion before and behind them. The people in crowds fly out of the country, and the frontier is guarded by lines of troops, not to exclude an enemy, but to prevent the escape of the inhabitants.

At the beginning of his consideration of the Company's abuses he had set out four conditions. He goes on:

> I am now come to my last condition, without which, for one, I will never

readily lend my hand to the destruction of any established government; which is, that in its present state, the government of the East India Company is absolutely incorrigible.

Of this great truth I think there can be little doubt, after all that has appeared in this House. It is so very clear, that I must consider the leaving any power in their hands, and the determined resolution to continue and countenance every mode and every degree of peculation, oppression, and tyranny, to be one and the same thing. I look upon that body as incorrigible, from the fullest consideration both of their uniform conduct, and their present real and virtual constitution.

If they had not constantly been apprized of all the enormities committed in India under their authority, if this state of things had been as much a discovery to them as it was to many of us, we might flatter ourselves that the detection of the abuses would lead to their reformation. I will go further: if the Court of Directors had not uniformly condemned every act which this House or any of its committees had condemned, if the language in which they expressed their disapprobation against enormities and their authors had not been much more vehement and indignant than any ever used in this House, I should entertain some hopes. If they had not, on the other hand, as uniformly commended all their servants who had done their duty and obeyed their orders, as they had heavily censured those who rebelled, I might say, 'These people have been in an error, and when they are sensible of it they will mend.' But when I reflect on the uniformity of their support to the objects of their uniform censure, and the state of insignificance and disgrace to which all of those have been reduced whom they approved, and that even utter ruin and premature death have been among the fruits of their favour, I must be convinced, that in this case, as in all others, hypocrisy is the only vice that never can be cured.

In concluding his main argument, when Burke says 'you' he is referring to the formal approval by the Commons of his Select Committee reports.

The fact is, that for a long time there was a struggle, a faint one indeed, between the Company and their servants. But it is a struggle no longer ... The Company has made a common cause, and identified themselves, with the destroyers of India. They have taken on themselves all that mass of enormity; they are supporting what you have reprobated; those you condemn they applaud; those you order home to answer for their conduct, they request to stay, and thereby encourage to proceed to their practices. Thus the servants of the East India Company triumph, and the representatives of the people of Great Britain are defeated.

I therefore conclude, what you all conclude, that this body, being totally perverted from the purposes of its institution, is utterly incorrigible; and because they are incorrigible, both in conduct and constitution, power ought to be taken out of their hands; just on the same principles on which have been made all the just changes and revolutions of government that have taken place since the beginning of the world.

This speech is qualitatively different from any of Burke's previous utterances over India. For the first time, he is speaking without constraint. He is speaking for a Bill designed to his own political specifications and written by himself. He has carried his party with him and overcome its waverings. He can now speak his own mind, because his mind now dominates his party, and he gives full expression to his hatred of oppression.

Many contemporaries thought the eulogy of Fox the finest part of the speech. This passage has a falsity, but it is a generous falsity, which is moving in its context:

It will be a distinction honourable to the age, that the rescue of the greatest number of the human race that ever were so grievously oppressed, from the greatest tyranny that was ever exercised, has fallen to the lot of abilities and dispositions equal to the task; that it has fallen to one who has the enlargement to comprehend, the spirit to undertake, and the eloquence to support, so great a measure of hazardous benevolence. His spirit is not owing to his ignorance of the state of men and things; he well knows what snares are spread about his path, from personal animosity, from court intrigues, and possibly from popular delusion. But he has put to hazard his ease, his security, his interest, his power, even his darling popularity, for the benefit of a people whom he has never seen. This is the road that all heroes have trod before him. He is traduced and abused for his supposed motives. He will remember, that obloquy is a necessary ingredient in the composition of all true glory: he will remember, that it was not only in the Roman customs, but it is in the nature and constitution of things, that calumny and abuse are essential parts of triumph. These thoughts will support a mind which only exists for honour, under the burthen of temporary reproach. He is doing indeed a great good; such as rarely falls to the lot, and almost as rarely coincides with the desires, of any man. Let him use his time. Let him give the whole length of the reins to his benevolence. He is now on a great eminence, where the eyes of mankind are turned to him. He may live long, he may do much. But here is the summit. He never can exceed what he does this day.

The falsity is obvious. Fox was not 'the author' of the Bill. Burke was. The great task to which Fox had, somewhat reluctantly, set himself did not simply 'fall to his lot', it was imposed on him by the awe which Burke inspired in him. Fox did indeed 'well know what snares are spread about his path' and he had tried not to go any further down that path. It was Burke who, by a vigorous application of the Eleventh Report, had driven him on. These falsities of form are dictated by the parliamentary setting, in which Burke's praise must be couched in a form appropriate to Fox's position as leader, and to his own as follower. The realities were different, yet there is a genuine warmth in the praise. The feelings involved are not those of a follower applauding a leader, but of a teacher applauding a pupil. That had been the relation of Fox to Burke from the beginning, and so it remained. On the Indian question, the great teacher had been worried about his beloved, brilliant, wayward pupil. Being worried, he had been stern with him. The sternness had worked, the pupil had done well, and praise is now called for. The warmth of the praise reflects affection for the pupil, admiration for his great talents, and also the depth of Burke's relief that Fox is still with him.

The vote at which Burke's speech was aimed – a vote to go into committee – passed handsomely: 217 to 103. Shortly afterwards, however, the Bill went to the Lords and to its fate. On 11 December, the King sprang his trap on the Fox–North coalition. He gave his confidant Lord Temple the following statement in writing: 'His Majesty allowed Earl Temple to say, that whoever voted for the India Bill was not only not his friend, but would be considered by him as an enemy; and if these words were not strong enough, Earl Temple might use whatever words he might deem stronger and more to the purpose.' This was, of course, a terrifying threat to any lord: it meant being completely cut off from all state patronage, both for oneself and one's family. So it is not surprising that the East India Bill was decisively defeated in the Lords on 17 December 1783.

Next day, the King sent the following message to North: 'Lord North is by this required to send me the seals of his Department, and to acquaint Mr Fox to send those of the Foreign Department.' Burke's own dismissal, as Paymaster-General, followed on 19 December. The King had not been alone in preparing this coup; he was working closely with his confidential agents and advisers, Charles Jenkinson, John Robinson and Richard Atkinson (the last of whom was acting for the East India Company). This was the court intrigue that Burke had warned about in his speech in December. This was what he meant by his expression 'the double Cabinet'. A set of confidential advisers – what would now be called a 'kitchen Cabinet' – was conspiring with the King to use his prerogative to destroy the official Cabinet.

After dismissing North and Fox, the King first sent for the chosen instrument of their destruction to be chief minister. Temple accepted, but resigned three days later (possibly fearing impeachment). The King then sent for William Pitt, then aged twenty-four. Pitt, although he knew himself to be in a minority in the Commons, continued as chief minister for three months, enduring repeated voting defeats and violent Whig attacks for unconstitutional conduct.

When the Commons met, on 17 December, Mr Baker of Hertford, a personal friend of Burke, rose in his place and proposed a resolution in the following terms:

> That it is now necessary to declare that to report any opinion or pretended opinion of His Majesty upon any Bill or other proceedings depending on either House of Parliament, with a view to influencing the votes of the Members, is a high crime and misdemeanour derogatory to the honour of the Crown, a breach of the fundamental privilege of Parliament, and subversive of the constitution of this country.

Against this resolution, Pitt moved the Order of the Day, but was defeated. The resolution was obviously intended as a prelude to the impeachment of Lord Temple, and this would have followed had the Fox–North majority in the Commons remained stable, but this was not to be. Pitt held on grimly as chief minister, and Jenkinson and Robinson went to work on the Northites – their former party colleagues – showing them that the way back into royal favour was to start voting for Pitt.

About fifty succumbed to mingled royal favours and threats, and the Fox–North majority steadily dwindled.

By March 1784 Fox's majority was reduced to just one vote. Pitt now felt politically strong enough to go to the country. By this time Robinson and Atkinson had completed their homework in the boroughs, using public funds, Company funds, secret service funds and promises of titles. Meanwhile, most of the London press portrayed the East India Bill sponsored by the Fox–North coalition as having aimed not at reform, but at getting the loot of India into the same unprincipled hands as had clutched at power through coalition. Much of this press campaign was fuelled and paid for by the East India Company, and by Paul Benfield in particular.

So when Pitt dissolved Parliament in March, the membership of the new House was no longer in doubt. Lists of the Members who had been agreed upon were already being handed around in Westminster. These elections were, accordingly, a disaster for the followers of Fox and North, who lost eighty-nine seats.

FROM NADIR TO IMPEACHMENT

Burke's situation as the 1784 parliamentary session opened was deeply depressing. The measure that had brought down the Fox–North coalition was his East India Bill, which was also central to Pitt's successful election campaign. On Burke's shoulders, therefore, rested most of the responsibility for the political demise of 'Fox's Martyrs', as the eighty-nine coalition followers who lost their seats were known. One might expect, therefore, that he would have little influence over his colleagues in the new Parliament. One might expect, in particular, that any attempt by him to suggest India as a focus for opposition in the new Parliament would be treated with derision: there was no more unpromising topic. Yet against all the odds, Burke was to carry not only his own colleagues but eventually a majority of this very Parliament to vote for the impeachment of Warren Hastings before the bar of the House of Lords. This extraordinary achievement is a measure of the persuasive powers he exerted when engaged on a matter about which he felt deeply and had thought deeply.

A year earlier, in the previous Parliament, Burke had entered into a solemn pledge to God, to his country, to the House and to the unfortunate people of India, that he would 'bring to justice as far as in him lay, the greatest delinquent that India ever saw'. In the new Parliament he set out to fulfil it.

The first opportunity came on 28 July, when he rose to oppose Pitt's East India Bill. He opposed it for its inadequacies, as compared with Fox's, but he did not attack it very strongly, for it appeared to be a serious reform measure partly along the lines of Fox's Bill. His main object in speaking was to signal the renewal of his attack on Warren Hastings. That attack took up most of his speech, and furnished its conclusion:

> that he had no personal cause of dislike to Mr Hastings; he felt no prejudice against him: on the contrary, when he first sat in the Select Committee he felt a strong prepossession in his favour, from the lofty panegyrics he had heard of him; so much so, that the friends of Sir Elijah Impey had upbraided him with being greatly partial to the Governor-General. If that partiality was now no more, it was because it had been rooted out by the discoveries he had made in the Company's records, while he sat in the Select Committee. All he wanted was that the House would give him an opportunity to defend the reports, and to make good all the charges they had brought against the Governor-General. Since he saw he was not likely to obtain that, he would not say anything more against the Bill, but simply to enter his protest against it in the name of the injured natives of India, whose grievances were to be enquired into and redressed by – those who had occasioned them.

Two days later, he made his Speech on Almas Ali Khan, in which he dealt with Warren Hastings' dealings with Almas Ali Khan, the largest revenue administrator in Oudh, a principality then subject to Hastings' absolute and arbitrary rule. Burke had come into possession of Hastings' instructions sent to John Bristow, the Resident at Lucknow, on 23 October 1782 concerning how to deal with Almas Ali Khan:

> If he has been guilty of any criminal offence to the Nabob his master, for which no immunity is provided in the engagement, or he shall break any one of the conditions of it, I do most strictly enjoin you, and it must be your special care to endeavour, either by force or surprise, to secure his person, and bring him to justice: by bringing him to justice, I mean that you urge the Nabob, on due conviction, to punish him with death, as a necessary example

to deter others from the commission of the like crimes; nor must you desist till this is effected. – I cannot prescribe the means: but to guard myself against that obloquy to which I may be exposed by a forced misconstruction of this order, by those who may hereafter be employed in searching our records for cavils and informations against me, I think it proper to forbid, and protest against, the use of any fraudulent artifice or treachery to accomplish the end which I have prescribed; and as you alone are privy to the order, you will of course observe the greatest secrecy that it may not transpire: but I repeat my recommendation of it as one of the first and most essential duties of your office.

Knowing the political conditions in Oudh, and Hastings' *modus operandi*, Burke saw that the instructions were a euphemistic order to have Almas Ali Khan murdered so that his money could be seized.

Alas! the situation and property of this man, like a great many of his countrymen, destroyed him, attracted the attention, stimulated the avarice, and brought down the vengeance of the British on his head. The crime of having money was imputed to this unfortunate prince, which, like the sin against the Holy Ghost in Christian theology, in Indian politics can never be forgiven. It seemed impossible, in this instance, to plunder without murder. The bloody edict is therefore issued. Mark how soon the fatal science in that country is brought to perfection! No matter what is done, provided the manner of doing it be properly managed. Yet he had heard of a letter, and of a murder, or something very like it, recited in that letter; an extract of which had come to his hand. From this extract he learned that orders had been sent to arrest Almas Ali Khan: but this gentleman-like business must be done in the most gentleman-like manner. The chief must be taken, and he must also be put to death; but all this must be contrived as to imply no treachery. Here was honour of a very singular and nice description – Plunder, peculation, and even assassination, without treachery! – Such was the extreme refinement which distinguished the cruelties of the East. All possible delicacy was even to be shown in the exercise of a ferocity, the foulest and the most atrocious that ever blackened the prostitution of usurped authority.

Burke's speeches on India in 1783 and 1784 were often met with derisive laughter, but it seems that the laughter during this one was more persistent and concerted than usual, and that the head of the new administration, the young William Pitt, was giving a lead. Burke challenged him on it:

> It became the Minister of a great and generous nation, instead of laughing at the miseries of his fellow creatures, to regard these important calls with all his attention. Good God! he exclaimed, what must the whole world think of a young man who could hear of oppression, peculation, rapine, and even murder, not with insensibility only, but with levity – with laughter! Whatever sport it was to the Treasury bench, it was, he could assure them, no sport to the poor helpless men who daily saw the effects of their industry, the means of their subsistence, extorted from them, and their families reduced to abjection and want!

There is reason to believe that this went home: Pitt was later to acknowledge that his contemptuous treatment of Burke's case, in the early years of his administration, was unwarranted.

The ever-present religious dimension in Burke's thinking about India is most obvious in this speech. And his negative feelings about England find more open expression than ever before. The following passage comes from deep down in Burke's psyche:

> He, for his own part, thought the dreadful procedure of Providence was so strongly and obviously marked as to have escaped no man but those who wished not to observe it – He believed from his heart, the vengeance of heaven to be raised against this country. By authorizing the massacres which had been so foully perpetrated and repeated in India, Britain was now become a land of blood – Much innocent blood had been shed, and he doubted was still shedding – But an avenger would certainly appear and plead the cause of the wronged with those who had wronged them – Yes, the arm of God was abroad – His righteous visitation was already begun, and who could tell where it might end? He knew with accuracy how to discriminate the good from the bad, those who had from those who had not imbrued their hands in the blood of their fellow creatures. The instruments of his wrath were infinite and would be exercised without ceasing or interval till the redress of the wretched and the punishment of the oppressors were completed. This great work Providence was visibly carrying on against a country, who, by its crooked policy, had ripened itself for destruction. What were the infatuation which seized us so generally, the debt which hung about

our neck, with a weight which precipitated our downfall; our want of union, our want of principle, and our want of consequence, but certain indications of a malediction which the dreadful wretchedness we had entailed on a people much better than we, had brought at last on our own heads?

Burke's next Indian speech, On the Nabob of Arcot's Debts, delivered on 28 February 1785, is one of his greatest, and marks a turning point in the debate over India. The Almas Ali Khan and Nabob of Arcot speeches are mostly in different keys, but the melody is the same. The second is generally the cooler and less emotional, but at its close the same emotions appear.

The speech unravels one of the most extraordinary extortion rackets of all time. Paul Benfield and his colleagues in the council at Madras were in the habit of lending, or purporting to lend, huge sums of money to the Nabob of Arcot, who was their prisoner and puppet at Madras, just as the Nabob of Oudh was the prisoner and puppet of Hastings in Bengal. By autumn 1784, the Company's Court of Directors had decided that a fund from the revenues of the Carnatic – south-eastern India – should be set up for debt repayment, but the directors insisted that claims on the fund could be accepted only after some form of examination. The directors were, however, overruled by the new Board of Control set up under Pitt's India Act. The board decided that the Nabob's debts, as stated by his creditors, were to be paid, in full, without enquiry of any kind. Burke believed that this startling decision by the board was the result of a corrupt agreement reached between Henry Dundas (who, as well as being Navy Treasurer, handled India affairs for Pitt, and picked the Board of Control) and the Nabob's 'creditors', in exchange for their financial and other assistance to the Pitt campaign in the elections of 1784.

Burke directed his attack against Dundas and Pitt. Dundas was particularly vulnerable because in the previous Parliament he had been a leading ally of Burke's in exposing Indian abuses. Dundas was now himself involved in the very type of transaction that he had formerly sought to expose. But Pitt was also vulnerable, though in a different way. Like his father, Chatham, the younger Pitt had a high reputation for probity, which he valued and liked to flaunt. The Nabob transaction did not sit well with such a reputation. As he listened to Burke's Speech on the Nabob of Arcot's Debts, Pitt must have suffered, and that suffering probably contributed to his volte-face over Warren Hastings the following year.

Burke asked:

> Whether the Chancellor of the Exchequer, and the Treasurer of the Navy [Pitt and Dundas], acting as a Board of Control, are justified by law or policy in suspending the legal arrangements made by the Court of Directors, in order to transfer the public revenues to the private emolument of certain servants of the East India Company, without the enquiry into the origin and justice of their claims, prescribed by an Act of Parliament?

Why, that is, were Pitt and Dundas prepared to open the public coffers to fund fraudulent claims by a group of conspirators? Burke lays down a general principle, to which he senses resistance:

> Fraud, injustice, oppression, peculation, engendered in India, are crimes of the same blood, family and cast, with those that are born and bred in England. To go no farther than the case before us; you are just as competent to judge whether the sum of four millions sterling ought, or ought not, to be passed from the public treasury into a private pocket, without any title except the claim of the parties, when the issue of fact is laid in Madras, as when it is laid in Westminster.

As Burke knew, of course, if the millions in question were to come from the British taxpayer, the scandal of their transfer would have brought down Pitt's administration. But as the money was to be paid by natives of India, parliamentary interest in the transaction was limited.

Burke then returned to 'the young Minister', linking Pitt personally with Benfield and his associates, and with their unaccountable fortunes, and going on to describe succinctly the working of the Nabob of Arcot's debts:

> If this body of private claims of debt, real or devised, were a question, as it is falsely pretended, between the Nabob of Arcot as debtor, and Paul Benfield and his associates as creditors, I am sure I should give myself but little trouble about it. If the hoards of oppression were the fund for satisfying the claims of bribery and peculation, who would wish to interfere between such litigants? If the demands were confined to what might be drawn from the

treasures which the Company's records uniformly assert that the Nabob is in possession of; or if he had mines of gold or silver or diamonds (as we know that he has none), these gentlemen might break open his hoards or dig in his mines without any disturbance from me. But the gentlemen on the other side of the House know as well as I do, and they dare not contradict me, that the Nabob of Arcot and his creditors are not adversaries, but collusive parties, and that the whole transaction is under a false colour and false names. The litigation is not, nor ever has been, between their rapacity and his hoarded riches. No; it is between him and them combining and confederating on one side, and the public revenues, and the miserable inhabitants of a ruined country, on the other. These are the real plaintiffs and the real defendants in the suit. Refusing a shilling from his hoards for the satisfaction of any demand, the Nabob of Arcot is always ready, nay, he earnestly, and with eagerness and passion, contends for delivering up to these pretended creditors his territory and his subjects. It is therefore not from treasuries and mines, but from the food of your unpaid armies, from the blood withheld from the veins, and whipped out of the backs of the most miserable of men, that we are to pamper extortion, usury, and peculation, under the false names of debtors and creditors of state.

Then Burke swoops on Dundas, who in supporting payment of the creditors' claims in full had rashly pointed out that this had been approved by the Company's Presidency, or council, at Madras (on which Benfield and his extortionist colleagues had a majority). Turning to Dundas, Burke said:

The right hon. gentleman, with an address peculiar to himself, every now and then slides in the Presidency of Madras, as synonymous to the Company. That the Presidency did approve the debt is certain. But the right hon. gentleman, as prudent in suppressing as skilful in bringing forward his matter, has not chosen to tell you that the Presidency were the very persons guilty of contracting this loan; creditors themselves, and agents, and trustees for all the other creditors. For this the Court of Directors accuse them of breach of trust; and for this the right hon. gentleman considers them as perfectly good authority for those claims.

Burke recalls how the creditors themselves, in 1781, had been willing to abate their claims by 25 per cent. Then he turns on Pitt, who in his capacity as Chancellor of the Exchequer had met the creditors' claims in full:

> But what corrupt men, in the fond imaginations of sanguine avarice, had not the confidence to propose, they have found a Chancellor of the Exchequer in England hardy enough to undertake for them. He has cheered their drooping spirits. He has thanked the peculators for not despairing of their commonwealth. He has told them they were too modest. He has replaced the twenty-five per cent which, in order to lighten themselves, they had abandoned in their conscious terror. Instead of cutting off the interest, as they had themselves consented to do, with the fourth of the capital, he has added the whole growth of four years' usury of twelve per cent to the first overgrown principal; and has again grafted on this meliorated stock a perpetual annuity of six per cent to take place from the year 1781. Let no man hereafter talk of the decaying energies of nature. All the acts and monuments in the records of peculation; the consolidated corruption of ages; the patterns of exemplary plunder in the heroic times of Roman iniquity, never equalled the gigantic corruption of this single act. Never did Nero, in all the insolent prodigality of despotism, deal out to his Praetorian guards a donation fit to be named with the largesse showered down by the bounty of our Chancellor of the Exchequer on the faithful band of his Indian sepoys.

After much detailed and cogent argument, the emotional temperature rises, and that imagery of physical corruption makes its appearance, indicating, as so often, that the Irish element of Burke's psyche is roused:

> That debt forms the foul putrid mucus in which are engendered the whole brood of creeping ascarides, all the endless involutions, the eternal knot, added to a knot of those inexpugnable tape-worms which devour the nutriment, and eat up the bowels of India . . .
>
> It is difficult for the most wise and upright government to correct the abuses of remote delegated power, productive of unmeasured wealth, and protected by the boldness and strength of the same ill-got riches. These abuses, full of their own wild native vigour, will grow and flourish under mere neglect. But where the supreme authority, not content with winking at the rapacity of its inferior instruments, is so shameless and corrupt as openly to give bounties and premiums for disobedience to its laws; when it will not trust to the activity of avarice in the pursuit of its own gains; when it secures

public robbery by all the careful jealousy and attention with which it ought to protect property from such violence; the commonwealth then is become totally perverted from its purposes; neither God nor man will long endure it; nor will it long endure itself. In that case, there is an unnatural infection, a pestilential taint fermenting in the constitution of society, which fever and convulsions of some kind or other must throw off; or in which the vital powers, worsted in an unequal struggle, are pushed back upon themselves, and by a reversal of their whole functions, fester to gangrene, to death; and instead of what was but just now the delight and boast of the creation, there will be cast out in the face of the sun, a bloated, putrid, noisome carcass, full of stench and poison, an offence, a horror, a lesson to the world.

When Burke finally sat down, it was to an extremely hostile reception. Despite a cry of questions from every part of House, Pitt made no attempt to reply. No serious reply was possible. Burke was on absolutely solid ground, as contemporaries and historians have agreed. From the point of view of a practical politician such as Pitt, the best answer to Burke's speech consisted not of rational argument but of shouting – from his followers – and then voting, with the majority supplied by the 1784 election overwhelming Burke by 164 to 69.

But Pitt, as well as being an excellent practical politician, was a fastidious human being. He cannot have enjoyed the speech, nor his own inability to answer, nor the bawling of his own troops. He was perhaps already wondering whether for his reputation's sake he should go on standing between Burke and the abuses in India. Towards the end of the speech, Burke acknowledged and emphasized his own isolation. But the sheer force of his case began to change the situation. By the following year, Burke had not only Fox but Pitt too helping him towards the impeachment of Hastings.

Only a few faint strains of Burke's great melody can be heard over the next three years, before it fully resumes, with the impeachment itself. Burke spent the intervening period rallying his own party to the cause and then presenting the case to the Commons.

In February 1785, Hastings, troubled by reports of proceedings in Parliament, sailed for home. On 20 June, Burke gave notice to the Commons 'that if no other gentleman would undertake the business, he would, on a future day, make a motion respecting the conduct of a gentleman just returned from India'. This was the first specific move towards impeachment. By the end of the year, Fox was worried about where Burke was heading, and tried to moderate his plans. But Burke was determined to decide and prosecute Indian policy without deference to the views of his party leader. He was going to go ahead against Hastings; his party and his leader could follow or not as they chose. And it was the party that gave in, not Burke. Before the new sessions began, in January 1786, Burke was able to secure a united opposition. A meeting at the Duke of Portland's house 'decided to adopt the impeachment as an opposition measure'. His speeches and unyielding determination had made their impact on Fox and his friends.

In February, Burke declared his intention to impeach Warren Hastings and ruled out an alternative legal procedure:

> His invincible objection to a Bill of pains and penalties would of course lead him to the proposition of another mode; and this, at once ancient and constitutional, was a Bill of impeachment ... With their permission, he should move for papers, from the contents of which he would endeavour to collect the several articles into their necessary points of view, and ... move for an impeachment at the bar of the House of Lords.

Pitt, in reply, was cautious, but not unyielding: 'Every paper which was material to elucidate the subject ought to be produced. He was neither a determined friend nor foe to Mr Hastings; but he was resolved to support the principles of justice and equity.' Pitt added: 'Should the right hon. gentleman bring fully home to Mr Hastings the violent imputations of atrocious crimes, he, for his own part, far from screening, would wish to bring down upon him the most exemplary punishment.'

In the event, Burke got most, though not all, of the papers he needed. He was making more progress than he had expected. On 4 April 1786, he presented to the House of Commons several Articles of Charge, formally accusing Hastings of high crimes and misdemeanours. Hastings appeared before the Commons to offer his defence on 1 May. It was generally admitted that the defence was a disaster. It was extremely long and boring, and abounded in prevarications, some of which later had to be withdrawn and replaced by others, to the great embarrassment of his supporters. In seeking to prove that his 'political conduct was invariably regulated by truth, justice and good faith', he had set himself an impossible task. Had he pleaded necessity of state, and the need for rigour in the governance of India, he could probably have averted impeachment. As it was, his defence did his cause great harm. A number of respected independent country gentlemen now began to support the impeachment. Yet the impeachment was still uphill work in the Commons. On 2 June, the first article – Hastings' conduct of the Rohilla War – was defeated by 116 votes to 67.

Then on 13 June, the breakthrough came. This was in the debate over the article concerning Hastings' treatment of Rajah Chait Singh. Pitt declared himself convinced by one element: 'The fine which [Hastings] determined to levy was beyond all proportion exorbitant, unjust and tyrannical; he [Pitt] should therefore, certainly, on the present charge, agree to the motion that had been made, not considering himself as thereby committed to a final vote of impeachment.' After that declaration, the article was carried by 119 to 79. Subsequent charges were also carried, whether Pitt voted for them or not. It seems that Pitt's vote was taken as a signal that the question of impeachment was no longer a party matter, but one on which Members were free to vote according to their consciences. And it soon became clear that under those conditions a majority of Members were by now convinced that Hastings deserved to be impeached.

Pitt's decision to vote for impeachment on the Benares article astonished Members on both sides at the time, and has been the subject of much speculation since. Marshall lists several of the 'ingenious explanations' offered, but finds that 'it seems to have been the unanimous opinion of all those who were in close contact with him that he had judged the case entirely on what he had believed to be its merits, and without any ulterior calculations.' The opinion of the independent Members had been moving against Hastings over the past two months, and even Hastings' followers had been dismayed by his incredible defence. Pitt must have realized that it was not politic to appear to be protecting him. To do so might remind people of that shady transaction over the Nabob of Arcot's debts, and Pitt would want that forgotten as soon as possible. Such considerations must have occurred to him, but he did also make a serious study of the case. As his penetrating mind explored the records, his feelings may have been similar to those of Burke when he undertook the same exercise in 1781. When he realized the extent of the Indian oppressions, he too probably became somewhat ashamed of his record on India.

The remaining articles were adjourned into the next session. Burke was in no hurry. Opinion was likely to be still more favourable after the recess. In February 1787, Richard Brinsley Sheridan introduced the article on Oudh, which was the strongest set of charges against Hastings. He began by referring to the vote in favour of impeachment on the Benares charge. That vote, he told the Members, had 'vindicated the character of his right hon. friend (Mr Burke) from the slanderous tongue of ignorance and perversion. They had, by their vote on that question, declared that the man who brought the charges was no false accuser; that he was not motivated by envy, by malice, nor by any unworthy motives to blacken a spotless name; but that he was the indefatigable, persevering, and, at length, successful champion of oppressed multitudes against their tyrannical oppressor.'

This endorsement marks Burke's greatly enhanced position within his party, thanks to the progress of the impeachment in the previous year. Sheridan (1751–1816) had not previously been an enthusiast for the India cause; in November 1783 he had even been the intermediary in the attempted deal with Hastings. After the 1784 election, Sheridan was among the Members who wanted to hear no more about India. If now he was fully behind Burke, so was the whole of his party – for the time being. The Oudh article carried by a vote of more than two to one: yeas, 175; noes, 68 – much better than the Benares article. The impeachment by the Commons was now unstoppable.

On 2 April, in a tactical move for the sake of 'unanimity', Burke accepted a procedural point from Pitt in preference to one from Fox. This symbolized that there was no longer any difference between the parties, but an effective unity over the impeachment. For Burke, it was an ecstatic moment, the consummation of six years of unstinting effort:

The effects of the enquiry with a view to impeachment had been glorious both in that House and without doors. Without doors men's minds had been changed, rooted prejudice had been eradicated, conviction had followed, and all the world confessed that the House of Commons were engaged in a grave and important proceeding essential to the establishment of the national character for justice and equity. Within doors all the various modes and styles of eloquence had been called forth, to the admiration of the House . . . softening almost into a common bond of union the hitherto obdurate hearts of violently contending politics; sheathing the sword of embattled party and lowering its hostile front.

On 25 April 1787, according to the *Parliamentary History*, 'Mr Burke brought up the first seven Articles of Impeachment against Mr Hastings, which were read *pro forma* at the table and ordered to be printed.' On 9 May, two Members protested against sending the impeachment to the Lords. Pitt sternly reprimanded them, saying that he

> felt himself totally at a loss to conceive how it could be reconciled to the honour, the conscience or the justice of that House to stop short of sending up the impeachment to that place, where alone it ought to undergo its ultimate discussion. He admitted that he once was of opinion that the language of those who chiefly promoted the present proceedings was too full of acerbity, and much too passionate and exaggerated; but when he found what the nature of the crime alleged was, and how strong was the presumption that the allegations were true, he confessed that he could not expect that gentlemen, when reciting what they thought actions of treachery, actions of violence and oppression, and demanding an investigation into those actions, should speak a language different from that which would naturally arise from the contemplation of those actions.

Generations of critics have found Burke's language against Hastings 'too full of acerbity, and much too passionate and exaggerated'. But this declaration by the greatest of his contemporary opponents, a notably cool and temperate politician, suggests that it was not in excess of the facts, and that Pitt had accepted this after due reflection.

The next day, the following motion was carried: 'That Mr Burke go to the Lords, and, at their bar, in the name of the House of Commons and of all the Commons of Great Britain, do impeach Warren Hastings Esquire, late Governor-General of Bengal, of high crimes and misdemeanours; and acquaint the Lords, that this House will, with all convenient speed, exhibit articles against him and make good the same.' The *Parliamentary History* goes on: 'The majority of the House immediately attended Mr Burke to the bar of the House of Peers, where Mr Burke solemnly impeached Mr Hastings ... On the 14th [May] Mr Burke carried the Articles of Impeachment up to the Lords.' And on 10 December 1787 – that is, after an interval proportionate to the dignity of their House – 'The Lords acquainted the Commons that they had appointed the 13 February next for the Trial of Warren Hastings Esq at the bar of the House of Lords.'

IMPEACHMENT BEFORE THE LORDS

Macaulay later wrote a famous description of the scene at Westminster Hall as the impeachment opened:

> The place was worthy of such a trial. It was the great hall of William Rufus; the hall which had resounded with acclamations at the inauguration of thirty kings; the hall which had witnessed the just sentence of Bacon and the just absolution of Somers; the hall where the eloquence of Strafford had for a moment awed and melted a victorious party inflamed with just resentment; the hall where Charles had confronted the High Court of Justice with the placid courage which has half redeemed his fame. Neither military nor civil pomp was wanting. The avenues were lined with grenadiers. The streets were kept clear by cavalry. The peers, robed in gold and ermine, were marshalled by the heralds under Garter King-at-Arms. The judges, in their vestments of state, attended to give advice on points of law. Near a hundred and seventy lords, three-fourths of the Upper House, as the Upper House then was, walked in solemn order from their usual place of assembling to the tribunal ... The long galleries were crowded by such an audience as has rarely excited the fears or the emulation of an orator. There were gathered together, from all parts of a great, free, enlightened, and prosperous realm, grace and female loveliness, wit and learning, the representatives of every science and of every art. There were seated round the Queen the fair-haired young daughters of the house of Brunswick. There the ambassadors of great kings and commonwealths gazed with admiration on a spectacle which no other country in the world could present. There Siddons, in the prime of her majestic beauty, looked with emotion on a scene surpassing all the imitations of the stage. There the historian of the Roman Empire thought of the days when Cicero pleaded the cause of Sicily against Verres; and when, before a senate which had still some show of freedom, Tacitus thundered against the oppressor of Africa. There were seen, side by side, the greatest painter and the greatest scholar of the age. The spectacle had allured Reynolds from that easel which has preserved to us the thoughtful foreheads of so many writers and statesmen, and the sweet smiles of so many noble matrons ...

For Burke, at the centre of that gorgeous scene, 13 February 1788 was a day of pride, but also of anxiety. As manager and opener of the case which the House of Commons was to present to the Lords, he occupied, at that moment, a more central position in the political order than he ever had before or ever would again. His feelings towards that order were, however, ambivalent, and he knew that his chances of success in this great enterprise were small. In the Lords, the influence of the Crown and of the Company were stronger than in the Commons, and both were favourable to Hastings. There were also the lawyers in the Lords to be considered. What was impending in the Lords was a legal proceeding, a trial, whereas what had taken place in the Commons had been a political debate. Burke had had to do no more than convince the Commons of the probability that serious crimes had been committed in India under Hastings. But before the Lords, he would be required to do much more: to prove beyond reasonable doubt that Hastings personally had committed these crimes or ordered others to commit them.

Both Hastings and Burke himself thought such proof impossible under the ordinary rules of evidence. Burke was later to quote to the Lords words that Hastings had uttered about the impossibility of obtaining proof of oppression: 'In the charge of oppression, although supported by the cries of the people and the most authentic representations, it is yet impossible to obtain legal proofs of it.' This was why Burke had argued in the Commons, as he was now to argue in the Lords, that an impeachment should not be held to the ordinary standards of proof and rules of evidence that applied to common crime in the ordinary courts. What should apply, he argued, were 'the enlarged and solid principles of state morality'. By this he meant that a high official, under impeachment, should be found guilty if it could be shown that the governmental system which he operated was criminally oppressive, even if it could not be shown that he personally had explicitly directed any specific act of criminal oppression.

This argument may have been reasonable, but Burke can have had little hope that it would prevail. Lawyers brought up on the rules of evidence were unlikely to be impressed by a layman such as Burke – who had studied law but never practised – talking about the principles of state morality. Then there was the additional handicap that the Articles of Impeachment were not lawyerly documents. They had been drawn up by Burke and Francis at a time when they did not believe there was much prospect of carrying the impeachment through the Commons to the Lords. So they were in a form calculated not to secure a conviction in the Lords, but to make an impact on public opinion. And if all that were not enough, Burke knew that the Lord Chancellor who would preside over the impeachment, Baron Thurlow (1731–1806), was friendly towards Hastings, having been at Westminster School with both Hastings and Sir Elijah Impey.

So as Burke entered Westminster Hall the prospects did not look bright. But then they had not looked bright in the Commons either, until Pitt's astonishing conversion. In any case, when committed to a course, Burke did not allow himself to be daunted or deflected by the improbability of success. He had stuck to his American course for more than fifteen years, during most of which success seemed most improbable. His Indian campaign lasted fourteen years, from 1781, when he first became fully committed to it, to 1795, when it ended with the dismissal of the charges against Hastings. Now, in February 1788, he had half of that course yet to run.

Fanny Burney records her impression of him as the proceedings began:

> I shuddered, and drew involuntarily back, when, as the doors were flung open, I saw Mr Burke, as head of the committee, make his solemn entry. He held a scroll in his hand, and walked alone, his brow knit with corroding care and deep labouring thought, – a brow how different to that which had proved so alluring to my warmest admiration when first I met him! so highly as he had been my favourite, so captivating as I had found his manners and conversation in our first acquaintance, and so much as I had owed to his zeal and kindness to me and my affairs in its progress! How did I grieve to behold him now the cruel prosecutor (such to me he appeared) of an injured and innocent man!

Fanny Burney was a lady-in-writing to the Queen, who was even more inclined to think well of Hastings than most of the rest of the Court (although the King had his doubts). But Fanny Burney was also an acute observer, with a good eye for theatrical business. Having reported Thurlow's speech calling on Warren Hastings to be ready to answer the charges, she detected what would prove to be a crucial feature of the trial, Thurlow's favourable disposition towards Hastings: 'This speech, uttered in a calm, equal, solemn manner, and in a voice mellow and penetrating, with eyes keen and black, yet softened into some degree of tenderness while fastened full upon the prisoner.'

Burke's opening speech lasted for four days, and was generally felt, even by hostile critics, to be worthy of the occasion. Fanny Burney's account of the second day is evidence of the remarkable impression he made on a highly intelligent witness who was strongly disposed to support the accused:

All I had heard of his eloquence, and all I had conceived of his great abilities was more than answered by his performance. Nervous, clear, and striking was almost all that he uttered: the main business, indeed, of his coming forth was frequently neglected, and not seldom wholly lost; but his excursions were so fanciful, so entertaining, and so ingenious, that no miscellaneous hearer, like myself, could blame them. It is true he was unequal, but his inequality produced an effect which in so long a speech was perhaps preferable to greater consistency, since, though it lost attention in its falling off, it recovered it with additional energy by some ascent unexpected and wonderful. When he narrated, he was easy, flowing, and natural; when he declaimed, energetic, warm, and brilliant. The sentiments he interspersed were as nobly conceived as they were highly coloured; his satire had a poignancy of wit that made it as entertaining as it was penetrating; his allusions and quotations, as far as they were English and within my reach, were apt and ingenious; and the wild and sudden flights of his fancy, bursting forth from his creative imagination in language fluent, forcible, and varied, had a charm for my ear and my attention wholly new and perfectly irresistible.

Were talents such as these exercised in the service of truth, unbiased by party and prejudice, how could we sufficiently applaud their exalted possessor? But though frequently he made me tremble by his strong and horrible representations, his own violence recovered me, by stigmatizing his assertions with personal ill-will and designing illiberality. Yet, at times I confess, with all that I felt, wished, and thought concerning Mr Hastings, the whirlwind of his eloquence nearly drew me into its vortex.

From the start, Burke told the Lords that much more was at stake than an individual's guilt:

My lords, the business of this day is not the business of this man, it is not solely whether the prisoner at the bar be found innocent or guilty, but whether millions of mankind shall be made miserable or happy.

Your lordships will see, in the progress of this cause, that there is not only a long, connected, systematic series of misdemeanours, but an equally connected system of maxims and principles invented to justify them. Upon both of these you must judge. According to the judgment that you shall give upon the past transactions in India, inseparably connected as they are with the principles which support them, the whole character of your future government in that distant empire is to be unalterably decided. It will take its perpetual tenor, it will receive its final impression, from the stamp of this very hour.

It is not only the interest of India, now the most considerable part of the British Empire, which is concerned, but the credit and honour of the British nation itself will be decided by this decision. We are to decide by this judgment, whether the crimes of individuals are to be turned into public guilt and national ignominy, or whether this nation will convert the very offences which have thrown a transient shade upon its government into something that will reflect a permanent lustre upon the honour, justice, and humanity of this kingdom.

Formally, Burke is speaking on behalf of the Commons of Great Britain, but it is hardly the Commons of Great Britain that put that last sentence into his mouth. Burke's personal ambivalence towards England can be heard here: in the impeachment of Warren Hastings, England herself is on trial, for Burke. If Hastings is found guilty, England is innocent; and vice versa. From here he puts the trial in its constitutional context. The impeachment represents all that is good about the British constitution as Burke saw it, for it holds not only subjects but governors to be accountable. This description of 'the great circulation of responsibility' anticipates his famous panegyric on the British constitution and its provisions against arbitrary rule in *Reflections on the Revolution in France*:

My lords, there is another consideration, which augments the solicitude of the Commons, equal to those other two great interests I have stated, those of our empire and our national character – something that, if possible, comes more home to the hearts and feelings of every Englishman: I mean, the interests of our constitution itself, which is deeply involved in the event of this cause. The future use and the whole effect, if not the very existence, of the process of an impeachment of high crimes and misdemeanours before the peers of this kingdom upon the charge of the Commons will very much be decided by your judgment in this cause. This tribunal will be found (I hope it will always be found) too great for petty causes: if it should at the same time be found incompetent to one of the greatest – that is, if little offences, from their minuteness, escape you, and the greatest, from their magnitude, oppress you – it is impossible that this form of trial should not in the end vanish out of the constitution. For we must not deceive ourselves: whatever does not stand with credit cannot stand long. And if the constitution should be deprived, I do not mean in form, but virtually, of this resource, it is virtually deprived of everything else that is valuable in it. For this process is the cement which binds the whole together; this is the individuating principle that makes England what England is. In this court it is that no subject, in no part of the empire, can fail of competent and proportionable justice; here it is that we provide for that which is the substantial excellence of our constitution – I mean the great circulation of responsibility by which (excepting the supreme power) no man, in no circumstance, can escape the account which he owes to the laws of his country. It is by this process that magistracy, which tries and controls all other things, is itself tried and controlled. Other constitutions are satisfied with making good subjects; this is a security for good governors. It is by this tribunal that statesmen who abuse their power are accused by statesmen and tried by statesmen, not upon the niceties of a narrow jurisprudence, but upon the enlarged and solid principles of state morality. It is here that those who by the abuse of power have violated the spirit of law can never hope for protection from any of its forms; it is here that those who have refused to conform themselves to its perfections can never hope to escape through any of its defects. It ought, therefore, my lords, to become our common care to guard this your precious deposit, rare in its use, but powerful in its effect, with a religious vigilance, and never to suffer it to be either discredited or antiquated. For this great end your lordships are invested with great and plenary powers: but you do not suspend, you do not supersede, you do not annihilate any subordinate jurisdiction; on the contrary, you are auxiliary and supplemental to them all.

Burke then argued that ordinary rules of evidence should not apply to an impeachment, that justice to the Indians required an enlargement of judicial procedure:

> But your lordships will maintain, what we assert and claim as the right of the subjects of Great Britain, that you are not bound by any rules of evidence, or any other rules whatever, except those of natural, immutable, and substantial justice.
>
> I have too much confidence in the learning with which you will be advised, and the liberality and nobleness of the sentiments with which you are born, to suspect that you would, by any abuse of the forms, and a technical course of proceeding, deny justice to so great a part of the world that claims it at your hands. Your lordships always had an ample power, and almost unlimited jurisdiction; you have now a boundless object. It is not from this district or from that parish, not from this city or the other province, that relief is now applied for: exiled and undone princes, extensive tribes, suffering nations, infinite descriptions of men, different in language, in manners, and in rites, men separated by every barrier of nature from you, by the providence of God are blended in one common cause and are now become suppliants at your bar. For the honour of this nation, in vindication of this mysterious providence, let it be known that no rule formed upon municipal maxims (if any such rule exists) will prevent the course of that imperial justice which you owe to the people that call to you from all parts of a great disjointed world. For situated as this kingdom is, an object, thank God, of envy to the rest of the nations, its conduct in that high and elevated situation will undoubtedly be scrutinized with a severity as great as its power is invidious.

With great boldness, Burke next argued that the Lords might be bribed, and that the results of bribery might take the form of a decision that the ordinary rules of evidence were to apply.

> It is well known that enormous wealth has poured into this country from India through a thousand channels, public and concealed; and it is no particular derogation from our honour to suppose a possibility of being corrupted by that by which other empires have been corrupted, and assemblies almost as respectable and venerable as your lordships' have been directly or indirectly vitiated. Forty millions of money, at least, have within our memory been brought from India into England. In this case the most

sacred judicature ought to look to its reputation . . . No direct false judgment is apprehended from the tribunals of this country; but it is feared that partiality may lurk and nestle in the abuse of our forms of proceeding. It is necessary, therefore, that nothing in that proceeding should appear to mark the slightest trace, should betray the faintest odour of chicane. God forbid that when you try the most serious of all causes, that when you try the cause of Asia in the presence of Europe, there should be the least suspicion that a narrow partiality, utterly destructive of justice, should so guide us that a British subject in power should appear in substance to possess rights which are denied to the humble allies, to the attached dependants of this kingdom, who by their distance have a double demand upon your protection, and who, by an implicit (I hope not a weak and useless) trust in you, have stripped themselves of every other resource under heaven!

I do not say this from any fear, doubt, or hesitation concerning what your lordships will finally do – none in the world; but I cannot shut my ears to the rumours which you all know to be disseminated abroad. The abusers of power may have a chance to cover themselves by those fences and entrenchments which were made to secure the liberties of the people against men of that very description. But God forbid it should be bruited from Peking to Paris that the laws of England are for the rich and the powerful, but to the poor, the miserable, and defenceless they afford no resource at all! God forbid it should be said, no nation is equal to the English in substantial violence and in formal justice – that in this kingdom we feel ourselves competent to confer the most extravagant and inordinate powers upon public ministers, but that we are deficient, poor, helpless, lame, and impotent in the means of calling them to account for their use of them! An opinion has been insidiously circulated through this kingdom, and through foreign nations too, that in order to cover our participation in guilt and our common interest in the plunder of the East, we have invented a set of scholastic distinctions, abhorrent to the common sense and unpropitious to the common necessities of mankind, by which we are to deny ourselves the knowledge of what the rest of the world knows, and what so great a part of the world both knows and feels.

In that passage, which is at the core of Burke's case against Hastings, the negative side of Burke's feelings towards the English ruling class and system of government is evident. He explains that he is putting a system of iniquity upon trial in the person of its chief practitioner, Warren Hastings.

As to the criminal, we have chosen him on the same principle on which we selected the crimes. We have not chosen to bring before you a poor, puny, trembling delinquent, misled perhaps by those who ought to have taught him better, but who have afterwards oppressed him by their power, as they had first corrupted him by their example. Instances there have been many, wherein the punishment of minor offences, in inferior persons, has been made the means of screening crimes of an high order, and in men of high description. Our course is different. We have not brought before you an obscure offender, who, when his insignificance and weakness are weighed against the power of the prosecution, gives even to public justice something of the appearance of oppression: no, my lords, we have brought before you the first man of India, in rank, authority, and station. We have brought before you the chief of the tribe, the head of the whole body of Eastern offenders, a captain-general of iniquity, under whom all the fraud, all the peculation, all the tyranny in India are embodied, disciplined, arrayed, and paid. This is the person, my lords, that we bring before you. We have brought before you such a person, that, if you strike at him with the firm and decided arm of justice, you will not have need of a great many more examples. You strike at the whole corps, if you strike at the head.

Central to Hastings' defence was the contention that actions in India were not to be judged by the moral standards that applied in Europe. Towards the close of the second day of his speech, Burke vigorously attacked this contention:

My lords, we positively deny that principle. I am authorized and called upon to deny it. And having stated at large what he [Hastings] means by saying that the same actions have not the same qualities in Asia and in Europe, we are to let your lordships know that these gentlemen have formed a plan of geographical morality, by which the duties of men, in public and in private situations, are not to be governed by their relation to the great Governor of the Universe, or by their relation to mankind, but by climates, degrees of longitude, parallels, not of life, but of latitudes: as if, when you have crossed the equinoctial, all the virtues die, as they say some insects die when they cross the line; as if there were a kind of baptism, like that practised by seamen, by which they unbaptize themselves of all that they learned in Europe, and after which a new order and system of things commenced.

This geographical morality we do protest against; Mr Hastings shall not screen himself under it; and on this point I hope and trust many words will not be necessary to satisfy your lordships. But we think it necessary, in justification of ourselves, to declare that the laws of morality are the same everywhere, and that there is no action which would pass for an act of extortion, of peculation, of bribery, and of oppression in England that is not an act of extortion, of peculation, of bribery, and oppression in Europe, Asia, Africa, and all the world over. This I contend for not in the technical forms of it, but I contend for it in the substance.

Mr Hastings comes before your lordships not as a British governor answering to a British tribunal, but as a subahdar, as a bashaw of three tails. He says, 'I had an arbitrary power to exercise: I exercised it. Slaves I found the people: slaves they are – they are so by their constitution; and if they are, I did not make it for them. I was unfortunately bound to exercise this arbitrary power, and accordingly I did exercise it. It was disagreeable to me, but I did exercise it; and no other power can be exercised in that country.' This, if it be true, is a plea in bar. But I trust and hope your lordships will not judge by laws and institutions which you do not know, against those laws and institutions which you do know, and under whose power and authority Mr Hastings went out to India. Can your lordships patiently hear what *we* have heard with indignation enough, and what, if there were nothing else, would call these principles, as well as the actions which are justified on such principles, to your lordships' bar, that it may be known whether the peers of England do not sympathize with the Commons in their detestation of such doctrine? Think of an English governor tried before you as a British subject, and yet declaring that he governed on the principles of arbitrary power! His plea is that he did govern there on arbitrary and despotic, and, as he supposes, oriental principles. And as this plea is boldly avowed and maintained, and as, no doubt, all his conduct was perfectly correspondent to these principles, the principles and the conduct must be tried together.

In these first two days of his opening speech, Burke laid down what he called 'the general grounds' of the charges against Hastings. The second two days dealt with particulars. One case raised by Burke on the third day has been a focus of adverse comment on his conduct of the impeachment. This was the case of Rajah Devi Singh, tax-farmer of

Rangpur. Burke came across it at a late stage of preparation of the impeachment. He first mentions it in a letter to Philip Francis on 3 January 1788. A note in the *Correspondence* establishes the background:

> This letter introduces one of the most controversial episodes in the impeachment: Burke's use of the reports of atrocities in the collection of revenue in Rangpur. Rangpur was a district in northern Bengal which, together with Dinajpur and Edrakpur, had been farmed in 1781 at a high assessment for which Raja Devi Singh was security. In February 1783 there were widespread disturbances in Rangpur against Devi Singh's collectors. John Paterson (d. 1809), a servant of the East India Company, was instructed by the Supreme Council to inquire into the causes of the unrest, and reported that it had been provoked by extortionate demands enforced by the use of torture, of which he provided lurid and detailed descriptions.

Writing to Francis, Burke shows himself determined to use the Paterson report on torture, but worried about how to use it: 'Oh! what an affair – I am clear that I must dilate upon that; for it has stuff in it that will, if anything, work upon the popular sense. But how to do this without making a monstrous and disproportioned member, I know not.'

On his third day in the Lords, Burke examined the system of extortion, the seizure of money and property: 'I come now to the last stage of their miseries,' he said. 'Everything visible and vendible was seized and sold. Nothing but the bodies remained.' Then he came to Paterson's report:

> And here, my lords, began such a scene of cruelties and tortures as I believe no history has ever presented to the indignation of the world – such as I am sure, in the most barbarous ages, no politic tyranny, no fanatic persecution, has ever yet exceeded. Mr Paterson, the commissioner appointed to enquire into the state of the country, makes his own apology and mine for opening this scene of horrors to you in the following words: 'That the punishments inflicted upon the riots, both of Rangpur and Dinajpur, for non-payment, were in many instances of such a nature that I would rather wish to draw a veil over them than shock your feelings by the detail, but that however disagreeable the task may be to myself, it is absolutely necessary, for the sake of justice, humanity, and the honour of government, that they should be exposed, to be prevented in future.'

My lords, they began by winding cords round the fingers of the unhappy freeholders of those provinces, until they clung to and were almost incorporated with one another; and then they hammered wedges of iron between them, until, regardless of the cries of the sufferers, they had bruised to pieces and forever crippled those poor, honest, innocent, laborious hands, which had never been raised to their mouths but with a penurious and scanty proportion of the fruits of their own soil; but those fruits (denied to the wants of their own children) have for more than fifteen years past furnished the investment for our trade with China, and been sent annually out, and without recompense, to purchase for us that delicate meal with which your lordships, and all this auditory, and all this country, have begun every day for these fifteen years at their expense. To those beneficent hands that labour for our benefit, the return of the British government has been cords and hammers and wedges. But there is a place where these crippled and disabled hands will act with resistless power. What is it that they will not pull down, when they are lifted to heaven against their oppressors? Then what can withstand such hands? Can the power that crushed and destroyed them? Powerful in prayer, let us at least deprecate and thus endeavour to secure ourselves from the vengeance which these mashed and disabled hands may pull down upon us. My lords, it is an awful consideration: let us think of it.

It might have been better if Burke had ceased his recital of torture there, at the end of that moving passage, leaving one atrocity to speak for all. He decided otherwise. He recited the catalogue of torture contained in the Paterson report, including details of revolting cruelties perpetrated in Rangpur against women. A contemporary account describes the impact of this recital on Burke himself, and on his audience: 'Here Mr B. leant his head upon his lap unable to proceed, so greatly was he oppressed by the horror which he felt at this relation. The effect of it was visible through the whole audience; a lady, who was in the Great Chamberlain's box, fainted away.' The eminent Shakespearean critic and editor Edmund Malone wrote to Lord Charlemont:

I suppose you have heard much of Burke's astonishing performance on the business of Hastings. I had the good fortune to hear him on the first, second and fourth day; but could not get a ticket on the third, when he gave so pathetic a description of the tortures that had been practised in India. All the papers have made sad stuff of his most delicate touches, on a point of so nice a nature that nothing but the most consummate art could have guarded him against ridicule.

Paterson's report had accused Devi Singh and his agents, not Hastings, but this was a distinction without a difference. Hastings had appointed Devi Singh tax-farmer in Rangpur. Devi Singh was part of the system of extortion headed by Hastings, and so were the tortures practised by his agents. It is true that a subsequent commission into what Paterson had reported found that 'the most dreadful of the cruelties stated in Mr Paterson's letter to have been exercised to enforce the payment of revenue ... have no existence'; but that commission had been set up by Hastings. It too was part of the system.

The relation of Devi Singh's fief to Hastings' empire is well established by a passage in the commission's conclusions concerning Richard Goodlad, the Company's – that is to say Hastings' – collector in Rangpur: 'Paterson's report alleged that Devi Singh's agents had collected an extortionate revenue by the use of torture, and that Richard Goodlad, the collector of Rangpur, had made no attempt to restrain them.' Goodlad defended himself by pleading ignorance, claiming that 'if this tyranny and extortion actually prevailed, no complaints were ever preferred to me to induce me to suspect it', and he was acquitted by the Supreme Council. With rather more candour, he admitted to another Company servant that 'had he gone out of his way to hear complaints, the collection of revenue from the district would have fallen short of the assessed total.' The Supreme Council which acquitted Goodlad was under Hastings' full control.

Hastings' own comprehensive verdict on the Rangpur affair was characteristic:

> I entirely acquit Mr Goodlad of all the charges: he has disproved them. It was the duty of the accuser to prove them. Whatever crimes may be established against Rajah Devi Sing, it does not follow that Mr Goodlad was responsible for them; and I so well know the character and abilities of Rajah Devi Sing, that I can easily conceive that it was in his power both to commit the enormities which are laid to his charge, and to conceal the grounds of them from Mr Goodlad, who had no authority but that of receiving the accounts and rents of the district from Rajah Devi Sing, and occasionally to be the channel of communication between him and the committee.

This passage was quoted by Burke on the fourth day of his speech. It was presumably because Hastings 'so well knew the character and abilities of Rajah Devi Singh' that he appointed him as tax-farmer in Rangpur. He intended such 'enormities' as he admits Devi Singh was capable of committing as the means of extorting the greatest possible sums from the people of Rangpur. The case of Devi Singh, then, was one of the best-documented examples of the workings of Hastings' system.

Finally, after four days of exposition, Burke summed up the significance of the impeachment, saying that he was committing 'the interests of India and of humanity' into the hands of the Lords.

> Therefore it is with confidence, that, ordered by the Commons,
> I impeach Warren Hastings Esquire of high crimes and misdemeanours.
> I impeach him in the name of the Commons of Great Britain in Parliament assembled, whose parliamentary trust he has betrayed.
> I impeach him in the name of all the Commons of Great Britain, whose national character he has dishonoured.
> I impeach him in the name of the people of India, whose laws, rights, and liberties he has subverted, whose properties he has destroyed, whose country he has laid waste and desolate.
> I impeach him in the name and by virtue of those eternal laws of justice which he has violated.
> I impeach him in the name of human nature itself, which he has cruelly outraged, injured, and oppressed, in both sexes, in every age, rank, situation, and condition of life.

The immediate reply was not promising. According to the *Parliamentary History*, the Lord Chancellor 'left the woolsack and opened his speech by pronouncing a very fine eulogium on Mr Burke, for his mode of opening his charges'. He then declared, 'I shall hold Mr Burke to the proof of all he has asserted', and ruled that 'the managers should complete the whole of their case before Mr Hastings said a word in his defence ... In the present impeachment, he trusted their lordships would not depart from the known established laws of the land.'

Thurlow had dealt Burke's cause two deadly blows. By ruling out any departure from 'the known established laws of the land', he had rejected the case for 'enlarged principles of state morality'; this made it virtually impossible to secure a conviction of Hastings on the basis of the known iniquities of his system of government. And by ruling that 'the managers should complete the whole of their case before Mr Hastings said a word in his defence', Thurlow was destroying Burke's hopes of arousing public opinion against Hastings. Without the drama of Hastings answering each charge as it was made, the public would lose interest in the case long before he came to make his general answer to the charges as a whole. Burke had now no real hope of success, but he was determined to do his duty.

The path he had now to tread was an increasingly lonely one. He soon became aware that Pitt's administration, while it had supported the principle of impeachment, would give little help. As Marshall writes, 'No member of the administration served on the committee, which meant that, for the first time since the Revolution of 1688, the crown law officers were not associated in the prosecution of an impeachment.'

Far from actively supporting the impeachment, the administration actually harassed its managers until 1790. As early as April 1788, the Treasury was complaining to Burke about the mounting costs. Burke replied:

> We conceive that justice for the people of India is an object which will warrant a large expense ... We know the attention that ought to be paid to the frugal expenditure of the public treasure, but we shall always steadily avow our opinion that some thousands of pounds from the many millions taken with so free and so strong an hand from the people of India are properly expended in an attempt to obtain justice for the injuries they have suffered.

Pitt, with his safe majority in the Commons, could have called off the impeachment at any time. Instead he let it drag on until 1795. His reasons for doing so are plain. It was consuming the time and talents of Burke and other opposition leaders, and diverting them from the Commons to the Lords. If Pitt had nipped the impeachment in the bud, he would have had Burke back in the Commons, attacking him for shielding corruption and oppression in India. It is unlikely that Pitt had forgotten his exposure during the Speech on the Nabob of Arcot's Debts, or that he wished for any repetition of that experience. When he supported the passage of the impeachment through the Commons, Pitt may have been moved by compassion for the Indians, but once it reached the Lords, his attitude was dictated by calculations of political expediency.

What was worse for Burke was that his own colleagues soon tired of the impeachment and became resentful of his commitment to it. On 20 November 1788, Georgiana, Duchess of Devonshire, noted in her diary: 'Sheridan, who is heartily tired of Hastings trial, and fearful of Burke's impetuosity, says that he wishes Hastings would run away and Burke after him.'

In May 1789, as a result of an expression used by Burke in the course of the impeachment, the Commons expressed its exasperation with him, and Burke rebuffed the censure of the House. The matter in hand was critically important; the Commons must either back him or dismiss him. In opening the sixth article – bribery and corruption – against Hastings, he summed up the fate of Nuncomar by saying that Hastings had 'murdered this man by the hands of Sir Elijah Impey'. Immediately, Hastings' agent in the Commons, Major Scott, petitioned the House to protect Hastings from allegations not included in any of the articles. Burke declined to take part in the subsequent Commons debate, which, he realized, would have cast him as a defendant. Instead he sent a letter to the House, to be read by Frederick Montagu. It is impressive and implacable:

The House having, upon an opinion of my diligence and fidelity (for they could have no other motive), put a great trust into my hands, ought to give me an entire credit for the veracity of every fact I affirm or deny; but if they fail with regard to me, it is at least in my power to be true to myself. I will not commit myself in an unbecoming contention with the agents of a criminal whom it is my duty to bring to justice ... I will not violate my trust by turning myself into a defendant, and bringing forward, in my own exculpation, the evidence which I have prepared for his conviction. I will not let him know on what documents I rely; I will not let him know who the witnesses for the prosecution are, nor what they have to depose against him. Though I have no sort of doubt of the constancy and integrity of those witnesses, yet because they are men, and men to whom, from my own situation, I owe protection, I ought not to expose them either to temptation or to danger. I will not hold them out to be importuned or menaced, or discredited, or run down, or possibly to be ruined in their fortunes, by the power and influence of this delinquent, except where the national service supersedes all other considerations. If I must suffer, I will suffer alone! . . .

The only favour I have to supplicate from the House is that their goodness would spare to the weakest of their Members any unnecessary labour by letting me know, as speedily as possible, whether they wish to discharge me from my present office. If they do not, I solemnly promise them that with God's assistance, I will, as a member of their committee, pursue their business to the end – that no momentary disfavour shall slacken my diligence in the great cause they have undertaken – that I will lay open, with the force of irresistible proof, this dark scene of bribery, peculation, and gross pecuniary corruption which I have begun to unfold, and in the midst of which my course has been arrested.

This poor Indian stratagem, of turning the accuser into a defendant, has been too often and too uniformly practised by Devi Sing, Mr Hastings, and Gunga Goom'd Sing, and other banyans [agents], black and white, to have any longer the slightest effect upon me, whom long service in Indian committees has made well acquainted with the politics of Calcutta . . .

I hope I have in no moment of this pursuit (now by me continued, in one shape or other, for near eight years) shown the smallest symptom of collusion or prevarication. The last point in which I should wish to show it is in this charge concerning pecuniary corruption – a corruption so great and so spreading, that the most unspotted characters will be justified in taking measures for guarding themselves against suspicion. Neither hope, nor fear, nor anger, nor weariness, nor discouragement of any kind, shall move me from this trust – nothing but an act of the House, formally taking away my commission or totally cutting off the means of performing it.

The Commons voted by 135 to 66 that the words complained of by Hastings' man 'should not have been spoken', but Pitt did not respond to Burke's challenge by calling on the parliamentary majority to discharge Burke from the management of the impeachment. Burke's party colleagues, led by Fox, had defended him quite warmly in the debate, as well as voting against the motion of censure. Fox said that Burke 'had done justice to God and man, and he deserved no censure'.

Facing the Lords, Burke did not so much apologize for using the word 'murdered' as reinforce it:

Your lordships do not imagine, I hope, that I used that word in any other than a moral and popular sense, or that I used it in the legal and technical sense of the word murder. Your lordships know that I could not bring before this bar any commoner of Great Britain on a charge for murder. I am not so ignorant of the laws and constitution of my country. I expressed an act which I conceived to be of an atrocious and evil nature, and partaking of some of the moral evil consequences of that crime. What led me into that error? Nine years' meditation upon that subject.

Burke knew that the impeachment could not be stopped in mid career. He had challenged Pitt on that point, and Pitt had drawn back. Many contemporaries found Burke's persistence absurd and futile, but if the welfare of the peoples of India is taken into consideration, his constancy of purpose, under adversity and ridicule, for fourteen years, has in it something of the sublime. He set out to establish a principle that was quite new in relation to the governance of India: that the servants of the East India Company, from highest to lowest, should be held accountable for their treatment of Indians. Until then no Company servant had ever been held so accountable. By holding Warren Hastings pinned at the bar of the House of Lords for nearly eight years, Burke established the principle of accountability in a way that nobody connected with the government of India, or of the empire generally, would ever forget. The ultimate acquittal did not erase the memory of the ordeal.

Hastings' successor, Lord Cornwallis, brought an end to the system of extortion that had prevailed for a quarter of a century of British rule in India. The beginning of the reform preceded the impeachment, but its impetus had been provided for the most part by Burke, from 1781 on, through the reports of his Select Committee, and the adoption of these by the Commons.

Only a Commons majority could terminate the mandate of the managers. Fox now wished to do so, but did not control a majority, and Burke, repenting of his former party constraints over India, was now indifferent to considerations of party – including the known wishes of his nominal leader. By the end of 1789, relations between the two men were clearly strained. Burke wrote to Philip Francis on 17 December of the 'desertion and treachery of friends' – aiming at Fox. The two had seen less of one another that year than formerly. This was partly due to the volume of work that Burke had undertaken, and partly a result of their divergence over the impeachment.

Burke wrote to Fox on 11 May 1789: 'It is unlucky that things are so circumstanced that we seldom can meet; and that, with us, an explanation cannot always follow on the heels of a misapprehension.' This was a careful fence-mending letter, written just after the crisis over his use of the word 'murdered'. If in the second half of 1789 their relations had been as cordial as before, they would have met and talked privately about the French Revolution as it flared. Had they done so, the quarrel – and the consequent split in the Whig party – might have been avoided. If Burke had been able to communicate to Fox his own misgivings over the revolution – at a stage when they were no more than misgivings – Fox's rising enthusiasm for it would have been significantly cooled, because of his immense respect for Burke. As it was, Fox had publicly committed himself before he was aware how Burke was thinking on the subject. And if Burke had not already been angry with Fox over India, he would have sought him out, for private remonstrance, at the first signs of Fox's enthusiasm for the French Revolution, manifested privately in November 1789 and publicly in February 1790. As it was, the old teacher publicly denounced his formerly beloved pupil, regarding him as doubly delinquent, over France and over India.

Burke had been committed to India since 1781, and by January 1790 he was committed to denouncing the French Revolution. He now saw Fox as opposing him over both, and was impelled by the elemental forces of his nature to thrust Fox aside so as to honour his commitments to India, to France, and, more obscurely, to Ireland.

V: France 1789–91

FIRST REACTION TO THE FRENCH REVOLUTION

The earliest known comment by Edmund Burke on the French Revolution is in a letter to Lord Charlemont of 9 August 1789:

> As to us here, our thoughts of everything at home are suspended by our astonishment at the wonderful spectacle which is exhibited in a neighbouring and rival country – what spectators, and what actors! England gazing with astonishment at a French struggle for liberty and not knowing whether to blame or to applaud! The thing indeed, though I thought I saw something like it in progress for several years, has still something in it paradoxical and mysterious. The spirit it is impossible not to admire; but the old Parisian ferocity has broken out in a shocking manner. It is true that this may be no more than a sudden explosion: if so no indication can be taken from it. But if it should be character rather than accident, then that people are not fit for liberty, and must have a strong hand like that of their former masters to coerce them. Men must have a certain fund of natural moderation to qualify them for freedom, else it become[s] noxious to themselves and a perfect nuisance to everybody else. What will be the event it is hard I think still to say. To form a solid constitution requires wisdom as well as spirit, and whether the French have wise heads among them, or if they possess such, whether they have authority equal to their wisdom, is to be seen; in the meantime the progress of this whole affair is one of the most curious matters of speculation that ever was exhibited.

By the end of the following month, Burke's negative view of the

Revolution had hardened. His friend William Windham (1750–1810), who was MP for Norwich and who visited Paris from mid August to 6 September, wrote to him on 15 September in an optimistic vein: 'What is said of the disorder and irregularity of the National Assembly has, I think, a great deal of exaggeration: at least, if a due consideration be had of all the circumstances. My prediction was (and accounts which I heard since my being there, have contributed to confirm it) that they would very soon become perfectly orderly.'

This expectation that things would settle down was widespread in the months immediately after the fall of the Bastille, especially among Burke's friends, the Whigs. It became still more general in 1790, a year of apparent tranquillity. Burke never shared it. In his reply to Windham, on 27 September, he civilly but firmly rejects his assessment:

That they should settle their constitution without much struggle, on paper, I can easily believe; because at present the interests of the Crown have no party, certainly no armed party, to support them; but I have great doubts whether any form of government which they can establish will procure obedience; especially obedience in the article of taxations. In the destruction of the old revenue constitution they find no difficulties – but with what to supply them is the opus. You are undoubtedly better able to judge; but it does not appear to me, that the National Assembly have one jot more power than the King; whilst they lead or follow the popular voice, in the subversion of all orders, distinctions, privileges, impositions, tythes, and rents, they appear omnipotent; but I very much question, whether they are in a condition to exercise any function of decided authority – or even whether they are possessed of any real deliberate capacity, or the exercise of free judgment in any point whatsoever, as there is a mob of their constituents ready to hang them if they should deviate into moderation, or in the least depart from the spirit of those they represent.

Here we find already the essentials of the view of the constitution-forming phase of the revolution that Burke was to develop in the following year in *Reflections on the Revolution in France*.

Ten days later an event occurred which suggested that Burke, not Windham, had been right. On 5 and 6 October, a crowd of 30,000 Parisians, men and women, marched to Versailles and forced their way into the palace shouting '*A Paris! A Paris!*' Louis XVI, prompted by

Lafayette, gave way, with the words: 'My friends, I shall go to Paris, with my wife and my children: it is to the love of my good and faithful subjects that I entrust my most precious possessions.' The Royal Family then made their way from Versailles to the Tuileries, in the midst of the crowd, which included women carrying pikes. The significance of the *journées* of 5 and 6 October is assessed by a modern French historian as follows: 'The sun had ceased to set at Versailles in the splendid isolation determined by Louis XIV. The October rain brought the King back to the Tuileries, which he was not to leave, except for prison, and then the scaffold.'

The news of the fateful *journées* reached Burke on 10 October. He wrote to his son Richard:

This day I heard from Laurence, who has sent me papers confirming the portentous state of France – where the elements which compose human society seem all to be dissolved, and a world of monsters to be produced in the place of it – where Mirabeau presides as the Grand Anarch; and the late Grand Monarch makes a figure as ridiculous as pitiable. I expect to hear of his dismissing the regiment he has called to his aid, for drinking his health, and [for] their listening to a French God Save the King, and that he has chosen a corps of Paris Amazons for his bodyguard.

On 4 November a young Parisian acquaintance of the Burkes, Charles-Jean-François Depont (1767–96), wrote Burke the letter to which *Reflections on the Revolution in France* was to be, in form, a reply. Depont asks for assurance 'that the French are worthy to be free; that they will know how to distinguish liberty from licence, and a legitimate government from a despotic power [and] that the revolution which has begun will succeed'. Burke's original reply – later greatly expanded to become the *Reflections* – is mild and judicious in tone, without any of the subsequent fierceness. In his letter, Depont had said he would never forget that his heart had beaten for the first time at the name of liberty 'when I heard you talk about it'. Burke takes this up:

Permit me then to continue our conversation, and to tell you what the freedom is that I love and that to which I think all men entitled. It is not solitary, unconnected, individual, selfish liberty. As if every man was to regulate the whole of his conduct by his own will. The liberty I mean is *social* freedom. It is that state of things in which liberty is secured by the equality of restraint; a constitution of things in which the liberty of no one man and no body of men and no number of men can find means to trespass on the liberty of any person or any description of persons in the society. This kind of liberty is indeed but another name for justice, ascertained by wise laws, and secured by well constructed institutions. I am sure that liberty, so incorporated, and in a manner identified, with justice must be infinitely dear to everyone who is capable of conceiving what it is. But whenever a separation is made between liberty and justice, neither is, in my opinion, safe . . .

When therefore I shall learn that in France the citizen, by whatever description he is qualified, is in a perfect state of legal security, with regard to his life, to his property, to the uncontrolled disposal of his person, to the free use of his industry and his faculties; – when I hear that he is protected in the beneficial enjoyment of the Estates to which, by the course of settled law, he was born, or is provided with a fair compensation for them; – that he is maintained in the full fruition of the advantages belonging to the state and condition of life in which he had lawfully engaged himself, or is supplied with a substantial, equitable equivalent; – when I am assured that a simple citizen may decently express his sentiments upon public affairs without hazard to his life or safety, even though against a predominant and fashionable opinion; when I know all this of France, I shall be as well pleased as everyone must be who has not forgot the general communion of mankind, nor lost his natural sympathy in local and accidental connections.

Burke addresses his young friend about his own future, in revolutionary times:

You are now to live in a new order of things; under a plan of government of which no man can speak from experience. Your talents, your public spirit, and your fortune give you fair pretensions to a considerable share in it. Your settlement may be at hand; but that it is still at some distance is more likely. The French may be yet to go through more transmigrations. They may pass, as one of our poets says, 'thro' many varieties of untried being' before their state obtains its final form. In that progress through chaos and darkness, you will find it necessary (at all times it is more or less so) to fix rules to keep your life and conduct in some steady course. You have theories enough concerning the rights of men. It may not be amiss to add a small degree of attention to their nature and disposition. It is with man in the concrete, it is with common human life and human actions you are to be concerned. I have taken so many liberties with you that I am almost got the length of venturing to suggest something which may appear in the assuming tone of advice. You will however be so good as to receive my very few hints with your usual indulgence, though some of them I confess are not in the taste of this enlightened age, and indeed are no better than the late ripe fruit of mere experience. – Never wholly separate in your mind the merits of any political question from the men who are concerned in it. You will be told, that if a measure is good, what have you [to] do with the character and views of those who bring it forward? But designing men never separate their plans from their interests; and if you assist them in their schemes, you will find the pretended good in the end thrown aside or perverted, and the interested object alone compassed, and that perhaps through your means. The power of bad men is no indifferent thing.

By the end of 1789, Burke had made up his mind about the character and probable future course of the French Revolution, 'through chaos and darkness'. But his emotions were not yet engaged, and he did not yet feel it incumbent upon him personally to oppose it. That engagement registers first in January 1790, in the closing sentences of a letter to an unknown correspondent: 'But so it is. I see some people here are willing that we should become their scholars too, and reform our state on the French model. They have begun; and it is high time for those who wish to preserve *morem majorum* [ancestral traditions], to look about them.'

Burke's decision to sound the alarm against English sympathizers with the French Revolution was reached in the third week of January, when he read a pamphlet containing the proceedings of the Revolution Society in the previous November. The Revolution Society was an old established body, consisting mainly of Dissenters, which existed to commemorate the English Revolution of 1688. The society met annually on 4 November, William III's birthday. The 1789 meeting was the first since the fall of the Bastille, and the participants used the occasion to celebrate and extol the French Revolution. The proceedings consisted of a sermon by a well-known dissenting minister, the Rev. Richard Price; a resolution carried by the society; a dinner in the London Tavern, and an address sent to the National Assembly. In the *Reflections*, Burke concentrates on Price's sermon, but it was the pamphlet as a whole that inflamed him. The pamphlet firmly placed the British welcome for the French Revolution in a context of anti-Popery. The resolution carried by the Revolution Society at the London Tavern on the evening following Price's sermon ran:

> This society, sensible of the important advantages arising to this country by its deliverance from Popery and arbitrary power, and conscious that, under God, we owe that signal blessing to the revolution which seated our deliverer King William the Third on the throne, do hereby declare our firm attachment to the civil and religious principles which were recognized and established by that glorious event and which have preserved the succession in the Protestant line; and our determined resolution to maintain and, to the utmost of our power, to perpetuate, those blessings to the latest posterity.

Price also moved the congratulatory address to the National Assembly in Paris, which was duly carried, conveyed to the Assembly, and warmly welcomed there.

Thus, a society set up to celebrate the English Revolution of 1688 was emphasizing the anti-Catholic character of that revolution and welcoming the French Revolution, which had already assumed an anti-Catholic character, notably through the annexation of church property in November 1789. Burke was bound to be alarmed, and it didn't help that Dr Price was a protégé of Lord Shelburne (who by now was Marquess of Lansdowne), whom Burke suspected of having fomented the Gordon Riots. Burke's feelings about what he read of the excesses of the Paris revolutionary mob in 1789 blended, in his imagination, with his still vivid memories of that London Protestant mob of nine years before. In his writing and speeches on the French Revolution, Burke frequently refers to the Gordon Riots. Nor was it entirely an imagined association. The London Corresponding Society, which has been described as 'the most active, the most extreme and the best organized' of the pro-Jacobin societies, was founded by a Scot named Thomas Hardy, a disciple of Lord George Gordon. Lord George himself is said to have sung the French revolutionary hymn *Ça Ira!* in Newgate Prison immediately before he died on 1 November 1793. The link between Protestant zealotry and British zeal for the French Revolution was real.

The language of the resolution carried by the society reminded Burke of just how anti-Catholic the Glorious Revolution, which he revered, had actually been. It made his Jacobite ancestors walk, and reproach him for having betrayed his people. As over India, nine years earlier, with similar forces in operation, the inner conflict released tremendous psychic energies, urging Burke on in a passionate commitment to another cause: France, as well as India, with Ireland as ultimate driving force. Burke had sound intellectual reasons for the positions he adopted over both India and France, and set them out cogently. Furthermore, he opposed the French Revolution on intellectual grounds before his emotions became involved. But the element of the obsessive, discerned by contemporaries in the passion and pertinacity of his commitment in both cases, owes much to an intense internal conflict over his Irish loyalties.

Anti-Catholicism was the aspect of the French Revolution that made the greatest emotional impact on him, but he did not wish to emphasize this in controversy. He knew only too well that many Englishmen were well disposed towards the revolution precisely because of its anti-Catholicism. So in his campaign against the revolution he stressed what he called its atheism. Burke knew, of course, that almost all the revolutionary leaders regarded themselves – or at least presented themselves – as deists, not atheists, but he chose not to observe this distinction. In his eyes it was a distinction without a difference. People who denied all revealed religion and mocked all churches were as bad as atheists. And it was effective in a controversy to call the revolutionaries atheists. That made them uncomfortable company for preachers such as Dr Price.

Immediately after contemplating the Revolution Society's proceedings, he set out to expand the letter to Depont into his greatest tract, *Reflections on the Revolution in France*, which was published the following November. In the meantime he took the earliest opportunity to make a parliamentary statement, strongly hostile to the revolution. The leader of the Whigs, Charles James Fox, had been gushing with enthusiasm for the revolution ever since the news of the fall of the Bastille reached England. 'How much the greatest event it is that has ever happened in the world and how much the best!' Fox had written in a letter, with sublime confidence, on 30 July 1789. Burke can hardly have known of that particular expression of enthusiasm for the revolution, but the enthusiasm itself was known to the whole political world. Burke now fired a warning shot across the bows of his leader in the Commons.

The debate in which Burke made his first parliamentary statement on the revolution was on the army estimates in early February 1790, a little less than seven months after the fall of the Bastille. Burke spoke, as was usually his way, late in the debate, on the second day (9 February) after Fox and Pitt had each spoken twice. Declaring his uncompromising and comprehensive hostility to the revolution, and his fears about British friendship towards it, Burke said:

The French had shown themselves the ablest architects of ruin that had hitherto existed in the world. In that very short space of time they had completely pulled down to the ground, their monarchy, their Church, their nobility, their law, their revenue, their army, their navy, their commerce, their arts and their manufactures. Our friendship and our intercourse with that nation had once been, and might again become more dangerous to us than their worst hostility.

Fox had applauded the extension of revolutionary citizenship to the soldiers of the French army. Now, gently but gravely, Burke remonstrated with him, and revealed that the strength of his hostility to the revolution was so great that it could lead to a breach between him and the Whigs:

He was sorry that his right hon. friend [Mr Fox] had dropped even a word expressive of exultation on that circumstance, or that he seemed of opinion that the objection from standing armies was at all lessened by it. That it was with a pain inexpressible he was obliged to have even the shadow of a difference with his friend, whose authority would be always great with him, and with all thinking people. That the House must perceive, from his coming forward to mark an expression or two of his best friend, how anxious he was to keep the distemper of France from the least countenance in England, where he was sure some wicked persons had shown a strong disposition to recommend an imitation of the French spirit of reform. He was so strongly opposed to even the least tendency towards the means of introducing a democracy like theirs, as well as to the end itself, that much as it would affect him if such a thing could be attempted and that any friend of his could concur in such measures (he was far, very far, from believing they could), he would part with his best friends and join with his worst enemies to oppose either the means or the end; and to resist all violent exertions of the spirit of innovation, so distinct from all principles of true and safe reformation; a spirit well calculated to overturn states, but perfectly unfit to amend them.

Fox seems to have been altogether unprepared for this, for he rose, according to the *Parliamentary History*, 'with a concern of mind which it was almost impossible to describe'. He acknowledged his immense intellectual indebtedness to Burke, and went on: 'Never would he lend himself to support any cabal or scheme, formed in order to introduce any dangerous innovation into our excellent constitution.' Burke accepted this olive branch with a civility within which we can sense a degree of reserve: 'What he said had drawn from his right hon. friend an explanation [no less] satisfactory to his mind than he was persuaded it was to the House and to all who heard it.'

Such reconciliation as there was, however, was immediately marred by an intervention by Sheridan, the next in eminence at this time to Fox and Burke among the Whig leaders. Sheridan said that he felt it 'a duty to declare that he differed decidedly from his right hon. friend in almost every word that he uttered respecting the French Revolution'. Burke curtly replied that 'henceforth his hon. friend [Sheridan] and himself were separated in politics.'

Pitt wound up the debate by declaring that 'he agreed with Mr Burke in every point he had urged relative to the late commotions in France.'

Burke remained, formally, a member of the parliamentary opposition and a follower of Fox for more than a year after that exchange. But he was no longer at home, politically or spiritually, in the party of Fox and Sheridan. For Burke, the difference over the revolution in France nullified the remaining areas of agreement. The enormous dangers stemming from the revolution changed the priorities of British politics. As far as Burke was concerned, the dour struggle that he and his friends had waged against the influence of the Crown ever since 1766 was now over. The new threat to the very existence of all monarchy made it necessary for true friends of the British constitution to abate their criticisms of George III.

Burke quietly gave notice of this shift in his priorities in an intervention on 10 March 1790, a month after his first challenge to Fox. He took an opportunity – a rather tenuous one, in terms of parliamentary procedure – to raise the matter of Dunning's resolution in favour of diminishing the power of the Crown: 'He was well known not only to have taken a part in laying down the principle stated in the resolution in question, but to have acted upon it in more than one instance.' Burke then added: 'That the resolution did not apply at present in anything like the proportion it had applied at the time it was voted.' He was giving notice that the French Revolution had already taken him out of the ranks of active opposition.

REFLECTIONS

The grand distinguishing feature of the *Reflections* is the power of Burke's insight into the character of the French Revolution, which was then at an early stage. This insight was so acute as to amount to a prophetic power. He saw where the revolution was heading, as no one else seems to have done at the time. The spring and summer of 1790, the period in which Burke wrote the *Reflections*, was apparently the most tranquil stage of the revolution. It was a period of constitution-making, of benevolent rhetoric and of peaceful jubilation, as in the Déclaration de Paix au Monde of 21 May 1790 or the Fête de la Fédération on 14 July 1790, celebrating the first anniversary of the fall of the Bastille. Contemplating that attractive scene, most people seem to have assumed that the revolution had finished, and that all that remained was to reap its benign consequences. Burke, however, sensed that the revolution was only beginning. In the penultimate paragraph of the *Reflections*, he repeated his warning to Depont that the French 'commonwealth' could hardly remain in the form it had taken in 1790, 'but before its final settlement it may be obliged to pass, as one of our poets says, "through great varieties of untried being", and in all its transmigrations to be purified by fire and blood'.

The most terrible events of the revolution – the September Massacres, the Terror, the executions of the King and Queen – all lay in the future when the *Reflections* was written and published. And yet they seem already to be present in it, in the ferocious dynamic which Burke ascribes to the revolution and which became visible to the world in those events of 1792–94. Burke foresaw not only 'transmigrations, fire and blood', but how they would end in military despotism:

> It is known that armies have hitherto yielded a very precarious and uncertain obedience to any senate or popular authority; and they will least of all yield it

to an Assembly which is to have only a continuance of two years ... In the weakness of one kind of authority, and in the fluctuation of all, the officers of an army will remain for some time mutinous and full of faction, until some popular general, who understands the art of conciliating the soldiery, and who possesses the true spirit of command, shall draw the eyes of all men upon himself. Armies will obey him on his personal account. There is no other way of securing military obedience in this state of things. But the moment in which that event shall happen, the person who really commands the army is your master; the master (that is little) of your King, the master of your Assembly, the master of your whole republic.

The seizure of power by Napoleon Bonaparte – the event predicted in this remarkable passage – occurred on 9 November 1799, nine years after the publication of the *Reflections* and more than two years after the death of the author.

Burke's astonishing capacity to see how events were moving derived from penetrating powers of observation, judicious inference from what was observed, and thorough analysis of what was discerned by observation and inference. He had immense respect for circumstances, and observed them with proportionate attentiveness. There is a passage about circumstances, in relation to liberty, very near the beginning of the *Reflections*, which is fundamental to Burke's political thinking generally. He is referring to the congratulations conveyed by the English Revolution Society to the French National Assembly in November 1789 on France's achievement of liberty:

I flatter myself that I love a manly, moral, regulated liberty as well as any gentleman of [the Revolution] Society, be he who he will; and perhaps I have given as good proofs of my attachment to that cause, in the whole course of my public conduct. I think I envy liberty as little as they do, to any other nation. But I cannot stand forward, and give praise or blame to any thing which relates to human actions, and human concerns, on a simple view of the object, as it stands, stripped of every relation, in all the nakedness and solitude of metaphysical abstraction. Circumstances (which with some gentlemen pass for nothing) give in reality to every political principle its distinguishing colour and discriminating effect. The circumstances are what render every civil and political scheme beneficial or noxious to mankind. Abstractedly speaking, government, as well as liberty, is good; yet could I, in common sense, ten years ago, have felicitated France on her enjoyment of a government (for she then had a government) without enquiry what the nature of that government was, or how it was administered? Can I now congratulate the same nation upon its freedom? Is it because liberty in the abstract may be classed amongst the blessings of mankind that I am seriously to felicitate a madman who has escaped from the protecting restraint and wholesome darkness of his cell on his restoration to the enjoyment of light and liberty? Am I to congratulate an highwayman and murderer who has broke prison, upon the recovery of his natural rights? This would be to act over again the scene of the criminals condemned to the galleys, and their heroic deliverer, the metaphysic Knight of the Sorrowful Countenance.

When I see the spirit of liberty in action, I see a strong principle at work; and this, for a while, is all I can possibly know of it. The wild *gas*, the fixed air is plainly broke loose: but we ought to suspend our judgment until the first effervescence is a little subsided, till the liquor is cleared, and until we see something deeper than the agitation of a troubled and frothy surface. I must be tolerably sure, before I venture publicly to congratulate men upon a blessing, that they have really received one. Flattery corrupts both the receiver and the giver; and adulation is not of more service to the people than to kings. I should therefore suspend my congratulations on the new liberty of France, until I was informed how it had been combined with government; with public force; with the discipline and obedience of armies; with the collection of an effective and well-distributed revenue; with morality and religion; with the solidity of property; with peace and order; with civil and social manners. All these (in their way) are good things too; and, without them, liberty is not a benefit whilst it lasts, and is not likely to continue long. The effect of liberty to individuals is that they may do what they please: We ought to see what it will please them to do, before we risk congratulations, which may be soon turned into complaints. Prudence would dictate this in the case of separate insulated private men; but liberty, when men act in bodies, is *power*. Considerate people, before they declare themselves, will observe the use which is made of *power*; and particularly of so trying a thing as *new* power in *new* persons, of whose principles, tempers, and dispositions, they have little or no experience, and in situations where those who appear the most stirring in the scene may possibly not be the real movers.

Burke's passionate indignation against the French Revolution – and above all against any attempt to imitate it in the British Isles – is evident in the *Reflections*, sustains it, and is the source of a part of its force. There is an emotional undercurrent throughout, and when it occasionally breaks through to the surface, the rhetoric is spectacular. The most spectacular passage – about the Queen of France as Burke saw her in 1773 – has been quoted far more than anything else in the book, and repetition of this has created the misleading impression that the *Reflections* consist mostly of gorgeous rhetoric. Yet for all its impact, there is actually very little rhetoric. Most of the book is made up of plain and cogent argument. Passion is present, but Burke keeps it under control, except on rare deliberate occasions. When it is evident, it is used to reinforce the rational, for Burke is convinced that the revolution in France is defective both in reason and in feeling.

'But it seems', he writes, 'as if it were the prevalent opinion in Paris, that an unfeeling heart, and an undoubting confidence are the sole qualifications for a perfect legislator.' This is a crucial insight, relevant to Burke's approach to Ireland, America, India and France. Burke sees over-confidence of decision-makers as necessarily cruel in its consequences. In combating the Protestant ascendancy in Ireland, the taxers and punishers of the American colonists, the extortionist rulers of India and finally the Jacobins, Burke was fighting a long war, on changing fronts, against the arrogance of power.

By the second half of 1790, the atrocities that had accompanied the first phase of the revolution, between July and October 1789, were fading from memory. The Whigs and radicals glossed over them as transient episodes in the early history of a revolution of which the generally benign character seemed well established in 1790. Burke, on the other hand, regarded these atrocities as inherent in the revolution and indicative of its future course. So Burke recalled a day which the Whigs would prefer to forget, the *journées révolutionnaires*, 6 and 7 October 1789:

History will record that on the morning of the 6th of October 1789, the King and Queen of France, after a day of confusion, alarm, dismay, and slaughter, lay down, under the pledged security of public faith, to indulge nature in a few hours of respite, and troubled melancholy repose. From this sleep the Queen was first startled by the voice of the sentinel at her door, who cried out to her to save herself by flight – that this was the last proof of fidelity he could give – that they were upon him, and he was dead. Instantly he was cut down. A band of cruel ruffians and assassins, reeking with his blood, rushed into the chamber of the Queen, and pierced with an hundred strokes of bayonets and poniards the bed from whence this persecuted woman had but just time to fly, almost naked, and through ways unknown to the murderers had escaped to seek refuge at the feet of a King and husband not secure of his own life for a moment.

This King, to say no more of him, and this Queen and their infant children (who once would have been the pride and hope of a great and generous people) were then forced to abandon the sanctuary of the most splendid palace in the world, which they left swimming in blood, polluted by massacre and strewed with scattered limbs and mutilated carcases. Thence they were conducted into the unprovoked, unresisted, promiscuous slaughter which was made of the gentlemen of birth and family who composed the King's bodyguard. These two gentlemen, with all the parade of an execution of justice, were cruelly and publicly dragged to the block, and beheaded in the great court of the palace. Their heads were stuck upon spears and led the procession, whilst the royal captives who followed in the train were slowly moved along, amidst the horrid yells and shrilling screams, and frantic dances, and infamous contumelies and all the unutterable abominations of the furies of hell in the abused shape of the vilest of women. After they had been made to taste, drop by drop, more than the bitterness of death, in the slow torture of a journey of twelve miles, protracted to six hours, they were, under a guard composed of those very soldiers who had thus conducted them through this famous triumph, lodged in one of the old palaces of Paris now converted into a Bastille for kings.

This narration is the prelude to the most famous passage in all of Burke's writings:

It is now sixteen or seventeen years since I saw the Queen of France, then the Dauphiness, at Versailles; and surely never lighted on this orb, which she hardly seemed to touch, a more delightful vision. I saw her just above the horizon, decorating and cheering the elevated sphere she just began to move in, – glittering like the morning-star, full of life, and splendour, and joy. Oh! what a revolution! and what an heart must I have, to contemplate without emotion that elevation and that fall! Little did I dream when she added titles of veneration to those of enthusiastic, distant, respectful love, that she should ever be obliged to carry the sharp antidote against disgrace concealed in that bosom; little did I dream that I should have lived to see such disasters fallen upon her in a nation of gallant men, in a nation of men of honour and of cavaliers. I thought ten thousand swords must have leaped from their scabbards to avenge even a look that threatened her with insult. – But the age of chivalry is gone. – That of sophisters, economists, and calculators, has succeeded; and the glory of Europe is extinguished for ever. Never, never more, shall we behold that generous loyalty to rank and sex, that proud submission, that dignified obedience, that subordination of the heart which kept alive, even in servitude itself, the spirit of an exalted freedom. The unbought grace of life, the cheap defence of nations, the nurse of manly sentiment and heroic enterprise is gone! It is gone, that sensibility of principle, that chastity of honour, which felt a stain like a wound, which inspired courage whilst it mitigated ferocity, which ennobled whatever it touched, and under which vice itself lost half its evil, by losing all its grossness.

This passage was written at a fairly early stage in the composition of the *Reflections*, and in the white heat of the emotions aroused in Burke by his discovery of the proceedings of the Revolution Society. The reasoned arguments which make up most of the book were probably the products of later stages of composition. In February 1790, Burke sent 'the manuscript draft and the proofs for the early part of the work' to Philip Francis. From Francis's reply, dated 19 February, we know that the draft and proofs already contained the romantic passage about the Queen. Burke had asked for Francis's critical comments. He got them:

Waiving all discussion concerning the substance and general tendency of this printed letter, I must declare my opinion that what I have seen of it is very loosely put together. In point of writing at least, the manuscript you showed me first was much less exceptionable. Remember that this is one of the most singular, that it may be the most distinguished and ought to be one of the most deliberate acts of your life. Your writings have hitherto been the delight and instruction of your own country. You now undertake to correct and instruct another nation, and your appeal in effect is to all Europe. Allowing you the liberty to do so in an extreme case, you cannot deny that it ought to be done with special deliberation in the choice of the topics, and with no less care and circumspection in the use you make of them. Have you thoroughly considered whether it be worthy of Mr Burke, of a Privy Counsellor, of a man so high and considerable in the House of Commons as you are, and holding the station you have obtained in the opinion of the world, to enter into a war of pamphlets with Doctor Price? . . . In my opinion all that you say of the Queen is pure foppery. If she be a perfect female character you ought to take your ground upon her virtues. If she be the reverse it is ridiculous in any but a lover to place her personal charms in opposition to her crimes. Either way I know the argument must proceed upon a supposition; for neither have you said anything to establish her moral merits, nor have her accusers formally tried and convicted her of guilt.

Francis's brusquely negative reaction was not limited to the passage about the Queen. He ended his letter by calling on Burke – in the rather painfully jocular tone which had characterized much of the correspondence between these two men – to abandon the whole enterprise which was to become the *Reflections*:

Look back, I beseech you and deliberate a little, before you determine that this is an office that perfectly becomes you. If I stop here it is not for want of a multitude of objections. The mischief you are going to do yourself is, to my apprehension, palpable. It is visible. It will be audible. I snuff it in the wind. I taste it already. I feel it in every sense and so will you hereafter when I *vow to God* (a most elegant phrase) it will be no sort of consolation to me to reflect that I did everything in my power to prevent it. I wish you were at the De—l for giving me all this trouble. And so farewell.

Burke was deeply hurt by Francis's letter, which he answered on the following day. He was especially hurt by Francis's reaction to the passage about the Queen:

I tell you again that the recollection of the manner in which I saw the Queen of France in the year 1774 [actually 1773] and the contrast between that brilliancy, splendour, and beauty, with the prostrate homage of a nation to her, compared with the abominable scene of 1789 which I was describing did draw tears from me and wetted my paper. These tears came again into my eyes almost as often as I looked at the description. They may again. You do not believe this fact, or that these are my real feelings, but that the whole is affected, or as you express it, 'downright foppery'. My friend, I tell you it is truth – and that it is true, and will be true, when you and I are no more, and will exist as long as men with their natural feelings exist. I shall say no more on this foppery of mine.

Burke, as we might expect, was altogether unshaken in his determination to persevere in his enterprise: 'But I intend no controversy with Dr Price or Lord Shelburne or any other of their set. I mean to set in a full view the danger from their wicked principles and their black hearts; I intend to state the true principles of our constitution in Church and state – upon grounds opposite to theirs.' The letter ends: 'Believe me always sensible of your friendship; though it is impossible that a greater difference can exist on earth between any sentiments on those subjects than unfortunately for me there is between yours and mine.'

Francis did not reply; but immediately after the book was published, on 1 November 1790, he sent Burke his comments in a letter that put him, for Burke, in the ranks of the enemy. Burke's reply, dated 19 November, is the end of a strained friendship, within a genuine alliance, which had subsisted between them for eight years.

> Your paper has much more the character of a piece in an adverse controversy carried on before the tribunal of the nation at large, than of the animadversion of a friend on his friend's performance ... All that you have said against the despotism of monarchies, you must be sensible that I have heard a thousand times before, though certainly not so neatly and sharply expressed ... I decline controversy with you; because I feel myself overmatched in a competition with such talents as yours.

It seems likely that Burke is here telling Francis that he knows him to be Junius, and does not hold Junius in particularly high esteem.

At the end of his letter, Burke indicates the terms on which he wishes his relations with Francis to be conducted for the future. 'These are opinions I have not lightly formed, or that I can lightly quit. Therefore let us end here all discussion on the subject. There is another, on which I have the happiness of more agreement with you.' In short, the two were to remain allies over Warren Hastings, but no more than allies.

It is rather surprising that Francis swallowed the rebuff, and continued the relationship within the terms laid down by Burke. He had been put in his place, and accepted that. This seems out of character. Both as Junius and as the avenger of Nuncomar, Francis had been vindictiveness personified. His meekness when reproved by Burke is therefore remarkable. It is true that he had an interest in continuing the alliance against Hastings, but even after Burke had snubbed him over the *Reflections*, Francis wrote about him with a deep respect such as he is never known to have accorded to any other human being whom he knew personally. Referring to the Ninth Report of the Select Committee on India, he wrote, in April 1791:

> As to the Ninth Report, which is indeed a masterpiece of human wisdom, the fact is I wrote a very small part of it, and, as to the composition, corrected the whole.
>
> On memory only, and speaking without book, I think I can say with truth that there is not one material principle or deduction in it which may not be fairly and honestly traced back to some antecedent opinions of my own, dilated on and expanded by a superior power. In some respect I am the acorn. But, if you want to see the oak in all its beauty, dignity, and strength, read the Ninth Report, the sole undoubted property of the commanding mastermind of Edmund Burke.
>
> It is true he sucked the saccharine juices out of all vegetation, even from such a wild weed as myself, and turned it to his purpose; but he alone was the wonderful artificer who made the wax, the comb and the honey.

Not least among the remarkable achievements of Edmund Burke was the taming of Junius.

Burke had expected 'the miscreants' of the pro-Jacobin faction to 'darken the air with their arrows' when the *Reflections* appeared, and they did. Among the many pamphlets attacking the book were Mary Wollstonecraft's *A Vindication of The Rights of Man* (1790) and Thomas Paine's *The Rights of Man* (1791–92), which was by far the most successful, in popular readership and acclaim. Another was *Vindiciae Gallicae* (1791) by James Mackintosh, who at this time thought little of Burke's arguments, but was impressed by the resourcefulness of his rhetoric:

> He can cover the most ignominious retreat by a brilliant allusion. He can parade his arguments with masterly generalship where they are strong. He can escape from an intolerable position into a splendid declamation. He can sap the most impregnable conviction by pathos and put to flight a host of

syllogisms with a sneer. Absolved from all the laws of vulgar method, he can advance a group of magnificent horrors to make a breach in our hearts, through which the most undisciplined rabble of arguments may enter in triumph.

But like many another, Mackintosh had his early admiration for the French Revolution completely dispelled by the events of 1792–94, and by the end of the decade he had completely reversed his judgment and come to see the magnificence of Burke's rhetoric as concealing not the weakness but the force of his arguments. According to the Mackintosh of 1799, Burke 'is only not esteemed the most severe and sagacious of reasoners, because he was the most eloquent of men, the perpetual force and vigour of his arguments being hid from vulgar observation by the dazzling glories in which they were enshrined'.

THE QUARREL WITH FOX, APRIL–MAY 1791

Burke decided from the beginning to ignore extra-parliamentary attacks on his book by radical 'miscreants'. His concern was with reactions among the parliamentary Whigs, to whom he still nominally belonged. For nearly six months there were no clear public developments among the Whigs that called for a reaction on Burke's part. Most Whigs disapproved of the *Reflections*, but there seems to have been a tacit agreement to avoid public discussion of the book. Still, there was a question that would not go away: could the author of the *Reflections* remain in a party that was led by an enthusiast for the French Revolution?

It was Fox himself who precipitated Burke's negative answer, in a Commons debate on 15 April 1791, recorded in the *Parliamentary History*:

Now that the situation of France had altered, that she had erected a government from which neither insult nor injustice was to be dreaded by her neighbours, he was extremely indifferent concerning the balance of power. With regard to the change of system that had taken place in that country, Mr Fox said that he knew different opinions were entertained on that point by different men, and added that he for one admired the new Constitution of France, taken together, as the most stupendous and glorious edifice of liberty which had been erected on the foundation of human integrity in any time or country.

(As it happened, the Constitution that Fox so admired was to be unceremoniously scrapped by the revolutionaries themselves in the following year, but Fox continued to eulogize the revolution even without that 'most stupendous and glorious edifice'.)

'As soon as Mr Fox sat down, Mr Burke rose, in much visible emotion, but the cry of "Question" being general, he unwillingly gave way to the division which immediately after took place.' According to a footnote to the record, 'Mr Fox is known to have regretted the injudicious zeal of those who would not suffer Mr Burke to answer him on the spot. The contention, he said, might have been fiercer and hotter, but the remembrance of it would not have settled so deep, nor rankled so long in the heart.'

It probably would not have made any substantial difference. It is hard to believe that Fox, when he produced – on the floor of the House, in Burke's presence – that effusion of superlatives about the French Constitution, did not intend to drive Burke from the party. The intention may not have been fully conscious (and Fox's subsequent conduct suggests that it was not), but it must have been active. Fox knew how strongly Burke felt, and a breach had been threatened in February of the previous year. In the circumstances, and after the publication of the *Reflections*, Fox's extravagant praise of the French Constitution was an intolerable provocation. Fox may have begun to resent Burke's intellectual and moral ascendancy over him at the time when it had cost him and the party dear over the East India Bill, and it seems that now, egged on by Sheridan, he was in revolt against that ascendancy.

Because Fox retained much of his old affection and veneration for Burke, it was a painful revolt, but he persisted, through a sustained parliamentary struggle. It began with Fox's provocation of 15 April, and continued through three further days of parliamentary debate, 21 April, 6 May and 11 May. The drama was the greater because the antagonists were two of the three greatest debaters of the period (the third being Pitt). And in a parliamentary duel between champions of debate, it was difficult for either to give way.

The business before the House on 21 April was the Quebec Bill. Burke saw an opportunity to discuss the French Revolution, on the rather tenuous pretext that Quebec, being a French-speaking province, might conceivably be offered the new French Constitution. Fox tried in vain to dissuade him from raising the subject, perhaps now hoping to avoid the breach he had already provoked. The two men walked to Westminster and entered the House together.

Fox began the debate by saying that 'when the Bill came again to be discussed, from the great respect which he entertained for some of his friends, he should be extremely sorry to differ from them, but he should never be backward in delivering his opinion, and he did not wish to recede from anything which he had formerly advanced.' Burke's reply was measured, but unyielding.

Mr Burke said he did not wish to call forth public opinion unnecessarily, or to provoke a debate with the right hon. gentleman, because he was his friend, and so he wished to consider him, but his principles were even dearer to him than his friendship. He did not wish to meet his friend as his adversary and antagonist. If it should so happen that he must defend his principles he would do it; though it would distress his body and mind to think that he and his friend must have that difference. He thought when he rose before, he had spoken guardedly. He did not know whether anything which he said had occasioned the remarks which had been made. His opinions on government he thought, were not unknown: the more he had considered the French Revolution, the more sorry he was to see it. On the 12th of February [actually 9 February 1790] he had thought it necessary to speak his opinion very fully on the French Revolution but since that time he had never mentioned it [in the Commons] either directly or indirectly; no man, therefore could charge him with having provoked the conversation that had passed.

Burke seems to imply here that he believed that the discussion of 9 February had been followed by an implicit parliamentary truce between Fox and himself. Fox was free to say what he liked about the revolution outside Parliament, and Burke was free to write about it. But the two men could work together as members of the same parliamentary party only if the topic on which they were so strongly opposed was avoided within the walls of Parliament. And there was no present difficulty about avoiding it, for there was no mention of the revolution on the parliamentary agenda for 1791. France and England were still at peace.

To bring the subject up in debate that year, MPs had to drag it into discussion of some other topic. Fox had done this first, by dragging it into a debate about Russia, on 15 April. Burke now retaliated by dragging it into the debate on Quebec, on 21 April.

Burke was not alone in believing that there should be a parliamentary truce over the French Revolution unless the business of the House should require otherwise. A Member spoke in that sense at the outset of the debate of 21 April. 'Mr Powys complained that the debate had turned irregularly both in retrospect [15 April] and anticipation [21 April], and hinted that Mr Fox should have imitated the example of Mr Burke, in writing, rather than speaking there in the House of Commons of the French Revolution.' So it is clear from the record that it was Fox, not Burke, who had initiated the parliamentary quarrel over the French Revolution.

Burke ended his speech on a conciliatory note towards Fox personally, but without any concessions of principle:

He thought it right to say that it was his intention to give his opinion on certain principles of government at the proper moment in the future progress of the Bill. Whether they should agree or disagree, the debate on the Bill, whenever it came, would show; but he believed he was most likely to coincide in sentiment with the other side of the House. Mr Burke said he did not believe his right hon. friend did mean the other night to allude offensively to the affairs of France, though at the moment he had thought it necessary to rise and make some observations which accident prevented.

This exchange of 21 April was a prelude only: the substantive and decisive debate came on 6 May, when the House resumed discussion of the Quebec Bill. Burke used that Bill as a pretext for a frontal assault on the French Constitution that Fox had unreservedly extolled:

Were we to give [the people of Quebec] the French Constitution – a constitution founded on principles dramatically opposed to ours, that could not assimilate with it on a single point: as different from it as wisdom from folly, as vice from virtue, as the most opposite extremes in nature – a constitution founded on what was called the rights of man? As soon as this system arrived among [the French], Pandora's box, replete with every mortal evil, seemed to fly open, hell itself to yawn, and every demon of mischief to overspread the face of the earth. [In Haiti] blacks rose against whites, whites against blacks, and each against one another in murderous hostility; subordination was destroyed, the bonds of society torn asunder, and every man seemed to thirst for the blood of his neighbour.

> Black spirits and white
> Blue spirits and grey
> Mingle, mingle, mingle.

All was toil and trouble, discord and blood, from the moment that this doctrine was promulgated among them; and he verily believed that wherever the rights of man were preached, such ever had been and ever would be the consequences.

France, who had generously sent them the precious gift of the rights of man, did not like this image of herself reflected in her child, and sent out a body of troops, well seasoned too with the rights of man, to restore order and obedience. These troops, as soon as they arrived, instructed as they are in the principle of government, felt themselves bound to become parties in the general rebellions and, like most of their brethren at home began asserting their rights by cutting off the head of their general. Ought this example to induce us to send to our colonies a cargo of the rights of man? As soon would he send them a bale of infected cotton from Marseilles.

Burke looked on the French Constitution 'not with approbation but with horror, as involving every principle to be detested, and pregnant with every consequence to be dreaded and abominated'. He and Fox were now in absolute opposition to one another on a specific point: the French Constitution of 1790–91. The clash of principles was irreparable. Personally, however, they had so far treated one another with respect. But now in reply to Burke's fierce attack on the French Constitution, Fox resorted to sarcasm, which envenomed the debate.

Mr Fox thought his right hon. friend could hardly be said to be out of order. It seemed that this was a day of privilege, when any gentleman might stand up, select his mark, and abuse any government he pleased, whether it had reference or not to the point in question. Although nobody had said a word on the subject of the French Revolution, his right hon. friend had risen up and abused that event. He might have treated the [Hindu] government, or that of China, or the government of Turkey, or the laws of Confucius precisely in the same manner, and with equal appositeness to the business of the House. Every gentleman had a right that day to abuse the government of every country as much as he pleased, and in as gross terms as he thought proper, or any government, either ancient or modern, with his right hon. friend.

Fox's implication that Burke was out of order was taken up by his followers, who interrupted Burke's reply with calls of 'Order! Order!' This deeply angered Burke, who saw the interruptions as a deliberate tactic arranged by Fox. The interruptions were probably spontaneous, but responsive to a suggestion in Fox's sarcastic reply, and Fox does not seem to have discouraged them. The *Parliamentary History* goes on:

Mr Burke replied that he understood his right hon. friend's irony, but his conclusions were very erroneously drawn from his premisses. If he was disorderly, he was sorry for it. His right hon. friend had also accused him of abusing government in very gross terms. He conceived his right hon. friend meant to abuse him in unqualified terms. He had called him to account for the decency and propriety of his expressions. Mr Burke said he had been accused of creating dissension among nations. He never thought the National Assembly was imitated so well as in the debate then going on. M. Cazales [a right-wing member of the Assembly] could never utter a single sentence in that Assembly without a roar. [Two Members call Burke to order; one defends him.]

Mr Burke said he meant to take the sense of the committee, whether or not he was in order. He declared he had not made any reflection, nor did he mean any, on any one gentleman whatever. He was as fully convinced as he could be, that no one gentleman in that House wanted to alter the constitution of England. The reason why, in the first regular opportunity that presented itself, he had been anxious to offer his reflections on the subject, was because it was a matter of great public concern, and occasion called for his observations. As long as they held to the constitution he should think it his duty to act with them; but he would not be the slave of any whim that might arise. On the contrary he thought it his duty not to give any countenance to certain doctrines which were supposed to exist in this country, and which were intended fundamentally to subvert the constitution. They ought to consider well what they were doing. [Here there was a loud cry of Order! Order! and Go on!] Mr Burke said, there was such an enthusiasm for order that it was not easy to go on. If the French revolutionaires were to mind their own affairs, and had shown no inclination to go abroad and to make proselytes in other countries, Mr Burke declared that neither he nor any other Member of the House had any right to meddle with them. If they were not as much disposed to make proselytes as Louis XIV had been to make conquests, he should have thought it very improper and indiscreet to have touched on the subject. He said he would quote the National Assembly itself, and a correspondent of his at Paris [Anacharsis Cloots], who had declared he appeared as the ambassador of the whole human race. [Repeated calls of order.] Mr Burke said an attempt was now being made, by one who had been formerly his friend, to bring down upon him the censure of the House.

Under the strain of being shouted down by his own colleagues, sitting all around him, Burke had reached breaking-point with Fox. Always, up to this moment, Burke had referred to Fox as his friend. Now, Fox has become 'one who was formerly his friend'. Burke went on:

It was unfortunate for him, he said, sometimes to be hunted by one party, and sometimes by another. He considered himself to be unfairly treated by those gentlemen with whom he had been accustomed to act, but from whom he now received extreme violence. He should, he said, if the tumult of order abated, proceed in the account he was going to give of the horrible consequences flowing from the French idea of the rights of man.

At this point, a Whig member, Lord Sheffield, put the charge of disorder into the form of a motion: 'That dissertations on the French Constitution, and to read a narrative of the transactions in France, are not regular or orderly on the question, that the clauses of the Quebec Bill be read a second time, paragraph by paragraph.' Pitt, who must have relished the sight and sound of the Whigs engaged in shouting down one of the most illustrious of their own number, now intervened on Burke's side, over the question of order:

Mr Pitt begged leave to observe, that the question of discretion and the question of order, ought to be kept perfectly separate. Whatever he might feel for himself, he must beg leave to be understood to do complete justice to the motives of the right hon. gentleman [Burke], which he could trace to no other source than a pure regard to the constitution of his country. But as to the motive in the hands of the chairman, as to the question of order when they were considering what was to be the best constitution for Canada, or for any other of the dependencies of Great Britain, it was strictly in order to allude to the constitution of other countries.

Pitt's statement ensured that the Commons, as a body, would not find Burke to be out of order, since Pitt had a large and disciplined majority. Lord Sheffield's motion could not carry (and was in fact withdrawn at the close of the debate, at Pitt's request). Fox now rose, however, to support that motion. It appears that he had not heard, or else had not understood, Burke's reference to 'one who was formerly his friend'. In support of the motion, Fox said:

On the French Revolution he did indeed differ from his right hon. friend. Their opinions, he had no scruple to say, were wide as the poles asunder. But what had a difference of opinion on that, which to the House was only matter of theoretical contemplation, to do with the discussion of a practical point, on which no such difference existed? On the revolution, he adhered to his opinion, and never would retreat any syllable of what he had said. He repeated that he thought it, on the whole, *one of the most glorious events in the history of mankind*. But when he had on a former occasion mentioned France, he had mentioned the revolution only, and not the Constitution: the latter remained to be modified by experience, and accommodated to circumstances.

This is curious. Fox here forgets – or retrospectively corrects – what he had actually said. The statement of 15 April that had provoked the parliamentary crisis between him and Burke was specifically in praise of the French Constitution. But perhaps word had reached Fox in the meantime that the Constitution, though still unfinished, was no longer *à la mode* among advanced revolutionaries. Robespierre had become President of the Jacobins in March. The constitution-makers were already near to being marked down for the guillotine.

Fox went on:

The arbitrary system of government was done away; the new one had the good of the people for its object, and this was the point on which he rested. If the committee should decide that his right hon. friend should pursue his argument on the French Constitution he would leave the House, and if some friend would send him word when the clauses of the Quebec Bill were to be discussed, he would return and debate them. And when he said this, he said it from no unwillingness to listen to his right hon. friend: he always had heard him with pleasure, but not where no practical use could result from his argument. When the proper period for discussion came, feeble as his powers were, compared with those of his right hon. friend, whom he must call his master, for he had taught him everything he knew in politics, yet he should be ready to maintain the principles he had asserted, even against his right hon. friend's superior eloquence to maintain, that the rights of man, which his right hon. friend had ridiculed as chimerical and visionary, were in fact the basis and foundation of every rational constitution, and even of the British constitution itself. Having been taught by his right hon. friend, that no revolt of a nation was caused without provocation, he could not help feeling a joy ever since the Constitution of France became founded on the rights of man, on which the British constitution itself was founded. If such were principles dangerous to the constitution, they were the principles of his right hon. friend, from whom he had learned them. During the American War they had together rejoiced at the success of a Washington, and sympathized, almost in tears, at the death of a Montgomery. From his right hon. friend he had learned that the revolt of a whole people could never be countenanced and encouraged, but must have been provoked.

These last reminders incensed Burke, who felt that friendly private conversations of the past were being exploited in order to worst him in public debate. The *Parliamentary History* goes on:

Mr Burke commenced his reply in a grave and governed tone of voice, observing that although he had been called to order so many times, he had sat with perfect composure, and had heard the most disorderly speech that perhaps ever was delivered in that House. His words and his conduct throughout had been misrepresented, and a personal attack had been made upon him from a quarter he never could have expected, after a friendship and intimacy of more than two-and-twenty years; and not only his public conduct, words and writings, had been alluded to in the severest terms, but confidential views and opinions had been brought forward, with a view of proving that he acted inconsistently. The practice now was, upon all occasions, to praise, in the highest strain, the French Constitution ... So fond were gentlemen of this favourite topic, that whoever disapproved of the anarchy and confusion that had taken place in France, or could not foresee the benefits that were to arise out of it, were stigmatized as enemies to liberty and to the British constitution – charges that were false, unfounded, and every way unfair. Doctrines of this kind, he thought, were extremely dangerous at all times and much more so if they were to be sanctioned by so great a name as that of the right hon. gentleman, who always put whatever he said in the strongest and most forcible view in which it could possibly appear. After what had been said, nobody could impute to him [Burke] interested or personal motives for his conduct. Those with whom he had been constantly in habits of friendship and agreement [attacked him] and from the other side of the House he was not likely to have much support; yet all he did was no more than his duty. It was a struggle, not to support any man, or set of men, but a struggle to support the British constitution, in doing which he had incurred the displeasure of all about him, and those opposite to him, and what was worst of all, he had induced the right hon. gentleman to rip up the whole course and tenure of his life, public and private, and that not without a considerable degree of asperity. His failings and imperfections had been keenly exposed, and, in short, without the chance of gaining one new friend, he had made enemies, it appeared malignant enemies, of his old friends: but, after all, he esteemed his duty far beyond any friendship, any fame, or any other consideration whatever. The right hon. gentleman in the speech just made, had treated him in every sentence with uncommon harshness. In the first place, after being fatigued with skirmishes of order, which were wonderfully managed by his light troops, the right hon. gentleman brought down the whole strength and heavy artillery of his own judgment, eloquence and abilities, upon him to crush him at once, by declaring a censure upon his whole life, conduct and opinions.

Notwithstanding this great and serious, though on his part unmerited attempt to crush him, he would not be dismayed; he was not yet afraid to state his sentiments in that House, or anywhere else, and he would tell all the world that the constitution was in danger.

Burke appears to have believed that Fox had organized a walk-out during his speech. 'In carrying on the attack against him, the right hon. gentleman had been supported by a corps of well-disciplined troops, expert in their manoeuvres, and obedient to the word of their commander [Mr Grey here called Mr Burke to order, considering that it was disorderly to mention gentlemen in that way, and to ascribe improper motives to them].' Here the *Parliamentary History* has a footnote:

> It is probable that a little incident which happened in the course of Mr Burke's reply contributed to draw from him the expressions considered as disorderly by Mr Grey. In his speech Mr Fox had intimated an intention of leaving the House, if the committee should suffer Mr Burke to proceed. While the latter gentleman was speaking, the former, being perhaps now resolved on a rejoinder, accidentally went toward the lobby for some light refreshment, with which he soon after returned to his place. But in the meantime about twenty other gentlemen, of those most personally attached to him, mistaking his departure for the execution of his declared intention, rose from their seats, and followed him out of the House.

Burke next recapitulated the political questions 'upon which he had differed from right hon. gentleman upon former occasions', and went on to say that

> in the course of their long acquaintance, no one difference of opinion had ever before for a single moment interrupted their friendship. It certainly was indiscreet at any period, but especially at his time of life, to parade enemies, or give his friends occasion to desert him; yet if his firm and steady adherence to the British constitution placed him in such a dilemma, he would risk all; and as public duty and public experience taught him, with his last words exclaim, 'Fly from the French Constitution.'

Fox here whispered that 'there was no loss of friends'. Burke said 'Yes, there was a loss of friends – he knew the price of his conduct – he had done his duty at the price of his friend, their friendship was at an end.' The *History* continues:

> *Mr Fox* rose to reply, but his mind was so much agitated, and his heart so much affected by what had fallen from Mr Burke, that it was some minutes before he could proceed. Tears trickled down his cheeks, and he strove in vain to give utterance to feelings that dignified and exalted his nature. The sensibility of every member of the House appeared uncommonly excited upon the occasion. Recovered at length from the depression under which he

had risen, Mr Fox proceeded to answer the assertions which had caused it. He said that however events which have altered the mind of his right hon. friend, for so he must call him notwithstanding what had passed – because, grating as it was to anyone to be unfriendly treated by those to whom they felt the greatest obligations, and whom, notwithstanding their harshness and severity, they found they must still love and esteem – he could not forget that, when a boy almost, he had been in the habit of receiving favours from his right hon. friend, but their friendship had grown with the years, and that it had continued for upwards of twenty-five years, for the last twenty of which they had acted together, and lived on terms of the most familiar intimacy. He hoped, therefore, that notwithstanding what had happened that day, his right hon. friend would think on past times, and, however any imprudent words or intemperance of his might have offended him, would show that it had not been at least intentionally his fault. His right hon. friend had said, and said truly, that they had differed formerly on many subjects, and yet it did not interrupt their friendship ... He enumerated, severally, what those differences of opinion had been, and appealed to his right hon. friend, whether their friendship had been interrupted on any one of these occasions.

At that point there appeared a possibility that the personal friendship might be preserved, to some extent, despite the clash of principle. If Fox had stopped there, that possibility would have remained, but the great debater is driven to carry on the debate and win it. Fatally, Fox goes on: 'In particular,' he said, 'on the subject of the French Revolution, the hon. gentleman well knows that his sentiment differed widely from his own; he knew also, that as soon as his book on the subject was published, he condemned that book both in public and private, and every one of the doctrines which it contained.'

That settled it. By formally and absolutely condemning the *Reflections* on the floor of the House, Fox had made it impossible for Burke to continue a member of his party. In personal terms, Fox's condemnation of the *Reflections* negated the appeal to friendship with which he had begun. Fox had apparently failed to notice Burke's fierce resentment, already declared, of his use of recollections of private conversations to furnish debating points against his old friend. Now he offered more in the same vein:

With regard to his right hon. friend's enthusiastic attachment to our constitution, in preference to all others, did he remember when His Majesty's speech was made in 1783 on the loss of America, in which His Majesty lamented the loss the provinces had sustained, in being deprived of the advantages resulting from a monarchy, how he had ridiculed that speech, and compared it to a man's opening the door after he had left a room, and saying, 'At our parting, pray let me recommend a monarchy to you'? In that ridicule, Mr Fox said, he had joined heartily at the time ...

Fox ends his speech:

The course he should pursue ... would be to keep out of his right hon. friend's way, till time and reflection had fitted his right hon. friend to think differently upon the subject; and then, if their friends did not contrive to unite them, he should think their friends did not act as they had a right to expect at their hands. If his right hon. friend wished to bring forward the question of the French Revolution on a future day, in that case he would discuss it with him as temperately as he could; at present he had said all that he thought necessary, and, let his right hon. friend say what he would more on the subject, he would make him no farther reply.

Burke rose once again:

He began with remarking that the tenderness which had been displayed in the beginning and conclusion of Mr Fox's speech was quite obliterated by what had occurred in the middle part. He regretted, in a tone and manner of earnestness and fervency, the proceedings of that evening, which he feared might long be remembered by their enemies to the prejudice of both. He was unfortunate enough to suffer the lash of Mr Fox, but he must encounter it. Under the mask of kindness a new attack, he said, was made upon his character and conduct in the most hostile manner, and his very jests brought up in judgment against him. He did not think the careless expressions and playful triflings of his unguarded hours would have been recorded, mustered up in the form of accusations, and not only have had a serious meaning imposed upon them which they were never intended to bear, but one totally inconsistent with any fair and candid interpretation. Could his most inveterate enemy have acted more unkindly towards him? The events of that night, in debates in which he had been interrupted without being suffered to explain, in which he had been accused without being heard in his defence, made him at a loss to understand what was either party or friendship. His arguments had been misrepresented. He had never affirmed that the English, like every other constitution, might not in some points be amended. He had never mentioned that to praise our own constitution the best way was to abuse all others. The tendency of all that had been said was to represent him as a wild inconsistent man, only for attaching bad epithets to a bad subject. With the view of showing his inconsistency, allusions had been made to his conduct in 1780 [and over] the American War ... If he thought, in 1780, that the influence of the Crown ought to be reduced to a limited standard, and with which Mr Fox himself at the time seemed to be satisfied, it did not follow that the French were right in reducing it with them to nothing. He was favourable to the Americans because he supposed they were fighting not to acquire absolute speculative liberty, but to keep what they had under the English constitution ... In France, it had been asserted by the right hon. gentleman that the largest religious tolerance prevailed. It would be judged of what nature that toleration was when it was understood that there the most cruel tests were imposed ... The treatment of the nuns was too shocking almost to be mentioned. These wretched girls, who could only be animated by the most exalted religious enthusiasm, were engaged in the most painful office of humanity, in the most sacred duty of piety, visiting and attending the hospitals. Yet these had been dragged into the streets; these had been scourged by the sovereigns of the French nation, because the priest from whom they had received the sacrament had not submitted to the test. And this proceeding had passed not only unpunished but uncensured. Yet in the country in which said proceedings had happened, the largest religious toleration was said to prevail ... Mr Burke said he was sorry for the occurrence of that day. 'Sufficient for the day was the evil thereof.' Yet if the good were to many, he would willingly title the evil to himself ... With regards to pretences of friendship, he must own that he did not like them, where his character, as in the present instance, had been so materially attacked and injured.

Fox, as he had promised, made no reply. Pitt, speaking at the close of the debate, noted that Fox had found Burke to be disorderly, in discussing the French Revolution, but that Fox himself had made two speeches on that subject. Pitt found Burke to be still in order, but added, characteristically, that 'he could not but think that every asperity and censure on that event had, for various reasons, better be avoided.' Yet he went on: 'He thought Mr Burke entitled to the gratitude of his country, for having that day, in so able and eloquent a manner, stated his sense of the degree of danger to the constitution that already existed.' This was neat. In the guise of a compliment to Burke, Pitt was making one of his sidelong, feline forays against the leader of the opposition in the Commons, insinuating that Fox was either unaware of, or collusive towards, the danger to the constitution that Burke had rightly identified.

Unlike either Burke or Fox, Pitt had every reason to be pleased with the course and outcome of the debate of 6 May 1791. Pitt had come under the fire of Burke's oratorical big guns – especially in the Speech on the Nabob of Arcot's Debts – and he knew their power so well that he had been happy to encourage Burke to find another target, through the impeachment of Warren Hastings. But that Fox should have become Burke's target was a splendid parliamentary windfall for him. From then on, Burke was Pitt's ally against Fox, although only implicitly so up to April 1792. It was a reluctant partnership, reserved and suspicious on both sides, but it was to become an effective working alliance. From the beginning it significantly strengthened Pitt's parliamentary position. As it grew, during the few remaining years of Burke's parliamentary career, it greatly strengthened Pitt's hand.

The breach between Burke and Fox had become irreparable by the close of parliamentary proceedings on 6 May. But the Commons debate between the two was to rumble on for a further parliamentary day, like the last few peals of a dying thunderstorm. The occasion was the resumption, on 11 May 1791, of the Quebec Bill debate. It started quietly. Fox began by raising a technicality. Burke discussed the technicality and then indicated that he held to his principles, but would stay within the rules of order this time:

> Situated as he was, an isolated being, perfectly separated, banished from his party, there was a voice which cried to him, 'Beware'. For the short time he would remain in Parliament (and it would be but a very short time), he would support those principles of government which were founded upon the wisdom of antiquity, and sanctioned by the experience of time. On the present Bill, necessary as it was for him to be careful of what he should say, he would state the arguments that occurred to him, as they should arise, upon every clause.

Fox spoke again, uncontroversially, and with a guardedly respectful reference to Burke. However, at this stage Burke apparently got wind of some stories that the Whigs were putting out about him, and also of a press release, which was to be published on the following day in the Whig paper, the *Morning Chronicle*. The press release ran: 'The great and firm body of the Whigs of England, true to their principles, have decided on the dispute between Mr Fox and Mr Burke, and the former is declared to have maintained the pure doctrines by which they are bound together, and upon which they have invariably acted.' The clear implication that Burke had failed to maintain 'the pure doctrines' was calculated to infuriate Burke, and it did.

Mr Burke rose. He began with observing that he had served the House and the country in one capacity or another, for twenty-six years, twenty-five of which had been spent within these walls. He had wasted so much of his life to a precious purpose, if that House should [not] at least counteract a most insidious design to ruin him in reputation and crown his age with infamy. For the best part of the time, he had been a very laborious and assiduous, though a very unimportant servant of the public. He had not, he declared, been treated with friendship; but if he was separated from his party, if sentence of banishment had been pronounced against him, he hoped to meet a fair, open hostility, to which he would oppose himself in a fair and manly way, for the very short period that he should continue a Member of that House.

The 'insidious design' was the circulation of a rumour that Burke was plotting with Pitt to ruin Fox's reputation by making out that he was a republican. This would keep Fox out of office, and Burke would be rewarded with a place in Pitt's administration. 'In saying what he had said on the subject,' Burke concluded,

he was conscious that he had done his duty, and he hoped he had in some measure averted what otherwise might have effected the downfall of the British constitution. That being the case, separate and unsupported as he was, let not the party who had excommunicated him imagine that he was deprived of consolation – although all was solitude without, there was sunshine and company enough within.

This final remark was a reference to Alexander Pope's 'sunshine of the soul', the reward of a person who has done his duty.

This would have been a satisfactory close to the debate for Burke, but his experienced antagonist could see this, and moved to spoil the effect. Fox made an offer to which Burke was obliged to reply: 'With regard to the right hon. gentleman's declaration that he was separated from the party, if he was so separated, it must be his own choice; and if he should repent that separation, he might be assured his friends would ever be ready to receive him, to respect him, and to love him, as heretofore.'

Burke's reply was cold and brief:

> He took notice of what had been said, that, if he would repent, he would be received. He stood, he said, a man publicly disgraced by his party, and therefore the right hon. gentleman ought not to receive him. He declared he had gone through his youth without encountering any party disgrace; and though he had then in his age been so unfortunate as to meet it, he did not solicit the right hon. gentleman's friendship, nor that of any man, either on one side of the House or the other.

And that was all. The *Parliamentary History*'s report of that last speech carries the footnote: 'Thus ended the friendship between Mr Burke and Mr Fox – a friendship which had lasted for more than the fourth part of a century.'

AFTER THE BREACH

Burke made no further parliamentary interventions on French affairs during 1791, but as a writer he was particularly active. He published two major tracts: *Letter to a Member of the National Assembly* and *Appeal from the New to the Old Whigs*. He also wrote two memoranda for private circulation, *Hints for a Memorial to Monsieur de M.M.* and *Thoughts on French Affairs*. Thereafter, he did not write about France until the following December (*Heads for Consideration on the Present State of Affairs*), but by then the revolution had entered its most dramatic and violent phase, with the 'deposition' of Louis XVI in August 1792.

During 1791, the revolutionary leaders were aiming at stability under new conditions by instituting a constitutional monarchy. It suited both them and Louis to pretend that the King was giving his free consent to the National Assembly's revolutionary programme. Foreign admirers of the revolution, such as Fox and almost all the rest of the Whigs, accepted this version of events, but Burke had scornfully rejected it as early as 10 October 1789, when he wrote about 'the late Grand Monarch' making 'a figure as ridiculous as pitiable'. In the *Reflections*, and again in *Letter to a Member of the National Assembly*, he correctly presented Louis XVI and Marie Antoinette as prisoners already.

The King's status as prisoner from October 1789 onwards was no sentimental side-issue, as some later pro-revolutionary commentators would suggest. It was central, because, at this stage, the royal prisoner was officially chief executive. From then on, France was a country without an executive. The Paris mob, prompted by a faction, had transferred the nominal executive from Versailles to Paris. Henceforward, ultimate power rested with the Paris mob, and thus, in any particular crisis, with whatever revolutionary factions could most effectively manipulate the mob. Burke had seen that clearly at the time.

Fox and most of the Whigs, by contrast, took the superficial and wishful view, and continued to do so. They believed that the violence of 1789 had been an aberration, that the Constitution of 1790-91 was all it purported to be, and that France, under its benign sway, was about to enjoy the blessings of an unexampled peace, stability and liberty.

These illusions ought to have been punctured when, on the night of 20-21 June 1791, the Royal Family tried to escape from France, but were captured at Varennes and returned to revolutionary Paris under the grimly watchful eyes of huge, silent crowds. The English Whigs, however, clung to their illusions. These events were an aberration, they thought, just like those of October 1789. The noble edifice of the French Constitution was still intact. And the Whigs even remained complacent at the macabre completion of the process on 14 September, when the prisoner-King swore fidelity to a Constitution devised by the people from whom he had tried to escape.

The King and the leaders of the National Assembly were now acting in concert over an agreed but incredible fiction. This official fiction was that Louis had not tried to escape at all, but had been abducted. Yet when Louis fled, he had left behind a declaration revoking his assent to all measures which had been laid before him while he was under restraint. This document is the definitive corroboration of Burke's view of the King's status as a prisoner from 1789. Yet it suited both the King and the National Assembly's leaders to pretend that no such document existed, and that the King had been, and remained, a loyal partner in the revolutionary process. That Parisians were not fooled became clear in the following year, as the mob brought down all who had subscribed to the official fiction, killing off most of them.

Burke's pamphlet *A Letter to a Member of the National Assembly*, written in January 1791, before his parliamentary quarrel with Fox or the flight to Varennes, is essentially a postscript to the *Reflections*. The greatest of its afterthoughts is the majestic onslaught on Rousseau as the grand inspiration of the revolutionaries. This was a topical subject. On 22 December 1790, the National Assembly had decreed that 'there shall be erected to the author of *Emile* and *du Contrat Social* a statue bearing the inscription: *La Nation Française libre à J. J. Rousseau...*' Burke writes:

The Assembly recommends to its youth a study of the bold experimenters in morality. Everybody knows that there is a great dispute amongst their leaders which of them is the best resemblance to Rousseau. In truth, they all resemble him. His blood they transfuse into their minds and into their manners. Him they study; him they meditate; him they turn over in all the time they can spare from the laborious mischief of the day, or the debauches of the night ... If an author had written like a great genius on geometry, though his practical and speculative morals were vicious in the extreme, it might appear that in voting the statue they honoured only the geometrician. But Rousseau is a moralist or he is nothing. It is impossible, therefore, putting the circumstances together, to mistake their design in choosing the author with whom they have begun to recommend a course of studies.

Their great problem is to find a substitute for all the principles which hitherto have been employed to regulate the human will and action. They find dispositions in the mind of such force and quality as may fit men far better than the old morality for the purposes of such a state as theirs, and may go much further in supporting their power and destroying their enemies. They have therefore chosen a selfish, flattering, seductive, ostentatious vice, in the place of plain duty. True humility, the basis of the Christian system, is the low but deep and firm foundation of all real virtue. But this, as very painful in the practice and little imposing in the appearance, they have totally discarded. Their object is to merge all natural and all social sentiment in inordinate vanity. In a small degree, and conversant in little things, vanity is of little moment. When full grown, it is the worst of vices, and the occasional mimic of them all. It makes the whole man false. It leaves nothing sincere or trustworthy about him. His best qualities are poisoned and perverted by it, and operate exactly as the worst. When your lords had many writers as immoral as the object of their statue (such as Voltaire and others) they chose Rousseau, because in him that peculiar vice which they wished to erect into a ruling virtue was by far the most conspicuous.

We have had the great professor and founder of *the philosophy of vanity* in England. As I had good opportunities of knowing his proceedings almost from day to day, he left no doubt in my mind that he entertained no principle either to influence his heart or to guide his understanding but *vanity*. With this vice he was possessed to a degree little short of madness. It is from the same deranged eccentric vanity that this, the insane *Socrates* of the National Assembly, was impelled to publish a mad Confession of his mad faults, and to attempt a new sort of glory, from bringing hardily to light the obscure and vulgar vices which we know may sometimes be blended with eminent talents. He has not observed on the nature of vanity, who does not know that it is omnivorous; that it has no choice in its food; that it is fond to talk even of its own faults and vices, as what will excite surprise and draw attention, and what will pass at worst for openness and candour. It was this abuse and perversion, which vanity makes even of hypocrisy, which has driven Rousseau to record a life not so much as chequered, or spotted here and there, with virtues, or even distinguished by a single good action. It is such a life he chooses to offer to the attention of mankind. It is such a life that, with a wild defiance, he flings in the face of his Creator, whom he acknowledges only to brave. Your Assembly, knowing how much more powerful example is found than precept, has chosen this man (by his own account without a single virtue) for a model. To him they erect their first statue. From him they commence their series of honours and distinctions.

It is that new-invented virtue which your masters canonize, that led their moral hero constantly to exhaust the stores of his powerful rhetoric in the expression of universal benevolence, whilst his heart was incapable of harbouring one spark of common parental affection. Benevolence to the whole species and want of feeling for every individual with whom the professors come in contact form the character of the new philosophy. Setting up for an unsocial independence, this their hero of vanity refuses the just price of common labour, as well as the tribute which opulence owes to genius, and which, when paid, honours the giver and the receiver; and then he pleads his beggary as an excuse for his crimes. He melts with tenderness for those only who touch him by the remotest relation, and then, without one natural pang, casts away, as a sort of offal and excrement, the spawn of his disgustful amours, and sends his children to the hospital of foundlings. The bear loves, licks, and forms her young; but bears are not philosophers. Vanity, however, finds its account in reversing the train of our natural feelings. Thousands admire the sentimental writer; the affectionate father is hardly known in his parish.

Under this philosophic instructor in the *ethics of vanity*, they have attempted in France a regeneration of the moral constitution of man. Statesmen like your present rulers exist by everything which is spurious, fictitious, and false; by everything which takes the man from his house, and sets him on a stage, which makes him up an artificial creature with painted theatric sentiments, fit to be seen by the glare of candlelight, and formed to be contemplated at a due distance. Vanity is too apt to prevail in all of us, and in all countries. To the improvement of Frenchmen it seems not absolutely necessary that it should be taught upon system. But it is plain that the present rebellion was its legitimate offspring, and it is piously fed by that rebellion, with a daily dole.

If the system of institution recommended by the Assembly is false and theatric, it is because their system of government is of the same character. To that, and to that alone, it is strictly conformable. To understand either, we must connect the morals with the politics of the legislators. Your practical philosophers, systematic in everything, have wisely begun at the source. As the relation between parents and children is the first among the elements of vulgar, natural morality, they erect statues to a wild, ferocious, low-minded, hard-hearted father of fine general feelings; a lover of his kind, but a hater of his kindred. Your masters reject the duties of this vulgar relation as contrary to liberty; as not founded in the social compact and not binding according to the rights of men, because the relation is not, of course, the result of *free election*; never so on the side of the children, not always on the part of the parents.

As well as this penetrating attack on the philosophy of vanity, Burke's *Letter to a Member of the National Assembly* contains two striking examples of his powers of predictive insight. At a time of no apparent threat to the King's person, Burke predicted his execution, almost exactly two years before he was guillotined on 21 January 1793:

In spite of their solemn declarations, their soothing addresses, and the multiple oaths which they have taken, and forced others to take, they will assassinate the King when his name will no longer be necessary to their designs; but not a moment sooner. They will probably first assassinate the Queen, whenever the renewed menace of such assassination loses its effect upon the anxious mind of an affectionate husband. At present, the advantage which they derive from the daily threats against her life is her only security for preserving it. They keep their sovereign alive for the purpose of exhibiting him, like some wild beast at a fair, as if they had a Bajazet in a cage. They chose to make monarchy contemptible by exposing it to derision, in the person of the most benevolent of their kings.

Burke is wrong only about the order of the two executions. Marie Antoinette was guillotined, but not until 16 October 1793.

Burke's capacity to predict events years before they happened – intensification of the revolution; execution of the King and Queen; emergence of a military despotism – came from his early and profound insight into the character and tendencies of the revolution. This also enabled him to predict the rise to power of hardliners such as Robespierre. This would follow the ousting of the self-deceiving moderates who led the Assembly from 1789 to 1791, of whom he wrote:

They are a sort of people who affect to proceed as if they thought that men may deceive without fraud, rob without injustice, and overturn everything without violence. They are men who would usurp the government of their country with decency and moderation. In fact they are nothing more or better than men engaged in desperate designs, with feeble minds. They are not honest; they are only ineffectual and unsystematic in their iniquity. They are persons who want not the dispositions, but the energy and vigour that is necessary for great evil machinations. They find that in such designs they fall at best into a secondary rank, and others take the place and lead in usurpation, which they are not qualified to obtain or to hold ... But these men naturally are despised by those who have heads to know and hearts that are able to go through the necessary demands of bold, wicked enterprises. They are naturally classed below the latter description, and will only be used by them as inferior instruments. They will be only the Fairfaxes of your Cromwells.

Here, in January 1791, Burke predicts the transition of revolutionary power of the second half of 1792.

Second in importance after the *Reflections* in the canon of Burke's writings on the controversy over the French Revolution is the pamphlet fully entitled *An Appeal from the New to the Old Whigs in consequence of some late discussions in Parliament relative to the Reflections on the French Revolution*. It was written immediately after Burke's parliamentary quarrel with Fox in April–May 1791, and its general purpose was to defend Burke against the charges of inconsistency levelled against him. The Whigs claimed that Burke's position over the revolution was inconsistent both with the Whig tradition and with his own words and actions in relation to the American Revolution and the power of the Crown. Published anonymously in August 1791, the pamphlet speaks of Burke in the third person:

I pass to the next head of charge – Mr Burke's inconsistency. It is certainly a great aggravation of his fault in embracing false opinions, that in doing so he is not supposed to fill up a void, but that he is guilty of a dereliction of opinions that are true and laudable. This is the great gist of the charge against him. It is not so much that he is wrong in his book (that, however, is alleged also) as that he has therein belied his whole life. I believe, if he could venture to value himself upon anything, it is on the virtue of consistency that he would value himself the most. Strip him of this, and you leave him naked indeed.

In the case of any man who had written something, and spoken a great deal, upon very multifarious matter during upwards of twenty-five years' public service, and in as great a variety of important events as perhaps have ever happened in the same number of years, it would appear a little hard, in order to charge such a man with inconsistency, to see collected by his friend a sort of digest of his sayings, even to such as were merely sportive and jocular. This digest, however, has been made, with equal pains and partiality, and without bringing out those passages of the writings which might tend to show with what restrictions any expressions quoted from him ought to have been understood. From a great statesman he did not quite expect this mode of inquisition. If it only appeared in the works of common pamphleteers, Mr Burke might safely trust to his reputation. When thus urged, he ought, perhaps, to do a little more. It shall be as little as possible; for I hope not much is wanting. To be totally silent on his charges would not be respectful to Mr Fox. Accusations sometimes derive a weight from the persons who make them to which they are not entitled from their matter.

He who thinks that the British constitution ought to consist of the three members, of three very different natures, of which it does actually consist, and thinks it his duty to preserve each of those members in its proper place and with its proper proportion of power, must (as each shall happen to be attacked) vindicate the three several parts on the several principles peculiarly belonging to them. He cannot assert the democratic part on the principles on which monarchy is supported, nor can he support monarchy on the principles of democracy, nor can he maintain aristocracy on the grounds of the one or of the other or of both. All these he must support on grounds that are totally different, though practically they may be, and happily with us they are, brought into one harmonious body. A man could not be consistent in defending such various, and at first view discordant, parts of a mixed constitution, without that sort of inconsistency with which Mr Burke stands charged.

As any one of the great members of this constitution happens to be endangered, he that is a friend to all of them chooses and presses the topics necessary for the support of the part attacked, with all the strength, the earnestness, the vehemence, with all the power of stating, of argument, and of colouring, which he happens to possess, and which the case demands. He is not to embarrass the minds of his hearers, or to encumber or overlay his speech, by bringing into view at once (as if he were reading an academic lecture) all that may and ought, when a just occasion presents itself, to be said in favour of the other members. At that time they are out of the court; there is no question concerning them. Whilst he opposes his defence on the part where the attack is made, he presumes that for his regard to the just rights of all the rest he has credit in every candid mind. He ought not to apprehend that his raising fences about popular privileges this day will infer that he ought on the next to concur with those who would pull down the throne; because on the next he defends the throne, it ought not to be supposed that he has abandoned the rights of the people.

A man, who, among various objects of his equal regard, is secure of some, and full of anxiety for the fate of others, is apt to go to much greater lengths in his preference of the objects of his immediate solicitude than Mr Burke has ever done. A man so circumstanced often seems to undervalue, to vilify, almost to reprobate and disown, those that are out of danger. This is the voice of nature and truth, and not of inconsistency and false pretence. The danger of anything very dear to us removes, for the moment, every other affection from the mind . . .

If the principles of a mixed constitution be admitted, [Mr Burke] wants no more to justify to consistency everything he has said and done during the course of a political life just touching to its close. I believe that gentleman had kept himself more clear of running into the fashion of wild, visionary theories, or of seeking popularity through every means, than any man perhaps ever did in the same situation.

He was the first who, on the hustings, at a popular election, rejected the authority of instruction from constituents – or who, in any place, has argued so fully against it. Perhaps the discredit into which that doctrine of compulsive instructions under our constitution is since fallen may be due in a great degree to his opposing himself to it in that manner and on that occasion.

The reforms in representation, and the Bills for shortening the duration of Parliaments, he uniformly and steadily opposed for many years together, in contradiction to many of his best friends. These friends, however, in his better days, when they had more to fear from his loss than now they have, never chose to find any inconsistency between his acts and expressions in favour of liberty and his votes on those questions. But there is a time for all things . . .

At popular elections the most rigorous casuists will remit a little of their severity. They will allow to a candidate some unqualified effusions in favour of freedom without binding him to adhere to them in their utmost extent. But Mr Burke put a more strict rule upon himself than most moralists would put upon others. At his first offering himself to Bristol . . . he thought himself bound to tell to the electors, both before and after his election, exactly what a representative they had to expect in him.

'The *distinguishing* part of our constitution,' he said, 'is its liberty. To preserve that liberty inviolate is the *peculiar* duty and *proper* trust of a Member of the House of Commons. But the liberty, the *only* liberty, I mean is a liberty connected with *order*; and that not only exists *with* order and virtue, but cannot exist at all *without* them. It inheres in good and steady government, as in *its substance and vital principle*.'

The liberty to which Mr Burke declared himself attached is not French liberty. That liberty is nothing but the rein given to vice and confusion. Mr Burke was then, as he was at the writing of his *Reflections*, awfully impressed with the difficulties arising from the complex state of our constitution and our empire, and that it might require in different emergencies different sorts of exertions, and the successive call upon all the various principles which uphold and justify it. This will appear from what he said at the close of the poll.

'To be a good member of Parliament is, let me tell you, no easy task — especially at this time, when there is so strong a disposition to run into the perilous extremes of *servile* compliance or *wild popularity*. To unite circumspection with vigour is absolutely necessary, but it is extremely difficult. We are now Members for a rich commercial *city*; this city, however, is but a part of a great *nation*, the interests of which are *various, multiform, and intricate*. We are Members for that great *nation* which, however, is itself but part of a great *empire*, extended by our virtue and our fortune to the farthest limits of the East and of the West. *All* these widespread interests must be *considered* — must be *compared* — must be *reconciled*, if possible. We are Members for a *free* country; and surely we all know that the machine of a free constitution is no *simple* thing, but as *intricate* and as *delicate* as it is valuable. We are Members in a *great and ancient* MONARCHY, and we must preserve religiously the true, legal rights of the sovereign, which form the keystone that binds together the noble and well-constructed arch of our empire and our constitution. A constitution made up of *balanced powers* must ever be a critical thing. As such I mean to touch that part of it which comes within my reach.'

In this manner, Mr Burke spoke to his constituents seventeen years ago. He spoke, not like a partisan of one particular member of our constitution, but as a person strongly, and on principle, attached to them all. He thought these great and essential members ought to be preserved, and preserved each in its place, and that the monarchy ought not only to be secured in its peculiar existence, but in its pre-eminence too, as the presiding and connecting principle of the whole. Let it be considered whether the language of his book, printed in 1790, differs from his speech at Bristol in 1774.

With equal justice his opinions on the American War are introduced, as if in his late work he had belied his conduct and opinions in the debates which arose upon that great event. On the American War he never had any opinions which he has seen occasion to retract, or which he has ever retracted. He, indeed, differs essentially from Mr Fox as to the cause of that war. Mr Fox has been pleased to say that the Americans rebelled 'because they thought they had not enjoyed liberty enough'. This cause of the war, *from him*, I have heard of for the first time. It is true that those who stimulated the nation to that measure did frequently urge this topic. They contended that the Americans had from the beginning aimed at independence, that from the beginning they meant wholly to throw off the authority of the Crown and to break their connection with the parent country. This Mr Burke never believed. When he moved his second conciliatory proposition, in the year 1776, he entered into the discussion of this point at very great length, and, from nine several heads of presumption, endeavoured to prove that charge upon that people not to be true.

If the principles of all he has said and wrote on the occasion be viewed with common temper, the gentlemen of the party will perceive that on a supposition that the Americans had rebelled merely in order to enlarge their liberty, Mr Burke would have thought very differently of the American cause. What might have been in the secret thoughts of some of their leaders it is impossible to say. As far as a man so locked up as Dr Franklin could be expected to communicate his ideas, I believe he opened them to Mr Burke. It was, I think, the very day before he set out for America that a very long conversation passed between them, and with a greater air of openness on the Doctor's side than Mr Burke had observed in him before. In this discourse, Dr Franklin lamented, and with apparent sincerity, the separation which he feared was inevitable between Great Britain and her colonies. He certainly spoke of it as an event which gave him the greatest concern. America, he said, would never again see such happy days as she had passed under the protection of England. He observed that ours was the only instance of a great empire in which the most distant parts and members had been as well governed as the metropolis and its vicinage, but that the Americans were going to lose the means which secured to them this rare and precious advantage. The question with them was not whether they were to remain as they had been before the troubles – for better, he allowed, they could not hope to be – but whether they were to give up so happy a situation without a struggle. Mr Burke had several other conversations with him about that time, in none of which, soured and exasperated as his mind certainly was, did he discover any other wish in favour of America than for a security to its *ancient* condition. Mr Burke's conversation with other Americans was large, indeed, and his enquiries extensive and diligent. Trusting to the result of all these means of information, but trusting much more in the public presumptive indications I have just referred to, and to the reiterated solemn declarations of their assemblies, he always firmly believed that they were purely on the defensive in that rebellion. He considered the Americans as standing at that time and in that controversy, in the same relation to England as England did to King James II in 1688. He believed that they had taken up arms from one motive only; that is, our attempting to tax them without their consent, to tax them for the purposes of maintaining civil and military establishments. If this attempt of ours could have been practically established, he thought, with them, that their assemblies would become totally useless – that under the system of policy which was then pursued, the Americans could have no sort of security for their laws or liberties, or for any part of them, and that the very circumstance of *our* freedom would have augmented the weight of *their* slavery.

Considering the Americans on that defensive footing, he thought Great Britain ought instantly to have closed with them by the repeal of the taxing act. He was of opinion that our general rights over that country would have been preserved by this timely concession. When, instead of this, a Boston Port Bill, a Massachusetts Charter Bill, a Fishery Bill, an Intercourse Bill, I know not how many hostile Bills, rushed out like so many tempests from all points of the compass, and were accompanied first with great fleets and armies of English, and followed afterwards with great bodies of foreign troops, he thought that their cause grew daily better, because daily more defensive – and that ours, because daily more offensive, grew daily worse. He therefore, in two motions, in two successive years, proposed in Parliament many concessions beyond what he had reason to think in the beginning of the troubles would ever be seriously demanded.

So circumstanced, he certainly never could and never did wish the colonists to be subdued by arms. He was fully persuaded that if such should be the event, they must be held in that subdued state by a great body of standing forces, and perhaps of foreign forces. He was strongly of opinion that such armies, first victorious over Englishmen in a conflict for English constitutional rights and privileges and afterwards habituated (though in America) to keep an English people in a state of abject subjection, would prove fatal in the end to the liberties of England itself; that in the meantime this military system would lie as an oppressive burden upon the national finances; that it would constantly breed and feed new discussions, full of heat and acrimony, leading possibly to a new series of wars; and that foreign powers, whilst we continued in a state at once burdened and distracted, must at length obtain a decided superiority over us. On what part of his late publication, or on what expression that might have escaped him in that work, is any man authorized to charge Mr Burke with a contradiction to the line of his conduct and to the current of his doctrines on the American War? The pamphlet is in the hands of his accusers: let them point out the passage, if they can.

Having read everything that Burke is known to have written, and everything he is recorded as saying, I find this defence against the charge of inconsistency fully justified. There were inconsistencies in his career; the greatest was the fundamental incompatibility between his earlier and later speeches over India. But even his great change of mind about India tells us something about his underlying principles. For if his later speeches about India were based on an implacable resistance to the abuse of power, the earlier ones were based on a reluctance to take from men their established rights and privileges. When he opposed the French Revolution, he was opposing a cataclysm which united both of these impulses, for it was both a massive abuse of power and a negation of all established rights. A statement Burke made when speaking against Warren Hastings on 1 December 1783 sums up the basic principle on which he was to resist the revolution. In explaining his initial reluctance to attack the East India Company's rule, Burke had expressed his 'insuperable reluctance . . . to destroy any established system of government upon a theory'. Burke thus succinctly defined the intellectual basis of what became his opposition to the French Revolution, nearly six years before the revolution began. Never were charges of inconsistency more lightly made, or more perfunctorily sustained, than the charges of inconsistency levelled by the Whigs and radicals – and some later historians – against Edmund Burke over the French Revolution.

The most eloquent and the most profound passage in *An Appeal* is Burke's defence of what he calls 'natural aristocracy' (a term to which he gives a wide definition) against the levelling tendencies and projects of the French revolutionaries:

A true natural aristocracy is not a separate interest in the state, or separable from it. It is an essential integral part of any large body rightly constituted. It is formed out of a class of legitimate presumptions, which, taken as generalities, must be admitted for actual truths. To be bred in a place of estimation; to see nothing low and sordid from one's infancy; to be taught to respect oneself; to be habituated to the censorial inspection of the public eye; to look early to public opinion; to stand upon such elevated ground as to be enabled to take a large view of the widespread and infinitely diversified combinations of men and affairs in a large society; to have leisure to read, to reflect, to converse; to be enabled to draw the court and attention of the wise and learned wherever they are to be found; to be habituated in armies to command and to obey; to be taught to despise danger in the pursuit of honour and duty; to be formed to the greatest degree of vigilance, foresight, and circumspection, in a state of things in which no fault is committed with impunity and the slightest mistakes draw on the most ruinous consequences; to be led to a guarded and regulated conduct from a sense that you are considered as an instructor of your fellow citizens in their highest concerns, and that you act as a reconciler between God and man; to be employed as an administrator of law and justice, and to be thereby amongst the first benefactors to mankind; to be a professor of high science, or of liberal and ingenuous art; to be amongst rich traders, who from their success are presumed to have sharp and vigorous understandings, and to possess the virtues of diligence, order, constancy, and regularity, and to have cultivated an habitual regard to commutative justice: these are the circumstances of men that form what I should call a *natural* aristocracy, without which there is no nation.

The state of civil society which necessarily generates this aristocracy is a state of nature – and much more truly so than a savage and incoherent mode of life. For man is by nature reasonable; and he is never perfectly in his natural state but when he is placed where reason may be best cultivated and predominates. Art is man's nature. We are as much at least, in a state of nature in formed manhood as in immature and helpless infancy. Men, qualified in the manner I have just described, form in nature, as she operates in the common modification of society, the leading, guiding, and governing part. It is the soul to the body, without which the man does not exist. To give, therefore, no more importance, in the social order, to such descriptions of men than that of so many units is a horrible usurpation.

'Art is man's nature.' Burke had long rejected the eighteenth century's tendency to oppose the natural to the artificial, and to exalt the former over the latter. His first book, published in 1756, was called *A Vindication of Natural Society*. The title, like the book itself, was ironic. Burke was seeking to show that the arguments for 'natural religion' – that is, religion without revelation, church or dogma – could be turned into a case for a 'natural society' devoid of its existing institutions. In the preface to the second edition of *A Vindication*, he abandoned the ironic mode and directly explained the purpose of the book: 'The design was to show that, without the exertion of any considerable forces, the same engines which were employed for the destruction of religion might be employed with equal success for the subversion of government.'

They might be, and in France they were, assiduously, during the thirty-three years that separated the publication of *A Vindication* from the outbreak of the French Revolution. The 'engines which were employed for the destruction of religion' by the *philosophes*, led by Voltaire, also subverted the French system of government (inadvertently, as far as Voltaire was concerned). They did so by desacralizing, delegitimizing and ultimately dislodging the keystone of that system, the monarchy. The King of France was held to have been peculiarly guilty, being the principal beneficiary of a prolonged fraud, organized by a hated Church; and the nobility, of whose honour the Most Christian King had been the fount, were made to look like secondary beneficiaries in a great ecclesiastical swindle. The guillotine awaited all of these criminals.

In *A Vindication of Natural Society*, Burke had described the nature of the pre-revolutionary process, then at a very early stage. *A Vindication* is therefore an outstanding example of Burke's capacity to foresee what was about to happen, out of the depths of his insight into what was already happening. Burke understood the long-term effects of the activity of the anti-Christian *philosophes* at a time when they themselves had no idea that they were subverting the state through their attacks on the Church. *A Vindication* is also an outstanding example of Burke's consistency, over a third of a century. He had denounced, in its embryo, in 1756, the phenomenon he was to fight in its mature form from 1790 to his death in 1797, forty-one years after the publication of *A Vindication*.

It may seem strange that in his *Appeal to the Old Whigs*, where his principal object is to establish his consistency, Burke should make no mention of *A Vindication*. But Burke is consistent even in his omissions, and this one is linked, I believe, with a striking omission in that earlier book. *A Vindication* is an attack on the anti-Christian phase of the Enlightenment, which by the 1750s had made significant progress in France – under the brilliant leadership of Voltaire – and little progress anywhere else. The main carriers of what Burke was talking about were French intellectuals, led by an enemy worthy of Burke's steel, Voltaire. Yet in *A Vindication* he makes no mention of Voltaire or of any of the other French *philosophes*, whose depredations he certainly has in mind. His ostensible target is a relatively minor figure, Henry St John, Viscount Bolingbroke, an early-eighteenth-century politician and Voltaire's leading British intellectual disciple.

In the 1750s as in the 1790s, Burke's primary targets were British importers of French ideas which he found abhorrent and dangerous. The importers targeted were Bolingbroke in the 1750s, and Richard Price and his friends in the 1790s. The articles of importation in each case were early and late products of the same philosophical manufactory, and Burke condemned them in 1756 as in the 1790s. But in *A Vindication* – quite unlike the *Reflections* – there is no mention of the original manufacturers. *A Vindication* contains no direct mention of Voltaire. The nearest Burke comes to referring to the French anti-Christian *philosophes* is in the preface: 'such are the reasonings which this noble writer and several others have been pleased to dignify with the name of philosophy.'

As so often when in Burke's pronouncements there is an unexpected silence, a failure to refer to something obviously relevant, or a cryptically guarded formulation, the probable explanation is to be found in his Irish conscience. The omissions in both *A Vindication* and *An Appeal* relate to Burke's sensitivity over Catholicism. In the 1750s, in his public persona as a good Protestant Whig, he could appropriately condemn Bolingbroke for attemping to subvert the Church of England, and so inadvertently subverting the British constitution. But Bolingbroke's mentor, Voltaire, was best known for attacking Roman Catholicism. So to condemn Voltaire for attacking religion would be to emerge as a defender of Roman Catholicism. And the omission from *An Appeal* of any reference to *A Vindication* is similar. If he had cited *A Vindication*, and demonstrated its relevance to the pre-revolutionary process in France, he could have triumphantly established his own personal consistency in resisting the ideological trends behind the revolution. But he would also have raised questions about his orthodoxy as a Protestant Whig. He had done his best to filter the anti-Catholic element out of Whiggery, and with considerable success, through his influence over Rockingham, Fox and others. But enough of that feeling was still around, even in 1790, to put him on his guard.

The last of Burke's writings and speeches on the French Revolution in the period 1789–91 – and his last while France was still ostensibly a monarchy – was *Thoughts on French Affairs*. The *Thoughts*, making a detailed case for breaking off relations with France, were prepared not for publication but for the eyes of Grenville, Pitt and possibly the King. Much of the memorandum is taken up by a *tour d'horizon* of the European powers in relation to revolutionary France towards the end of 1791, the last full year of European peace. In this context, the most important part is a passage unparalleled in Burke's public writings, comparing the French Revolution to the Reformation. Having noted that England's Glorious Revolution 'did not extend beyond its territory', he goes on:

> The present revolution in France seems to me to be quite of another character and description; and to bear little resemblance or analogy to any of those which have been brought about in Europe upon principles merely political. *It is a revolution of doctrine and theoretic dogma.* It has a much greater resemblance to those changes which have been made upon religious grounds, in which a spirit of proselytism makes an essential part.
>
> The last revolution of doctrine and theory which has happened in Europe is the Reformation. It is not for my purpose to take any notice here of the merits of that revolution, but to state one only of its effects.
>
> That effect was *to introduce other interests into all countries, than those which arose from their locality and natural circumstances.* The principle of the Reformation was such, as by its essence, could not be local or confined to the country in which it had its origin. For instance, the doctrine of 'Justification by Faith or by the Works', which was the original basis of the Reformation, could not have one of its alternatives true as to Germany and false as to every other country. Neither are questions of theoretic truth and falsehood governed by circumstances any more than by places. On that occasion, therefore, the spirit of proselytism expanded itself with great elasticity upon all sides; and great divisions were everywhere the result.
>
> These divisions however, in appearance merely dogmatic, soon became mixed with the political; and their effects were rendered much more intense from this combination. Europe was for a long time divided into two great factions, under the name of Catholic and Protestant, which not only often alienated state from state, but also divided almost every state within itself. The warm parties in each state were more affectionately attached to those of their own doctrinal interest in some other country than to their fellow citizens, or to their natural government, when they or either of them happened to be of a different persuasion. These factions, wherever they prevailed, if they did not absolutely destroy, at least weakened and distracted

the locality of patriotism. The public affections came to have other motives and other ties.

It would be to repeat the history of the last two centuries to exemplify the effects of this revolution.

Although the principles to which it gave rise did not operate with a perfect regularity and constancy, they never wholly ceased to operate. Few wars were made, and few treaties were entered into in which they did not come in for some part. They gave a colour, a character, and direction to all the politics of Europe.

These principles of internal, as well as external division and coalition, are but just now extinguished. But they who will examine into the true character and genius of some late events must be satisfied that other sources of faction, combining parties among the inhabitants of different countries into one connection, are opened, and that from these sources are likely to arise effects full as important as those which had formerly arisen from the jarring interests of the religious sects. The intention of the several actors in the change in France is not a matter of doubt. It is very openly professed.

In the modern world, before this time, there has been no instance of this spirit of general political faction, separated from religion, pervading several countries, and forming a principle of union between the partisans in each. But the thing is not less in human nature.

If Burke had used that comparison in his public works, he would have been making the largest possible present to Protestant sympathizers with the French Revolution, which is the very last thing he wanted to do. But *Thoughts on French Affairs* is essentially a state paper, containing an *argumentum ad hominem* aimed at Pitt. The message Burke sought to convey to Pitt was that the French Revolution was potentially as explosive an event, in social, political and military terms, as the Reformation had been. That warning was amply borne out, from early in the following year, throughout the remainder of the century, into the next one, and even beyond it into our own. But in late 1791, the Pitt administration was not inclined to listen. Lord Grenville, the Foreign Secretary, returned *Thoughts on French Affairs* 'without a word of observation'. Pitt, who also had a copy, said nothing either. Burke was hurt, and very much alone.

Now that Burke had left the Whigs, his connections with the government were complex. The French Revolution had transformed his relations with George III. Once Burke had made up his mind against the revolution, he dropped his long struggle to curb the power of the court. Emphasizing the need for limits to the power of the monarch was no longer appropriate when the very existence of monarchy was being challenged. And in any case the struggle was no longer necessary.

On the King's side, relations were transformed when he read the *Reflections*. George had long appreciated Burke's capacities, and now Burke became almost the apple of the royal eye. On 21 March 1791, Jane Burke proudly reported to her brother-in-law a conversation between the King and her husband: 'You have been of use to us all, it is a general opinion, is it not so Lord Stair? ... It is, said Lord Stair; – Your Majesty's adopting it, sir, will make the opinion general, said Ned – I know it is the general opinion, and I know that there is no man who calls himself a gentleman that must not think himself obliged to you, for you have supported the cause of the gentlemen.' The King also approved of the *Letter to a Member of the National Assembly*. A correspondent at court wrote to Burke on 5 May 1791: 'I lose no time in informing you that I have this morning had an opportunity of knowing, from the best authority, that His Majesty has perused it with much attention, and that he expressed very great satisfaction at the whole of it, particularly those parts which relate to Rousseau, Mirabeau and the new organization of the Courts of Justice.'

If George III had dominated the government in 1791 as he had done through Lord North from 1770 to 1782, Burke's advice to break off relations with France would have been heeded, and Burke might have been called to join the administration. But George no longer dominated as he had in the period of the American Revolution. The effective head of the administration was now the chief minister. That was how Burke and the rest of the Whigs had always thought it should be. They had won their struggle, but they were the losers by it. Paradox was piled on paradox. The ultimate eighteenth-century beneficiary of the long constitutional efforts of the Whigs, the Tory William Pitt, had come to office in 1784 through the most blatant exercise of royal initiative and authority that the reign had known. Yet this in itself had drained the King's authority and left Pitt his own master. George could not do without Pitt, and Pitt knew it. The King had been driven to stage the coup of 1784 by his desperation to rid himself of the Whigs, who had broken his will over America; but once Pitt had replaced the Fox–North coalition, George could not afford to offend Pitt by refusing to take his advice, because if he did he ran the risk of another coalition with Whigs in it, inevitably including the hated Fox. This was the stable basis of Pitt's authority.

The King, whatever the political constraints upon him, might not have accepted Pitt's authority so meekly if his own character had remained what it was in the 1770s. But his character seems to have been changed as a result of his bout of mental illness between November 1788 and February 1789. On 24 February, after his recovery, Burke observed: 'But his mind is subdued and broken; perfectly under the command of others.' On 4 April, he wrote: 'The King goes through ordinary conversations pretty much in his ordinary manner, but otherwise he is much and materially altered. He is in the most complete subjection to those who are called his attendants and in reality are his keepers. With regard to others, all jealousy with regard to his authority, a distinguishing feature of his mind, is completely gone.'

Politically, both George III and Burke were stuck with Pitt, because both now depended on him to keep the Whigs out. As far as Burke was concerned, Pitt was not nearly as hostile to the French Revolution as he should have been, but he was at least hostile in his own tepid way, whereas Fox and his friends actually supported it. So Burke had no alternative but to support Pitt, and Pitt knew this too. Burke was an extremely useful ally to Pitt, but not one Pitt particularly wished to cultivate.

Temperamentally and in political background, Burke and Pitt were remote from one another. Temperamentally, Burke was warm-hearted, hot-tempered, given to exaggeration when his emotions were aroused. Pitt was cold, and cultivated coldness. It was part of his authority. He appeared in the character of the phlegmatic Englishman, given to understatement and impervious to enthusiasm. With Pitt as the foil, Burke's Irishness showed especially strongly, and Pitt seems deliberately to have exploited this in debate in the mid 1780s in order to show Burke up as an overheated outsider.

The political background was no more conducive to friendship than their temperaments. Pitt's father, the Earl of Chatham, by accepting office in 1767 without the Rockinghams, broke the ranks of the Whigs, which led to fifteen years in the wilderness for Burke and his friends. Chatham's acceptance was regarded by the Rockinghams, and especially by Burke, as a betrayal. Burke, who was rarely uncharitable towards political opponents (with the exception of Shelburne), was startlingly vindictive towards Chatham. The savage sentence in his account of the end of the dying Chatham's famous last speech in the House of Lords, on 7 April 1778, is unique in the whole canon of Burke's writing, in its combination of bitterness and callousness: 'Lord Chatham fell upon the bosom of the Duke of Portland, in an apoplectic fit, after he had spit his last venom.' That remark was in a private letter and Pitt would probably not have known of it. But he would have known, in a general way, of Burke's antagonism to his father, and the younger Pitt was not disposed to view with favour the enemies of the elder.

Still, cool as it was, the political alliance between the two men lasted through the rest of Burke's parliamentary career, which ended in 1794.

New Whigs and Old

After his great parliamentary quarrel with Fox in May 1791, Burke did not speak again in the Commons on French affairs until 30 April 1792. Not one of the Whigs in either House had publicly taken his side against Fox, yet he knew that privately several were in substantial agreement with him and were worried about Fox's enthusiasm for the revolution. Yet they liked Fox and, perhaps more important, they detested Pitt, especially for what they regarded as his unconstitutional part, in collusion with George III, in the crisis of 1783 and the elections of 1784.

From February 1790 on, Burke never desisted from his attack on the French Revolution and its English sympathizers. But he was careful to choose the ground for his assaults. During the second half of 1791 and the first quarter of 1792, he fought the battle through correspondence, through conversation with powerful individuals, and above all through his great series of political tracts. In the Commons he held his peace.

After his break with Fox, his object in parliamentary politics was to win over the leading Foxite Whigs. The most important of these were the Duke of Portland and Earl Fitzwilliam, who were Whig magnates in the Rockingham tradition: high-minded, virtuous, cautious and conservative, liberal in tendency and a little slow. Both had great influence when they chose to exert it, which was seldom. Portland was the nominal leader of the party, and had presided over what was known as the Fox–North coalition, though in practice, both in government and in opposition, he allowed Fox to take the lead until 1794. Burke, however,

was much closer to Fitzwilliam than to Portland, and it was through
Fitzwilliam that he hoped to win over Portland also.

Fitzwilliam (1748–1833) was Rockingham's heir in material terms, and
he saw himself as Rockingham's heir in moral and intellectual terms also.
On Rockingham's death in July 1782, Burke had transferred his
allegiance, almost formally, not to Portland or Fox, the heirs to the
parliamentary leadership, but to Fitzwilliam:

> You have his place to fill and his example to follow; and you are the only
> man in the world to whom this would not be a work of the greatest difficulty.
> But to you it is so natural that it is only going on in your own course and
> inclining with the bent of your ordinary dispositions. You are Lord
> Rockingham in everything. To say this is not to flatter you; and I think it
> impossible it should displease you. I am so much convinced of this, that I
> have no doubt that you will take it in good part that his old friends, who
> were attached to him by every tie of affection and of principle, and among
> others myself, should look to you, and should not think it an act of
> forwardness and intrusion to offer you their services.

Fitzwilliam, for his part, knowing Rockingham's respect for Burke's
judgment, always heard him attentively and was often swayed by him.
When he resisted Burke's advice, he felt uneasy about doing so.

Fitzwilliam's inheritance from Rockingham included the patronage of
the borough of Malton, for which Burke sat in the Commons from 1780
to his retirement in 1794. Fitzwilliam was also Burke's patron in a
pecuniary sense, for on various occasions Burke accepted quite large
sums of money from him, as he had done from Rockingham. Yet none of
this made Burke into Fitzwilliam's mouthpiece. His public campaign
against the French Revolution was acutely uncomfortable for Fitzwilliam.
It was personally awkward because of Fitzwilliam's close friendship with
Fox, and it was politically awkward because it played into the hands of
the detested Pitt. Yet Fitzwilliam's regard for Burke was such that the
cordial tone of their correspondence is troubled only slightly at this time,
when Fitzwilliam twice attempts to renew his financial subventions to
Burke and Burke twice refuses, giving as his reason their continuing
political divergence.

Burke realized that to keep on attacking Fox in the Commons while
Fitzwilliam and Portland were still giving him general support in the

Lords would only hinder his campaign to win them over. But there was another consideration too: Burke had to wait for the French Revolution to catch up with his predictions. To many of his people, his ideas seemed almost crazily alarmist. The month of the break with Fox saw the promulgation by the National Assembly of the Déclaration de Paix au Monde (22 May 1790), a document that deeply moved Wordsworth and the German poet Friedrich Klopstock, along with many other impressionable souls. This was the high-water mark of pacific revolutionary internationalism: the happy flowering of Enlightenment cosmopolitanism. Burke's position seemed unreasonable.

The following month, with Louis XVI's flight and recapture, may have sobered the revolution's admirers a little, but after that things seemed to stabilize, with further messages of reassurance to the world. Yet Burke knew that these appearances were utterly deceptive and that harder revolutionaries would take the place of the men of 1789–91. By late 1791, these fiercer men were beginning to force events, but this was not yet perceptible to most outsiders. On the contrary, Louis XVI's acceptance of the Constitution in September appeared to inaugurate a new era in which the fruits of the revolution might be secured without undue violence. Burke would not speak again in Parliament on the subject until the real change had become unmistakable and alarming, in April 1792.

Meanwhile he was active not only in his writings but in international correspondence. The *Reflections* had made him famous throughout Europe – hated by the revolutionaries, revered by their enemies. He became the intellectual focal point, in Britain, for the European counter-revolution. Louis's brothers, the Comte de Provence (later Louis XVIII) and the Comte d'Artois (later Charles X), had succeeded in escaping from France in June 1791, and Burke's hopes for a restoration (with limited reforms) now centred on these exiled princes, for he had given up Louis for lost. He favoured counter-revolutionary war against the French regime of which Louis was the nominal head. 'I am afraid', he wrote on 16 August 1791, 'that the war in favour of monarchy must be against the monarch as well as against the rebels.'

Burke sent his son, Richard, to Coblenz in August to meet the Comte de Provence, who was next in line to the throne after Louis XVI and the Dauphin. The Comte, who was clever and an author of pamphlets, admired the *Reflections*. He and his exiled court received Richard warmly. This mission indicates Edmund Burke's unique significance in the European politics of the 1790s. He neither held any office, nor belonged to any party, and he never would again. In the political life of Great Britain he appeared to be entirely isolated, although he was in fact on the eve of a breakthrough. Yet even at the apparent nadir of his political fortunes, the radiations of his mind and the resonance of his words reached the entire civilized world. Princes thought about him and so did revolutionaries. Marie Antoinette read his passage about her in her youth, and wept as she read. The King of Poland wrote to him and so did the Pope.

In Britain too, even in his deepest isolation, Burke remained a force to be reckoned with. The Whigs as a body now hated and feared him. Pitt and his ministers valued him as an ally against them, but knew him to be an uncontrollable ally, and therefore one to be handled warily and with respect.

IRELAND 1790–92: THE BURKES AND THE CATHOLIC COMMITTEE

In the early 1790s Burke once more had an opportunity to be of direct service to the Irish Catholics. On 13 August 1790, Thomas Hussey, later president of Maynooth College and first Catholic Bishop of Waterford, wrote to Burke transmitting a letter from the Catholic Committee to his son Richard 'as a professional gentleman'. This overture asked Richard for his help in drafting an appeal to the nation. A year later came an offer of appointment as agent to the committee. With his father's approval, Richard accepted in September. Edmund took a strong interest in Richard's activities as agent, though they sat rather awkwardly with his position on the French Revolution.

The Catholic Committee had been in existence since the 1760s, but had become inactive after 1783 after the Irish Volunteers' convention in Dublin avoided committing itself to Catholic enfranchisement. The committee revived suddenly in 1790 under the stimulus of the French Revolution and the Declaration of the Rights of Man and of the Citizen, which proclaimed the spirit of the age to be explicitly at odds with disfranchisement on religious grounds.

But as exemplified by the French Revolution, the spirit of the age was also fostering a new Irish radicalism. Under the influence of Theobald Wolfe Tone, a skilful and energetic lawyer and publicist, radical

Dissenters founded the Society of United Irishmen in Belfast in October 1791 and in Dublin the following month. The society was open to all Irishmen, irrespective of religion, and was firmly committed to full enfranchisement of Catholics and removal of all legal and political impediments, as part of a general enlargement of the franchise and the espousal of a more radical politics.

On those grounds alone, the leaders of the Catholic Committee valued the United Irishmen as allies. Yet some eminent Catholics, such as the leading landowner Lord Kenmare, broke with the Catholic Committee partly because of its association with radicals from the north. Thomas Hussey, who had acted as intermediary between the committee and the Burkes, also had misgivings. His ambivalence appeared shortly after he had put Richard in touch with the Catholic Committee. He wrote to Richard:

> Hitherto the Catholics ... have proceeded with proper deference and sub-mission to the laws in their application for redress ... Sublimated, how-ever, as men's minds are by the *French disease* (as it is not improperly called), one cannot foresee what a continuation of oppressive laws may work upon the minds of people: and those of the Irish Catholics are much altered within my own memory, and they will not in future bear the lash of tyranny and oppression which I have seen inflicted upon them without their resisting or even complaining.

In September 1791, when Richard Burke agreed to serve as agent for the Catholic Committee, 'the *French disease*' of radicalism was rife, and Richard, with his father's approval, found himself in a kind of tacit alliance with ideological enemies of the author of the *Reflections*. The leaders of the Catholic Committee were discreet, but they tended to share the outlook of their United Irish friends, who by no means agreed with the *Reflections*. So why did they employ Burke's son? It is generally agreed that they did so in order to ensure Burke's support. But his support for the enfranchisement of Catholics had been apparent for nearly thirty years, often to his detriment. It looks as if what was wanted was a sign of approval specifically for the Catholic Committee, which was then engaged on a controversial and not obviously Burkean course. Richard's appointment would tend to reassure Catholics who were worried about 'the *French disease*'.

It might have been expected that Burke would wish to separate the Catholic Committee from its United Irish allies, yet instead he opposed any such separation in 1791–92. Burke saw the stigmatized condition of the Irish Catholics as the most important factor laying them open to the seductions of Jacobin ideology. He thought that if they were fully enfranchised they would fall more under the influence of their natural leaders – Catholic clergy, gentry and merchants – who themselves would be more resistant to radical influences once their own status was securely accepted. In short, Burke accepted a degree of tactical alignment with the radicals in order to defeat them later on. As often, though not always, an apparent contradiction on Burke's part turns out to exemplify a deep coherence of thought, feeling and purpose.

Burke's optimism about what might be achieved through this tactical alignment yielded to foreboding in February 1792, when the Irish Parliament contemptuously rejected the Catholic petition for enfranchisement. The concession of full enfranchisement might perhaps have turned the Catholics away from the radicals, but this rejection of enfranchisement implied the sealing of an alliance between Catholics and radicals, with potential revolutionary implications.

Richard Burke had inherited some part of his father's political insight and powers of expression, but his own political efforts were unfortunate. He was tactless in the extreme. He talked down to important people, including Portland and Fitzwilliam, and wrote them didactic letters of inordinate length. His indiscretions earned him many enemies in Britain, Ireland and Europe, and there are scathing accounts of him from people of widely differing political views. Probably the fairest account comes from Wolfe Tone, who succeeded him in the summer of 1792 as agent to the Catholic Committee:

> Richard Burke, with a considerable portion of talents from nature and cultivated, as may be well supposed, with the utmost care by his father, who idolized him, was utterly deficient in judgment, in temper and especially the art of managing. In three or four months, during which he remained in Ireland, he contrived to embroil himself and, in a certain degree, the committee, with all parties in Parliament, the opposition as well as the government . . .

The evidence of intelligence, especially in Richard's many letters to his father, is hard to reconcile with the abundant evidence of his blundering in practice. But there is something feverish about many of his letters and about his reported conduct. It may be that the tuberculosis which was to kill him in 1794, blighting his father's last three years of life, was already at work in 1791. But even if Richard had been a more effective agent, he could not have accomplished what the Catholic Committee wanted him to do. A majority in the Irish Parliament, which had enjoyed 'legislative independence' since 1782, was implacably opposed in 1791-92 to Catholic enfranchisement (as distinct from forms of relief which did not admit Catholics to any share of power). Real political authority still resided in the British government, so the Catholic Committee wanted Richard Burke (no doubt with his father's assistance) to persuade Pitt's administration to put enough pressure on the Irish Parliament to bring about Catholic enfranchisement. But Pitt did not want to do this at the time.

In principle, Pitt was in favour of Catholic enfranchisement. In practice, his administration, like most others, usually wanted Ireland to be governed with as little trouble and cost as possible. On the whole, the course that promised the least trouble was to refrain from irritating the Irish ruling class, who were now embattled under the new and provocative title of the 'Protestant Ascendancy'. This meant leaving the Catholics disfranchised. The calculations that led Pitt to pursue this policy were not likely to be changed by long letters from Richard Burke. Richard could report no progress and was in consequence dismissed by his impatient employers in July 1792. He never accepted his dismissal, which was ambiguously worded, and as it happened his most effective work by far towards achieving the committee's objectives was performed at the end of that year under dramatically altered circumstances.

Up to now, where Irish affairs were concerned, Burke had always preferred to work behind the scenes as much as possible. On America, India and France, he had made major speeches in Parliament and written major tracts for publication. But on Ireland he had spoken relatively little, often in self-defence, and often cryptically. The 'corruption' passage in the 1780 Bristol Guildhall speech had been a quite exceptional cry from the heart concerning the condition of the Irish Catholics (and of the Burkes). The *Tract Relative to the Laws against Popery*, of the early 1760s, was intended for circulation among influential people, not for publication, and was not published in his lifetime. So his first major public statement on Ireland was the *Letter to Sir Hercules Langrishe*, dated 3 January 1792.

In form it is a personal letter, but its presentation and length – sixty printed pages – suggest it was always intended to be published, as it was, in February. Feeling unable to give effective support to the Irish Catholics either behind the scenes or on the floor of the House, Burke decided to try an appeal to the Irish Parliament itself, through one of its most distinguished members. He knew that the chances of making any impact there were low, but such considerations seldom deterred him from trying, if only for acquittal of conscience. (A subsidiary motive was probably to help Richard with the Catholic Committee.) Now that he was free from all party ties and political ambitions, he was probably glad to speak freely in public about matters on which he had so long remained reticent.

At the time, Langrishe was proposing measures in the Irish House of Commons to remove Catholic disabilities in four fields: law, education, intermarriage and apprenticeships. These later carried, but they did not provide for enfranchisement. Now Burke set out to try to convince Langrishe and others that further resistance to Catholic enfranchisement would drive the Catholics into the arms of the radical Dissenters, and ultimately of the Jacobins.

Explaining his 'Herculean' proposals for limited Catholic relief in a letter to Burke of 10 December 1791, Langrishe had offered a constitutional argument which touched Burke at the most sensitive point in his political psyche. The state had to be fully Protestant, Langrishe had argued, because 'it was declared so at the Revolution'. In his *Letter*, Burke rebuts this argument by establishing a distinction never before publicly pointed out by him, although always implicit in his long commitment to Catholic relief. This is a distinction between the general principles of the Glorious Revolution and some of its actual practices, especially in Ireland, and in relation to Catholics:

[I] come to what seems to be a serious consideration in your mind: I mean the dread you express of 'reviewing, for the purpose of altering, the *principles of the Revolution*'. This is an interesting topic, on which I will, as fully as your leisure and mine permits, lay before you the ideas I have formed.

First, I cannot possibly confound in my mind all the things which were done at the Revolution with the *principles* of the Revolution. As in most great changes, many things were done from the necessities of the time, well or ill understood, from passion or from vengeance, which were not only not perfectly agreeable to its principles, but in the most direct contradiction to them. I shall not think that the *deprivation of some millions of people of all the rights of citizens, and all interest in the constitution, in and to which they were born*, was a thing conformable to the *declared principles* of the Revolution. This I am sure is true relatively to England (where the operation of these *anti-principles* comparatively were of little extent); and some of our late laws, in repealing Acts made immediately after the Revolution, admit that some things then done were not done in the true spirit of the Revolution. But the Revolution operated differently in England and Ireland, in many and these essential particulars. Supposing the principles to have been altogether the same in both kingdoms, by the application of those principles to very different objects, the whole spirit of the system was changed, not to say reversed. In England it was the struggle of the *great body* of the people for the establishment of their liberties, against the efforts of a very *small faction* who would have oppressed them. In Ireland it was the establishment of the power of the smaller number at the expense of the civil liberties and properties of the far greater part, and at the expense of the political liberties of the whole. It was, to say the truth, not a revolution, but a conquest: which is not to say a great deal in its favour. To insist on everything done in Ireland at the Revolution would be to insist on the severe and jealous policy of a conqueror, in the crude settlement of his new acquisition, as a *permanent* rule for its future government.

There follows a brief description of the situation in Ireland in the aftermath of the Glorious Revolution:

The new English interest was settled with as solid a stability as anything in human affairs can look for. All the penal laws of that unparalleled code of oppression, which were made after the last event, were manifestly the effects of national hatred and scorn towards a conquered people, whom the victors delighted to trample upon and were not at all afraid to provoke. They were not the effect of their fears, but of their security. They who carried on this system looked to the irresistible force of Great Britain for their support in their acts of power. They were quite certain that no complaints of the natives would be heard on this side of the water with any other sentiments than those of contempt and indignation. Their cries served only to augment their torture

... Indeed, in England, the double name of the complainants, Irish and Papists (it would be hard to say which singly was the most odious) shut up the hearts of everyone against them. Whilst that temper prevailed (and it prevailed in all its force to a time within our memory), every measure was pleasing and popular just in proportion as it tended to harass and ruin a set of people who were looked upon as enemies to God and man, and, indeed, as a race of bigoted savages who were a disgrace to human nature itself.

These passages completely demolished (without mentioning) the idyllic picture of Ireland's share in the blessings of the British constitution which Burke had presented to the Commons eighteen years before in his Speech on Conciliation with America. They also seriously qualify the no less idyllic picture of the Glorious Revolution he had given much more recently in the peroration of *An Appeal from the New to the Old Whigs*. The ageing Burke has dropped the old pretences and emerged from concealment in matters of great moment to him. The pretences had been only occasional, and the two examples cited are the chief ones among his published works. But the concealment had been habitual since boyhood, and must have been hard to break. He had never concealed his detestation of the penal laws themselves, but with the exception of the isolated outburst in the Bristol Guildhall speech of 1780, he had concealed the extent of his emotional identification with the conquered people. This new openness was a final sacrifice in the cause of the Irish Catholics, whose emancipation he hoped to help to complete before his death, by unreserved support for the efforts of the Catholic Committee.

In writing to Langrishe, Burke stresses the continuity of his own thinking on these matters: 'Though my hand but signs it, my heart goes with what I have written. Since I could think at all, those have been my thoughts.' We may be sure that these had indeed always been his thoughts, but during most of his life his strategy with regard to Irish affairs had been such as to preclude Ireland's becoming a major theme of his pronouncements. Ireland profoundly affected the great melody of his oratory and his writings, but usually indirectly, through inflections, mainly on the themes of India and France, and sometimes on America. So most of that part of the great melody that refers directly to Ireland is contained in this late work, the *Letter to Sir Hercules Langrishe*.

Burke knew that the most effective argument at his disposal, in relation to the Parliament of which Langrishe was a Member, was that it was no longer safe to keep the Catholics disfranchised. If members of the Established Church insisted on that, they would push the Catholics into the arms of the radical Dissenters, the United Irishmen, and so in the direction of revolution:

> You are to weigh, with the temper [moderation] which is natural to you, whether it may be for the safety of our establishment that the Catholics should be ultimately persuaded that they have no hope to enter into the constitution but through the Dissenters...
>
> Suppose the people of Ireland divided into three parts. Of these (I speak within compass), two are Catholic; of the remaining third, one half is composed of Dissenters. There is no natural union between those descriptions. It may be produced. If the two parts Catholic be driven into a close confederacy with half the third part of Protestants, with a view to a change in the constitution in Church or state or both, and you rest the whole of their security on a handful of gentlemen, clergy, and their dependents, compute the strength *you have in Ireland* to oppose to grounded discontent, to capricious innovation, to blind popular fury, and to ambitious, turbulent intrigue.

A Letter to Sir Hercules Langrishe was ill received in Dublin Castle. The Lord Lieutenant, Lord Westmorland, in a letter to Pitt, referred to Richard Burke as bent on 'inflammation' in Ireland and went on: 'If the father is a friend of peace, it was most injudicious to publish that inflammatory Letter to Sir Hercules Langrishe.' Burke was certainly a sincere 'friend of peace', and believed that Catholic enfranchisement would promote it. Yet Westmorland had a point too: language such as Burke was using did have an inflammatory effect, as long as enfranchisement was denied. Burke, however, put the blame for the inflammation, not unreasonably, on the unjust and unwise denial of enfranchisement, and not on his own critique of that policy.

THE REVOLUTION SPREADS FROM FRANCE, 1792–93

In 1792, the French Revolution began unmistakably to match Burke's vision of it. On 20 April, the National Assembly declared war on Austria. The declaration affirmed, in the name of the National Assembly, that it 'adopts in advance all foreigners who, abjuring the cause of its enemies, range themselves under its banners and consecrate their efforts to the defence of its liberty'. Jacques Brissot, the leader of the dominant Girondin faction in the Assembly, proclaimed the war to be 'a universal crusade for liberty'. At the popular level, the slogan was one of class war: 'War on the castles, peace to the cabins.' French revolutionary expansionism, both military and ideological, was now in full spate.

The supposition of Fox and Sheridan that the revolution was no more than a French internal affair was now in ruins. The pro-French radical societies with which they had flirted ceased to look like groups of harmless enthusiasts and now appeared in the sinister guise of people who might be 'ranged under the banners' of a foreign revolutionary Assembly. In particular, the formation by a group of younger Whig parliamentarians of the Association of the Friends of the People – established a few days before the proclamation of the 'universal crusade for liberty' – was acutely embarrassing to the Whig leaders. The time had come for Burke to break his parliamentary silence over these matters.

The occasion, on 30 April 1792, was well suited to his purposes. It was a debate about parliamentary reform of the kind favoured by pro-French clubs, and had been proposed by the young Charles Grey, one of the radical Whigs of the Association of Friends of the People. Burke's remaining Whig friends, headed by Portland and Fitzwilliam, strongly disapproved of Grey and his associates, and Burke now had an excellent opportunity to win them over by attacking the young radicals. His assault, as recorded in the *Parliamentary History*, was short and sharp:

> There were in this country men who scrupled not to enter into an alliance with a set in France of the worst traitors and regicides that had ever been heard of – the club of the Jacobins. He asked if this was a time for encouraging visionary reforms in this country.

Burke's use of the words 'regicides' is remarkable. Louis XVI was still on his throne, and there were as yet no legal charges against him. But Burke had believed from very early on that regicide was implicit in the nature of the French Revolution.

Fox's reply was vague, low-key, and cannot have been satisfactory to Grey and his friends. It seems to have encouraged Burke in the hope that

Fox might distance himself from the sympathizers with the revolution, now that its dangerous character had become so patent. He soon had a chance to make a public overture to Fox. On 11 May 1792, the anniversary of the last of the encounters that broke off their friendship, there was a debate on Fox's 'motion for the repeal of certain statutes respecting religious opinions'. The overture to Fox was an awkward affair: a little stilted, a little hollow, as if Burke were forcing himself, in a good cause. He began by praising 'the delicacy used by the right hon. gentleman [Fox] in matters of religion', and, still more artificially, claimed to have arrived, through Fox's speech, at a most satisfactory 'discovery'. This was 'that the House was untainted by those false principles which had been so amply circulated without doors'. The so-called discovery was really an offer: if Fox would now repudiate 'those false principles', Burke was prepared to forget that Fox had ever been tainted by them.

This time Fox's reply was uncompromisingly negative: 'His opinions of the French Revolution were precisely the same now as they had ever been. The right hon. gentleman's book was a libel on every free constitution in the world.' Whatever the French revolutionaries might actually do, Charles James Fox would remain true to the idealized view of the revolution that he had formed at the very beginning, in July 1789. Burke, for his part, saw the news from France as irrefutable confirmation of the validity of his analysis in the book that Fox now once again condemned. So the chasm between them actually widened during the debate.

Rebuffed by Fox, Burke concentrated on splitting the Whigs, bringing as many of them as possible to support Pitt's ministry in preparation for the coming war with France. In the Commons, the able and energetic William Windham (1750–1810) set up a small Burkean 'third party' and became a target of bitter hostility from his former Whig colleagues. But Burke's main hopes rested with Earl Fitzwilliam and the Duke of Portland. Fitzwilliam at least was now thoroughly alarmed. Both Fitzwilliam and Portland were slowly overcoming their objection to a coalition, but their ideas were still unrealistic. Portland was thinking of a coalition not headed by Pitt, and including Fox. Pitt, well aware of the disarray of the opposition, had no intention of agreeing to anything of the kind.

Some Whigs, during this pivotal year, were torn between loyalty to

Fox and growing awareness of the weight of Burke's argument over the French Revolution. One such was a contemporary of Windham who later became a full disciple of Burke, Sir Gilbert Elliot (1751–1814). There is a remarkable letter in which he expressed the torment of mind he felt at having to resist Burke's 'authority'. Elliot, who had long been on friendly terms with Burke, mainly over Indian affairs, had written to Burke proposing to visit him at Beaconsfield on 7 April and received a reply agreeing. He sent on the reply to his wife. Noting 'a little stiffness' in it, he went on:

> The truth is that I have had a horror at this meeting, and that he does not know how to feel on the subject either. I believe his disposition towards me to be affectionate and kind as usual, but I know his sanguine character so well that I cannot doubt of his being at heart deeply hurt and affected at my withdrawing myself from the [Indian] proceeding of last year. My own wish, and a very anxious one it is, is to return to the most unlimited cordiality and affection with him in point of private and personal friendship; but besides that I am unable to go all lengths with him on the subject which most engrosses his mind – the *French question* – I have felt so sensibly the evil of admitting any sway over my mind so powerful and sovereign as his was, and have found myself so often led to a fluctuation of opinion on important points by yielding first to the influence of his authority and then having to combat the same point with my own reason, and I think the particular subject of his present attention is so likely to lead to questions of immense moment on which every man should form an opinion of *his own*, and regulate his conduct by an unbiased and *temperate* judgment, that I cannot again surrender myself so unconditionally even to Burke; and this is a resolution which I *must* acquaint him with.

This is the only first-hand account that has come down to us of what it felt like to come within the Burkean field of force and to offer resistance to it. Elliot's experience is a clue to much in the political behaviour of Rockingham, Fox and Fitzwilliam, and even, though to a much lesser extent, of Pitt. It is therefore a clue to a great part of the political pattern of the late eighteenth century. Elliot's account establishes the folly of estimating Burke's political influence by the magnitude of the offices he held. Elliot was not responding to a former Paymaster of the Forces. He was struggling to resist 'any sway over my mind so powerful and sovereign as his was'. Later, Elliot came round completely to Burke's view.

In July and August, the French Revolution made another surge in the direction predicted by Burke. The Girondins, heirs to the constitution-makers of 1790–91, had opted for war in the hope of generating patriotic enthusiasm, uniting the nation behind them, and silencing the more radical revolutionaries who accused them of betraying the revolution. There was no mistake about the patriotic enthusiasm – the 'Marseillaise' was written in the first days of the war with Austria – but the rest of the Girondin programme went badly wrong. The war itself went badly at first, and military failures were blamed on the treachery of the King and his pseudo-revolutionary allies.

The blow fell on 10 August, when an insurrectionary republican Commune massacred the King's Swiss Guard and overthrew the monarchy. The Girondins were discredited and doomed. The Constitution of 1790–91 had collapsed, as Burke had said it would. And as Burke had also predicted, a new generation of revolutionaries, harder and more purposeful – Danton, Robespierre and others – took the places of the Utopian innovators who had opened the way for them. The Royal Family were transferred to prison in the Temple. Other prisons were full of suspects arrested as counter-revolutionaries, including many clergy. The Prussian Army besieged Verdun and threatened Paris. For four days, armed revolutionary mobs roamed the city, entering the prisons and massacring prisoners. The mobs were encouraged by the Commune and unchecked by an Assembly where the members were terrified for their own lives.

On 17 August, Burke wrote to James Bland Burges, the Foreign Under-Secretary, who had just sent him some of the accounts received by the government about the fall of the French monarchy and imprisonment of the Royal Family. He wrote: 'I am infinitely obliged to you for your constant attention to my feelings. I certainly am much interested in what happens in France, the effects and example of which I am certain cannot be confined to that kingdom. Even if they could, there is enough to shock and afflict any person whose heart is not wholly alienated from his species. I looked for some such an event for a long time. But let these things be never so much expected they still confound one when they happen.'

Burke went on to put a question intended to push Pitt in the direction of a breach with the new republic. It concerned the position of Lord Gower, then British ambassador in Paris. Gower had, of course, been accredited to Louis, who was now in effect deposed. So Burke asked: 'Will Lord Gower continue in Paris? If he should, will his old commission and credentials serve him, or must he have a new one to the new power set up by the Jacobins? I do by no means envy his situation; which, whatever other advantages it may have, does not shine in point of dignity.' On the day he wrote that, a despatch was sent to Lord Gower 'instructing him to return to England, reiterating the King's neutrality on the internal affairs of France and his solicitude for the personal situation of their Most Christian Majesties and their Royal Family'. This was much less than what Burke wanted, which was a complete break with revolutionary France, followed by war. But the recall of the British ambassador was a step in the right direction.

On the same day, Burke wrote to Fitzwilliam, giving him the news from France and striking while the iron was hot. After an introductory paragraph about sheep-breeding – a hobby the two had in common – Burke got down to business:

All Europe seems to me to be collecting from various causes and on various principles some new and grievous malady, from the contagion of which I am far from thinking that this country is likely to be exempted. The events which have lately happened in France, though by me, and by most others I believe, perfectly foreseen in all the extent of their atrocity, are nearly as shocking and disgusting to me as if they had come upon me quite unexpectedly. I have not, I confess, the same humane sympathy with the actors in all these horrors which has made many gentlemen think that the blessings of the French system of the rights of man had been bought at an unusually cheap purchase: but it is paid for by instalments – and the price may to them at last appear more adequate to the real value of the object. Their appetite is pretty sharp – but be their hunger for the destruction of everything to which the vulgar idea of dignity had hitherto been annexed be never so sharp (and I know how sharp it is), one would think it has been nearly satiated. I know the bitter hatred which many persons in a certain party entertain against priests, nobility, and kings, but one would think they might relent a little at the murder of such a multitude of clergy and the famine and dispersion of such numbers more, an hundred thousand at least of both sexes. The expatriation, spoliation, and ruin of twenty-five thousand princes, noblemen, and gentlemen – and truly as to kings and queens, it is hard to satisfy their hunger and thirst for their persecution, if they are not now glutted. I do suppose, that such a termination of the misery and captivity of three years, attended with humiliations and mortification of every sort, could hardly be exceeded by any effort of imagination; and this but preparatory to the dreadful death that awaits them.

So far, Burke is on common ground; he knew Fitzwilliam's feelings about all this were the same as his own. But now he points the political moral, first against Fox, Fitzwilliam's friend, and then against Fitzwilliam himself:

Surely all this will be enough to satiate even Mr Fox, and Mr Sheridan, or Dr Priestley – or whoever carries these triumphs the farthest. If this King and Queen had been guilty of all the crimes that ever were committed by kings and queens from the beginning of the world, they have surely expiated them all in their own persons. Yet Mr Fox's newspaper chooses to tell the people of England and of Europe that the horrors of this tragic narration, many facts of which it details correctly, was owing, to the 'want of *candour*' (want of candour truly) in the miserable victims, and that they themselves were the authors of all the crimes from which they suffered. Mr Fox's paper only describes the calamities of these unfortunate people to aggravate the load of their affliction. This paper professes to convey to France the sentiments of the independent people of England. This paper for two years past has stimulated the French to all their excesses. It laments indeed the excesses which have been committed, but it laments them only on account of the ill consequences they may have on their blessed scheme of liberty. Thank God that I have been completely separated from all the partisans of that sort of liberty. If I cannot, as I cannot, preserve the freedom of others from its tyranny, I have hitherto at least preserved my own. I am not in the way of being witness to the insolent triumph and savage joy of these philosophic and patriotic fomentors of all that degrades and debases human nature. I know that the faction in France which looked not a little to names in England could not have stood their ground without English countenance. It is most certain, though very extraordinary, that these people had their eyes fixed on England for everything, and that even an alehouse club was important to them. How much more the first and most splendid names in this country, carrying with them the weight and sanction of great parties.

That last startling sentence is the nub of the whole letter. Here Burke implicitly accused Fitzwilliam and Portland of a share in responsibility – through the 'countenance' they had given and were continuing to give to Fox's policy – for the bloody and destructive course of the French Revolution. Burke was prone to torture himself if ever he felt he had been complicit with evil, or even insufficiently successful in opposing it, and he wished to prevent his friends too from becoming fellow travellers. Subsequent developments were to show that his words were not wasted on Fitzwilliam, though they took effect more slowly than Burke wished.

Two weeks later came the September Massacres, the news of which could only reinforce Burke's message. As the year 1792 closed, the French Revolution was intensifying and expanding. On 20 September, the Duke of Brunswick's invading force was defeated at Valmy. The newly elected National Convention proclaimed the republic 'one and indivisible'. On 19 November, the Convention, in the First Propagandist Decree, declared 'that it will grant fraternity and aid to all peoples'. In December, the Austrian Netherlands was annexed, under the name of 'Belgium'. Savoy, Nice and the Rhineland were also declared to be returned to the Motherland.

Fitzwilliam and Portland hoped that the eyes of Fox and Sheridan would be opened by the course of events in Europe. On the contrary, Fox seemed to be exhilarated by the triumphs of the revolution he had loved so steadfastly from its beginnings. By late November, Portland was beginning to suspect Fox of wanting a revolution in England. As the Duke put it, in his rather mealy-mouthed way, 'I am sorry to say that I fear I observed symptoms of no very strong indisposition to submit to the experiment of a new and possibly a republican system of government.' His fears were to be confirmed in the following month. On 4 December, at the Whig Club, Fox toasted 'the friends of liberty all over the world' and professed himself 'an advocate for the rights of the people'. Fitzwilliam gloomily commented: 'When coupled with the times ... his commenting upon them at all does not meet with my approbation.' But Fox was already reconciling himself to the probable loss of Fitzwilliam and Portland and their following: 'I grow doubtful of preserving those connections which I love and esteem as much as ever.' The Whig party was moving inexorably towards disintegration, with Burke and Fox, from their opposing sides, driving the process on.

On 11 December 1792, in Paris, the trial of Louis XVI for treason began. Two days later, the new session of Parliament opened at Westminster, following scenes of turmoil in Britain itself. In the Commons, the Address of Thanks moved by Pitt included the words: 'That we learn with concern, that not only a spirit of tumult and disorder has shown itself in acts of insurrection, which required the interposition of a military force in support of the civil magistrate, but that the industry employed to excite discontent has appeared to proceed from a design to attempt, in concert with persons in foreign countries, the destruction of our happy constitution, and the subversion of all order of government.'

Fox denied it all, and his followers were in surprisingly boisterous mood. When Windham rose to speak, he was 'interrupted with loud cries'. Burke came to Windham's aid with a point of order and went on to speak himself: 'He, for his own part, declared himself to be not a defender of ministry or opposition, but of the country. The French had declared war against all kings, and of consequence against this country, if it had a King. The question now was not whether we shall carry an address to the King, but whether we should have a King at all.' Burke did not, at this stage, attack Fox. But Fox intervened again, stating flatly: 'France had justice completely on her side' – an astonishing form of words, considering the nature of the judicial proceedings unfolding in France as he was speaking, and virtually treasonous too. He thought that Britain 'ought immediately to acknowledge the government of France and to adopt all honourable means of procuring peace'. He therefore urged that the British ambassador be sent back to Paris.

Burke replied rather mildly, considering the provocation:

And what was the peculiar time when we were desired to despatch an ambassador to them? At the very moment perhaps when the merciless savages had their hands red with the blood of a murdered King. The Koran which France held out was the declaration of the rights of man and universal fraternity; and with the sword she was determined to propagate her doctrines, and conquer those whom she could not convince.

Still Fox drove on. Five days later, he introduced in the Commons a formal 'motion for sending a minister to Paris to treat with the provisional government of France'. Burke's speech against this showed, in its conclusion, that his patience was wearing thin: 'Let no ambassador go thither from Great Britain. If we condescend to acknowledge them by sending an ambassador, might they not insult him by saying "Who sent you? The King or the people?" ... I say we are now engaged in actual war ... If there must be a war, it had arisen from the proceedings of those among themselves who, by their seditious practices, had provoked it.'

As the execution of Louis drew nearer, Fox's Whigs showed signs that they knew they had gone too far. On 20 and 21 December, the Commons debated the situation of the French Royal Family. Opening for the Whigs, Sheridan appealed to the French authorities for 'justice, mercy and magnanimity'. Burke would have none of this: 'Mr Burke was not one who looked up to the leaders of the revolution in France for justice, magnanimity or mercy – he was not willing to apply to them, in any way, for the exercise of those virtues. The truth was, the King was in the custody of assassins who were both his accusers and his judges, and his destruction was inevitable.'

During this debate, Pitt's administration presented a copy of 'the instructions dated 17 August sent to Earl Gower, His Majesty's ambassador to the Most Christian King, signifying His Majesty's pleasure that he should quit Paris'. The instructions expressed 'solicitude for the personal situation of their Most Christian Majesties' and warned 'that any acts of violence could not fail to produce one universal sentiment of indignation throughout every country in Europe'. Fox declared his 'concurrence' with these instructions, and so did Sheridan. The *Parliamentary History* records Burke as observing that these 'manly declarations' by Fox and Sheridan 'deserved the highest approbation', but this did not presage any reconciliation.

A week later, Burke again strongly attacked Fox, saying that 'any person who had seen the French business in the bud, and who now saw it fully blown and matured, and yet still wished to maintain any connection between France and this country must, in every respect, meet with his entire disapprobation'. This speech of 21 December became famous as the 'dagger speech'.

He mentioned the circumstances of three thousand daggers having been bespoke at Birmingham by an Englishman, of which several had been delivered. It was not ascertained how many of these were to be exported, and how many were intended for home consumption. [Here Mr Burke drew out a dagger which he had kept concealed, and with much vehemence of action threw it to the floor.] This, said he, pointing to the dagger, is what you are to gain by an alliance with France: wherever their principles are introduced, their practice must follow.

The Foxites naturally ridiculed this bit of business, and it was probably a mistake on Burke's part to be so theatrical. Yet at this time Burke was at the height of his influence in relation to the French Revolution. No sensible person, by the end of 1792, could any longer regard Burke's diagnosis in the *Reflections* as alarmist. He had indeed, at the beginning of 1790, 'seen the French business in the bud', and all could see it now 'fully blown and matured'. The Foxites might jeer, but others contemplated him with immense respect, and Pitt took care to consult him in the midst of the great European crisis of the winter of 1792–93.

Since the final fall of the French monarchy in August, Burke had been urging Pitt to declare war on revolutionary France. His case became stronger with the King's execution on 21 January 1793. Three days later, the Foreign Secretary, Grenville, informed the French ambassador that his functions were 'now entirely terminated by the fatal death of his late Most Christian Majesty' and that 'the King can no longer permit your residence here'. The National Assembly retaliated, on 1 February, by declaring war on 'the King of England'.

On the eve of war with France, Burke was in close contact with ministers, and on 8 February 1793, when the French declaration reached England, Pitt immediately sent him a copy. Consultations between them continued after the outbreak of war, and Burke is reported to have attended a meeting of the Cabinet on 13 February. On 6 March, Burke, Windham and Sir Gilbert Elliot met Pitt and Dundas. Elliot left a valuable account of how Burke exerted his influence on that occasion:

Pitt was of course all civility, and desired that we would never make the smallest scruple of applying for any information we wished, or suggesting anything we thought useful, promising to attend to it with great care, and assuring us of a perfectly confidential communication of all information. He gave us a good deal of satisfaction concerning naval preparations, and on all other points gave us encouraging information. Burke gave him a little political instruction, in a very respectful and cordial way, but with the authority of an old and most informed statesman; and although nobody ever takes the whole of Burke's advice, yet he often, or rather always, furnishes very important and useful matter, *some part* of which sticks and does good. Pitt took it all very patiently and cordially.

IRELAND AT WAR

Over Irish affairs too, the conditions of late 1792 and early 1793 were conducive to the taking of some of Burke's advice. This was the time of Burke's greatest influence with Pitt, and he used it to bring about a major measure of Catholic emancipation. On 3 December, the General Committee of the Roman Catholics of Ireland, a new and popularly elected body, drew up a petition to the King to be given a share 'in the advantages of the constitution'. The strategy of petitioning the King directly, bypassing the Irish administration and Parliament, was one that Edmund and Richard Burke had recommended. The Catholic petitioners arrived in London on 18 December. They relied on Richard as their agent, despite his earlier dismissal by the Catholic Committee the previous July, and following a private interview between Richard and Pitt on Christmas Day 1792, the delegates were presented to George III on 2 January.

A major Catholic Relief Bill followed in the Irish Parliament in April, and was carried with the decisive support of the British administration (despite the fiction of 'legislative independence'). The Catholic Relief Act of 1793 removed almost all the remaining Catholic disabilities. By far the most important exception was that Catholics, though admitted to the franchise, were still excluded from Parliament. More than two years later, an attempt to remove that exception – inspired, ultimately, by Burke – was to end in disaster. But for the present Burke was happy, having achieved much of what he had hoped for Ireland.

Pitt's motive in bringing about this major measure of Catholic relief was to reduce the danger of insurrection in case of a French landing. Yet the danger would not go away. Burke was acutely aware of it in the months immediately after the French declaration of war. This appears from a letter he wrote to Henry Grattan on 8 March 1793 to congratulate him on the Catholic Relief Act. Burke refers to 'the mutinous spirit which is in the very constitution of the lower part of our compatriots of every description, and now begins to ferment with tenfold force by the leaven of republicanism, which always existed, though without much noise in the northern parts of the kingdom, but now becomes more evident and requires no small degree both of firm and of prudent management'. He is referring to what we are likely to think of, in retrospect, as early rumblings of the Great Rebellion which broke out in 1798, the year after his death.

Among the main carriers of revolutionary ideas in Ireland were the United Irishmen. Ostensibly, at its inception, the Society of the United Irishmen had purely constitutional objectives centred on reform of the franchise, and no doubt many of its members aimed at no more. But there is some evidence that its founders had bolder ambitions. Entries in Wolfe Tone's journal are conspiratorial from the beginning:

> *October 12 [1791]*: Mode of doing business [of the United Irishmen] by a secret committee who are not known or suspected of co-operating, but who in fact direct the movement of Belfast.
> *17 August 1792: The King of France dethroned*. Very glad of it . . .
> *25 October 1792: This is* [the anniversary of] *the King's accession. How many more accessions shall we have?*
> *26–31 January, 1793*. The King of France was beheaded on the 21st January. *I am sorry it was necessary*.

Burke would have been horrified if he had known that these were the real sentiments of the man who had succeeded his son as agent of the Catholic Committee. Burke was right about that 'leaven of republicanism', but he did not realize how near that leaven was to the committee whose declared objectives he and his son supported.

In the course of their agitation, the middle-class Catholics of the committee had also made contact with the other main carrier of revolutionary feelings and ideas: a complex social and political movement among Catholics called the Defenders. This movement had agrarian, sectarian, millenarian and revolutionary aspects, and was broadly anti-Protestant and anti-English. In the early 1790s, then, the Defenders were awkward potential partners for the non-sectarian United Irishmen, but in the second half of the decade the two apparently quite disparate societies became overlapping parts of one large and confused revolutionary movement.

In the meantime, in its radical phase, from 1790 onwards, the Catholic Committee was in touch with both the United Irishmen and the Defenders. There is an element of paradox about Burke, the great counter-revolutionary, being involved with the radical Catholic Committee. But while Burke was conservative in relation to Britain, being determined to defend the constitution against its Jacobin and pro-Jacobin enemies, he was not conservative in relation to Ireland, where the full benefits of the British constitution were still denied to the majority of the population, including his relatives. He did not want Jacobinism to spread to Ireland, but he knew that fear of its spread was the best hope of securing full Catholic enfranchisement. The Catholic Committee, in its cordial relations with the United Irishmen, was exploiting that fear, and Edmund Burke was not above abetting it, within limits.

Burke and Tone – who met only once – were utterly at odds over the French Revolution. But they were allies, in the early 1790s, in relation not only to the principle of Catholic enfranchisement but in support for the Catholic Committee's programme for securing it, through popular agitation with an implicit threat behind it. They were agreed, tacitly, on an immediate objective, and on a tactic for achieving it. But while Burke hoped that the removal of all Catholic disabilities would have a tranquillizing effect, diminishing the attractions of Jacobinism and strengthening the connection between Ireland and Great Britain, Wolfe Tone hoped that the struggle for enfranchisement, the resistance to it, and the spread of revolutionary ideas would destroy sectarian differences and produce a new Ireland, emancipated both from British rule and from Catholic superstition. Neither dream was to be fulfilled, and both turned to nightmare in 1795–98.

Yet in 1793–94, the first two years of the war with France, the thought of possible revolution in Ireland, though never entirely absent from Burke's mind, was not among his most pressing preoccupations. Richard Burke's connection with the Catholic Committee had come to an end in 1792, and the committee itself went into abeyance in 1793, perhaps partly because of the Catholic Relief Act of that year, but mainly because of the great difficulty of conducting open, popular agitation in time of war. At the same time the Society of United Irishmen, in its original form, dwindled to nearly nothing. With Britain at war with France, pro-French propaganda became almost impossible, and in any case the French Revolution no longer looked attractive to many of those who had idealized it in 1790–91. The real revolutionaries, probably a minority of the original membership, bided their time, or went underground.

Concern about Ireland was perennial with Burke, and always linked to his other concerns. But his prime focus, from 1793 on, was prosecution of the war with revolutionary France. His major contribution was to be the consolidation of parliamentary support for the war by ensuring the defection of as many Whigs as possible from Fox's opposition. In February, when a resolution of the Whig Club confirmed its attachment to Fox and repudiated 'calumnies' against him, Burke and about forty others, including Windham and Elliot, resigned from the Club.

As Fitzwilliam and Portland had approved the pro-Fox resolution of the Whig Club, Burke's resignation in protest was an implicit rebuke to them. In September, he made the rebuke explicit, with *Observations on the Conduct of the Minority*, an indictment, under fifty-four heads, of Fox's misdeeds in relation to the French Revolution. In the covering letter with which he sent this formidable document to Portland, he pointed the moral: '[There is] no man who is connected with a party which professes publicly to admire or may be justly suspected of secretly abetting this French Revolution, who must not be drawn into its vortex and become the instrument of its designs.' As George III and Lord North had found over America, and as Hastings and Pitt had found over India, so Portland and Fitzwilliam now found over France that Burke was hard to deflect.

October 1793 brought the trial and execution of Marie Antoinette. 'Oh God!' wrote Burke. 'The charge! and the last article particularly!' (The last article stated that Marie Antoinette 'committed indecencies with her own son, too shocking to mention'.) 'All this', Burke went on, 'is but the unfolding of the Jacobin system.' That Burke had foreseen the system's consequences did not lessen his horror as he contemplated events in France and the acceptance of them by his former friends. For even the advent of the Terror made no change in the attitude of the Foxites.

At the end of 1793, Burke wrote to Fitzwilliam declining an offer of financial assistance, because he regarded Fitzwilliam's continued support for Fox as incompatible with confidence in Burke himself:

I send back enclosed the papers, which you were so good to send to me, with a thousand thanks. My dear lord, the debt of gratitude is never to be cancelled; and whilst honour, virtue, and benignity are entitled to the love and esteem of mankind you ever must have an uncontrovertible title to my cordial and respectful attachment: but when confidence and good opinion on your side no longer exist, you must be sensible that an intercourse of this kind cannot continue ... I am not at all surprised that the Jacobins should represent me after *their* manner. That their representations should have so much weight with you is not what I equally expected – but the thing is done and I say no more of it in the way of discussion. I shall only say in justice to my intentions that I am not conscious to myself of having been wanting to the demands of public principle or private friendship. I am however come to a time of life in which it is not permitted that we should trifle with our existence. I am fallen into a state of the world that will not suffer me to play at little sports or to enfeeble the part I am bound to take by smaller collateral considerations. I cannot proceed as if things went on in the beaten circle of events such as I have known them for towards half a century. The moral state of mankind fills me with dismay and horror. The abyss of hell itself seems to yawn before me. I must act, think, and feel according to the exigencies of this tremendous season.

Both Fitzwilliam and Portland now capitulated and broke with Fox. On Christmas Day, Portland told Fitzwilliam of his intention to notify Fox of his determination 'to support the war with all the effect and energy in my power'. Although Fox led the Whigs in the Commons, Portland ranked as leader of the party as a whole. In that capacity, he invited Burke to the Whigs' eve-of-session meeting on 20 January 1794, at Burlington House. It must have been a most uncomfortable meeting. Portland 'made a strong and decisive speech declaring his support for the [Pitt] ministry', and urged the same course on his followers. Henceforward, in both Houses, the Portland Whigs were a separate party, speaking and voting against the Foxites, in favour of the war and of measures of repression against Jacobin propaganda. Rather like Fox's East India Bill, the Portland Whigs were essentially a Burkean creation, moulded by his thinking.

Fitzwilliam went with Portland. In February in the Lords, Burke's old bugbear, the former Earl of Shelburne, now Marquess of Lansdowne, proposed a motion for peace with France. Fitzwilliam opposed him, on thoroughly Burkean lines:

With regard to peace with France, we could have no hopes of it under the present system, unless we were prepared to sacrifice everything that was dear to us ... the safety of the country, the preservation of the constitution, of everything dear to Englishmen and to their posterity, depended upon the preventing the introduction of French principles and the new-fangled doctrine of the rights of man; and that this could only be effected by the establishment of some regular form of government in that country upon which some reliance might be placed.

The creation of the Portland Whigs, bringing new support to the war against the French Revolution, was a major victory for Burke. He was now to work to consolidate that victory by the creation of a coalition government.

INDIA: CLOSING THE IMPEACHMENT

In 1794, Burke finally acquitted himself of the impeachment of Warren Hastings, after more than six years. Its management had been a self-imposed and totally unrewarded labour in the service of the peoples of India. The Speech in Reply at its close was, and was intended to be, his last major speech, and his longest. It lasted from 28 May to 16 June. As a whole it is not among his greatest, although it has profound moments and contains the final strain of the Indian part of the great melody. Its mood is of grim determination in the discharge of duty. But Burke knew the end was likely to be bitter, as he soon made clear: 'The wreck and fragments of our cause (which has been dashed to pieces upon rules by which your lordships have thought fit to regulate its progress) await your final determination.' The rules that dashed Burke's hopes of success were those which required the managers to show that Warren Hastings personally had committed crimes, or directly and explicitly ordered their commission. Under such rules, the impeachment could not succeed.

When opening the impeachment, Burke had hoped to arouse public opinion sufficiently to make the Lords fear the consequences of acquitting Hastings and thus to persuade them to relax their interpretation of the rules. He had therefore played on the emotions of his audience. This might have worked if the hearings had been completed in 1788–89, when there was still intense public interest. But the Lord Chancellor and others interested in an acquittal had spun out the proceedings, to Burke's frustration, and by 1794 public opinion had been irretrievably lost. In France that summer, the Terror was raging. The impeachment was yesterday's news.

In his opening speech, before a fashionable throng in Westminster Hall, Burke had stressed the cruelty of Hastings' system. In his closing speech, with nobody listening but a few unimpressionable peers, he stressed the system's fraudulent nature. Perhaps he hoped that some peers who would scarcely be moved by the suffering of Indians might resent deceptions invented to defraud people like themselves. One such was the fiction that Hastings was the servant of the Company's Court of Directors, whereas in reality it was the other way round; another was the fiction that the Nabob of Oudh was an independent prince, whereas he was in reality Hastings' slave. There were many others. Burke presented himself as one who was giving the Lords a conducted tour behind the scenes of Hastings' India. This was, in particular, the theme of the fourth day of the speech:

> I only think it necessary that your lordships should truly know the actual state of that country, and the ground upon which Mr Hastings stood. Your lordships will find it a fairy land, in which there is a perpetual masquerade, where no one thing appears as it really is – where the person who seems to have the authority is a slave, while the person who seems to be the slave has the authority. In that ambiguous government, everything favours fraud, everything favours peculation, everything favours violence, everything favours concealment.

And then, after the production of a number of telling exhibits:

> Now, my lords, was there ever such a discovery made of the arcana of any public theatre? You see here, behind the ostensible scenery, all the crooked working of the machinery developed and laid open to the world. You now see by what secret movement the master of the mechanism has conducted the great Indian opera – an opera of fraud, deceptions, and harlequin tricks. You have it all laid open before you. The ostensible scene is drawn aside; it has vanished from your sight. All the strutting signors, and all the soft signoras are gone; and instead of a brilliant spectacle of descending chariots, gods, goddesses, sun, moon, and stars, you have nothing to gaze on but sticks, wire, ropes, and machinery. You find the appearance all false and fraudulent; and you see the whole trick at once.

A few such touches apart, the Speech in Reply is a dogged, conscientious, sustained exposition. But there is one long passage, from the first day, where the great melody is unmistakable. The passage is the extraordinary panegyric on 'sympathetic revenge', which concludes with a contingent curse on the House of Lords if they dare to acquit Hastings.

If it should still be asked why we show sufficient acrimony to exact a suspicion of being in any manner influenced by malice or a desire of revenge, to this, my lords, I answer, Because we would be thought to know our duty, and to have all the world know how resolutely we are resolved to perform it. The Commons of Great Britain are not disposed to quarrel with the divine wisdom and goodness, which has moulded up revenge into the frame and constitution of man. He that has made us what we are has made us at once resentful and reasonable. Instinct tells a man that he ought to revenge an injury; reason tells him that he ought not to be a judge in his own cause. From that moment, revenge passes from the private to the public hand; but in being transferred it is far from being extinguished. My lords, it is transferred as a sacred trust to be exercised for the injured, in measure and proportion, by persons who, feeling as he feels, are in a temper to reason better than he can reason. Revenge is taken out of the hands of the original injured proprietor, lest it should be carried beyond the bounds of moderation and justice. But, my lords, it is in its transfer exposed to a danger of an opposite description. The delegate of vengeance may not feel the wrong sufficiently: he may be cold and languid in the performance of his sacred duty. It is for these reasons that good men are taught to tremble even at the first emotions of anger and resentment for their own particular wrongs; but they are likewise taught, if they are well taught, to give the loosest possible rein to their resentment and indignation whenever their parents, their friends, their country, or their brethren of the common family of mankind are injured. Those who have not such feelings, under such circumstances, are base and degenerate. These, my lords, are the sentiments of the Commons of Great Britain. . .

To give up all the repose and pleasures of life, to pass sleepless nights and laborious days, and, what is ten times more irksome to an ingenuous mind, to offer oneself to calumny and all its herd of hissing tongues and poisoned fangs in order to free the world from fraudulent prevaricators, from cruel oppressors, from robbers and tyrants, has, I say, the test of heroic virtue, and well deserves such a distinction. The Commons, despairing to attain the heights of this virtue, never lose sight of it for a moment. For seventeen years they have, almost without intermission, pursued, by every sort of enquiry, by legislative and by judicial remedy, the cure of this Indian malady, worse ten thousand times than the leprosy which our forefathers brought from the East. Could they have done this, if they had not been actuated by some strong, some vehement, some perennial passion, which, burning like the Vestal fire, chaste and eternal, never suffers generous sympathy to grow cold in maintaining the rights of the injured or in denouncing the crimes of the oppressor?

My lords, the managers for the Commons have been actuated by this passion; my lords, they feel its influence at this moment; and so far from softening either their measures or their tone, they do here, in the presence of their Creator, of this House, and of the world, make this solemn declaration, and nuncupate this deliberate vow: *that they will ever flow with the most determined and unextinguishable animosity against tyranny, oppression, and peculation in all, but more particularly as practised by this man in India; that they never will relent, but will pursue and prosecute him, and it, till they see corrupt pride prostrate under the feet of justice.* We call upon your lordships to join us; and we have no doubt that you will feel the same sympathy that we feel or (what I cannot persuade my soul to think or my mouth to utter) you will be identified with the criminal whose crimes you excuse, and rolled with him in all the pollution of Indian guilt from generation to generation. Let those who feel with me upon this occasion join with me in this vow: if they will not, I have it all to myself.

Burke's eloquence in the Indian speeches is not the airy kind, off the top of a brilliant head. It is spun out of his very entrails. The 'perennial passion' that he ascribes to the Commons, in whose name he is conducting the impeachment, is very much his own. His is the 'determined and unextinguishable animosity against tyranny, oppression, and peculation', wherever they be found, and his the great melody against it. The words 'whenever their parents, their friends, their country and the common family of mankind are injured' are significant. In Burke's psyche, other voices, as well as those of Indians, were calling for revenge. Like Hamlet, Burke was listening to his father's ghost.

So Burke completed his work, not only in the impeachment, but in Parliament. Although the Lords did not hand down their verdict until the following year, Burke's toil ended on 16 June 1794, with the conclusion of this speech. Without delay he accepted the Chiltern Hundreds, and retirement. On 20 June 1794, his last day in the Commons, Pitt proposed a vote of thanks to the managers of the impeachment: 'It was a task of great length, labour and difficulty, and had been performed by the hon. managers with indefatigable industry, unparalleled assiduity, and laudable obedience to the desires of that House. He was confident that the example of Mr Hastings would deter other governors from a repetition of the practices which marked his administration.' Pitt added a word of warning to Hastings' friends in the House:

And he asked those who had shown themselves hostile for the impeachment to reflect seriously before they gave a negative to the motion; for he doubted much whether an unanimous vote of that House (honourable though it was) would be so honourable to the managers as a vote of thanks marked with the discriminating negative of those who felt themselves irritated and stung by the faithful and admirable discharge of the task imposed on them by their country.

Hastings' friends concentrated their attack on Burke. The first of their speakers remarked that he would not object to thanking the managers provided that thanks 'could be given without their bestowing their thanks at the same time on the leading manager, who had by his conduct disgraced and degraded the House of Commons'. Windham and Francis opposed any such proviso. So did Fox. Generously, in view of all that had passed, he said that he 'disclaimed all separation between the rest of the managers and the right hon. member so eminently qualified, not only by nature but by his particular study and attention, to be, as he was termed, their leader in this business, and with whom it was their boast and glory to be identified'.

The vote of thanks to the managers, including Burke, was carried by 50 votes to 21. The Speaker then conveyed the thanks of the House:

The subject to which your attention has been directed was intricate and extensive beyond example; you have proved that it was well suited to your industry and eloquence, the exertions of which have conferred honour not on yourselves only, but on this House, whose credit is intimately connected with your own. A forcible admonition has been given, on this occasion, to all persons in situations of national trust, that they can neither be removed by distance, nor sheltered by power, from the vigilance and authority of this House . . .

Burke replied on behalf of the managers:

Mr Burke said that by the orders of the House when the thanks were given, he and his brother managers were tongue-tied, and had no means whereby to express their gratitude but by their submission to those orders. But he thought he would be wanting in gratitude if he did not, the moment the penalty of silence was removed, seize the first opportunity to express his own satisfaction, and that of his fellow managers, on the occasion. They had laboured to discharge their duty, they had completed the task, and they were paid by the thanks of that House, the first reward men could receive.

TRAGEDY, AUGUST 1794

So ended a parliamentary career of nearly thirty years. Earl Fitzwilliam had agreed that Richard Burke would succeed to the seat at Malton for which his father had sat since his defeat for Bristol in 1780. Edmund and Richard travelled to Malton together, and Richard was elected for the borough on 18 July, 1794. Ten days later, tragedy struck. Richard suffered an acute and unmistakable attack of tuberculosis of the trachea. He died on 2 August, in the presence of his father and mother. As he lay dying, he asked if it was raining. His father told him that the noise was the wind rustling through the trees. Richard then spoke his last words: three lines from Adam's morning hymn in Book V of *Paradise Lost*, a favourite passage of his father's:

> His praise ye winds, that from four quarters blow,
> Breathe soft or loud; and wave your tops, ye pines,
> With every plant, in sign of worship wave.

Burke's devoted young friend and volunteer assistant, French Laurence, left an account of Edmund and Jane in the days immediately following Richard's death:

The behaviour of our two poor remaining friends is such as might be expected from them by those who rightly knew both their sensibility and their strength of reason: though perhaps for the exertion of the latter under so severe a dispensation, we hardly gave them sufficient credit. During the first day the father was at times, as I have heard, truly terrible in his grief. He occasionally worked him[self] up to an agony of affliction, and then, bursting away from all control, would rush to the room where his son lay, and throw himself headlong, as it happened, on the body, the bed, or the floor. Yet at intervals he attended and gave directions relative to every little arrangement, which their situation rendered necessary, pleasing himself most with thinking what would be most consonant to the living wishes and affections of his lost son: at intervals too he would argue against the ineffectual sorrows of his wife. She on the other hand sometimes broke into fits of violent weeping, sometimes showed a more quiet but more determined grief, and at other times again a more serene composure than her husband. Instead of dashing herself down, like him, she only lamented that when, on Thursday, by an accidental fall she sprained her wrist, 'it had not been her neck'; but when her husband attempted to persuade her that she had no business still to remain in the house, she answered steadily, '*No Edmund*, while he remains here, I will not go.' I am happy however to inform you, that on Saturday evening she took and gave a promise, that neither of them would ever enter more the chamber where their son lay. They have repented, but have fulfilled their mutual promises, and she has consented, notwithstanding her resolution above mentioned, to leave the house this day.

It seems that Burke, after his son's death, refused a peerage that Pitt had offered. Pitt's Victorian biographer, Earl Stanhope, writes:

It was now desired I cannot say with truth to honour Mr Burke, but rather to honour the peerage by his accession to its ranks. There was also, so I have heard, the design, as in other cases of rare merit, to annex by an Act of Parliament a yearly income to the title during two or three lives. Already was the title chosen as Lord Beaconsfield. Already was the patent preparing. Just then it pleased Almighty God to strike the old man to the very earth by the untimely death of his beloved son, his only child ... There ended Burke's whole share of earthly happiness. There ended all his dreams of earthly grandeur. Thenceforth a coronet was to him a worthless bauble which he must decline to wear.

Edmund Burke had a little less than three years to live. In personal terms, the years after the death of his son, with the blighting of all his fond and ardent hopes for him, were a period of utter desolation, as his letters and those of his friends attest. But his public activity was undiminished – even in some ways enhanced – until the very last months. The Burke scholar R. B. McDowell writes:

> What is remarkable is not that he was deeply afflicted, but how successfully he rallied and with what intellectual and emotional power he expressed himself during the following three years. It might almost be said that the blow of his son's death acted on him as a stimulus, bringing home to him the immediacy of catastrophe in the political sphere. If his happiness was shattered, Europe's future was imperilled, and Burke, like Job to whom he compared himself, drew general lessons from his afflictions.

From the frequent references to Richard in the correspondence of those years it is clear that Burke drew consolation from the causes he had shared with his son, in their common passionate commitments in France and Ireland. There is a sense of posthumous collaboration, and also of atonement, for Burke accused himself of having kept his son too much to himself, and perhaps of having asked too much of him. Yet these funereal or morbid preoccupations are evident only in asides. In intellectual combat, they became transmuted into exaltation. The last of Burke's published political writings, the *Letter to a Noble Lord* (1796) and *Letters on a Regicide Peace* (1796–97), are distinguished from his earlier writings and speeches not by melancholy undertones, but on the contrary by their exceptional élan, coruscating wit and reckless high spirits. They are marked by the quality that Yeats admired in Nietzsche, 'a curious, astringent joy'.

BURKE'S VICEROY, IRELAND 1794–95

In July 1794, the month between Edmund's retirement and Richard's death, a new coalition government was formed in London. Pitt's administration, under stress from French victories in Holland and Italy, was strengthened by the accession of the Portland Whigs. Four of these Burkean Whigs joined the administration, which then benefited from the support of their following in both Houses. Burke had been working for this coalition since 1791. Three of the new ministers – Portland,

Fitzwilliam and Windham – were his friends. Fitzwilliam was about to be made Viceroy of Ireland, and he, on Irish affairs, was Burke's disciple. He believed in the removal of all Catholic disabilities, and specifically in completing enfranchisement by giving Catholics the right to sit in Parliament. He also followed Burke in believing that nothing would go right in the administration of Ireland without the removal of what Burke called the 'junto', a tightly knit group of officials, well endowed with sinecures and resistant to Catholic claims. These officials were removable at the pleasure of the Viceroy, at least in theory.

Fitzwilliam's appointment is indicative of Burke's strong influence over the formation of the coalition. But Pitt never had any intention of allowing Fitzwilliam scope in Ireland to proceed as Burke wished. For Pitt, the advantage of allowing Fitzwilliam to go to Ireland was that it separated him from Portland. With Fitzwilliam at his side, and stiffened by Fitzwilliam's Burkean sense of purpose, Portland could be difficult, as he had shown in the coalition negotiations. But Portland on his own would be easy. William Pitt was an excellent judge of men, and a ruthless operator. And so Fitzwilliam went to Ireland and his political doom.

He arrived, amid popular rejoicing, on 4 January 1795. He immediately took on the junto, and by mid January he had removed five of its officials. He was complying with Burke's specific instructions: 'You must therefore directly criminate the Irish jobbery, or you are defeated; and defeated, I cannot well say with how much disgrace.' Pitt grumbled about the dismissals, irritated by the power Burke was indirectly exercising, but did not press the point. Instead, the issue that precipitated Fitzwilliam's fall was the freedom of Catholics to sit in Parliament. Although Burke believed in the justice of this, he was not anxious to press the point at an inappropriate moment, and in a long letter to Fitzwilliam he had characterized the matter as being of negligible importance, since so few would be in a position to benefit from it.

However, on 12 February 1795, Henry Grattan, after discussion with Fitzwilliam, formally asked leave to introduce his Catholic Relief Bill. Fitzwilliam strongly recommended acceptance, and was widely known to desire it. When Pitt showed the Viceroy's despatches to the King, George thundered against

letters from the Lord Lieutenant of Ireland, which to my greatest astonishment propose the total change of the principles of government which have been followed by every administration in the kingdom since the abdication of King James II . . . venturing to condemn the labour of ages and wanting an adoption of ideas which every man of property in Ireland and every friend to the Protestant religion must feel diametrically contrary to those he has imbibed in his youth.

Since George had already signed a number of Catholic Relief Acts, from 1778 to 1793, his reaction to this one may seem surprisingly violent. But it was hardly unprompted. Pitt would have made known to the King his sense that Fitzwilliam was going too far. And the King would have known that Fitzwilliam could be repudiated without the risk of losing Pitt.

Fitzwilliam was now doomed, and on 23 February, he was officially recalled. He departed from a mourning Dublin on 25 March 1795. Thomas Hussey was not alarmist but accurate when he wrote to Burke: 'The disastrous news, my dear sir, of Earl Fitzwilliam's recall is come; and Ireland is now on the brink of a civil war.' After the high hopes kindled by his known intentions, Fitzwilliam's recall set in motion the agitation, conspiracy and repression that were to result, after Burke's death, in the Great Rebellion of 1798. The concession of Catholic representation in Parliament, if made in 1795, would probably have given little joy to Catholics. As Burke said, it affected very few people. But the dismissal of a Viceroy for having been prepared to accept this measure of enfranchisement outraged Catholics generally and gave great encouragement to the revolutionaries among them.

To Burke, Fitzwilliam's recall was nothing less than the reversal of his hopes for Ireland. In these trying circumstances what is remarkable is how cool a head he kept, and how steady in his priorities he remained. He fiercely resented what Pitt had done, but he still saw Pitt as the indispensable leader in the anti-Jacobin cause. Everything else had to be subordinated to that, since the Jacobins threatened everything: England, Ireland, all Europe.

On 13 March 1795, when Fitzwilliam's recall was known, Burke wrote him a long, tenderly supportive letter:

Before I could abandon you, I must first abandon all my opinions, all my feelings, all my principles. Before I could abandon you, I must forget that I have a King, that I have a country, that I have a friend: I must forget that once I had a son – who at a very early period of his life risked it in the field rather than suffer the slightest glance upon your fame ... Whatever an enfeebled mind in an old and shattered carcass could do, I have done for this fortnight past. I thought, and do still think, Mr Pitt's power necessary to the existence of the ancient order in Europe. But that which nothing else could destroy he may destroy himself. I am in truth overwhelmed with grief, shame, and anguish. But my reason, such as it is, remains.

Burke was not about to break publicly with Pitt, or advise others to do so, even over Fitzwilliam's recall. He was distressed but not deflected from his course. His view of British politics became more pessimistic, and his feelings were reinforced by developments in the Hastings case. By 20 March, the committee of the House of Lords had rejected the first two charges against Hastings. Acquittal followed a month later. Burke wrote to Grattan: 'We have had an Eastern, and a Western chief governor before the public. Mr Hastings is acquitted by the House of Lords. Lord Fitzwilliam is condemned by the Cabinet. All this, however strange, is not contradictory.'

The deep ambivalence of Burke's feelings towards England and the heritage of the Glorious Revolution produced angel figures and devil figures in his mind. For many years, Rockingham had been the angel and Shelburne the devil. After Shelburne had been forced out of office and out of active politics, with Burke's help, Warren Hastings succeeded him in the devil role. After Rockingham's death, Fitzwilliam was the successor angel ('You are Lord Rockingham in everything'). So in commenting on 'an Eastern and a Western chief governor', Burke means that a devil has been acquitted and an angel condemned. The negative side of his feelings about England had gained an edge over the positive side. The idealized view of the British constitution, apparent in *On Conciliation with America* (1775), in the peroration of the speech opening the impeachment of Hastings (1788), in the *Reflections* (1790) and in the conclusion of *An Appeal from the New to the Old Whigs* (1791) made no more appearances after the first three traumatic months of 1795. The cloud-capped towers and gorgeous palaces that Burke had liked to evoke were now dismantled. In future, Burke's references to the working of British politics were to be bleak, and sometimes savagely sardonic.

At first Burke was puzzled about Pitt's reasons for treating Fitzwilliam as he did. It didn't seem in character. As he wondered about it, before the dismissal was known, the depth of Burke's respect for Pitt, even at such a trying moment, was apparent: 'the whole of this has I know not what air of chicanery and pettifogging in it; I do not know how to spell and put it together with the name of the most eloquent tongue, the clearest head, and the most powerful mind for official business of the time we live in.' After the dismissal, however, Burke discerned a deeper motive. In his letter to Grattan on 20 March, he says, 'It is possible they look to a Sansculotic peace.' He also shows himself aware of Pitt's hostility to himself, and makes a veiled reference to its relevance to Fitzwilliam's dismissal:

> God knows how earnestly I wished Mr Pitt's stability and greatness. I wish it still. I am afraid I am not equally regarded by him. Indeed it is natural, that he and the rest, from the summit of human glory and prosperity, should not discern me in the mud of my obscurity and wretchedness. I have done all I could to bring them together, to keep them together, and, after a breach, to reconcile them. I agree with you that this quarrel cannot be on its ostensible grounds. I have perhaps more reason than you have to think so. If it stood on those grounds I am quite sure that nothing on earth could more easily have been compromised. But to the last hour, no sort of compromise or treaty was listened to. There must be some sort of original sin. For something or other, Lord Fitzwilliam, in a signal and unexampled punishment, is to be made, at every hazard, a striking example.

The reference to 'the mud of my obscurity' rings false: it is one of Burke's not infrequent but never quite successful displays of humility. Burke had long known – at least since Pitt's abandonment of Warren Hastings – that Pitt's negative feelings towards him did not include contempt. Yet 'for something or other' Fitzwilliam was to be punished; the reason was Pitt's resentment of Burke's influence over members of his coalition administration.

In the following month, which brought peace between France and Prussia, Burke felt sure that Pitt was contemplating a British peace, and that this had been behind the treatment of his Viceroy. To Fitzwilliam, Burke wrote: 'Indeed the moment I found them determined finally to break with your lordship, I had no kind of doubt that they thought they had peace in prospect. Otherwise, the part they acted would be beyond the ordinary insanity of the violent passions.'

Superficially, this looks like one of Burke's wilder notions. That an Irish Viceroy should be removed because Pitt was aiming at peace with revolutionary France seems quite implausible. Yet it can be seen to fit. The Thermidorians who succeeded Robespierre in July 1794 were not proselytizing ideologists but pragmatists, after their fashion. Pitt, who was also above all a pragmatist, after his own fashion, thought it possible to do business with them, and was to make the attempt in 1795–96. It is likely that he had had such an overture in mind from about the time the coalition was formed, and it was always apparent that Fitzwilliam would be a most inconvenient member of an administration seeking peace with revolutionary France. According to Fitzwilliam's biographer, E. A. Smith, 'it was Fitzwilliam above all who had urged upon a seemingly reluctant Cabinet in June 1794 Burke's policy of total war against the revolution.' That stand had marked Fitzwilliam out, in Pitt's eyes, as the most potentially refractory member of his new coalition. In the event of a serious attempt at peace with France, Fitzwilliam would be the main source of trouble within the Cabinet, because he was the most attached to Burke's ideas. The last thing Pitt wanted was a convinced Burkean in the Cabinet who was liable to resign at the wrong moment, over the wrong issue, at the master's call. Against that background, Pitt's treatment of Fitzwilliam becomes more intelligible. To get rid of him over Irish affairs, about which few in Britain cared very much, was preferable to waiting for him to jump, in the midst of a major political crisis over a central issue: peace with France.

Pitt, being essentially a power politician – as distinct from that much rarer thing, a cause politician – had always considered Burke as a force that might enlarge, or advance, or encroach upon his own power, depending on the circumstances. Over Pitt's dubious Indian involvement in the mid 1780s, Burke had been a threat. Later, from the breach with Fox at the beginning of the 1790s, Burke offered the prospect of an accretion to Pitt's power-base, and was courted accordingly, although always with some reserve. But when the accretion materialized, in the form of the coalition, Pitt found that some of the Portland Whigs considered themselves not as his supporters, but as conditional allies under Burke's influence. That had to be stopped.

The Irish administration was now back in the hands from which Burke had tried to wrest it, and those in power were bent on a policy of pre-emptive repression of an incipient Catholic rebellion. Pitt's administration, through the recall of Fitzwilliam, had opted to give the junto its head. Pitt knew that repression might lead to disaster, but perhaps conciliation and repression were only alternative roads to the same disaster. And if the junto's policies – which were the practical embodiment of 'legislative independence' – were to fail, Pitt had a remedy in reserve: the Union of Great Britain and Ireland.

Burke, meanwhile, was committed to supporting Pitt's coalition as long as the alternative was Fox and a pro-Jacobin policy. The French Revolution, in Burke's mind, took precedence over everything else, including Ireland. But emotionally, that precedence was painful. His correspondence for this period reflects a high degree of ambivalence. He wrote to a friend in March 1795: 'Well! they all amaze me, – princes, dukes, marquesses, Chancellors of the Exchequer, secretaries of state! – My heart is sick; my stomach turns; my head grows dizzy; the world seems to me to reel and stagger. The crimes of democracy, and the madness and folly of aristocracy alike frighten and confound me. The only refuge is in God who sees through all these mazes.'

Burke was, of course, opposed to all Jacobins, Irish as well as English and French. But his feelings towards the Irish Jacobins were significantly different from his feelings towards the English ones. All of his many comments on the English Jacobins, from the moment he learnt of their existence in November 1789, are implacably hostile, and usually contemptuous. He does not often refer to the Irish Jacobins, but when he does his tone is more respectful. The most conspicuous of these men, in 1795, was Arthur O'Connor, a Member of the Irish Parliament who spoke there on 4 May 1795 along 'United Irish' lines, attacking the political and administrative abuses since Fitzwilliam's recall and hinting that if they were not speedily redressed, the Irish people might look for foreign aid. (O'Connor later escaped arrest by going to France, became a general in the French army, and married a daughter of Condorcet.) Burke wrote to Fitzwilliam:

It should seem as if young O'Connor gave himself his full swing. I am sorry

for it. He has good parts; and on his Uncle Longfield's death he will have a
large fortune. I saw him at Bath about three years ago. He was then an
enthusiast, an admirer of Rousseau and the French writers, but, as I thought,
very tractable; and had taken, on the whole, a very proper direction. What
became of him after that time I never knew: I saw he had a mind of great
energy, and was capable of much good or of much evil. I am very sorry to
say, that the course they are pursuing in Ireland will Jacobinize all the
energies and all the active talents of that country. These are very
considerable, and the popular mind is more susceptible of any emotion there
than it is here. Jacobinism is the vice of men of parts; and, in this age, it is the
channel in which all discontents will run.

Clearly O'Connor's speech made a strong impression on Burke, for he
refers to it again a few days later, in a letter to Thomas Hussey:

In Parliament the language of your friends (one only excepted) was what it
ought to be. But that one speech, though full of fire and animation, was not
warmed with the fire of heaven. I am sorry for it. I have seen that gentleman
but once. He is certainly a man of parts, but one who has dealt too much in
the philosophy of France.

O'Connor was on the wrong side, but there is something splendid
about him all the same. Burke never wrote in that vein about any of the
English Jacobins. He thought the circumstances very different. The Irish
revolutionaries had something to be revolutionary about; the English did
not. Burke saw that many Catholics were becoming Jacobinized, but he
did not cease to sympathize with them on that account. He put the blame
for the rapid spread of Jacobinism after Fitzwilliam's recall squarely onto
the shoulders of the Protestant Ascendancy (a term popularized in the
1790s by members of the Ascendancy itself, and replacing the older and
less offensive term 'Protestant interest').

The Protestant Ascendancy now took its place in a malign triad in
Burke's mind, together with 'Indianism' and Jacobinism. On 26 May
1795, Burke wrote to Hercules Langrishe:

In the Catholic question I considered only one point. Was [full enfranchise-
ment] at the time, and in the circumstances, a measure which tended to
promote the concord of the citizens? I have no difficulty in saying it was; and

as little in saying that the present concord of the citizens was worth buying, at a critical season, by granting a few *capacities*, which probably no one man now living is likely to be served or hurt by. When any man tells *you* and *me* that if these places were left in the discretion of a Protestant Crown, and these memberships in the discretion of Protestant electors, or patrons, we should have a Popish official system, and a Popish representation, capable of overturning the establishment, he only insults our understandings. When any man tells this to *Catholics*, he insults their understandings and he galls their feelings. It is not the question of the places and seats; it is the real hostile disposition, and the *pretended* fears, that leave stings in the minds of the people. I really thought that in the total of the late circumstances, with regard to persons, to things, to principles, and to measures, was to be found a conjunction favourable to the introduction, and to the perpetuation, of a general harmony, producing a general strength which to that hour Ireland was never so happy as to enjoy. My sanguine hopes are blasted, and I must consign my feelings on that terrible disappointment to the same patience in which I have been obliged to bury the vexation I suffered on the defeat of the other great, just, and honourable causes in which I have had some share; and which have given more of dignity than of peace and advantage to a long, laborious life. Though perhaps a want of success might be urged as a reason for making me doubt of the justice of the part I have taken, yet until I have other lights than one side of the debate has furnished me, I must see things, and feel them too, as I see and feel them. I think I can hardly overrate the malignity of the principles of Protestant Ascendancy as they affect Ireland; or of Indianism, as they affect these countries, and as they affect Asia; or of Jacobinism as they affect all Europe, and the state of human society itself. The last is the greatest evil. But it readily combines with the others, and flows from them. Whatever breeds discontent at this time will produce that great master-mischief most infallibly. Whatever tends to persuade the people that the *few*, called by whatever name you please, religious or political, are of opinion that their interest is not compatible with that of the *many*, is a great point gained to Jacobinism. Whatever tends to irritate the talents of a country, which have at all times, and at these particularly, a mighty influence on the public mind, is of infinite service to that formidable cause. Unless where heaven has mingled uncommon ingredients of virtue in the composition – *quos meliore luto finit proecordia Titan* [Whom Titan has fashioned with kindlier skill and a finer clay] – talents naturally gravitate to Jacobinism. Whatever ill humours are afloat in the state, they will be sure to discharge themselves in a mingled torrent in the *Cloaca Maxima* of Jacobinism. Therefore people ought well to look about them. First, the physicians are to take care that they do nothing to irritate this epidemical distemper. It is a foolish thing to have the better of the patient in a dispute. The complaint, or its cause, ought to be removed, and wise and lenient arts ought to precede the measures of vigour. They ought to be the *ultima*, not the *prima*, not the *tota* ratio of a wise government. God forbid that on a worthy occasion authority should want the means of force, or the disposition to use it. But where a prudent and enlarged policy does not precede it, and attend it too, where the hearts of the better sort of people do not go with the hands of the soldiery, you may call your constitution what you will, in effect it will consist of three parts (orders, if you please) – cavalry, infantry, and artillery – and of nothing else or better.

By the autumn of 1795, the cycle of seditious conspiracy and governmental repression was far advanced in Ireland, and already amounted to incipient civil war. Its epicentre, at this time, was in Co. Armagh, where Protestants were fighting Catholic Defenders and where the Orange Order was founded in September 1795. Its members immediately set about the mass expulsion of thousands of Catholics from rural areas. These disturbances were known as 'the Armagh outrages'. As Thomas Bartlett writes: 'It was on the anvil of these expulsions that the alliance between Defenders and United Irishmen was forged sometime early in 1796.' The Catholic Archbishop of Dublin, Dr Troy, issued a pastoral letter in August denouncing the Defenders and shortly afterwards parties of Defenders surrendered their arms. Burke disapproved of these developments, since he thought the Catholic clergy too inclined to advise their flocks to submission under repression and provocation. In February, he had written to Fitzwilliam: 'All the miseries of Ireland have originated in what has produced all the miseries of India, a servile patience under oppression, by the greatest of all misnomers called prudence.'

By the end of the year, Burke's position over Ireland was so complex and involved as to be almost untenable. His heart and head were at variance. He had first become emotionally committed to the anti-Jacobin cause in November 1789, on discovering that Protestant bigots in England were welcoming the French Revolution because of its anti-Catholic character. But by 1795 in Ireland, Protestant bigots were anti-

Jacobin, or at least were making use of anti-Jacobinism for anti-Catholic purposes. Burke's Catholic sympathies – and specifically his sympathies with those Catholics who were disposed to resist repression and provocation – drew him toward the side of the Irish Catholic pro-Jacobins, a category which included the Defenders.

Conditions in Ireland were now highly propitious to the spread of Jacobinism. Defender documents reveal a confusion of Catholic millenarian hopes with Jacobin jargon. There are references to 'the present United States of France and Ireland' and to 'the Tree of Liberty'. A Defender catechism of 1795 runs: 'Are you concerned? I am. To what? To the National Convention. What do you design by that cause? To quell all nations, dethrone all kings and to plant the true religion that was lost at the Reformation. Who sent you? Simon Peter, the head of the Church. Signed by order of the Chief Consul.'

The late rays of the Enlightenment, as they penetrated the mists of rural Ireland in the middle of the last decade of the eighteenth century, produced strange and ominous rainbows. Altogether the situation was so chaotic that it is not surprising that Burke's relation to it was confused. Politically, this mattered little: Burke's influence over Irish affairs, so significant over three decades, had collapsed. 'As to the rest,' he wrote to Thomas Hussey in September 1795, 'everything has gone beyond my reach. I have only to lament.'

Detractors Counter-attacked

Towards the end of 1795, the centre of Burke's attention was deflected from the doom-laden scene in Ireland by developments at Westminster which were to provide the genesis for his last published writings: *Letter to a Noble Lord* and *Letters on a Regicide Peace* (February and October 1796). The occasion for the composition of *Letter to a Noble Lord* was an attack in the Lords by two Whig peers, the Duke of Bedford and the Earl of Lauderdale, in November 1795, on the pension that Burke had been granted on retiring from Parliament. Although he had declined the offered peerage, Burke had accepted a pension of £1,200 a year, which enabled him to pay his debts and to be assured, during his last illness, that his widow would not face an old age of poverty. (Jane died in 1812, fifteen years after Edmund.) His many enemies, among the Whigs and radicals, were triumphant. The secret of Burke's 'apostasy', to use Lauderdale's word, was out. He had written the *Reflections* because he was in quest of the pension he finally secured four years later. That accounted for everything. It was the thirty pieces of silver. As Burke's biographer Carl B. Cone says: 'His representation as a Judas Iscariot and a sycophant was cruel and maddening as well as untrue.' But Burke had been on the receiving end of an enormous amount of abuse and innuendo in his long political career. In *Letter to a Noble Lord* he called it 'the hunt of obloquy, which ever has pursued me with a full cry through life'. Most of these attacks came from anonymous writers in the corrupt press, faceless and unaccountable tormentors. Burke never answered them.

The Duke of Bedford, on the other hand, was one of the leaders of the Whigs, and a marvellous target. The Bedford family, since the days of Henry VIII, had been beneficiaries of Crown patronage on a colossal scale. So by attacking Burke's modest pension, the Duke had laid himself open to the most devastating *argumentum ad hominem* in the history of English controversy. But *Letter to a Noble Lord* is more than that; it is also the nearest that Burke comes to an *apologia pro vita sua*. It contains, with much else, his grave and succinct reply to the charge of venality that dogged him throughout his life and has clung to his reputation ever since:

> His Grace thinks I have obtained too much. I answer, that my exertions, whatever they have been, were such as no hopes of pecuniary reward could possibly excite; and no pecuniary compensation can possibly reward them. Between money and such services, there is no common principle of comparison: they are quantities incommensurable.

In itself, this is no more than a rebuttal, but when we take into consideration the totality of Burke's writing and speeches, the rebuttal becomes a refutation. Those writings and speeches are indeed 'such as no hopes of pecuniary reward could possibly excite'.

Burke goes on to distinguish between his own efforts as a reformer and the revolutionary innovations defended by the Duke. Here he gives full vent to the horror and hatred that the French Revolution had inspired in him. The imagery of corruption that is associated with disturbance at the Irish level in Burke's psyche is strongly present:

It cannot at this time be too often repeated, line upon line, precept upon precept, until it comes into the currency of a proverb – *To innovate is not to reform*. The French revolutionists complained of everything; they refused to reform anything; and they left nothing, no, nothing at all, *unchanged*. The consequences are *before* us – not in remote history, not in future prognostication: they are about us; they are upon us. They shake the public security; they menace private enjoyment. They dwarf the growth of the young; they stop our way. They infest us in town; they pursue us to the country. Our business is interrupted, our repose is troubled, our pleasures are saddened, our very studies are poisoned and perverted, and knowledge is rendered worse than ignorance by the enormous evils of this dreadful innovation. The revolution harpies of France, sprung from Night and Hell, or from that chaotic anarchy which generates equivocally 'all monstrous, all prodigious things', cuckoo-like, adulterously lay their eggs, and brood over, and hatch them in the nest of every neighbouring state. These obscene harpies, who deck themselves in I know not what divine attributes, but who in reality are foul and ravenous birds of prey (both mothers and daughters), flutter over our heads, and souse down upon our tables, and leave nothing unrent, unrifled, unravaged, or unpolluted with the slime of their filthy offal.

Burke compares his own arduous public career with Bedford's situation:

I was not, like his Grace of Bedford, swaddled and rocked and dandled into a legislator: *'Nitor in adversum'* [I advance against adversity] is the motto for a man like me. I possessed not one of the qualities nor cultivated one of the arts that recommend men to the favour and protection of the great. I was not made for a minion or a tool. As little did I follow the trade of winning the hearts by imposing on the understandings of the people. At every step of my progress in life (for in every step was I traversed and opposed) and at every turnpike I met, I was obliged to show my passport, and again an again to prove my sole title to the honour of being useful to my country, b a proof that I was not wholly unacquainted with its laws and the whole syste n of its interests both abroad and at home. Otherwise, no rank, no toleration even, for me. I had no arts but manly arts. On them I have stood, and, please God, in spite of the Duke of Bedford and the Earl of Lauderdale, to the last gasp will I stand.

Here again Burke's self-assessment is borne out by his life and work. He was indeed 'not made for a minion or a tool'.

This first part of the tract is mainly defensive, but towards the middle, Burke suddenly attacks:

His Grace may think as meanly as he will of my deserts in the far greater part of my conduct in life. It is free for him to do so. There will always be some difference of opinion on the value of political services. But there is one merit of mine which he, of all men living, ought to be the last to call in question. I have supported with very great zeal, and I am told with some degree of success, those opinions, or, if his Grace likes another expression better, those old prejudices, which buoy up the ponderous mass of his nobility, wealth, and titles. I have omitted no exertion to prevent him and them from sinking to that level to which the meretricious French faction his Grace at least coquets with, omit no exertion to reduce both. I have done all I could to discountenance their enquiries into the fortunes of those who hold large portions of wealth without any apparent merit of their own. I have strained every nerve to keep the Duke of Bedford in that situation which alone makes him my superior . . .

The Duke of Bedford conceives that he is obliged to call the attention of the House of Peers to His Majesty's grant to me, which he considers as excessive and out of all bounds.

I know not how it has happened, but it really seems that whilst his Grace was meditating his well-considered censure upon me, he fell into a sort of sleep. Homer nods, and the Duke of Bedford may dream; and as dreams (even his golden dreams) are apt to be ill-pieced and incongruously put together, his Grace preserved his idea of reproach to *me*, but took the subject-matter from the Crown grants *to his own family*. This is 'the stuff of which his dreams are made'. In that way of putting things together his Grace is perfectly in the right. The grants to the House of Russell were so enormous as not only to outrage economy, but even to stagger credibility. The Duke of Bedford is the leviathan among all the creatures of the Crown. He tumbles about his unwieldy bulk, he plays and frolics in the ocean of the royal bounty. Huge as he is, and whilst 'he lies floating many a rood', he is still a creature. His ribs, his fins, his whalebone, his blubber, the very spiracles through which he spouts a torrent of brine against his origin, and covers me all over with the spray, everything of him and about him is from the throne. Is it for *him* to question the dispensation of the royal favour?

I really am at a loss to draw any sort of parallel between the public merits of his Grace, by which he justifies the grants he holds, and these services of mine, on the favourable construction of which I have obtained what his Grace so much disapproves. In private life I have not at all the honour of acquaintance with the noble Duke, but I ought to presume, and it costs me nothing to do so, that he abundantly deserves the esteem and love of all who live with him. But as to public service, why, truly, it would not be more ridiculous for me to compare myself, in rank, in fortune, in splendid descent, in youth, strength, or figure, with the Duke of Bedford, than to make a parallel between his services and my attempts to be useful to my country. It would not be gross adulation, but uncivil irony to say that he has any public merit of his own to keep alive the idea of the services by which his vast landed pensions were obtained. My merits, whatever they are, are original and personal; his are derivative. It is his ancestor, the original pensioner, that has laid up this inexhaustible fund of merit which makes his Grace so very delicate and exceptious about the merit of all other grantees of the Crown. Had he permitted me to remain in quiet, I should have said, "Tis his estate: that's enough. It is his by law: what have I to do with it or its history?' He would naturally have said, on his side, "Tis this man's fortune. He is as good now as my ancestor was two hundred and fifty years ago. I am a young man with very old pensions; he is an old man with very young pensions, that's all.'

Burke goes on to review the career of the founder of the Bedford family fortunes, a courtier of Henry VIII. And he warns the inheritor against his incongruous and unnatural allies, the Jacobins:

They are the Duke of Bedford's natural hunters, and he is their natural game. Because he is not very profoundly reflecting, he sleeps in profound security. They, on the contrary, are always vigilant, active, enterprising and, though far removed from any knowledge which makes men estimable or useful, in all the instruments and resources of evil their leaders are not meanly instructed or insufficiently furnished. In the French Revolution everything is new, and from want of preparation to meet so unlooked-for an evil, everything is dangerous. Never before this time was a set of literary men converted into a gang of robbers and assassins; never before did a den of bravoes and banditti assume the garb and tone of an academy of philosophers.

Let me tell his Grace that an union of such characters, monstrous as it seems, is not made for producing despicable enemies. But if they are formidable as foes, as friends they are dreadful indeed ...

Whatever his Grace may think of himself, they look upon him, and everything that belongs to him, with no more regard than they do upon the whiskers of that little long-tailed animal that has been long the game of the grave, demure, insidious, spring-nailed, velvet-pawed, green-eyed philosophers, whether going upon two legs or upon four.

From a whale and a mouse, Burke turns the hapless Duke into an ox, for the slaughter:

Is it not a singular phenomenon that whilst the Sansculotte carcass-butchers and the philosophers of the shambles are pricking their dotted lines upon his hide, and, like the print of the poor ox that we see in the shop windows at Charing Cross, alive as he is, and thinking no harm in the world, he is divided into rumps, and sirloins, and briskets, and into all sorts of pieces for roasting, boiling, and stewing, that, all the while they are measuring *him*, his Grace is measuring *me* – is invidiously comparing the bounty of the Crown with the deserts of the defender of his order, and in the same moment fawning on those who have the knife half out of the sheath? Poor innocent!

> Pleased to the last, he crops the flowery food,
> And licks the hand just raised to shed his blood.

PEACE WITH FRANCE? BURKE AGAINST PITT

The four *Letters on a Regicide Peace* are the last of Burke's great polemics against the French Revolution. As early as March 1795 he had foreseen that Pitt would make a move in the direction of peace with France. The move actually came that autumn, following the adoption in August by the new Directory of the 'Constitution of the Year III', of which Article I proclaimed: 'The rights of man in society are liberty, equality, security and property.' Fraternity had vanished, and in its place had come 'security and property'. Pitt interpreted this new Constitution as meaning that the French Revolution was now at last being consolidated. But Burke liked the new Constitution no better than its predecessor, and foresaw, correctly, that it would be no more effective.

As it turned out, the most significant political document of 1795–96 was not the Constitution of the Year III, but General Bonaparte's proclamation to the army of Italy on 27 March:

> Soldiers, you are naked, ill fed! The government owes you much; it can give you nothing. Your patience, the courage you display in the midst of these rocks, are admirable; but they procure you no glory, no fame is reflected upon you. I seek to lead you into the most fertile plains in the world. Rich provinces, great cities will be in your power. There you will find honour, glory, and riches. Soldiers of Italy, would you be lacking in courage or constancy?

Liberty, equality and fraternity here yielded to 'honour, glory and riches' as motivating forces for the revolutionary armies. The property rights guaranteed by the new Constitution were the rights of the French who owned property in 1796, but the property of France's neighbours was still an object of annexation by the French 'liberators'. In that sense, France was still a revolutionary nation. Loot, not liberty, was now the motivating force, but France was no less dangerous, and was not about to settle down within its old frontiers. France was decidedly more expansionist after Robespierre than it had been under him. General Bonaparte, the 'popular general' whose rise to supreme power Burke had predicted in the *Reflections*, was beginning his ascent. Pitt's peace initiative of 1795–96 could hardly have been more misguided.

The first definite intimation to Burke that peace with France was in the wind came with a letter from William Eden, Baron Auckland, enclosing a pamphlet of his own composition entitled *Some Remarks on the Apparent Circumstances of the War in the Fourth Week of October 1795*. This argued that the time had come for considering peace with France. Auckland was a friend and ally of Pitt's, and his nearest neighbour at Holwell. The pamphlet was probably written at Pitt's request, and it was probably also at Pitt's suggestion that the author sent a copy to Burke, in order to draw a reaction.

Burke's reply to Auckland was implacably negative: 'If the plan of politics there recommended (pray excuse my freedom) should be adopted by the King's councils, and by the good people of this kingdom (as, so recommended, undoubtedly it will), nothing can be the consequence but utter and irretrievable ruin to the ministry, to the Crown, to the succession, to the importance, to the very existence of this country.' Auckland forwarded Burke's letter to Pitt, who sent it back with the words 'I return Burke's letter, which is like other rhapsodies from the same pen, in which there is much to admire, and nothing to agree with.' But Pitt was a little premature: the real rhapsody was only then in the process of composition.

Burke's *Letters on a Regicide Peace* were written with a single purpose: to force Pitt to continue the war with revolutionary France until the restoration of the French monarchy. The *Letters* have neither the scope nor the profundity of the *Reflections*, and the proportion of rhetoric and invective to analysis is much higher. Yet the *Letters* are an astonishing production. They are the work of a dying man, yet they contain the fieriest and most animated passages of all Burke's writing. In his letter to Auckland, Burke had spoken of himself as 'a dejected old man, buried in the anticipated grave of a feeble old age, forgetting and forgotten in an obscure and melancholy retreat'; yet this late work of that dejected old man is distinguished beyond all by sheer exuberance and knockabout high spirits. The enjoyment Burke felt in writing it communicates itself on almost every page.

This was the fourth great occasion on which a period of constraint had been followed by a tremendous release of Burke's energy. The first was the silence over American affairs generally observed by the Rockinghams from 1768 to 1774. When the Rockinghams finally decided to protest against the penal Acts, the consequent release of energy produced two of Burke's greatest speeches, On American Taxation and On Conciliation with America. The second occasion had to do with India. Then, the period of constraint had extended from Burke's discovery, in 1773, that his heart was at variance with his party over Indian policy, until the time, ten years later, when he was able to bring his party round to his point of view. That was followed by a series of great speeches, including those on Fox's East India Bill and on the Nabob of Arcot's Debts. The period before the writing of the *Reflections* (1788–89) was also one of constraint, because of Burke's strained relations with Whig colleagues. Fox's enthusiasm for the French Revolution liberated Burke from that constraint, and so released a new burst of energy.

The period of constraint before the composition of *Letters on a Regicide Peace*, when Burke had to bottle up his feelings so as not to offend Pitt, was much shorter but probably more distressing than those that had gone before. It lasted from March 1795, with the news of Fitzwilliam's recall, to October of that year, when Burke learnt of Pitt's intention to seek peace with France. Burke had continued to support Pitt only because he considered him indispensable to the conduct of the indispensable war against revolutionary France. Now Pitt wanted to desert his post, and it became a congenial duty to drive him back to it. Burke's thraldom to Pitt, as long as Pitt was faithful to the war, had been profoundly uncongenial, because of Burke's feelings about the way Pitt had treated his friend Fitzwilliam and, along with him, Burke's own people, the Catholics of Ireland. The exuberance in the *Letters on a Regicide Peace* reflects his joy at being released from that self-imposed thraldom, and released from it by the very same sense of duty that had imposed it in the first place.

Burke nowhere in the *Letters* attacks Pitt personally, because he felt that Pitt was still needed, provided he could be persuaded to continue the war. He alludes to him on only one occasion, and then with restraint. It is with Pitt's minions that Burke clashes, addressing Pitt through them, implicitly.

Of the four *Letters on a Regicide Peace*, two were published on 26 October 1796, during Burke's lifetime; the other two were published posthumously. The first to be written was later called the fourth. Its target is Auckland's pamphlet, seen as Pitt's *ballon d'essai*. Burke refuses to accept the revolutionary government as the embodiment of France, arguing that it is instead a regicide usurpation. And he mocks and scorns Auckland's summary of the terms on which the Directory might agree to peace:

But hear still further and in the same good strain the great patron and advocate of amity with this accommodating, mild, and unassuming power, when he reports to you the law they give, and its immediate effects: 'They amount,' says he, 'to the sacrifice of powers that have been the most nearly connected with us, the direct or indirect annexation to France of all the ports of the Continent from Dunkirk to Hamburg' – an immense accession of territory – 'and, in one word, *the abandonment of the independence of Europe!*' This is the *law* (the author and I use no different terms) which this new government, almost as soon as it could cry in the cradle, and as one of the very first acts by which it auspicated its entrance into function, the pledge it gives of the firmness of its policy – such is the law that this proud power prescribes to abject nations. What is the comment upon this law by the great jurist who recommends us to the tribunal which issued the decree? 'An obedience to it would be' (says he) 'dishonourable to us, and exhibit us to the present age and to posterity as submitting to the law prescribed to us by our enemy.'

Here I recognize the voice of a British plenipotentiary: I begin to feel proud of my country. But, alas! the short date of human elevation! The accents of dignity died upon his tongue. This author will not assure us of his sentiments for the whole of a pamphlet; but in the sole energetic part of it he does not continue the same through an whole sentence, if it happens to be of any sweep or compass. In the very womb of this last sentence, pregnant, as it should seem, with a Hercules, there is formed a little bantling of the mortal race, a degenerate, puny parenthesis, that totally frustrates our most sanguine views and expectations, and disgraces the whole gestation. Here is this destructive parenthesis: 'Unless some adequate compensation be secured *to us*.' *To us!* The Christian world may shift for itself, Europe may groan in slavery, we may be dishonoured by receiving law from an enemy – but all is well, provided the compensation to us be adequate. To what are we reserved? An *adequate* compensation 'for the sacrifice of powers the most nearly connected with us'; an *adequate* compensation 'for the direct or indirect annexation to France of all the ports of the Continent from Dunkirk to Hamburg'; an *adequate* compensation 'for the abandonment of the independence of Europe'! Would that when all our manly sentiments are thus changed, our manly language were changed along with them, and that the English tongue were not employed to utter what our ancestors never dreamed could enter into an English heart!

On the repudiation by the Directory of the principle of equality, he writes:

The regicides, they say, have renounced the creed of the rights of man, and declared equality a chimera. This is still more strange than all the rest. They have apostatized from their apostasy. They are renegadoes from that impious faith for which they subverted the ancient government, murdered their King, and imprisoned, butchered, confiscated and banished their fellow subjects, and to which they forced every man to swear at the peril of his life. And now, to reconcile themselves to the world, they declare this creed, bought by so much blood, to be an imposture and a chimera. I have no doubt that they

always thought it to be so when they were destroying everything at home
and abroad for its establishment. It is no strange thing to those who look into
the nature of corrupted man to find a violent persecutor a perfect unbeliever
of his own creed. But this is the very first time that any man or set of men
were hardy enough to attempt to lay the ground of confidence in them by an
acknowledgment of their own falsehood, fraud, hypocrisy, treachery,
heterodox doctrine, persecution, and cruelty. Everything we hear from them
is new, and, to use a phrase of their own, *revolutionary*; everything supposes a
total revolution in all the principles of reason, prudence, and moral feeling. If
possible, this their recantation of the chief parts in the canon of the rights of
man is more infamous and causes greater horror than their originally
promulgating and forcing down the throats of mankind that symbol of all
evil.

Burke rejects a call for a change of heart towards the Directory,
expresses his own hatred of it, and explains that such hatred is natural
and essential to man:

A kind providence has placed in our breasts a hatred of the unjust and cruel,
in order that we may preserve ourselves from cruelty and injustice. They
who bear cruelty are accomplices in it. The pretended gentleness which
excludes that charitable rancour produces an indifference which is half an
approbation. They never will love where they ought to love, who do not
hate where they ought to hate.

The second of the *Letters* (published as the first) leaves Auckland's
pamphlet behind. Headed 'On the Overtures of Peace', it meditates on
how the ruin of the French monarchy, economy, society and civilization
threatens to ruin the rest of Europe as well:

Deprived of the old government, deprived in a manner of all government,
France, fallen as a monarchy, to common speculators might have appeared
more likely to be an object of pity or insult, according to the disposition of
the circumjacent powers, than to be the scourge and terror of them all: but
out of the tomb of the murdered monarchy in France has arisen a vast,
tremendous, unformed spectre, in a far more terrific guise than any which
ever yet have overpowered the imagination and subdued the fortitude of
man. Going straight forward to its end, unappalled by peril, unchecked by

remorse, despising all common maxims and all common means, that hideous phantom overpowered those who could not believe it was possible she could at all exist, except on the principles which habit rather than nature had persuaded them were necessary to their own particular welfare and to their own ordinary modes of action. But the constitution of any political being, as well as that of any physical being, ought to be known before one can venture to say what is fit for its conservation or what is the proper means of its power. The poison of other states is the food of the new republic . . .

The republic of regicide, with an annihilated revenue, with defaced manufactures, with a ruined commerce, with an uncultivated and half-depopulated country, with a discontented, distressed, enslaved, and famished people, passing with a rapid, eccentric, incalculable course from the wildest anarchy to the sternest despotism, has actually conquered the finest parts of Europe, has distressed, disunited, deranged, and broke to pieces all the rest . . .

He correctly predicts a long war, and then stresses its unique character:

We are not at an end of our struggle, nor near it. Let us not deceive ourselves: we are at the beginning of great troubles . . .

We are in a war of a *peculiar* nature. It is not with an ordinary community, which is hostile or friendly as passion or as interest may veer about; not with a state which makes war through wantonness and abandons it through lassitude. We are at war with a system, which, by its essence, is inimical to all other governments, and which makes peace or war as peace and war may best contribute to their subversion. It is with an *armed doctrine* that we are at war. It has, by its essence, a faction of opinion and of interest and of enthusiasm in every country. To us it is a Colossus which bestrides our Channel. It has one foot on a foreign shore, the other upon the British soil. Thus advantaged, if it can at all exist it must finally prevail. Nothing can so completely ruin any of the old governments, ours in particular, as the acknowledgment, directly or by implication, of any kind of superiority in this new power. This acknowledgment we make, if, in a bad or doubtful situation of our affairs, we solicit peace, or if we yield to the modes of new humiliation in which alone she is content to give us an hearing.

Burke's thesis of 'an armed doctrine' is open to question in the

post-Thermidorian period about which he was writing. As he himself
had noted in the first of these *Letters*, the Thermidorians had apostatized
from most of the doctrines which had been sacred to the revolutionaries.
Insofar as there was any 'doctrine' guiding the destinies of post-
Thermidorian France, it was that proclaimed by Bonaparte to his troops
in Italy: the doctrine of 'honour, glory and riches'. But that raw doctrine
was certainly an armed one, and of terrifying efficiency.

Yet whatever the nature of the 'armed doctrine', Burke was right to
see that post-Thermidorian France was a manically expansionist power,
with which peace could not be concluded without total submission. Pitt's
assumption that the Directory was an ordinary power, with which
business could be done, was unfounded, as Pitt was now beginning to
find out for himself. 'In one point we are lucky,' Burke writes.

> The regicide has received our advances with scorn. We have an enemy to
> whose virtues we can owe nothing, but on this occasion we are infinitely
> obliged to one of his vices. We owe more to his insolence than to our own
> precaution ... The pride of the regicide may be our safety. He has given
> time for our reason to operate, and for British dignity to recover from its
> surprise. From first to last he has rejected all our advances. Far as we have
> gone, he has still left a way open to our retreat.

Then Burke produces one of his last great set-pieces, the picture of the
royal ambassadors at the regicide levee:

> To those who do not love to contemplate the fall of human greatness, I do
> not know a more mortifying spectacle than to see the assembled majesty of
> the crowned heads of Europe waiting as patient suitors in the antechamber of
> regicide. They wait, it seems, until the sanguinary tyrant *Carnot* shall have
> snorted away the fumes of the undigested blood of his sovereign. Then,
> when, sunk on the down of usurped pomp, he shall have sufficiently indulged
> his meditations with what monarch he shall next glut his ravening maw, he
> may condescend to signify that it is his pleasure to be awake, and that he is at
> leisure to receive the proposals of his high and mighty clients for the terms
> on which he may respite the execution of the sentence he has passed upon
> them. At the opening of those doors, what a sight it must be to behold the
> plenipotentiaries of royal impotence, in the precedency which they will
> intrigue to obtain, and which will be granted to them according to the

seniority of their degradation, sneaking into the regicide presence, and, with the relics of the smile which they had dressed up for the levee of their masters still flickering on their curled lips, presenting the faded remains of their courtly graces to meet the scornful, ferocious, sardonic grin of a bloody ruffian, who, whilst he is receiving their homage, is measuring them with his eye, and fitting to their size the slider of his guillotine!

He reflects again on the revolutionary achievement in the sphere of manners, and emphasizes that manners are not trivial, not separate from questions of state, any more than philosophical ideas are:

Manners are of more importance than laws. Upon them, in a great measure, the laws depend. The law touches us but here and there, and now and then. Manners are what vex or soothe, corrupt or purify, exalt or debase, barbarize or refine us, by a constant, steady, uniform, insensible operation, like that of the air we breathe in. They give their whole form and colour to our lives. According to their quality, they aid morals, they supply them, or they totally destroy them. Of this the new French legislators were aware; therefore, with the same method and under the same authority, they settled a system of manners the most licentious, prostitute, and abandoned that ever has been known, and at the same time the most coarse, rude, savage, and ferocious. Nothing in the revolution, no, not to a phrase or a gesture, not to the fashion of a hat or a shoe, was left to accident. All has been the result of design; all has been matter of institution. No mechanical means could be devised in favour of this incredible system of wickedness and vice that has not been employed. The noblest passions, the love of glory, the love of country, have been debauched into means of its preservation and its propagation. All sorts of shows and exhibitions, calculated to inflame and vitiate the imagination and pervert the moral sense, have been contrived. They have sometimes brought forth five or six hundred drunken women calling at the bar of the Assembly for the blood of their own children, as being royalists or constitutionalists. Sometimes they have got a body of wretches calling themselves fathers to demand the murder of their sons, boasting that Rome had but one Brutus, but that they could show five hundred. There were instances in which they inverted and retaliated the impiety, and produced sons who called for the execution of their parents. The foundation of their republic is laid in moral paradoxes. Their patriotism is always prodigy. All those instances to be found in history, whether real or fabulous, of a doubtful public spirit, at which morality is perplexed, reason is staggered, and from which affrighted nature recoils, are their chosen and almost sole examples for the instruction of their youth.

His objection to Jacobin morality he summarizes in one sentence: 'They think everything unworthy of the name of public virtue, unless it indicates violence on the private.'

Some of those who had floated the idea of a 'regicide peace' had argued, by way of precedent, that European powers had not hesitated to conclude agreements with Algiers, a polity of pirates. Burke plays happily with this notion:

I never shall so far injure the Janizarian Republic of Algiers as to put it in comparison, for every sort of crime, turpitude, and oppression, with the Jacobin Republic of Paris. There is no question with me to which of the two I should choose to be a neighbour or a subject. But situated as I am, I am in no danger of becoming to Algiers either the one or the other. It is not so in my relation to the atheistical fanatics of France. I *am* their neighbour; I *may* become their subject. Have the gentlemen who borrowed this happy parallel no idea of the different conduct to be held with regard to the very same evil at an immense distance and when it is at your door? When its power is enormous, as when it is comparatively as feeble as its distance is remote? When there is a barrier of language and usages which prevents corruption through certain old correspondences and habitudes, from the contagion of the horrible novelties that are introduced into everything else? I can contemplate without dread a royal or a national tiger on the borders of Pegu. I can look at him with an easy curiosity, as prisoner within bars in the menagerie of the Tower. But if, by *Habeas Corpus*, or otherwise, he was to come into the lobby of the House of Commons whilst your door was open, any of you would be more stout than wise who would not gladly make your escape out of the back windows. I certainly should dread more from a wild cat in my bedchamber than from all the lions that roar in the deserts behind Algiers. But in this parallel it is the cat that is at a distance, and the lions and tigers that are in our antechambers and our lobbies. Algiers is not near; Algiers is not powerful; Algiers is not our neighbour; Algiers is not infectious. Algiers, whatever it may be, is an old creation; and we have good data to calculate all the mischief to be apprehended from it. When I find Algiers transferred to Calais, I will tell you what I think of that point.

Now, for the first time, Burke refers explicitly to Pitt, the implicit target of the whole polemic. The passage is a ceremonious and solemn warning and it contains an allusion to the recall of Fitzwilliam:

In wishing this nominal peace not to be precipitated, I am sure no man living is less disposed to blame the present ministry than I am. Some of my oldest friends (and I wish I could say it of more of them) make a part in that ministry. There are some, indeed, 'whom my dim eyes in vain explore'. In my mind, a greater calamity could not have fallen on the public than the exclusion of one of them. But I drive away that, with other melancholy thoughts. A great deal ought to be said upon that subject, or nothing. As to the distinguished persons to whom my friends who remain are joined, if benefits nobly and generously conferred ought to procure good wishes, they are entitled to my best vows; and they have them all. They have administered to me the only consolation I am capable of receiving, which is, to know that no individual will suffer by my thirty years' service to the public. If things should give us the comparative happiness of a struggle, I shall be found, I was going to say fighting (that would be foolish) but dying, by the side of Mr Pitt. I must add that if anything defensive in our domestic system can possibly save us from the disasters of a regicide peace, he is the man to save us. If the finances in such a case can be repaired, he is the man to repair them. If I should lament any of his acts, it is only when they appear to me to have no resemblance to acts of his. But let him not have a confidence in himself which no human abilities can warrant. His abilities are fully equal (and that is to say much for any man) to those which are opposed to him. But if we look to him as our security against the consequences of a regicide peace, let us be assured that a regicide peace and a constitutional ministry are terms that will not agree. With a regicide peace the King cannot long have a minister to serve him, nor the minister a King to serve ...

The third *Letter* is headed 'On the Genius and Character of the French Revolution as it regards other Nations'. It begins by acknowledging the redoubtable character of Burke's adversaries:

It is a dreadful truth, but it is a truth that cannot be concealed: in ability, in dexterity, in the distinctness of their views, the Jacobins are our superiors. They saw the thing right from the very beginning. Whatever were the first motives to the war among politicians, they saw that in its spirit, and for its objects, it was a *civil war*; and as such they pursued it. It is a war between the partisans of the ancient, civil, moral, and political order of Europe against a sect of fanatical and ambitious atheists which means to change them all. It is not France extending a foreign empire over other nations: it is a sect aiming at universal empire, and beginning with the conquest of France. The leaders of that sect secured the *centre of Europe*; and that secured, they knew that, whatever might be the event of battles and sieges, their *cause* was victorious. Whether its territory had a little more or a little less peeled from its surface, or whether an island or two was detached from its commerce, to them was of little moment. The conquest of France was a glorious acquisition. That once well laid as a basis of empire, opportunities never could be wanting to regain or to replace what had been lost, and dreadfully to avenge themselves on the faction of their adversaries.

As against that dreadful, calculating foresight, Burke evokes an image of the common run of British politicians, the kind of men who had laughed at his speeches:

In truth, the tribe of vulgar politicians are the lowest of our species. There is no trade so vile and mechanical as government in their hands. Virtue is not their habit. They are out of themselves in any course of conduct recommended only by conscience and glory. A large, liberal, and prospective view of the interests of states passes with them for romance, and the principles that recommend it for the wanderings of a disordered imagination. The calculators compute them out of their senses. The jesters and buffoons shame them out of everything grand and elevated. Littleness in object and in means to them appears soundness and sobriety. They think there is nothing worth pursuit but that which they can handle, which they can measure with a two-foot rule, which they can tell upon ten fingers.

Continuing his analysis of the energies released by the French Revolution, he considers the roles of philosophers and politicians:

In the Revolution of France, two sorts of men were principally concerned in giving a character and determination to its pursuits: the philosophers and the politicians. They took different ways, but they met in the same end. The philosophers had one predominant object, which they pursued with a fanatical fury, that is, the utter extirpation of religion. To that every question of empire was subordinate. They had rather domineer in a parish of atheists than rule over a Christian world. Their temporal ambition was wholly subservient to their proselytizing spirit, in which they were not exceeded by Mahomet himself.

They who have made but superficial studies in the natural history of the human mind have been taught to look on religious opinions as the only cause of enthusiastic zeal and sectarian propagation. But there is no doctrine whatever on which men can warm, that is not capable of the very same effect. The social nature of man impels him to propagate his principles, as much as physical impulses urge him to propagate his kind. The passions give zeal and vehemence. The understanding bestows design and system. The whole man moves under the discipline of his opinions . . .

The other sort of men were the politicians. To them, who had little or not at all reflected on the subject, religion was itself no object of love or hatred. They disbelieved it, and that was all. Neutral with regard to that object, they took the side which in the present state of things might best answer their purposes. They soon found that they could not do without the philosophers, and the philosophers soon made them sensible that the destruction of religion was to supply them with means of conquest, first at home, and then abroad. The philosophers were the active internal agitators, and supplied the spirit and principles: the second gave the practical direction . . .

Without question, to bring about the unexampled event of the French Revolution, the concurrence of a very great number of views and passions was necessary. In that stupendous work no one principle by which the human mind may have its faculties at once invigorated and depraved was left unemployed; but I can speak it to a certainty, and support it by undoubted proofs, that the ruling principle of those who acted in the revolution *as statesmen* had the exterior aggrandizement of France as their ultimate end in the most minute part of the internal changes that were made.

The point about aggrandizement was crucial to the debate of 1796. If the French were as bent on aggrandizement as Burke believed, then there was no hope of a tolerable peace, either with the Directory or any of its successors until expansionist France could be defeated in war:

From all this what is my inference? It is, that this new system of robbery in France cannot be rendered safe by any art; that it *must* be destroyed, or that it will destroy all Europe; that to destroy that enemy, by some means or other, the force opposed to it should be made to bear some analogy and resemblance to the force and spirit which that system exerts; that war ought to be made against it in its vulnerable parts. These are my inferences. In one word, with this republic nothing independent can coexist.

The fourth and last of the *Letters on a Regicide Peace* is a kind of postscript, for by this time the attempt at a peace had ended in humiliating failure. Lord Malmesbury, Pitt's envoy to the Directory, had been contemptuously expelled from France (19 December 1796). This final *Letter* (published as Letter III) is entitled: 'On the rupture of the negotiation; the terms of peace proposed; and the resources of the country for the continuance of the war.' It begins by summarizing a paper laid before Parliament which documented all the rebuffs suffered by the ambassador at Paris. But Burke then expresses his exasperation with those who still wanted to negotiate:

A laboured display of the ill consequences which have attended an uniform course of submission to every mode of contumelious insult, with which the despotism of a proud, capricious, insulting, and implacable foe has chosen to buffet our patience, does not appear to my poor thoughts to be properly brought forth as a preliminary to justify a resolution of persevering in the very same kind of conduct, towards the very same sort of person, and on the very same principles. We state our experience, and then we come to the manly resolution of acting in contradiction to it ... As it is not only confessed by us, but made a matter of charge on the enemy that he had given us no encouragement to believe there was a change in his disposition or in his policy at any time subsequent to the period of his rejecting our first overtures, there seems to have been no assignable motive for sending Lord Malmesbury to Paris, except to expose his humbled country to the worst indignities, and the first of the kind ... that have been known in the world of negotiation.

The parliamentary debate on the matter revealed, in Burke's view, the degradation of both the great parties:

On that day, I fear, there was an end of that narrow scheme of relations called our country, with all its pride, its prejudices, and its partial affections. All the little quiet rivulets that watered an humble, a contracted, but not an unfruitful field, are to be lost in the waste expanse and boundless, barren ocean of the homicide philanthropy of France. It is no longer an object of terror, the aggrandizement of a new power which teaches as a professor that philanthropy in the chair, whilst it propagates by arms and establishes by conquest the comprehensive system of universal fraternity. In what light is all this viewed in a great assembly? The party which takes the lead there [Pitt's] has no longer any apprehensions, except those that arise from not being admitted to the closest and most confidential connections with the metropolis of that fraternity. That reigning party no longer touches on its favourite subject, the display of those horrors that must attend the existence of a power with such dispositions and principles, seated in the heart of Europe. It is satisfied to find some loose, ambiguous expressions in its former declarations which may set it free from its professions and engagements. It always speaks of peace with the regicides as a great and an undoubted blessing, and such a blessing as, if obtained, promises, as much as any human disposition of things can promise, security and permanence. It holds out nothing at all definite towards this security. It only seeks, by a restoration to some of their former owners of some fragments of the general wreck of Europe, to find a plausible plea for a present retreat from an embarrassing position. As to the future, that party is content to leave it covered in a night of the most palpable obscurity. It never once has entered into a particle of detail of what our own situation, or that of other powers, must be under the blessings of the peace we seek . . .

As to the other party [Fox's Whigs], the minority of today, possibly the majority of tomorrow, small in number but full of talents and every species of energy, which, upon the avowed ground of being more acceptable to France, is a candidate for the helm of this kingdom, it has never changed from the beginning. It has preserved a perennial consistency. This would be a never failing source of true glory if springing from just and right; but it is truly dreadful if it be an arm of Styx which springs out of the profoundest depths of a poisoned soil. The French maxims were by these gentlemen at no time condemned. I speak of their language in the most moderate terms. There are many who think that they have gone much further: that they have always magnified and extolled the French maxims; that, not in the least disgusted or discouraged by the monstrous evils which have attended these maxims from the moment of their adoption both at home and abroad, they still continue to predict that in due time they must produce the greatest good to the poor human race. They obstinately persist in stating those evils as matter of accident, as things wholly collateral to the system.

Burke points out that while Parliament was again offering to negotiate, in December 1796, a great French fleet with a great army aboard was just leaving Bantry Bay. This was the expedition headed by Hoche. Wolfe Tone had successfully solicited its launch by the Directory and was himself aboard. The expedition failed because bad weather made it impossible to land the troops, and the fleet was dispersed by storms. But the knowledge that the French were serious about sending forces to Ireland gave hope and encouragement to those planning the rebellion that was to break out in 1798. Yet a declaration issued just as the French were leaving Bantry Bay committed Britain to engage in negotiations again should the Directory be willing. Burke comments:

> It was on the very day of the date of the wonderful pledge, in which we assumed the Directorial government as lawful, and in which we engaged ourselves to treat with them whenever they pleased – it was on that very day the regicide fleet was weighing anchor from one of your harbours, where it had remained four days in perfect quiet ... Whilst you are invoking the propitious spirit of regicide equity and conciliation, they answer you with an attack. They turn out the pacific bearer of your 'how do you dos', Lord Malmesbury; and they return your visit, and their 'thanks for your obliging enquiries', by their old practised assassin, *Hoche*. They come to attack – what? A town, a fort, a naval station? They come to attack your King, your constitution, and the very being of that Parliament which was holding out to them these pledges, together with the entireness of the empire, the laws, liberties, and properties of all the people. We know that they meditated the very same invasion, and for the very same purposes, upon this kingdom, and, had the coast been as opportune, would have effected it.

In the conclusion of this final *Letter*, Burke comes near to threatening Pitt with impeachment should he renew his effort to negotiate a peace with revolutionary France:

> As to the great majority of the nation, they have done whatever, in their several ranks and conditions and descriptions, was required of them by their relative situations in society: and from those the great mass of mankind cannot depart without the subversion of all public order. They look up to that government, which they obey that they may be protected. They ask to be led and directed by those rulers whom providence and the laws of their

country have set over them, and under their guidance to walk in the ways of safety and honour. They have again delegated the greatest trust which they have to bestow to those faithful representatives who made their true voice heard against the disturbers and destroyers of Europe ... They have in all things reposed an enduring, but not an unreflecting confidence. That confidence demands a full return, and fixes a responsibility on the ministers entire and undivided. The people stands acquitted, if the war is not carried on in a manner suited to its objects. If the public honour is tarnished, if the public safety suffers any detriment, the ministers, not the people, are to answer it, and they alone. Its armies, its navies, are given to them without stint or restriction. Its treasures are poured out at their feet. Its constancy is ready to second all their efforts. They are not to fear a responsibility for acts of manly adventure. The responsibility which they are to dread is lest they should show themselves unequal to the expectation of a brave people. The more doubtful may be the constitutional and economical questions, upon which they have received so marked a support, the more loudly they are called upon to support this great war, for the success of which their country is willing to supersede considerations of no slight importance. Where I speak of responsibility, I do not mean to exclude that species of it which the legal powers of the country have a right finally to exact from those who abuse a public trust: but high as this is, there is a responsibility which attaches on them from which the whole legitimate power of the kingdom cannot absolve them; there is a responsibility to conscience and to glory, a responsibility to the existing world, and to that posterity which men of their eminence cannot avoid for glory or for shame – a responsibility to a tribunal at which not only ministers, but kings and parliaments, but even nations themselves, must one day answer.

Those of the *Letters on a Regicide Peace* which were published in Burke's lifetime had success with the public: 'Unpleasant as was the prospect of a long war,' writes Carl B. Cone, 'people seemed to appreciate Burke's defiant and frank acknowledgement of it. They read his pamphlets eagerly and approvingly. Thirteen editions were issued.' And Burke's acute sense of timing had not deserted him. The publication of those two *Letters* on 20 October 1796 came just two days before Lord Malmesbury arrived in Paris on his ill-fated embassy to the Directory. This was a stroke comparable to the publication of the Eleventh Report of the Indian Select Committee at just the right moment to shatter Fox's attempts to make peace with Hastings.

In the long battle of wills and minds between Burke and Pitt, Pitt had beaten Burke over Fitzwilliam's viceroyalty, and hurt him deeply in the process. But in the battle over peace with the Directory, it was Burke who prevailed, because of his superior understanding of the French Revolution and of the military expansionism emerging out of it. Pitt, despite his strong personal inclination to peace, would be still at war with France when he died in 1806, nine years after Burke's death. And when peace eventually came, nine years later still, it was the kind of peace that Burke, not Pitt, had always insisted it must be: peace with a restored monarchy.

From 1795 on, Burke had little regard either for Pitt or Fox personally, but he was obliged to support Pitt, because the alternative was Fox: 'I have no partiality at all to him [Pitt] or to his measures, against which latter nothing but the accelerated motion of my illness could have hindered me from publishing my opinion before this time, but between my disapprobation of Mr Pitt's measure[s] and my horror of those of Mr Fox, there is some difference.'

IRELAND 1796-97

In the brief period of the revolutionary crisis when Burke was free to attack Pitt, his writing displays a great exuberance. But once Pitt's attempt to make peace had failed, Burke was compelled to renew support for him. This was especially painful in relation to Ireland, which was the chief topic of most of his last letters. Much in them is expressive of deep inner conflict.

In November 1796, John Keogh — Richard Burke's old chief in the Catholic Committee — wrote to Edmund offering to keep him 'truly informed' about the Irish situation, and to carry any message he might choose to send to the Catholics. Burke's reply was cold and guarded. By this time, he did not trust Keogh, regarding him as far gone in Jacobinism. Burke drew attention to his own declining health and to his total lack of influence 'for a good while' over Irish affairs. Then he took up, with marked ambivalence, a phrase of Keogh's, who had said, 'I know you are so uncourtly as to be a true Irishman.' Burke wanted Keogh to know that he is both a true Irishman and a true Englishman, but he had unusual difficulty in formulating the thought:

> You do me justice in saying in your letter of July, that I am a 'true Irishman'. Considering, as I do, England as my country, of long habit, of long obligation and of establishment, and that my primary duties are here, I cannot conceive how a man can be a genuine Englishman without being at the same time a true Irishman, though fortune should have made his birth on this side the water. I think the same sentiments ought to be reciprocal on the part of Ireland, and if possible with much stronger reason.

He goes on to attack all ideas of separating Ireland from England, and implicitly warns Keogh against his Protestant friends among the United Irishmen:

> I conceive that the last disturbances, and those the most important, and which have the deepest root, do not originate, nor have they their greatest strength, amongst the Catholics; but there is, and ever has been, a strong republican Protestant faction in Ireland, which has persecuted the Catholics as long as persecution would answer their purpose; and now the same faction would dupe them to become accomplices in effectuating the same purposes, and thus either by tyranny or seduction would accomplish their ruin.

Burke then alludes specifically to the founder of the United Irishmen, Wolfe Tone, and to his connections with the Catholic Committee. (Tone had left Ireland for America in June 1795, after it was discovered that he had been in contact with a captured French agent. By November 1796, he was in France, on the staff of General Hoche, awaiting orders to sail to Ireland, with the expedition that miscarried at Bantry Bay.) Burke tells Keogh:

> It was with grief I saw last year with the Catholic Delegates a gentleman who was not of their religion or united to them in any avowable bond of a public interest, acting as their secretary in their most confidential concerns. I afterwards found that this gentleman's name was implicated in a correspondence with certain Protestant conspirators and traitors who were acting in direct connection with the enemies of all government and all religion . . .

I never saw him but once, which was in your company, and at that time knew nothing of his connections, character, or dispositions.

In a letter to French Laurence, Burke described Keogh as 'a man that on the whole I think ought not to be slighted, though he is but too much disposed to Jacobin principles and connections in his own nature and is a Catholic only in name – not but that whole body contrary to its nature has been driven by art and policy into Jacobinism, in order to form a pretext to multiply the jobs and to increase the power of that foolish and profligate junto to which Ireland is delivered over as a farm.'

That last sentence was the nub, for it was Pitt who had driven the Irish Catholics into Jacobinism by delivering Ireland over to the Dublin Castle junto. And Burke was stuck with Pitt, because the alternative was Fox and the English Jacobins. He saw Jacobinism in England as fuelling both sides in the incipient civil war in Ireland. He wrote again to French Laurence on 23 November 1796: 'The Jacobin opposition take this up to promote sedition in Ireland; and the Jacobin ministry will make use of it to countenance tyranny in the same place.' He wrote also to Fitzwilliam: 'We are in a perpetual dilemma between tyranny and Jacobinism; the Jacobinism too tasting of tyranny, and the tyranny rankly savouring of Jacobinism.'

Writing from Maynooth in Ireland, Thomas Hussey informed Burke of the rapid spread of the United Irishmen, and their revolutionary programme: 'They are urging these cursed sentiments throughout the country; and under the name of United Irishmen this evil is extending beyond imagination. Many thousands, I am assured, are weekly sworn throughout the country in such a secret manner, and form, as to evade all the law in those cases.' He added: 'I am terrified at what I foresee regarding my own unfortunate native country. To pass by Parliament and break the connection with Great Britain is, I am informed, the plan of the United Irishmen.'

Hussey was right about the new United Irish programme. The original programme of the Society of United Irishmen had been of a Whig kind, aiming at reform of the Irish Parliament (though some of its members, including Tone, probably had more far-reaching designs from the start). But in May 1795, after Fitzwilliam's recall, a new oath-bound

United Irish Society was formed, with a separatist and revolutionary programme. The slide to full-scale rebellion was now irreversible.

Burke's reply to Hussey is the most important and comprehensive of his late writings on Ireland. The circumstances of its composition (sometime after 9 December 1796) are such as to justify our taking it as Burke's political testament with regard to Ireland. 'I dictate my answer from my couch, on which I am obliged to lie for a good part of the day,' it reads. 'I cannot conceal from you, much less can I conceal from myself, that in all probability I am not long for this world. Indeed things are in such a situation independently of the domestic wound [Richard's death] that I never could have less reason for regret in quitting the world than at this moment; and my end will be, by several, as little regretted.'

Burke goes on to draw a critical distinction between Jacobinism in general and the particular type of Jacobinism to which Irish Catholics are being driven by official policy in the second half of the 1790s:

> You state, what has long been but too obvious, that it seems the unfortunate policy of the hour to put to the far largest portion of the King's subjects in Ireland the desperate alternative between a thankless acquiescence under grievous oppression or a refuge in Jacobinism, with all its horrors and all its crimes. You prefer the former dismal part of the choice. There is no doubt but that you would have reasons if the election of one of these evils was at all a security against the other. But they are things very alliable and as closely connected as cause and effect. That Jacobinism which is speculative in its origin, and which arises from wantonness and fullness of bread, may possibly be kept under by firmness and prudence. The very levity of character which produces it may extinguish it. But the Jacobinism which arises from penury and irritation, from scorned loyalty and rejected allegiance, has much deeper roots. They take their nourishment from the bottom of human nature and the unalterable constitution of things, and not from humour and caprice or the opinions of the day about privileges and liberties. These roots will be shot into the depths of hell, and will at last raise up their proud tops to heaven itself. This radical evil may baffle the attempts of heads much wiser than those are, who in the petulance and riot of their drunken power are neither ashamed nor afraid to insult and provoke those whom it is their duty and ought to be their glory to cherish and protect.

This is as much as to say that for a people so oppressed as the Irish

Catholics in the 1790s, the resort to rebellion is justifiable. And Burke goes on to advise Hussey that as a minister of religion he need not collude with the Irish administration, even for the purpose of averting rebellion.

This was a perfectly understandable position for a sympathizer with the Catholics in 1796, and it is in accordance with the established pattern of Burke's views in Ireland. Yet the tension between this specific acceptance of Irish rebellion and Burke's fierce anti-Jacobinism must have been almost intolerable. This letter was written in December 1796, the month when a French fleet anchored in Bantry Bay. What would Burke's position have been if the French army carried by that fleet had been able to land in Ireland (as a much smaller French force did in 1798, after his death)? He was fully committed to fierce resistance to any such attempt. Yet such resistance would entail the bloody repression of rebels with whom Burke at heart sympathized. No wonder he told Hussey that he felt 'little reason for regret in quitting the world'. He knew that the longer he lived, the greater was the risk that he might witness, in the land where he was born, a war in which his head would be on one side, and his heart on the other. Had he lived just a year longer, into the summer of 1798, he would have witnessed just such a war. He would have followed his head, and the general anti-Jacobin cause, but at the cost of still greater emotional torments.

Meanwhile, the English Jacobins had also been busy. Burke had founded a school at Penn, near Beaconsfield, for the sons of royalist refugees from France. He gave much of his time to this project in his last years, and enjoyed the company of the boys. In January the school was attacked by a stone-throwing mob. The news was kept from Burke. A friend wrote that Jane Burke would tell her husband about it 'when she shall think his spirits equal to such a subject – he is certainly better than he has been for some months past, but still in a very precarious state, and of course his friends are very anxious to keep everything from him which may create *new griefs*, and these poor boys have been almost his only comfort since he lost his own son'.

In a letter of March 1797, he offered his friend and confidant French Laurence some deathbed reflections on his own career, and in particular on Ireland:

What I dictate may not be pleasing either to the great or to the multitude; but looking back on my past public life, though not without many faults and errors, I have never made many sacrifices to the favour of the great, or to the humour of the people. I never remember more than two instances in which I have given way to popularity; and those two are the things of which, in the whole course of my life, now at the end of it, I have the most reason to repent. Such has been the habit of my public life, even when individual favour and popular countenance might be plausibly presented to me as the means of doing my duty the more effectually. But now, alas! of what value to me are all those helps or all those impediments. When the damp chill sweat of death already begins to glaze our visage, of what moment is it to us whether the vain breath of man blows hot or cold upon it? But our duties to men are not extinguished with our regard to their opinions.

A country, which has been dear to us from our birth, ought to be dear to us, as from our entrance so to our final exit from the stage upon which we have been appointed to act; and in the career of the duties which must in part be enjoyments of our new existence, how can we better start, and from what more proper post, than the performance of those duties which have made occupations of the first part of the course allotted to us?

INDIA AND IRELAND 1796–97

India is less present than Ireland in the correspondence of Burke's last years, and yet the preoccupation is even more intense. The acquittal of Warren Hastings in 1795 was a bitter blow, though not an unexpected one. But what was exquisitely distressing was the decision by the Board of Control of the East India Company – which was responsible ultimately to Pitt's administration – to grant an annuity of £4,000 to Hastings. What distressed Burke most was a perceived symmetry between this and his own pension (although Hastings' annuity was more than three times greater). Furiously, Burke wrote on 6 March 1796 to Henry Dundas, who was responsible for Indian affairs:

It is with pain inexpressible I am driven to the step I *must* take. Costs and damages to an immense amount are given by you, on the public estate administered by the East India Company, to Mr Hastings, against the House of Commons. That House has charged him with robbing that fund and the people from whose labours the fund arises, and we reward that robbery by a new robbery. I cordially wished well to your India administration; and, except in one instance in the beginning, I never, even whilst I was otherwise in warm opposition, opposed it; hoping, that redress would be given to India and that this gang of thieves called the Court of Directors and Proprietors would be kept in some order. But there am I, acting under your own *individual* authority, as well as *public* authority, attempted to be disgraced with the present age, and with all posterity. But it shall never be said, either by the present age or by posterity, that the blood of India has been compromised by a pension to the accuser and another to the party accused. I shall therefore, I hope, before the end of next week, present a petition to the House of Commons, and know whether they will confess themselves false accusers – whether they will deliberately betray those whom they have employed in their accusation, and whether the only satisfaction they will give to undone nations as the result of their twenty-four years enquiry into their grievances is an enormous sum of money, from their substance, to reward the person they have charged as the author of their grievances.

He wrote in a similar vein to Fitzwilliam, to Portland, to Windham, to Speaker Addington and to Chancellor Loughborough. In the letter to Loughborough he returns to the blood-guilt theme:

Oh no! It shall never be said, never, never, that the cause of the people of India, taken up for twenty years in Parliament, has been compromised by pensions to the accused and the accuser. The blood of that people shall not be on my head.

The idea of a petition to the Commons, in the circumstances, was hopelessly impractical, and a product of emotional shock. Fitzwilliam, as a good friend should in such circumstances, gently talked Burke out of this project. Having pointed out the odds against success, he concludes:

No, my dear Burke, you cannot stir – You must rest the character of your cause upon the judgment of the last House of Commons, when all parties, contending about everything else, agreed alone on this – this, backed by the indelible notoriety of the crimes you laboured with such meritorious toil and efforts to bring to condign punishment, and thereby to vindicate the character of the country at large from any disgraceful concurrence with the crimes of an individual, must bear out your cause and character before that tribunal which will do it justice, an impartial posterity.

Burke acquiesced, with deep reluctance, and an increment of guilt. He wrote to French Laurence: 'But what a dreadful example it is to add myself to the number of those who have successively betrayed the poor people of India.'

Burke's strongest emotional preoccupation in his dying months was with India, at least overtly. It is on this issue – and apparently on this alone – that he craved vindication, through the preparation and publication of a history of the impeachment of Warren Hastings. On his retirement from Parliament in 1794, he had entrusted this task to French Laurence, who was co-adviser to Jane Burke as executrix of his will. In an impassioned passage in a letter written a little less than a year before his death, Burke reminds his friend of the charge laid upon him:

As it is possible that my stay on this side of the grave may be yet shorter than I compute it, let me now beg to call to your recollection the solemn charge and trust I gave you on my departure from the public stage. I fancy I must make you the sole operator in a work in which, even if I were enabled to undertake it, you must have been ever the assistance on which alone I could rely. Let not this cruel, daring, unexampled act of public corruption, guilt, and meanness go down to a posterity perhaps as careless as the present race without its due animadversion, which will be best found in its own acts and monuments. Let my endeavours to save the nation from that shame and guilt be my monument – the only one I ever will have. Let everything I have done, said, or written be forgotten but this. I have struggled with my active life, and I wish after death to have my defiance of the judgments of those who consider the dominion of the glorious empire given by an incomprehensible dispensation of the divine providence into our hands as nothing more than an opportunity of gratifying for the lowest of their purposes, the lowest of their passions – and that for such poor rewards, and for the most part, indirect and silly bribes, as indicate even more the folly than the corruption of these infamous and contemptible wretches. I blame myself exceedingly for not having employed the last year in this work and beg forgiveness of God for such a neglect. I had strength enough for it, if I had not wasted some of it in compromising grief with drowsiness and forgetfulness, and employing some of the moments in which *I* have been roused to mental exertion in feeble endeavours to rescue this dull and thoughtless people from the punishments which their neglect and stupidity will bring upon them for their systematic iniquity and oppression. But you are made to continue all that is good of me, and to augment it with the various resources of a mind fertile in virtues and cultivated with every sort of talent and of knowledge. Above all, make out the cruelty of this pretended acquittal, but in reality this barbarous and inhuman condemnation of whole tribes and nations, and of all the abuses they contain. If ever Europe recovers its civilization that work will be useful. Remember! Remember! Remember!

Burke wrote that letter from Bath, where his doctors had ordered him to take the waters. He also recorded his physical condition:

But my flesh is wasted in a manner which in so short a time no one could imagine. My limbs look about to find the rags that cover them. My strength is declined in the full proportion; and at my time of life new flesh is never supplied and lost strength is never recovered. If God has anything to do for me here – here he will keep me. If not, I am tolerably resigned to his divine pleasure.

In the following February, less than six months before his death, Burke again reminded his friend of that injunction over India:

But you remember, likewise, that when I came hither at the beginning of last summer, I repeated to you that dying request which I now reiterate: that if at any time, without the danger of ruin to yourself, or over-distracting you from your professional and parliamentary duties, you can place in a short point of view, and support by the documents in print and writing which exist with me, or with Mr Troward, or yourself, the general merits of this transaction, you will erect a cenotaph most grateful to my shade, and will clear my memory from that load, which the East India Company, King, Lords, and Commons, and in a manner the whole British nation (God forgive them) have been pleased to lay as a monument upon my ashes. I am as conscious as any person can be of the little value of the good or evil opinion of mankind to the part of me that shall remain, but I believe it is of some moment not to leave the fame of an evil example, of the expenditure of fourteen years labour, and of not less (taking the expense of the suit, and the costs paid to Mr Hastings, and the parliamentary charges) than near £300,000. This is a terrible example, and it is not acquittance at all to a public man, who, with all the means of undeceiving himself if he was wrong, has thus with such incredible pains both of himself and others, persevered in the persecution of innocence and merit. It is, I say, no excuse at all to urge in his apology that he has had enthusiastic good intentions. In reality, you know that I am no enthusiast, but [according] to the powers that God has given me, a sober and reflecting man. I have not even the other very bad excuse, of acting from personal resentment or from the sense of private injury – never having received any; nor can I plead ignorance, no man ever having taken more pains to be informed. Therefore *I* say, *Remember*.

At the time of that last 'Remember', Burke was still in Bath. The disease which was destroying him (believed to have been tuberculous enteritis) had hitherto been confined to his stomach. By February, it was beginning to affect his head. As he wrote in the same letter: 'They have taken the town and are now attacking the citadel.' As the phrase itself reveals, the citadel was still defended.

It may seem strange that the last letters should show him much more affected, in a personal way, by the affairs of India than by those of Ireland. Certainly there is nothing among the copious references to Ireland in his surviving letters of 1796-97 that corresponds to the throb of guilt and thirst for vindication that appear, with urgent and insistent repetition, in these last references to India. Yet superficially the affairs of India should now have given him much less concern than those of Ireland. With regard to India, he had fought against a system and against the man who had presided over and symbolized it. Against the man, the struggle was a stalemate, and Hastings' annuity was a deep affront. Yet regarding the system, Burke had won. The organized practice of maximum extortion, conducted by the servants of the Company which had flourished under Hastings, had been suppressed, in large part because of the reports of the Select Committee and their adoption by the House of Commons – all of which was almost entirely due to Burke's personal labours. By the end of his life, the people of India were incontestably better off by reason of his exertions on their behalf.

This was not the case with the people of Ireland, and specifically the Catholics, whom he had sought to serve not just for fourteen years, but throughout his life. Those people were now heading towards a disaster which was visibly looming up as he lay dying. And the chain of events leading immediately towards that disaster had begun with the recall of Fitzwilliam – that is to say, with the failure of Burke's long-prepared grand experiment, designed to save the Catholics of Ireland. Yet once that experiment had failed, Burke was constrained by his wider commitment, to oppose the French Revolution, not merely to leave the Irish to their fate, but to side with Pitt, who was ultimately responsible for the continuation of their oppression. Burke acknowledged that that people had just cause for rebellion. Yet when the justifiable rebellion should come, he would be obliged to support its repression.

Given the pattern of his life and the political pattern in the late 1790s, the dying Burke must have been afflicted by guilt about Ireland. But it is over India that he accuses himself and craves vindication. On an almost absurdly trivial ground – that of failing to present a petition to the Commons against Hastings' annuity – he speaks of adding himself 'to the number of those who have successively betrayed the poor people of India'. I believe that this is the psychological equivalent of a physiological 'referred pain'. All his life, Burke had been bottling up a large part of his feelings about Ireland. By 1796–97 the old reasons for doing this had passed, but a new and imperative one had taken their place. The guilt about Ireland was now too much for his conscious mind to bear, and was expressed in relation to India, where it was bearable because largely imaginary. The urgent need to forget certain things about Ireland lent the urgency to his repeated cry over India: Remember!

As he lay dying in Bath, Burke appeared as a religious figure to his intimates, as William Wilberforce, who visited him very near the end, tells us: 'Burke was lying on a sofa much emaciated; and Windham, Laurence, and some other friends, were round him. The attention shown to Burke by all that party was just like the treatment of Achitophel of old. "It was as if one went to inquire of the oracle of the Lord".'

Wilberforce brought Burke the news of the mutiny of Spithead: 'And it was with Burke's emphatic demand for strong measures [against the mutineers] ringing in his ears that Windham left to attend a Cabinet meeting in London.' The Spithead and Nore mutinies – the most dangerous period for England in the whole war with France – darkened Burke's last months. He wrote to French Laurence on 12 May 1797: 'I should not be surprised at seeing a French army convoyed by a British Navy to an attack upon this kingdom.' It is against that background that we have to understand Burke's otherwise startling last instructions – given orally to his kinsman Edward Hoyle, three days before his death – concerning his own burial: he wanted to be buried 'unknown, the spot unmarked and separate from his son, wife and brother on *account of the French revolutionists*'.

That the revolutionaries might conquer England was a reasonable contingency to provide for in the summer of 1797; they never looked nearer to attaining this objective than at that moment. Nor was it unreasonable to consider that some of the victorious French revolutionaries (or of their English allies) might desecrate Burke's grave. It is true that Jacobinism, by this late date, was no longer the dominant force in Paris that Burke sometimes suggested it was: the driving force was no longer an egalitarian ideology, but militant French nationalism, fuelled by a devouring appetite for loot and glory. But the militant French nationalists hated Burke quite as much as the original Jacobins had done. If the revolution had spread to England, zealots might well have dug up Burke's bones and dumped them on some kind of dung-heap. His desperate precaution was tragic, but not fanciful.

Some short time before Burke's death, Fox made an attempt 'to arrange a last reconciliatory meeting with him'. Jane Burke wrote back, on Edmund's behalf.

Mrs Burke presents her compliments to Mr Fox, and thanks him for his obliging enquiries. Mrs Burke communicated his letter to Mr Burke, and, by his desire, has to inform Mr Fox that it has cost Mr Burke the most heartfelt pain to obey the stern voice of his duty in rending asunder a long friendship, but that he deemed this sacrifice necessary; that his principles remained the same; and that in whatever of life yet remained to him, he conceives that he must live for others and not for himself. Mr Burke is convinced that the principles which he has endeavoured to maintain are necessary to the welfare and dignity of his country, and that these principles can be enforced only by the general persuasion of his sincerity. For herself, Mrs Burke has again to express her gratitude to Mr Fox for his enquiries.

There seems at first sight a contradiction between this rebuff and the last words of Burke's will and testament, written nearly three years before: 'If the intimacy which I have had with others has been broken off by a political difference on great questions concerning the state of things existing and impending, I hope they will forgive whatever of general human infirmity or my own particular infirmity has entered into that contention. I heartily entreat their forgiveness. I have nothing more to say.' Why, if Burke was implicitly prepared to 'entreat' Fox to forgive him, was he not prepared to forgive Fox? Because of the difference between forgiveness and the kind of reconciliation that Fox wanted. Forgiveness was a personal matter, and Burke as a devout Christian no doubt forgave all his enemies, as individuals, in preparing himself for death. But the 'last reconciliatory meeting' that Fox proposed would have had political implications, which Burke refused. The meeting would have signified that the differences of principle, to which Burke had attached such importance in his lifetime, were not of such great importance after all, in the final perspective. But Burke wanted the political world to know that these principles remained of transcendent importance to him, and that Fox was still outside the pale in terms of those principles.

If Burke and Fox had both lived until after Waterloo, Burke might have received Fox. But to receive the great French apologist in the shadow of French triumphs in the summer of 1797 would have been striking the flag of resistance in the face of the advancing enemy. A print published that summer, entitled 'French Telegraph making Signals in the Dark', shows Fox signalling with a dark lantern to a fleet which is advancing from a coast marked '*République*'. There is no defending fleet in sight. This was the scene of Burke's last nightmare: a mutinous English fleet carrying a French army towards British ports. Burke did regard Fox as sending welcoming signals in that direction, which is why Charles James Fox was not admitted to the deathbed of Edmund Burke.

Burke died shortly after midnight on 9 July. Jane was with him, and French Laurence, who reported Burke's 'dying advice and request' to Fitzwilliam 'steadily to pursue that course in which he now is. He can take no other that will not be unworthy of him.' Burke feared that Fitzwilliam might be about to rejoin the Foxites. Laurence goes on: 'Mrs Burke, of whom you and Lady Fitzwilliam will I am sure be most anxious to hear, shows a fortitude truly worthy of the character which we have ever known her to possess. She feels that she has duties to discharge, for the sake of which she thinks herself bound to take every care of life, though in itself it has no longer any pleasure for her. Her behaviour is most unaffectedly heroic.' The letter ends:

> Oh! my dear lord, what an incalculable loss have his family, his friends, and
> his countrymen suffered in that wonderful man, pre-eminent no less in
> virtues than in genius and in learning! So kind to all connected with him, so

partial to those whom he esteemed, ever preferring them in all things to himself; yet so zealous and resolute a champion in the cause of justice, social order, morals and religion. The private vanishes before the public calamity. When he fell, these kingdoms, Europe, the whole civilized world, lost the principal prop that remained, and were shaken to their very centres.

The funeral service at Beaconsfield, on 15 July 1797, according to the Anglican rite, had the character of a solemn tribute to a pillar of the state. The pall-bearers were William Windham, the Secretary of State for War; Murrough O'Brien, Earl of Inchiquin; Earl Fitzwilliam; the Duke of Devonshire; Sir Gilbert Elliot; Henry Addington, Speaker of the House of Commons; the Duke of Portland; and Lord Loughborough, the Lord Chancellor. The combined presence of Fitzwilliam and Portland is worthy of note. The two men, formerly close friends and colleagues, had not met since Portland had dismissed Fitzwilliam from his Irish post, in harrowing circumstances, more than two years before. French Laurence, inviting Fitzwilliam to be pall-bearer wrote:

> Will you, my dear lord, allow me to name your lordship for one of the pall-bearers, to show the last respect to the memory of a man who while living ever loved you most affectionately and ardently? It may however be right to advertise your lordship that from some late most kind messages, and from his having borne the pall over poor young Richard, it will be impossible to pass over the Duke of Portland on this melancholy occasion.

No force less than that of their common reverence for Edmund Burke could have induced those two men to take part together in any public event.

The chief bond between the pall-bearers was their common hostility to the French Revolution. Burke's other three great causes were less clearly represented. Ireland was worthily represented by Fitzwilliam, who had paid dearly for his commitment to Burke's ideas with the revoking of his viceroyalty. Sir Gilbert Elliot had worked closely with Burke over India in the management of the impeachment of Warren Hastings. But America, the earliest of Burke's public causes, was not represented. Of Burke's closest collaborators in that cause, three were dead (Rockingham, Dowdeswell and Lord John Cavendish); the fourth, Charles James Fox, knew that he would not be welcome.

Few Foxites would have wished to be present in Beaconsfield on that July day, especially after Burke's deathbed rebuff to their leader. Yet one Foxite Member of Parliament was in the crowd of mourners. This was Philip Francis. He had been dismissed into outer darkness by Burke seven years before, because of his scoffing reaction to the *Reflections*; and Francis agreed with Fox, not Burke, over the French Revolution. Yet he came to Beaconsfield, to an uncongenial gathering and what must have been a chilly reception. He is a lonely figure in that crowd, and a moving one. He was a proud and selfish man, yet he deliberately went to face what he knew would be an uncomfortable experience, and a somewhat humiliating one. And he did so only in order to show respect to a man who had snubbed him.

Francis had changed indeed. The dark bond of India had held under the rending strain of France. It was a complex and ambiguous bond, and it was a haunted one. Over Burke's India fell the shadow of Ireland, and Philip Francis, in that cortège, was attended as always by the shade of Nuncomar.

Remember!

Index

Anne, Queen, 39
Annual Register, 47
anti-Catholicism, 36, 91, 116, 211,
    212, 303; American, 48–50; *see
    also* Catholics; Protestants
*An Appeal from the New to the Old
    Whigs*, 240, 246–53, 254, 255,
    270, 297
Arcot, Nabob of, *see* Carnatic,
    Nabob of
Ardesoif, Abraham, 12
Armagh outrages (1795), 303
Association of the Friends of the
    People, 272
Aston, Sir Richard, 21
Atkinson, Richard, 173, 174
Auckland, William Eden, Baron,
    310–11, 312–13
Austria, Austrian Netherlands;
    France declares war on (1792),
    271–2, 275; annexation of, 278

Bagot, Sir William 23, 27
Baker of Hertford, Mr, 173
Ballitore, Co. Kildare, Burke
    attends boarding school at, 8
Ballyduff, Co. Cork, 5, 6–7, 68
Bartlett, Thomas, 303
Barwell, Richard, 140, 142, 144
Bastille, fall of the (July 1789), 207,
    210, 213, 215
battle of the Saints, West Indies
    (1782), 117
Beasley, Jerry, C., 16
Bedford, Duke of, 304, 305–9
Benfield, Paul, 140, 154, 155, 156–7,
    174, 178, 179
Bengal, 133, 145, 146, 154, 156, 157,

158–9, 160, 166, 178; East India
    Company in, 138–42; Rangpur
    affair, 197–200
Bengal Judicature Act (1781),
    158–60
Bengal Supreme Court, 145
Blackwater Valley, Shanballymore,
    6, 7, 70; Burke's birth in (1729),
    4
Burges, James Bland, 274
Bolingbroke, Henry St John,
    Viscount, 255
Boston Port Act (1774), 62–3, 105,
    251
Boston Tea Party (1773), 62
Boulter, Archbishop Hugh, 2
Bowen, Mr (uncle), 5
Brandywine, battle of (1777), 84
Brissot, Jacques, 272
Bristol, Frederick Augustus
    Hervey, Earl of, and Bishop of
    Derry, 124, 125
Bristol, 95; Burke elected MP for
    (1774–80), 29–40, 66–8, 97, 127;
    Burke's Guildhall speech (1780),
    36, 158, 267, 270
Bristow, John, Resident at
    Lucknow, 175–6
British Constitution, Burke on, 70,
    191–2, 233, 247–9, 297; *see also*
    French Constitution
Brunswick, Duke of, 278
Buck, Andrew, 11, 12, 13
Buckinghamshire, Earl of, Lord
    Lieutenant of Ireland, 94
Bunker Hill, battle of (1775), 73
Burgoyne, General John, 75, 84,
    85, 86, 89, 92, 125, 150

Conway, General Henry, 111, 112, 118

Copeland, Thomas, 9, 15, 24

Cornwall, Charles, 64

Cornwallis, General Charles, 2nd Earl, 204; surrender to Washington at Yorktown (1781), 102, 111, 121

Correspondence, 9–11, 15, 130, 197

Council for Bengal (1773), 142–3, 144, 148, 149

Courts of Justice, French, 158

Cromwell, Oliver, 5, 116

Cruger, John, Speaker of New York Assembly, 48, 61–2

Cullen, Paul, Archbishop of Dublin, 8

Culloden, battle of (1746), 11

Danton, Georges Jacques, 275

d'Artois, Charles Comte (later Charles X), 263

Day, Sir John, 152

Déclaration de Paix au Monde (1790), 215, 263

Declaratory Act (1766), 50–2, 53, 54, 63, 124; Burke's speeches on, 51–2, 58, 80, 82

Defenders, Catholic, 283, 303, 304

Dennis, William, 11, 12, 13, 15

Dependency of Ireland Act (1719), 124

Depont, Charles-Jean-François, 208, 212, 215

Devi Singh, Rajah, 196–7, 199–200, 203

Devonshire, Duke of, 339

Devonshire, Georgiana, Duchess of, 202

Directory, French, 312, 313–14, 316, 321, 322, 324, 326; adoption of Constitution of Year III by, 309–10

Dowdeswell, William, Chancellor of the Exchequer, 45, 46, 56, 68, 339

Dublin, 4, 5–6, 8; Irish Volunteers parade through (1779), 96–7; Irish Volunteers convention (1783), 125, 126–7, 264; *see also* Trinity College

Dundas, Henry, 159–60, 178–9, 180, 281, 331–2

Dungannon convention of Irish Volunteers (1782), 122

Dunning, John, 107–8, 214

East India Bill, Fox's (1783), 146, 161–74, 175, 225, 286, 311

East India Act, Pitt's (1784), 175, 178

East India Company, 62, 129, 130–43, 138, 139–40, 154–5, 252, 334; extortion, bribery and corruption practised by, 133–4, 136, 139, 141–2, 153–4, 156, 169–70, 178–82, 197–200, 201, 202; arrest and deposition of Lord Pigot, 136, 146, 154–5; Court of Directors, 132, 140, 141, 156, 163, 170, 178, 179, 288, 332; Court of Proprietors, 156–7, 160, 161, 163, 332; liaison between George III and, 155, 160–1; defeat of Fox's East India Bill, 146, 161–74; Board of

241, 242, 263; deposition of
(1792), 240, 275, 281, 283; trial
of (1792), 278–9; execution of
(1793), 215, 244–5, 280, 281, 283
Lyall, Sir Alfred, 62, 148–9

Macartney, Lord, 150
Macaulay, Thomas Babington, 187
McDowell, R. B., 96–7, 294
Mackintosh, James, *Vindiciae
Gallicae*, 223–4
Macpherson, Sir John, 150
Madras, 136, 140, 146, 154, 155, 156,
157, 178, 180
Mahratta War (India), 150–1, 157,
158
Malmesbury, Lord, 322, 326
Malone, Edmund, 198–9
Malton, Edmund Burke's election
as MP for (1780–94), 110, 262,
292; Richard Burke's election as
MP for (1794), 292
Marie Antoinette, Queen of
France, 218–20, 221, 241, 264,
275, 277; execution of (1793),
215, 245, 285
Marshall, P. J., 160, 162, 201
Massachusetts Bay Regulation Bill,
65–6
Massachusetts Charter Bill, 251
Meredith, Sir William, 44
Middle Temple, Burke's legal
studies in, 14–15
Mir Jafar, Nabob of Bengal, 139,
140
Mir Qasim, Nabob of Bengal,
139–40
Mirabeau, Honoré-Gabriel-Victor,

Comte de, 208, 258
Mohun, Matthew, 12, 13
Monson, Colonel George, 142, 143,
148
Musgrave, Sir Richard, *Memoirs*,
15–16
Monanimy Castle, Ballyduff, 6, 68
Montagu, Frederick, 202–3
Morley, John, 35–6
Mutiny Act (1765), 54, 55, 100–1,
102

Nagle family, Nagle country, 4, 5,
6, 7, 23, 70, 90
Nagle, James (uncle), 4
Nagle, Patrick (uncle), 5
Nagle, Sir Richard, of
Carrigacunna, 6, 70
Napoleon I Bonaparte, Emperor,
216, 310, 316
natural aristocracy, Burke's
defence of, 252–3
natural religion, Burke's notion of,
253–4
New York Assembly, 48, 49, 54–5,
61–2, 63; Townshend's proposal
to suspend, 54–5
Newcastle, Duke of, 22
Noble, John, 29–30, 35
Nore mutiny (1797), 336
North, Frederick, Lord, 53, 58, 65,
76, 94, 98, 105, 106, 107–8, 109,
112, 113, 114–15, 120, 142, 159,
161, 173, 174, 258, 285;
'Conciliatory Propositions to the
Americans' of, 86–7; Fox–North
Coalition (1783), 119–20, 121,
126, 161, 162, 172–3